New Perspectives on

MICROSOFT®
OUTLOOK® 2000

INTRODUCTORY

ROBIN M. ROMER

APPROVED COURSEWARE

COURSE
TECHNOLOGY
™
THOMSON LEARNING

Australia • Canada • Mexico • Singapore • Spain • United Kingdom • United States

COURSE TECHNOLOGY

THOMSON LEARNING

Microsoft® Outlook® 2000—Introductory

is published by Course Technology.

Managing Editor
Greg Donald

Senior Editor
Donna Gridley

Series Technology Editor
Rachel Crapser

Senior Product Manager
Kathy Finnegan

Associate Product Manager
Melissa Dezotell

Editorial Assistant
Jessica Engstrom

Developmental Editor
Rachel Biheller Bunin

Production Editor
Jennifer Goguen

Compositor
GEX Publishing Services

Cover Designer
Efrat Reis

Text Designer
Meral Dabcovich

COPYRIGHT © 2001 Course Technology, a division of Thomson Learning, Inc. Thomson Learning™ is a trademark used herein under license.

Printed in the United States of America

1 2 3 4 5 6 7 8 9 BM 04 03 02 01

For more information, contact Course Technology, 25 Thomson Place, Boston, Massachusetts, 02210.

Or find us on the World Wide Web at: www.course.com

ALL RIGHTS RESERVED. No part of this work covered by the copyright hereon may be reproduced or used in any form or by any means—graphic, electronic, or mechanical, including photocopying, recording, taping, Web distribution, or information storage and retrieval systems—without the written permission of the publisher.

For permission to use material from this text or product, contact us by
Tel   (800) 730-2214
Fax (800) 730-2215
www.thomsonrights.com

Disclaimer
Course Technology reserves the right to revise this publication and make changes from time to time in its content without notice.

The Web addresses in this book are subject to change from time to time as necessary without notice.

Some of the product names and company names used in this book have been used for identification purposes only and may be trademarks or registered trademarks of their respective manufacturers and sellers.

Microsoft and the Office logo are either registered trademarks or trademarks of Microsoft Corporation in the United States and/or other countries. Course Technology is an independent entity from the Microsoft Corporation, and not affiliated with Microsoft in any manner. This text may be used in assisting students to prepare for a Microsoft Office User Specialist Exam for Outlook 2000. Neither Microsoft Corporation, its designated review company, nor Course Technology warrants that use of this text will ensure passing the relevant exam.

Use of the Microsoft Office User Specialist Approved Courseware Logo on this product signifies that it has been independently reviewed and approved in complying with the following standards: Acceptable coverage of all content related to the Microsoft Office Core and Expert Exams entitled *"Microsoft Outlook 2000";* and sufficient performance-based exercises that relate closely to all required content, based on sampling of text.

ISBN 0-619-02058-X

PREFACE

The New Perspectives Series

About New Perspectives

Course Technology's **New Perspectives Series** is an integrated system of instruction that combines text and technology products to teach computer concepts, the Internet, and microcomputer applications. Users consistently praise this series for innovative pedagogy, use of interactive technology, creativity, accuracy, and supportive and engaging style.

How is the New Perspectives Series different from other series?

The New Perspectives Series distinguishes itself by **innovative technology**, from the renowned Course Labs to the state-of-the-art multimedia that is integrated with our Concepts texts. Other distinguishing features include **sound instructional design**, **proven pedagogy**, and **consistent quality**. Each tutorial has students learn features in the context of solving a realistic case problem rather than simply learning a laundry list of features. With the **New Perspectives Series**, instructors report that students have a complete, integrative learning experience that stays with them. They credit this high retention and competency to the fact that this series incorporates critical thinking and problem solving with computer skills mastery. In addition, we work hard to ensure accuracy by using a multi-step quality assurance process during all stages of development. Instructors focus on teaching and students spend more time learning.

Choose the coverage that's right for you

New Perspectives applications books are available in the following categories:

Brief
2-4 tutorials

Brief: approximately 150 pages long, two to four "Level I" tutorials, teaches basic application skills.

Introductory
6 or 7 tutorials, or Brief + 2 or 3 more tutorials

Introductory: approximately 300 pages long, four to seven tutorials, goes beyond the basic skills. These books often build out of the Brief book, adding two or three additional "Level II" tutorials. The book you're holding is an Introductory book

Comprehensive
Introductory + 4 or 5 more tutorials. Includes Brief Windows tutorials and Additional Cases

Comprehensive: approximately 600 pages long, eight to twelve tutorials, all tutorials included in the Introductory text plus higher-level "Level III" topics. Also includes two Windows tutorials and three or four fully developed Additional Cases.

Advanced
Quick Review of basics + in-depth, high-level coverage

Advanced: approximately 600 pages long, covers topics similar to those in the Comprehensive books, but offers the highest-level coverage in the series. Advanced books assume students already know the basics, and therefore go into more depth at a more accelerated rate than the Comprehensive titles. Advanced books are ideal for a second, more technical course.

Office

Office suite components
+ integration + Internet

Custom Editions

Choose from any of the
above to build your own
Custom Editions or
CourseKits

Office: approximately 800 pages long, covers all components of the Office suite as well as integrating the individual software packages with one another and the Internet.

Custom Books: The New Perspectives Series offers you two ways to customize a New Perspectives text to fit your course exactly: *CourseKits*™ are two or more texts shrinkwrapped together, and offer significant price discounts. *Custom Editions*® offer you flexibility in designing your concepts, Internet, and applications courses. You can build your own book by ordering a combination of topics bound together to cover only the subjects you want. There is no minimum order, and books are spiral bound. Contact your Course Technology sales representative for more information.

What course is this book appropriate for?

New Perspectives on Microsoft Outlook 2000—Introductory can be used in any course in which you want students to learn the most important topics of Outlook 2000, including sending and receiving e-mail messages and managing their Inbox, scheduling appointments and meetings using the Calendar, creating and managing contacts, tasks and journal entries, using Outlook with the other Office applications, and using Outlook with the Internet. It is particularly recommended for a full-semester course on Outlook 2000 or as part of a course communicating with e-mail. This book assumes that students have learned basic Windows navigation and file management skills from Course Technology's *New Perspectives on Microsoft Windows 95—Brief*, or the equivalent book for Windows 98, 2000, or NT.

What is the Microsoft Office User Specialist Program?

The Microsoft Office User Specialist Program provides an industry-recognized standard for measuring an individual's mastery of an Office application. Passing one or more MOUS Program certification exam helps your students demonstrate their proficiency to prospective employers and gives them a competitive edge in the job marketplace. Course Technology offers a growing number of Microsoft-approved products that cover all of the required objectives for the MOUS Program exams. For a complete listing of Course Technology titles that you can use to help your students get certified, visit our Web site at *www.course.com*.

New Perspectives on Microsoft Outlook 2000—Introductory has been approved by Microsoft as courseware for the Microsoft Office User Specialist (MOUS) program. After completing the tutorials and exercises in this book, students may be prepared to take both the MOUS Core and Expert exam for Outlook 2000. For more information about certification, please visit the MOUS program site at *www.mous.net*.

Proven Pedagogy

CASE

Tutorial Case Each tutorial begins with a problem presented in a case that is meaningful to students. The case turns the task of learning how to use an application into a problem-solving process.

45-minute Sessions Each tutorial is divided into sessions that can be completed in about 45 minutes to an hour. Sessions allow instructors to more accurately allocate time in their syllabus, and students to better manage their own study time.

1.

2.

3.

Step-by-Step Methodology We make sure students can differentiate between what they are to do and what they are to *read*. Through numbered steps—clearly identified by a gray shaded background—students are constantly guided in solving the case problem. In addition, the numerous screen shots with callouts direct students' attention to what they should look at on the screen.

TROUBLE?

TROUBLE? Paragraphs These paragraphs anticipate the mistakes or problems that students may have and help them continue with the tutorial.

Tutorial Tips

Tutorial Tips Page This page, following the Table of Contents, offers students suggestions on how to effectively plan their study and lab time, what to do when they make a mistake, and how to use the Reference Windows, MOUS grids, Quick Checks, and other features of the New Perspectives series.

"Read This Before You Begin" Page Located opposite the first tutorial's opening page for each level of the text, the Read This Before You Begin Page helps introduce technology into the classroom. Technical considerations and assumptions about software are listed to save time and eliminate unnecessary aggravation. Notes about the Data Disks help instructors and students get the right files in the right places, so students get started on the right foot.

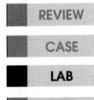

Quick Check Questions Each session concludes with meaningful, conceptual Quick Check questions that test students' understanding of what they learned in the session. Answers to the Quick Check questions are provided at the end of each tutorial.

Reference Windows Reference Windows are succinct summaries of the most important tasks covered in a tutorial and they preview actions students will perform in the steps to follow.

Task Reference Located as a table at the end of the book, the Task Reference contains a summary of how to perform common tasks using the most efficient method as well as references to pages where the task is discussed in more detail.

End-of-Tutorial Review Assignments and Case Problems Review Assignments provide students with additional hands-on practice of the skills they learned in the tutorial using the same case presented in the tutorial. These Assignments are followed by four Case Problems that have approximately the same scope as the tutorial case but use a different scenario. In addition, some of the Review Assignments or Case Problems may include Exploration Exercises that challenge students and encourage them to explore the capabilities of the program they are using, and/or further extend their knowledge.

File Finder Chart This chart, located in the back of the book, visually explains how a student should set up their Data Disk, what files should go in what folders, and what they'll be saving the files as in the course of their work.

MOUS Certification Chart In the back of the book, you'll find a chart that lists all the skills for the Microsoft Office User Specialist Core and Expert Exams on Outlook 2000. With page numbers referencing where these skills are covered in this text and where students get hands-on practice in completing the skills, the chart can be used as an excellent study guide in preparing for the Microsoft Outlook 2000 Core or Expert exam.

New Perspectives on Microsoft® Outlook® 2000—Introductory Instructor's Resource Kit contains:

- Electronic Instructor's Manual in Word 97 format
- Data Files
- Solution Files
- ExamView Testbank
- ExamView Engine
- Figure Files
- Sample Syllabus

These supplements come on CD-ROM. If you don't have access to a CD-ROM drive, contact your Course Technology customer service representative for more information.

The New Perspectives Supplements Package

Electronic Instructor's Manual Our Instructor's Manuals include tutorial overviews and outlines, technical notes, lecture notes, solutions, and Extra Case Problems. Many instructors use the Extra Case Problems for performance-based exams or extra credit projects. The Instructor's Manual is available as an electronic file, which you can get from the Instructor Resource Kit (IRK) CD-ROM or download it from **www.course.com**.

Data Files Data Files contain all of the data that students will use to complete the tutorials, Review Assignments, Case Problems, and Additional Cases. A Readme file includes instructions for using the files. See the "Read This Before You Begin" page for more information on Data Files.

Solution Files Solution Files contain every file students are asked to create or modify in the tutorials, Review Assignments, Case Problems, Extra Case Problems, and Additional Cases. A Help file on the Instructor's Resource Kit includes information for using the Solution files.

Figure Files Many figures in the text are provided on the IRK CD-ROM to help illustrate key topics or concepts. Instructors can create traditional overhead transparencies by printing the figure files. Or they can create electronic slide shows by using the figures in a presentation program such as PowerPoint.

ExamView® This textbook is accompanied by ExamView, a powerful testing software package that allows instructors to create and administer printed, computer (LAN-based), and Internet exams. ExamView includes hundreds of questions that correspond to the topics covered in this text, enabling students to generate detailed study guides that include page references for further review. The computer-based and Internet testing components allow students to take exams at their computers, and also save the instructor time by grading each exam automatically.

More innovative technology

Course CBT Enhance your students' Office 2000 classroom learning experience with self-paced computer-based training on CD-ROM. Course CBT engages students with interactive multimedia and hands-on simulations that reinforce and complement the concepts and skills covered in the textbook. All the content is aligned with the MOUS (Microsoft Office User Specialist) program, making it a great preparation tool for the certification exams. Course CBT also includes extensive pre- and post-assessments that test students' mastery of skills. These pre- and post-assessments automatically generate a "custom learning path" through the course that highlights only the topics students need help with.

Skills Assessment Manager (SAM) How well do your students *really* know Microsoft Office? SAM is a performance-based testing program that measures students' proficiency in Microsoft Office 2000. SAM is available for Office 2000 in either a live or simulated environment. You can use SAM to place students into or out of courses, monitor their performance throughout a course, and help prepare them for the MOUS certification exams.

CyberClass CyberClass is a Web-based tool designed for on-campus or distance learning. Use it to enhance how you currently run your class by posting assignments and your course syllabus or holding online office hours. Or, use it for your distance learning course, and offer mini-lectures, conduct online discussion groups, or give your mid-term exam. For more information, visit our Web site at: *www.course.com/products/cyberclass/index.html.*

WebCT WebCT is a tool used to create Web-based educational environments and also uses WWW browsers as the interface for the course-building environment. The site is hosted on your school campus, allowing complete control over the information. WebCT has its own internal communication system, offering internal e-mail, a Bulletin Board, and a Chat room. Course Technology offers pre-existing supplemental information to help in your WebCT class creation, such as a suggested Syllabus, Lecture Notes, Figures in the Book, Course Presenter, Student Downloads, and Test Banks in which you can schedule an exam, create reports, and more.

Acknowledgments

It's truly a pleasure to work with the Course Technology team. Greg Donald, managing editor, thank you for the opportunity to expand two earlier Outlook tutorials into a full book. Donna Gridley, senior editor, thanks for shepherding this book through the entire process. Jennifer Goguen, production editor, thanks for smoothly turning manuscript into a finished book.

Many thanks to reviewers Pat Hathaway, Paul D. Camp Community College; Mary McIntosh, Red River College; and Connie Poferl, for feedback that was constructive as well as encouraging. I very much appreciate the efforts of Alex White in Quality Assurance and QA testers Marianne Broughey and Justin Rand for their sharp attention to details as they worked their way through the tutorials.

A very special thank you to Rachel Biheller Bunin, developmental editor. Your keen editing, thoughtful comments and suggestions, and careful tracking of all the details helped bring this book to a higher level. Thanks also for your encouraging phone calls and ready supply of e-mail jokes. I look forward to the next time.

Thanks to my husband, Brian Romer, for making sure I ate and slept regularly throughout the creation of this book. Your love and encouragement makes this all possible. My family also plays an important role. In particular, thanks to my brothers Gregg Geller for testing the Exchange material and Mitch Geller for technical consultation throughout.

TABLE OF CONTENTS

Tutorial 3   OUT 3.01

Managing Contacts

Communicating with LinkUp's Members

Tutorial 4   OUT 4.01

Managing Your Inbox

Arranging a Crew for Speedy Cleaning Company

Tutorial 5   OUT 5.01

Integrating Outlook with Other Programs

Working with Homebuyers for Ace Realty

Tutorial 6   OUT 6.01

Customizing Outlook

Creating Contributor Contact Forms for Luminescence

Reference Window

Tutorial Tips

These tutorials will help you learn about Microsoft Outlook 2000. The tutorials are designed to be worked through at a computer. Each tutorial is divided into two sessions. Watch for the session headings, such as Session 1.1 and Session 1.2. Each session is designed to be completed in about 45 minutes, but take as much time as you need. It's also a good idea to take a break between sessions.

To use the tutorials effectively, read the following questions and answers before you begin.

Where do I start?

Each tutorial begins with a case, which sets the scene for the tutorial and gives you background information to help you understand what you will be doing. Read the case before you go to the lab. In the lab, begin with the first session of a tutorial.

How do I know what to do on the computer?

Each session contains steps that you will perform on the computer to learn how to use Microsoft Outlook 2000. Read the text that introduces each series of steps. The steps you need to do at a computer are numbered and are set against a shaded background. Read each step carefully and completely before you try it.

How do I know if I did the step correctly?

As you work, compare your computer screen with the corresponding figure in the tutorial. Don't worry if your screen display is somewhat different from the figure. The important parts of the screen display are labeled in each figure. Check to make sure these parts are on your screen.

What if I make a mistake?

Don't worry about making mistakes—they are part of the learning process. Paragraphs labeled "TROUBLE?" identify common problems and explain how to get back on track. Follow the steps in a TROUBLE? paragraph only if you are having the problem described. If you run into other problems:

- Carefully consider the current state of your system, the position of the pointer, and any messages on the screen.
- Complete the sentence, "Now I want to..." Be specific, because identifying your goal will help you rethink the steps you need to take to reach that goal.
- If you are working on a particular piece of software, consult the Help system.
- If the suggestions above don't solve your problem, consult your technical support person for assistance.

How do I use the Reference Windows?

Reference Windows summarize the procedures you will learn in the tutorial steps. Do not complete the actions in the Reference Windows when you are working through the tutorial. Instead, refer to the Reference Windows while you are working on the assignments at the end of the tutorial.

How can I test my understanding of the material I learned in the tutorial?

At the end of each session, you can answer the Quick Check questions. The answers for the Quick Checks are at the end of that tutorial.

After you have completed the entire tutorial, you should complete the Review Assignments and Case Problems. They are carefully structured so that you will review what you have learned and then apply your knowledge to new situations.

What if I can't remember how to do something?

You should refer to the Task Reference at the end of the book; it summarizes how to accomplish tasks using the most efficient method.

Before you begin the tutorials, you should know the basics about your computer's operating system. You should also know how to use the menus, dialog boxes, Help system, and My Computer.

How can I prepare for MOUS Certification?

The Microsoft Office User Specialist (MOUS) logo on the cover of this book indicates that Microsoft has approved it as a study guide for Microsoft Outlook 2000. At the back of this text, you'll see a chart that outlines the specific Microsoft certification skills for Microsoft Outlook 2000 that are covered in the tutorials. You'll need to learn these skills if you're interested in taking a MOUS exam. If you decide to take a MOUS exam, or if you just want to study a specific skill, this chart will give you an easy reference to the page number on which the skill is covered. To learn more about the MOUS certification program refer to the preface in the front of the book or go to *http://www.mous.net*.

Now that you've read the Tutorial Tips, you are ready to begin.

New Perspectives on

MICROSOFT®
OUTLOOK® 2000

Read This Before You Begin

To the Student

Data Disks

To complete the tutorials, Review Assignments, and Case Problems in this book, you need two Data Disks. Your instructor will either provide you with Data Disks or ask you to make your own.

If you are making your own Data Disks, you will need two blank, formatted, high-density disks. You will need to copy a set of folders from a file server or standalone computer or the Web onto your disks. Your instructor will tell you which computer, drive letter, and folders contain the files you need. You also could download the files by going to *www.course.com*, clicking Student Downloads, and following the instructions on the screen.

The following list shows you which folders go on each of your disks so that you will have enough disk space to complete all the tutorials, Review Assignments, and Case Problems:

Data Disk 1

Write this on the disk label: Data Disk 1: Tutorials 1, 2, 3, and 4

Put these folders on the disk: Tutorial.01, Tutorial.02, Tutorial.03, Tutorial.04

Data Disk 2

Write this on the disk label: Data Disk 2: Tutorials 5, 6, and 7

Put these folders on the disk: Tutorial.05, Tutorial.06, Tutorial.07

When you begin each tutorial, be sure you are using the correct Data Disk. See the inside front or inside back cover of this book for more information on Data Disk files, or ask your instructor or technical support person for assistance.

Using Your Own Computer

If you are going to work through this book using your own computer, you need:

- **Computer System:** Microsoft Office 2000 Professional (Outlook, Word, Access, Excel, and PowerPoint) and Windows 98, Windows 2000, or Windows NT must be installed on your computer. This book assumes a complete installation of Outlook 2000.

- **Data Disks:** You will not be able to complete the tutorials or exercises in this book using your own computer until you have Data Disks.

Set Up Notes

To complete the steps in these tutorials as they were written, you must have Outlook set up for the Corporate or Workgroup service option (not No E-mail or Internet Only). If you use a different service option, then not all features are available or work as described. If your system is set up for No E-mail, then you need to switch to Internet Only before you can switch to Corporate or Workgroup.

To find out which Outlook service option is set up on your system:

1. Click Help on the menu bar, and then click About Microsoft Outlook. The service option is listed below the version and copyright information.
2. Click the OK button to close the About Microsoft Outlook dialog box.

To switch from the No E-mail service option to the Internet Only service option:

1. Click Tools on the menu bar, and then click Accounts. The Internet Accounts dialog box opens.
2. Click the Add button, and then click Mail. The Internet Connection Wizard dialog box opens so you can set up a new account.

3. Type your name in the first Internet Connection Wizard dialog box, and then click the Next button.
4. Continue to enter the requested information in the Internet Connection Wizard dialog boxes. Click the Next button to move to the next dialog box.
5. Click the Finish button to have the wizard set up your account based on the information you entered. Outlook changes to the Internet Only option when you set up an Internet account.

To switch from the Internet Only service option to the Corporate or Workgroup service option:

1. Click Tools on the menu bar, and then click Options. The Options dialog box opens.
2. Click the Mail Delivery tab.
3. Click the Reconfigure Mail Support button to open the Outlook 2000 Startup wizard.
4. Click the Corporate or Workgroup option button, and then click the Next button. A dialog box opens, informing you that changing the Outlook configuration from Internet Only to Corporate or Workgroup will affect all users of Outlook on this machine and that you'll need to restart Outlook to have the change occur.
5. Click the Yes button to exit Outlook.
6. Restart Outlook. You may need to insert the Office 2000 CD-ROM to complete the switch to the Corporate or Workgroup option. Outlook opens with the Corporate or Workgroup service option.

Visit Our World Wide Web Site

Additional materials designed especially for you are available on the World Wide Web. Go to http://www.course.com.

To install fax service for Windows 98 after installing Office/Outlook:

1. Insert the Windows 98 CD-ROM in the CD-ROM drive, and run the program called Awfax.exe located in the folder tools\oldwin95\message\us. The message will say that you must have Outlook 97 installed; it works for Outlook 2000 as well.
2. Open the Control Panel.
3. Double-click Add/Remove Programs.
4. Click Microsoft Office 2000 and then click Add/Remove
5. Click the Repair Office button in the Microsoft Office 2000 Maintenance Mode dialog box.
6. Click the Repair Errors in My Office Installation option button.
7. Click Finish and then wait for the process to complete. (This can take 10–15 minutes or longer, depending on your system.)

To install the Net Folders add-in:

1. Click Tools on the menu bar, click Options, and then click the Other tab in the Options dialog box.
2. Click the Advanced Options button, and then click the Add-In Manager button.
3. If Net Folders does not appear in the Add-In Manager dialog box, click the Install button, and then double-click the fldpub.ecf file.
4. Click the Net Folders check box to insert a check mark, and then click the OK button in each dialog box.

To the Instructor

The Data Files are available on the Instructor's Resource Kit for this title. Follow the instructions in the Help file on the CD-ROM to install the programs to your network or standalone computer. For information on creating Data Disks, see the "To the Student" section above.

You are granted a license to copy the Data Files to any computer or computer network used by students who have purchased this book.

Set Up Notes

Before beginning the tutorials, students must verify that Outlook is set up with the Corporate or Workgroup service option. Students will need a profile, which you can create for them or they can create by following the steps in Tutorial 1, and an e-mail account and Internet access. Tutorial 5 uses the Fax service, which requires a manual installation in Windows 98; they'll need a modem and phone/fax line to complete all the steps. Tutorial 7 requires the Net Folders add-in. For more information, see the "To the Student" section above.

COMMUNICATING BY E-MAIL

Sending and Receiving Messages for The Express Lane

CASE

The Express Lane

The Express Lane is a complete and affordable online grocery store in the San Francisco Bay Area, specializing in natural and organic foods. When Alan Gregory and Lora Shaw began The Express Lane in 1998, fewer than 200,000 U.S. households were using online services to purchase food and other household goods and services; by 2007, this number is expected to reach 15 to 20 million (Andersen Consulting, January 20, 1998).

Unlike traditional grocers, The Express Lane does not have a storefront where customers come to shop. Instead it stores both packaged goods and fresh produce in its warehouse. Customers place orders through the company's Web site. The Express Lane staff confirms the order by e-mail, selects and packs the requested items, bills the customer's credit card for the cost of the groceries plus a $5 service fee, and delivers the groceries to the customer's front door at the day and time selected by the customer.

Alan focuses on the supplier end of the business, ensuring that the warehouse has the proper stock, locating new suppliers, and preparing budgets. Lora focuses on the customer end of the business, which includes finding new customers, responding to customer comments, and processing customer payments. To coordinate these activities, The Express Lane relies on **Microsoft Outlook 2000**, a personal information management program that helps you perform a wide range of communication and organizational tasks, such as sending, receiving, and filing e-mail; organizing contacts; scheduling appointments, events, and meetings; creating a to-do list and delegating tasks; and writing notes. Outlook is part of the Office 2000 Professional Suite. In this tutorial, you'll use Outlook's e-mail to send information about increasing an order to a supplier. You'll also set up a Personal Address Book, create entries for all the suppliers, and send a message to the group of suppliers.

**SESSION
1.1**

In this session, you'll learn about the Outlook components. First you'll start Outlook, view its window elements, and navigate between components. Then you'll create and send an e-mail message. Finally you'll create and organize a personal address book.

Exploring Outlook

Outlook is organized into six components, as described in Figure 1-1. With these six components you can perform all the communication, scheduling, and organizational tasks you need to work efficiently and effectively. Each component generates a specific **item**, the basic element that holds information in Outlook (similar to a file in other programs). Items include e-mail messages, appointments, contacts, tasks, journal entries, and notes. These items are organized by and stored in **folders**. Unlike other folders in Office programs, which you can view and open in Windows Explorer, Outlook folders are available only from within Outlook.

Figure 1-1	OUTLOOK COMPONENTS
COMPONENT	**DESCRIPTION**
Mail	A communication tool for receiving, sending, storing, and managing e-mail. The Inbox folder stores messages you receive; the Outbox folder stores outgoing messages you have written but not sent.
Calendar	A scheduling tool for planning your appointments, events, and meetings.
Contacts	An address book for compiling street addresses, phone numbers, e-mail and Web addresses, and other personal information about people with whom you communicate.
Tasks	A to-do list for organizing and tracking items you need to complete or delegate.
Notes	A notepad for jotting down ideas and thoughts, which you can group, sort, and categorize.
Journal	A diary for recording your activities, such as talking on the phone, sending an e-mail message, or working on a document.

Outlook has three installation options—No E-mail, Internet Mail Only, and Corporate or Workgroup. Each option changes the functions and features available to you. All three options set up Outlook as a personal information manager (PIM), which enables you to use the Calendar, Contacts, Journal, Notes, and Tasks folders, but not all the features for the folders are available in each option. The No E-mail option provides no access to the Mail component, and only some access to Outlook's other features. The Internet Mail Only option enables you to send and receive e-mail over only the Internet or an intranet using a modem and a dial-up Internet service provider, and provides access to most of Outlook's features. The Corporate or Workgroup option connects Outlook to any type of e-mail service, and gives you access to all of Outlook's capabilities. *The tutorials in this book assume you are using Outlook with the Corporate or Workgroup installation.*

Starting Outlook

Before you can use the Corporate or Workgroup installation of Outlook, you need a **profile**—a group of settings that specify how Outlook is set up for a user on a specific computer. A profile includes information that tells Outlook who you are and how Outlook works for you. If you use Outlook on multiple computers, you will need to set up a profile on each computer. A profile can include multiple **information services**, which are settings that specify how you send, receive, and store messages, addresses, and other items. Although each person can have multiple profiles, typically you need only one. When several people share one computer, they each should have a different profile to ensure that their Outlook information remains separate from the other users' information. The most complex part of using Outlook is setting up a profile because the options and required information change, depending on which information services you choose to install, your computer configuration, your e-mail or Internet service provider, and so forth. For example, when you add the Internet E-mail information service, you will need to know the incoming and outgoing server addresses among other information. These addresses are usually available from your ISP or network administrator. The setup wizard walks you through the steps of creating or adding information services to a profile.

Like most other programs, you can start Outlook in many ways: click the Outlook button on the Quick Launch toolbar, click the Outlook icon on your desktop, or use the Start menu. When you start Outlook, the default profile opens or you are prompted to create one. If there are multiple profiles already set up, you may be prompted to select a profile from an existing list.

To start Outlook:

1. Make sure that Windows is running on your computer and that the Windows desktop appears on your screen.

2. Click the **Start** button on the taskbar to display the Start menu, and then point to **Programs** to display the Programs menu.

3. Point to **Microsoft Outlook** on the Programs menu.

   TROUBLE? If you don't see Microsoft Outlook on the Programs menu, point to Microsoft Office and then point to Microsoft Outlook. If you still can't find Microsoft Outlook, click the Outlook icon on the Quick Launch toolbar or on your desktop. If none of the above is available, ask your instructor or technical support person for help.

4. Click **Microsoft Outlook**. What happens next depends on whether none, one, or multiple profiles are set up on your computer.

   TROUBLE? If you have the Internet Mail Only installation and need to switch to the Corporate or Workgroup Installation, click Tools on the menu bar, click the Options button, click the Mail Services tab, click the Reconfigure Mail Support button, click the Corporate or Workgroup option button, click the Next button, and then click the Yes button. You may have to restart Outlook and insert the Microsoft Office 2000 CD-ROM for the change to take effect.

5. Choose the next action to take by comparing your screen to the descriptions below:

   If the Choose Profile dialog box opens and you already have a profile, click the **Profile Name** list arrow, click your profile name, and then click the **OK** button. The Outlook program window opens, and you should read but not complete the next set of steps.

   If the Choose Profile dialog box opens and you need to create a profile, click the **New** button, and then continue with Step 3 in the next set of steps.

   If the Inbox Setup Wizard dialog box opens, then there are no profiles set up for Outlook. Skip to Step 3 in the next set of steps.

If the Outlook program window opens, then a default profile is set to open when Outlook starts. To create a new profile, complete the next set of steps. To restart Outlook with a different profile, click **Tools** on the menu bar, click **Options**, click the **Mail Services** tab, click the **Prompt for Profile** to be used option button, and then click the **OK** button. Click **File** on the menu bar, click **Exit**, and then restart Outlook.

If the Outlook Startup Setup Wizard dialog box opens, welcoming you to Outlook and offering to guide you through Configuring Outlook, follow the steps in the wizard.

The next set of steps walks you through the process of setting up a new profile. You need to do this only once. If you are working on a lab computer, your instructor or technical support person may have already set up a profile for you. If you are unsure whether you need to or have the access to set up a profile, check with your instructor or technical support person.

To set up a profile:

1. If necessary, click the **New** button to open the Microsoft Outlook Setup Wizard, and then click the **Show Profiles** button to open the Mail dialog box, which lists the existing profiles.

   TROUBLE? If the Inbox Setup Wizard dialog box opens instead of the Microsoft Outlook Setup Wizard, then no profiles exist for Outlook. Continue with Step 2.

   TROUBLE? If you need to set up a profile, but see only the main Outlook program window, do the following: Click the Start button on the taskbar, point to Settings, and then click Control Panel. Double-click Mail to open the Mail dialog box. Continue with Step 2. If you still have trouble, ask your instructor or technical support person for help.

2. Click the **Add** button to open the Inbox Setup Wizard dialog box. This dialog box lists available information services that you can add to your profile. See Figure 1-2.

Figure 1-2   INBOX SETUP WIZARD DIALOG BOX

information services available; your list may be different

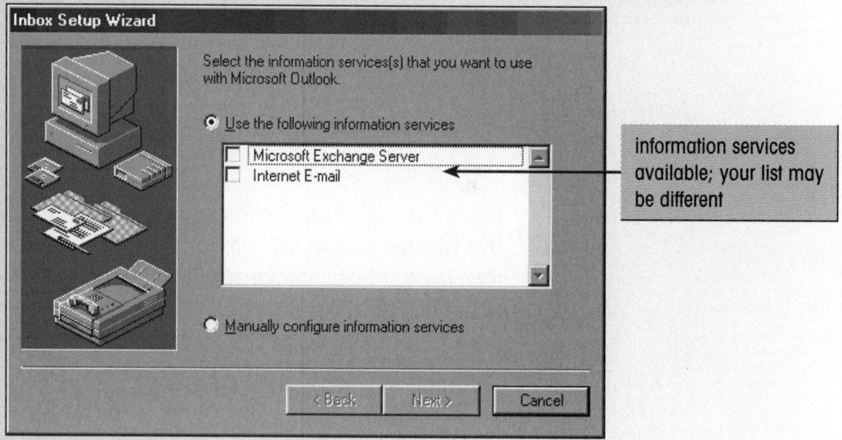

TROUBLE? If you see more information services than shown in Figure 1-2, it means that your installation of Outlook has other features available.

The more information services you add, the longer Outlook takes to open. So, add only those services you plan to use. For this tutorial, you'll need an e-mail service.

3. Click the **Internet E-mail** (or appropriate e-mail information service) check box to select it, and then click the **Next** button to display the next wizard dialog box.

4. Type your name in the Profile Name text box, and then click the **Next** button.

5. Click the **Setup Mail Account** button. The Mail Account Properties dialog box opens. See Figure 1-3.

| Figure 1-3 | MAIL ACCOUNT PROPERTIES DIALOG BOX |

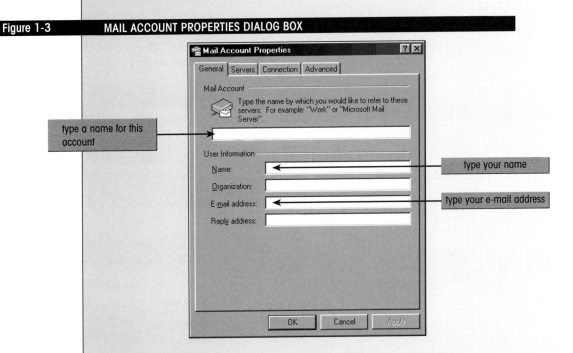

6. On the General tab, type **NP Outlook** as the name for this mail account. Notice the title bar changes to reflect what you type in this text box.

7. Press the **Tab** key, type your name (which will appear on every e-mail message you send) in the Name text box, and then type your e-mail address in the E-mail address text box. You need to enter a reply e-mail only if you want to receive messages at a different address than you send them from.

8. Click the **Servers** tab, and then type:

   ■ the server for messages you will receive in the Incoming mail (POP3) text box
   ■ the server for messages you will send in the Outgoing mail (SMTP) text box
   ■ your Internet account or user name in the Account name text box
   ■ your Internet password in the Password text box

If you want to ensure that anyone who accesses your Outlook profile cannot also access your e-mail, leave the Password text box empty and click the Remember password check box to remove the check mark; you then will have to enter your password each time you access your e-mail.

TROUBLE? If you don't know your server information, your account number, or your password, ask your instructor or technical support person for help.

9. Click the **Connection** tab, and then click the option button next to the type of connection you will use, such as Local Area Network or phone line. If you use your phone line, select the Dial-Up Networking connection for your modem.

You won't make any changes to the Advanced tab unless specified by your ISP or server administrator.

10. Click the **OK** button to return to the Inbox Setup Wizard dialog box, and then click the **Next** button. The Inbox Setup Wizard dialog box prompts you to indicate the location for your **personal folder file**—a special folder on your hard disk (not a network server) in which Outlook information, such as items, folders, and messages, are saved.

11. Click the **Browse** button, and then switch to the location specified by your instructor or technical support person, type your name in the File name text box, and then click the **Open** button.

12. Click the **Next** button, and then click the **Finish** button to set up your profile with the information services listed in the final Inbox Setup Wizard dialog box.

TROUBLE? If you opened the Mail dialog box through the Control Panel, click the Close button in the Mail dialog box.

13. If necessary, click the **Profile Name** list arrow in the Choose Profile dialog box, click your profile name, and then click the **OK** button.

After a short pause, the Outlook program window opens.

14. If necessary, click the **Maximize** button. Figure 1-4 shows the maximized Outlook window with the Inbox displayed.

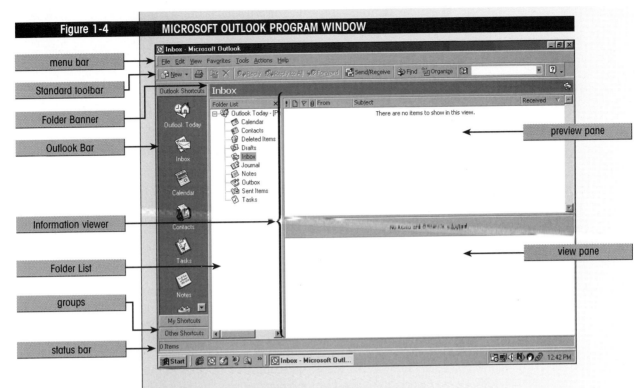

Figure 1-4   MICROSOFT OUTLOOK PROGRAM WINDOW

menu bar
Standard toolbar
Folder Banner
Outlook Bar
Information viewer
Folder List
groups
status bar

preview pane
view pane

TROUBLE? If your screen does not show the Outlook Bar, Folder List, status bar, or the Inbox, don't worry. You'll learn how to hide and display these shortly.

TROUBLE? Don't worry if your screen differs slightly from Figure 1-4. Although the figures in this book were created while running Windows 98 in its default settings, all Windows operating systems share the same basic user interface. Microsoft Outlook should run equally well using Windows 95, Windows 98 in Web style, Windows NT, or Windows 2000.

With your profile set up and Outlook started, you're ready to explore Outlook. The Outlook window contains some elements that might be familiar to you from other Microsoft Office programs. Other elements are specific to Outlook. The Outlook window includes the following (refer to Figure 1-4):

■ **Menu bar**—groups of related commands that are organized into lists, called **menus**. You use the menu commands to perform tasks. Menu commands vary, depending on the displayed Outlook folder.

■ **Standard toolbar**—a collection of shortcut icons to frequently used menu commands that you can click to quickly perform a task. The toolbar's buttons vary, depending on the displayed Outlook folder. Additional toolbars are available in different folders.

■ **Outlook Bar**—groups of shortcut icons that you can click to open frequently used folders, files, and Web sites. You can add more shortcut icons to quickly open other folders on your system or network.

■ **Groups**—collections of related shortcut icons to folders, files, and Web sites. Click a group button to display its contents.

■ **Folder List**—a hierarchy of the Outlook folders that you use to store and organize items.

■ **Folder Banner**—a bar that displays the name of the open folder (Inbox in Figure 1-4). To display a list of all folders, click the folder name.

■ **Information viewer**—the screen display of items stored in the selected folder; may be divided into panes. For example, in Figure 1-4, the Information viewer for the Inbox is divided into two panes. The upper pane displays the list of stored items, such as e-mail messages in the Inbox. The lower pane displays the item selected in the upper pane, such as the contents of the selected e-mail message.

■ **Status bar**—a banner of helpful details about the current view, such as the number of items that appear in that view.

No matter which component you use, these features of the Outlook window work in the same way. You can display or hide any of these elements, depending on your needs and preferences. For your work here, you'll customize the Outlook window to match Figure 1-4.

Customizing the Outlook Window

You'll use the View menu to change which features of the Outlook window are displayed. As with all the Office 2000 programs, when you first display any menu, a short, personalized menu may appear with the most recently used commands. After a short pause, the full menu appears. You can also click the double arrow at the bottom of the menu to display the full menu. Once you use a command on the full menu, it moves to the short menu. The first time you open Outlook, the menus and toolbars display all of the basic commands and buttons. As you work, however, Outlook personalizes the menus and toolbars based on how often you use the commands. Eventually, the menus and toolbars will display only the commands and toolbar buttons you use most often.

To customize the Outlook window:

1. Click **View** on the menu bar. Remember to pause a moment or click the double arrow to display the full menu, if necessary.

   Items that you can display or hide appear on the menu. Those that appear are preceded by a check mark or have the shortcut icon clicked to appear pressed in. Clicking those items hides them.

2. Click **Outlook Bar**. The Outlook Bar disappears from your screen.

   TROUBLE? If the Outlook Bar was not already displayed, then it appears rather than disappears. Skip to Step 4.

   You want to display the Outlook Bar, preview pane, status bar, and Folder List.

3. Click **View** on the menu bar, and then click **Outlook Bar**. The Outlook Bar reappears.

4. Use the View menu to display the Preview Pane, Status bar, and Folder List as necessary. Your screen should now look similar to Figure 1-4.

   TROUBLE? If you do not see Preview Pane on the view menu, then you are probably in a folder that doesn't have a preview pane. You'll learn how to switch to the Inbox in the next section. At that time, be sure Preview Pane is selected.

As you can see, the Folder List duplicates the information in the Outlook Bar. Both enable you to move between different Outlook folders. Your Folder List may have different items than the Outlook Bar if you customized either one.

Navigating Between Outlook Components

You can click any icon in the Outlook Bar to display its folder's contents in the Information viewer. The Outlook Bar is split into three groups (collections of related shortcut icons). For example, the Outlook Shortcuts group includes shortcuts to a variety of the built-in folders—Outlook Today, Inbox, Calendar, Contacts, Tasks, Notes, and Deleted Items. You click a group bar to display its contents. For example, you can click the My Shortcuts group bar to see shortcuts to the Drafts, Outbox, Sent Items, and Journal folders and the Outlook Update Web page. You can click the Other Shortcuts group to view the shortcuts to My Computer, and the My Documents and Favorites folders.

A second way to navigate between folders is with the Folder List. You can click any folder icon in the Folder List to display the folder's contents in the Information viewer. You'll practice working with both methods.

To navigate between Outlook components:

1. Click the **Outlook Shortcuts** group bar, if necessary, to display its shortcuts.

2. Click **Calendar** on the Outlook Bar to switch to the Calendar. Notice the daily planner, current and next month calendar, and the TaskPad. See Figure 1-5.

Figure 1-5	CALENDAR INFORMATION VIEWER

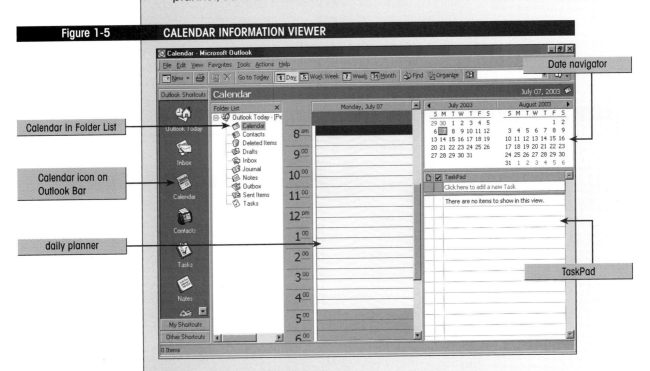

TROUBLE? If your Calendar looks different, then the view is not set to Day. Click the Day button on the Standard toolbar to change the view.

3. Click the **My Shortcuts** group bar. The My Shortcuts group fills the Outlook Bar so you can see its shortcuts.

4. Click **Journal** in the My Shortcuts group on the Outlook Bar to switch to the Journal. Notice that the Journal displays a timeline. If the Journal is turned on, you will see icons representing any e-mail messages, files, phone calls, tasks, and other items organized by date. Today's date is selected. See Figure 1-6.

| Figure 1-6 | JOURNAL INFORMATION VIEWER |

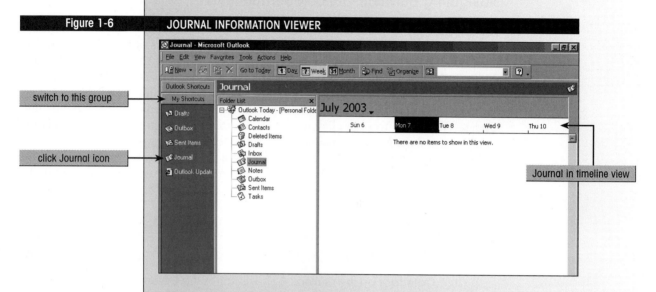

switch to this group

click Journal icon

Journal in timeline view

TROUBLE? If the Office Assistant or a dialog box appears, asking whether you want to turn on the Journal, click the No button.

5. Click the **Outlook Shortcuts** group bar and then click **Contacts**. Letter buttons appear on the right side of the screen. Each letter button, when clicked, will move you to contacts beginning with that letter. See Figure 1-7.

| Figure 1-7 | CONTACTS INFORMATION VIEWER |

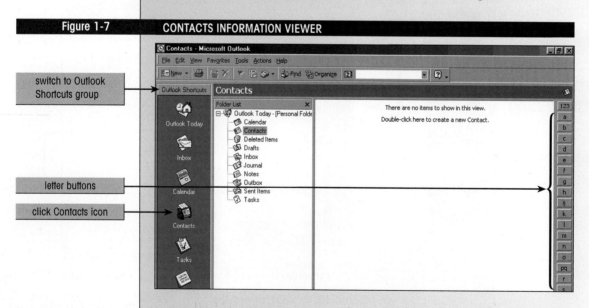

switch to Outlook Shortcuts group

letter buttons

click Contacts icon

You can also move between Outlook components using the Folder List.

6. Click the **Calendar** icon in the Folder List.

7. Click the **Inbox** icon in the Folder List.

You can switch quickly to any Outlook folder using either the Outlook Bar or the Folder List. To increase the space available on your screen for the Information viewer, you'll hide the Folder List.

8. Click the **Close** button in the upper-right corner of the Folder List. The Folder List closes and the Information viewer expands to fill the extra space.

The Information viewer displays the contents of the Inbox folder, from where you create e-mail messages.

Sending E-mail Messages

E-mail, the electronic transfer of messages between computers, is a simple and inexpensive way to stay in touch with friends around the corner, family across the country, and colleagues in the same building or around the world. You send messages whenever you have time. The messages are delivered immediately and stored until recipients can read those messages at their convenience. The Express Lane staff uses e-mail to correspond with its customers, suppliers, and each other. Staff members use e-mail for both internal and external communications because it is fast, convenient, and inexpensive. In addition, it saves the company the cost of additional supplies for paper, ink or toner, and so forth.

Before you can send and receive e-mail messages with Outlook, you must have access to an e-mail server or Internet service provider (ISP), an e-mail address, and a password. An **e-mail address** is a series of characters that you use to send and receive e-mail messages. It consists of a user ID and a host name separated by the @ symbol. A **user ID** (or user name or account name) is a unique name that identifies you to your mail server. The **host name** consists of the name of your Internet service provider's computer on the Internet plus its domain or level. For example, look how each of the parts makes up the following e-mail address in Figure 1-8.

Figure 1-8	PARTS OF AN E-MAIL ADDRESS

alan@expresslane.com

user ID   host name

Although many people might use the same host, each user ID is unique, enabling the host to distinguish one user from another. A **password** is a private code that you enter to access your account. (In this book, you'll use your own e-mail address to send all messages.)

Choosing a Message Format

Outlook can send and receive messages in three formats: HTML, Outlook Rich Text, and Plain Text. Although you specify one of these formats as the default for your messages, you can always switch formats for an individual message. **HTML** provides the most formatting features and options (including text formatting, numbering, bullets, paragraph alignment, horizontal lines, backgrounds, pictures and animated graphics, and multimedia files). **Outlook Rich Text** provides some formatting options (including text formatting, bullets, paragraph alignment, and embedded objects), but some recipients will not be able to see the formatting if you send messages over the Internet. **Plain Text** messages include no formatting, and the recipient specifies which font is used for the message. When you reply to a message, Outlook uses the same format in which the message was created. For example, if you reply to a message sent to you in Plain Text, Outlook sends the response in Plain Text.

So which message format should you use as your default? HTML is appropriate when you want to enhance your messages with formatting, although some recipients may not receive your messages properly. The Outlook Rich Text is best for recipients that also are using Outlook. Because you often do not know what program others are using, you'll usually want to stick to Plain Text. Plain Text ensures that all recipients can read your messages, no matter what e-mail program they are using. In addition, the Plain Text e-mail files are smaller, which means they take less time to travel to their destination and require less storage space.

You'll set the default message format to Plain Text to ensure everyone can read your messages and that they are the smallest size possible.

To choose a default message format:

1. Click **Tools** on the menu bar, and then click **Options**. The Options dialog box opens.

2. Click the **Mail Format** tab in the Options dialog box.

3. Click the **Send in this message format** list arrow, review the options, and then click **Plain Text** in the Send in this message format list box. See Figure 1-9.

Figure 1-9	OPTIONS DIALOG BOX

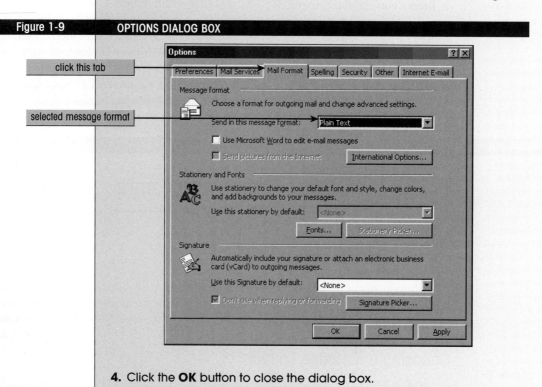

4. Click the **OK** button to close the dialog box.

Each time you create a message, Outlook will use the Plain Text format, unless you select a different format for that message.

Creating an E-mail Message

An e-mail message looks similar to a memo, which has separate header lines for the Date, To, From, Cc, and Subject followed by the body of the message. Outlook automatically fills in the Date line with the date on which you send the message and the From line with your name or e-mail address; these lines are not visible in the Message window. You complete the other lines. The To line lists the e-mail addresses of one or more recipients. The Cc line lists the e-mail addresses of anyone who will receive a courtesy copy of the message. An optional Bcc line lists the e-mail addresses of anyone who will receive a blind courtesy copy of the message; the Bcc recipients are not visible to each other or to the To and Cc recipients. You might use Bcc when you send notification messages to a large group of people, such as an address change notification to your entire e-mail list, but you don't want to publicize everyone's e-mail address. Do not add any spaces to e-mail addresses when you type them or your message will be returned. The Subject line provides a quick overview of the message topic, like a headline. The main part of an e-mail message is the message body.

Like any other type of communication, e-mail is governed by its own customs of behavior, called **netiquette** (short for Internet etiquette), to help prevent miscommunications and hard feelings. As you write and send e-mail messages, keep in mind the following guidelines:

- **Reread your messages.** Your words can have a lasting impact. Be sure they convey the thoughts you intended and want others to attribute to you. Your name and e-mail address are attached to every message that you send, and your e-mail can be forwarded swiftly to others.

- **Be concise.** The recipient should be able to read and understand your message quickly.

- **Use standard capitalization.** Excessive use of uppercase is considered shouting and exclusive use of lowercase is difficult to read.

- **Check spelling and grammar.** Create and maintain a professional image by using standard grammar and spelling. What you say is just as important as how you say it.

- **Avoid sarcasm.** Without vocal intonations and body language, a recipient may read your words as insulting or derogatory. To help convey emotions and feelings, you can use smileys or emoticons, such as :-). To learn additional smileys, there are many smiley dictionaries you can refer to on the Web. You can use your favorite search engine to search on the keywords "smiley dictionary" to find good sites or you can try:
  paul.merton.ox.ac.uk/ascii/smileys.html,
  www.eff.org/papers/eegtti/eeg_286.html,
  www.les.aston.ac.uk/it/smile.html, or
  www.gifford.co.uk/tribbles/other/smilies.html.

- **Don't send confidential information.** E-mail is not private and once you send it you lose control over where it may go and who might read it. Also, employers or schools usually can access their employees' or students' e-mail messages.

The adage "Act in haste; repent in leisure" is particularly apt for writing e-mail. For more e-mail netiquette guidelines, visit Web sites such as: **www.dtcc.edu/cs/rfc1855.html**, **www.iwillfollow.com/email.htm**, and **www.albion.com/netiquette**.

REFERENCE   WINDOW   **RW**

Sending an E-mail Message
- Click the New Mail Message button on the Standard toolbar.
- Type one or more e-mail addresses in the To, Cc, and Bcc boxes as needed (separate multiple addresses with semicolons).
- Type a message title in the Subject box.
- Type a message in the Message body box.
- Click the Send button on the Standard toolbar to send the message.
- If necessary, click the Send/Receive button on the Standard toolbar in the Inbox or Outbox.

You'll create an e-mail next. Although usually you would send messages to other people, you will be sending messages to yourself in this tutorial so you can practice sending and receiving messages.

To create an e-mail message:

1. Click the **New Mail Message button** 🖃 New on the Standard toolbar. A new Message window opens with the Plain Text format specified in the title bar. If necessary, maximize the window.

   TROUBLE? If the Office Assistant or a dialog box appears and asks whether you want to use Word as your e-mail editor for all messages, click the No button.

2. Type your e-mail address in the To box. You could send the e-mail to multiple recipients by typing a semicolon between each address.

3. Press the **Tab** key twice to move past the Cc box to the Subject box. You skipped the Cc box because you aren't sending a courtesy copy of this e-mail to anyone.

   TROUBLE? If the insertion point is not in the Subject box, then the Bcc box is displayed. Click the Tab key again to move to the Subject box, and then continue with Step 4.

4. Type **Mangoes Order** in the Subject box, and then press the **Tab** key to move to the message body.

   You'll type a concise message that includes some intentional errors that you'll correct in the next set of steps. In the next step, be sure to type the message with the errors shown.

5. Type **The Express Lane customers are enjiyng the mangoes form Maklin Produce. Please double our order for the next three weeks.**, press the **Enter** key twice, type **Thanks you,** (including the comma), press the **Enter** key, and then type your name. See Figure 1-10.

Figure 1-10	COMPLETED E-MAIL

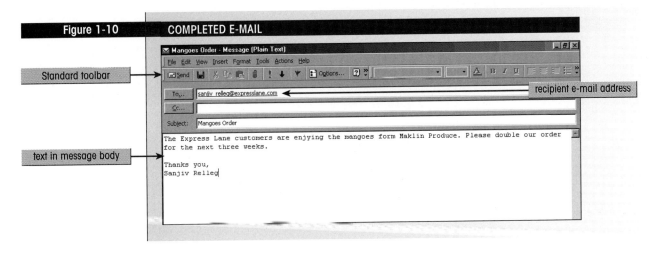

Standard toolbar

recipient e-mail address

text in message body

Though e-mail messages may take seconds to create, the time invested in correcting any grammar and spelling errors is well worth it. You don't want a reader to be distracted by the errors and ignore the message you want to convey.

Checking the Spelling of Messages

The Outlook spelling checker reviews the spelling of the subject and text of your message. Checking the spelling of messages helps to ensure that you correct any typographic errors before sending your message. When you check the spelling, Outlook compares the words in your message to its dictionary. Any words that do not appear in the dictionary are displayed in the Spelling dialog box. You then choose to correct the spelling, ignore the word (such as when it's a proper name), or add the word to a custom dictionary.

Before you check the spelling of your message, you'll verify what options are set for the spelling checker. You need to set these options only one time.

To check the spelling of a message:

1. Click **Tools** on the menu bar, and then click **Spelling**. The Spelling dialog box opens.

2. Click the **Options** button to display the Spelling tab in the Options dialog box.

3. Verify that the first and last check boxes are selected in the General options area. See Figure 1-11.

Figure 1-11   SPELLING OPTIONS

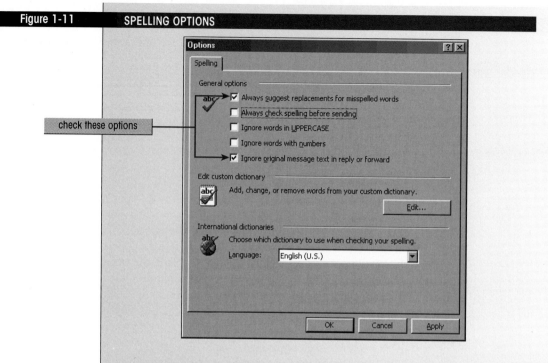

check these options

The first option has Outlook suggest alternate spellings for words not in its dictionary. The last option prevents Outlook from checking the spelling in messages you received.

4. Click the **OK** button to return to the Spelling dialog box. Notice that the first misspelled word is highlighted. See Figure 1-12.

Figure 1-12   OUTLOOK SPELLING CHECKER

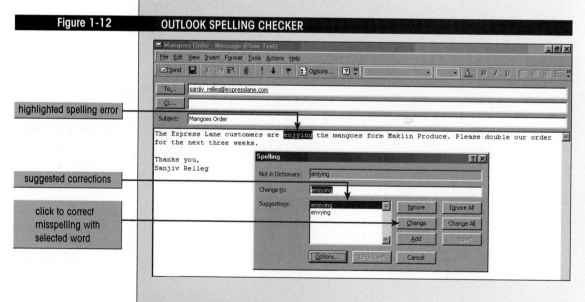

highlighted spelling error

suggested corrections

click to correct misspelling with selected word

5. Click **enjoying** in the Suggestions list box, if necessary, to select the correct spelling, and then click the **Change** button. If this word appeared multiple times in your message, you could click the Change All button to replace all instances of the misspelling with the correct word at one time.

The next misspelled word is flagged. Because Maklin is a proper name, it is correct as is. If this were a name you used frequently, you could add it to the custom dictionary by clicking the Add button. This time you will ignore the word.

6. Click the **Ignore** button. If this word appeared multiple times in your message, you could click the Ignore All button to skip all instances of the word in the message.

7. Continue to Change or Ignore highlighted words, as necessary. A dialog box opens when Outlook has finished checking the message.

8. Click the **OK** button to confirm the spelling check is complete.

Although the spelling check is complete, your message is not necessarily error-free. The spelling checker verifies the spelling of individual words, not their usage. Your message may still contain words that are spelled correctly, but used incorrectly. For example, Outlook does not notice that "thanks you" should be "thank you" because each individual word is spelled correctly. The same is true for the substitution of "form" for "from." The key to a completely error-free message is to proofread your work before sending it.

To proofread your message:

1. Verify that your e-mail address is typed correctly in the To box.

2. Verify that the text in the Subject box is typed correctly.

3. Double-click **form** and then type **from** to correct the error in the first line, click to the right of **Thanks** and then press the **Backspace** key to delete the letter s from "Thanks" in the closing. You can edit any text by selecting the word or words and retyping them or by clicking in the word, pressing the Backspace or Delete key to erase incorrect characters, and then typing the correct characters.

4. Verify that the message body contains no other spelling or grammar errors. This is also a good time to ensure that the content is accurate. Your finished message should match Figure 1-13.

Figure 1-13	CORRECTED E-MAIL

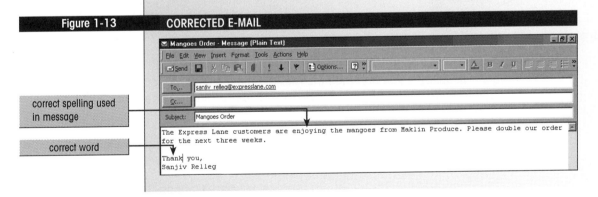

correct spelling used in message

correct word

Once you're sure that the message is error-free, you are ready to send it.

Sending Messages

After you finish creating your e-mail message, you move it to the **Outbox** (the outgoing message storage folder) to send. In most cases, your message is sent immediately along the path to its destination and you cannot see its brief stopover in the Outbox. If you are working offline (not connected to your e-mail server) or have a dial-up connection, the message remains in the Outbox until you choose to send it. In this case, it is usually efficient to create all of your messages before you send them.

You'll send the message now.

To send a message:

1. Click the **Send** button on the Standard toolbar. The message moves to the Outbox.

   If you are working on a LAN, Steps 2 through 4 occur automatically, and you should read but not complete them. If you are working with a dial-up connection, you'll need to manually send the message from the Outbox. Although you can send and receive e-mail from the Inbox or the Outbox, you'll switch to the Outbox to deliver this message.

2. Click the **My Shortcuts** group button on the Outlook Bar. The Outbox is followed by (1), which indicates that there is one outgoing message.

   TROUBLE? If you don't see the Outbox in the My Shortcuts group, click View on the menu bar, and then click Folder List to view the Outbox in the Folder List.

3. Click **Outbox** to view the message in the Information viewer of the Outbox. See Figure 1-14.

Figure 1-14	OUTBOX

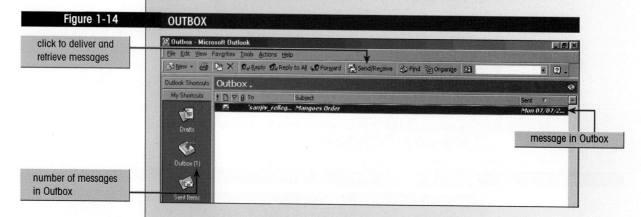

click to deliver and retrieve messages

number of messages in Outbox

message in Outbox

   TROUBLE? If you don't see the message in the Outbox, you are probably connected to the Internet and the message has already been sent. Just read the rest of the steps in this section.

4. Click **Tools** on the menu bar, and then click **Send** to send the message. Notice that the Outbox is empty and that the (1) has disappeared.

   TROUBLE? If Outlook requests a password, you might need to enter your password before you can send and receive your messages. Type your password, and then click the OK button.

A copy of the message is stored in the Sent Items folder, which provides a record of all the messages you sent. The time your e-mail takes to arrive at its destination will vary, depending on the size of the message, the speed of your Internet connection, and the number of other users on the Internet. When you send a message, your e-mail server identifies its final destination by the host name in the e-mail address. Rather than being sent directly to its final destination, your message passes from host to host until it arrives at the appropriate host. You may see a dialog box that shows the progress of the message to your mail server. While you're waiting for your message to arrive, you'll create a Personal Address Book.

Using a Personal Address Book

E-mail addresses neither contain a uniform number of characters nor follow a standard format. User names vary from complete first and last names separated by periods or underscores (First.Last) to first initial and last names (F_Last) to any combination of numbers and letters, including nicknames, titles, and cryptic abbreviations. In addition, the host name can range from a few characters to a long string of characters. All this variation could make it difficult to send e-mail messages. If you mistype someone's e-mail address by even one character, the message will either come bouncing back to you or go to the wrong person. Instead of relying on memory and accurate typing, you can compile all the e-mail addresses you use in an Address Book.

The **Address Book** is a collection of address lists that store names, e-mail addresses, fax numbers, and distribution lists. Whenever you want to send an e-mail message, you simply select the appropriate address from the address book. When using Outlook with the Corporate or Workgroup installation, you will have several address lists, including:

- **Outlook Address Book**—An address book created from any contacts in the Contacts folder.
- **Global Address List**—An address book created and maintained by a network administrator that contains all user, group, and distribution list e-mail addresses in your organization.
- **Personal Address Book**—A custom address book you create to store e-mail addresses you use frequently.

Creating a Personal Address Book

To create the Personal Address Book, you must first add it to your profile. This creates a file in the location you specify. Personal Address Book files have a .pab extension and can be copied to a disk. Once you create the Address Book file, you can enter the names and e-mail addresses of people with whom you correspond.

To create a Personal Address Book:

1. Click **Tools** on the menu bar, and then click **Services**. The Services dialog box opens, listing services set up for your profile.

2. Click the **Add** button to open the Add Service to Profile dialog box.

3. Click **Personal Address Book**, and then click the **OK** button to open the Personal Address Book dialog box. See Figure 1-15.

   TROUBLE? If a dialog box opens saying that the action cannot be completed because the information service has already been added to your profile and cannot be specified twice, click the OK button, click the Cancel button to return to the Add Service to Profile dialog box, click the Properties button to open the Personal Address Book dialog box, make sure the First name (John Smith) option button is selected to specify how names will appear in the Address Book, click the OK button, and then skip to the next series of steps to enter contacts in the Address Book.

Figure 1-15 PERSONAL ADDRESS BOOK DIALOG BOX

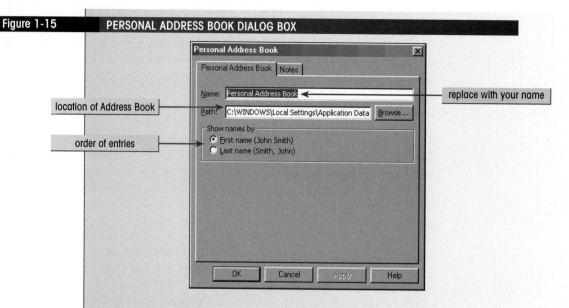

location of Address Book

replace with your name

order of entries

4. Type your name in the Name text box. Outlook uses this name for the Personal Address Book within Outlook.

5. Click the **Browse** button to open the Use Personal Address Book dialog box, type your first and last name in the File name text box, change the Look in list box to the location where you store your student files, and then click the **Open** button.

6. Make sure the **First name (John Smith)** option button is selected to specify how names will appear in the Address Book.

7. Click the **OK** button in the Use Personal Address Book dialog box.

8. Click the **OK** button in the dialog box, confirming that you must exit and restart Outlook before you can use the Personal Address Book. Notice that the Personal Address Book with your name is added to the list.

9. Click the **OK** button in the Services dialog box.

10. Click **File** on the menu bar, and then click **Exit and Log Off** to close Outlook and log off all messages services.

11. Restart Outlook, using your profile.

Because you want to be sure to use the correct addresses every time you send an order, you'll enter the addresses of The Express Lane's suppliers to the Address Book.

To enter contacts in the Address Book:

1. Click the **Address Book** button 🖳 on the Standard toolbar of the Inbox Information viewer. The Address Book window opens.

2. Click the **Show Names from the** list arrow, and then click your name.

3. Click the **New Entry** button 🖳 on the Address Book toolbar. The New Entry dialog box opens.

4. In the Put this entry area, click the **In the** list arrow, and then click your name. The Select the entry type list changes to show types available for the Personal Address Book and your profile. See Figure 1-16.

Figure 1-16	NEW ENTRY DIALOG BOX

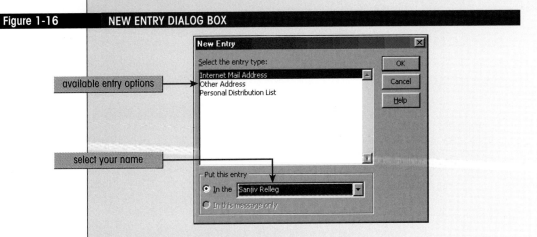

available entry options

select your name

5. Click **Internet Mail Address** in the Select the entry type list box, and then click the **OK** button. The New Internet Mail Address Properties dialog box opens ready for you enter contact information. See Figure 1-17.

Figure 1-17	NEW INTERNET MAIL ADDRESS PROPERTIES DIALOG BOX

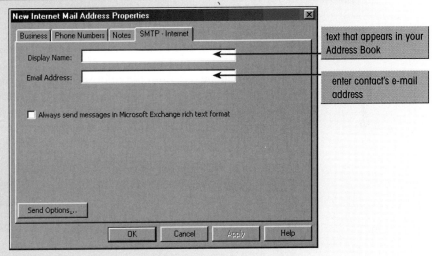

text that appears in your Address Book

enter contact's e-mail address

6. Type **Alicia Lindenberg** in the Display Name text box to specify how this contact appears in the Address Book, and then press the **Tab** key.

7. Type your e-mail address in the Email Address text box. For this tutorial, you'll use your own e-mail address.

You can enter additional information about this contact in the other tabs of the dialog box, such as company address and phone numbers. For now, you need only the e-mail address.

8. Click the **OK** button. Alicia's name appears in the Address Book.

9. Repeat Steps 2 through 9 to create address book entries for **Daniel O'Brien**,

Trey Jones, **Tory Anders**, **Leslie Katz**, and **Alan Gregory**, using your e-mail address for each additional entry. See Figure 1-18.

Figure 1-18	ADDRESS BOOK NAMES

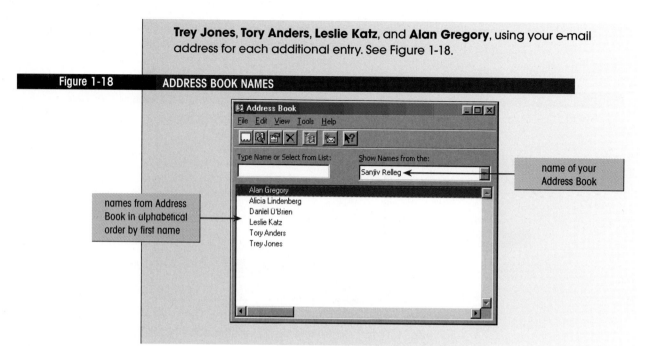

The next time you need to send a message to any of these people, you can select the name rather than typing their e-mail address in the To box.

Creating a Personal Distribution List

Sometimes you'll find that you repeatedly send one message—such as a weekly progress report or company updates—to the same group of people. Rather than manually selecting the names one by one from the Address Book, you can create a personal distribution list. A **personal distribution list** is a group of people to whom you frequently send the same messages, such as all suppliers. A distribution list saves time and insures that you don't inadvertently leave out someone. You can create multiple distribution lists to meet your needs, and individuals can be included in more than one distribution list.

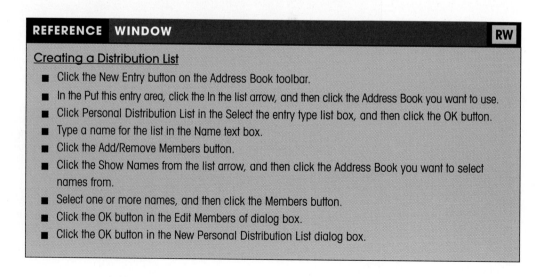

REFERENCE WINDOW   **RW**

Creating a Distribution List

- Click the New Entry button on the Address Book toolbar.
- In the Put this entry area, click the In the list arrow, and then click the Address Book you want to use.
- Click Personal Distribution List in the Select the entry type list box, and then click the OK button.
- Type a name for the list in the Name text box.
- Click the Add/Remove Members button.
- Click the Show Names from the list arrow, and then click the Address Book you want to select names from.
- Select one or more names, and then click the Members button.
- Click the OK button in the Edit Members of dialog box.
- Click the OK button in the New Personal Distribution List dialog box.

Alan asks you to create a distribution list of all The Express Lane suppliers, as he frequently needs to send the same information to all of them.

To create a personal distribution list:

1. Click the **New Entry** button 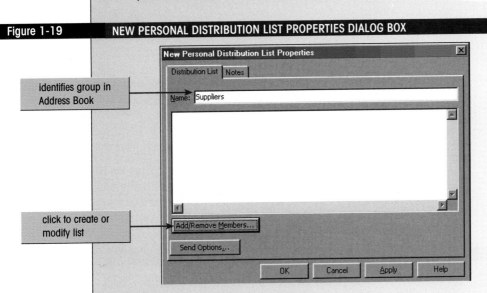 on the Address Book toolbar. The New Entry dialog box opens.

2. In the Put this entry area, click the **In the** list arrow, and then click your name.

3. Click **Personal Distribution List** in the Select the entry type list box, and then click the **OK** button. The New Personal Distribution List dialog box opens.

4. Type **Suppliers** in the Name text box. This identifies how the group will appear in your Address Book. See Figure 1-19.

Figure 1-19	NEW PERSONAL DISTRIBUTION LIST PROPERTIES DIALOG BOX

identifies group in
Address Book

click to create or
modify list

New Personal Distribution List Properties

Distribution List | Notes

Name: Suppliers

Add/Remove Members...

Send Options...

OK   Cancel   Apply   Help

5. Click the **Add/Remove Members** button. The Edit Members of Suppliers dialog box opens.

6. Click the **Show Names from the** list arrow, and then click your name. The names you entered in the Address Book appear in the list.

    You can select any or all the names to add to the distribution list. If you click the first name, hold down the Shift key, and click the last name, all entries between the first and last names will be selected. If you hold down the Ctrl key as you click names, only those names you click will be selected.

7. Click **Alicia Lindenberg**, press and hold the **Ctrl** key, click all the names *except* Daniel O'Brien and Alan Gregory, and then release the **Ctrl** key.

8. Click the **Members** button to move the selected names into the Personal Distribution List box. Your distribution list should match the one shown in Figure 1-20.

Figure 1-20   ADDING NAMES TO SUPPLIERS DISTRIBUTION LIST

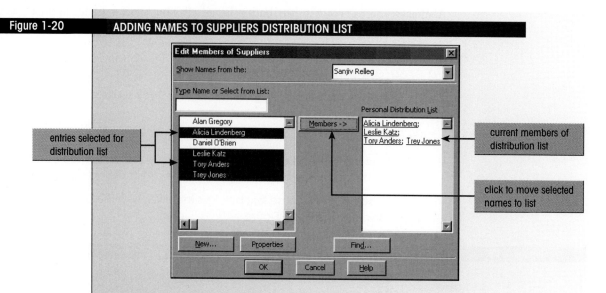

entries selected for distribution list

current members of distribution list

click to move selected names to list

TROUBLE? If your Suppliers list contains extra names, click the name in the Personal Distribution List box, and then press the Delete key.

9. Click the **OK** button to return to the New Personal Distribution List dialog box, which lists the four names you added to the Suppliers distribution list.

10. Click the **OK** button. The Suppliers distribution list appears in the Address Book marked with the group icon. The names that you added to the Suppliers distribution list also still appear as individuals in the address book. See Figure 1-21.

Figure 1-21   ADDRESS BOOK WITH SUPPLIERS DISTRIBUTION LIST

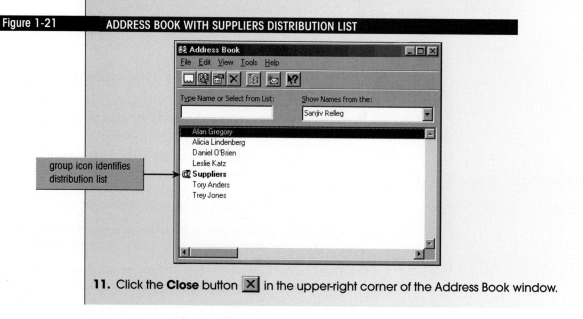

group icon identifies distribution list

11. Click the **Close** button ⊠ in the upper-right corner of the Address Book window.

Now you quickly can address an e-mail to multiple recipients at one time.

Sending an E-mail Message to Your Distribution List

Alan asks you to send a message to all the suppliers letting them know that the warehouse will closed on specific holidays—including New Year's Day, Memorial Day, Independence Day, Labor Day, and Christmas. Because you created the Suppliers distribution list, you can write and address the e-mail without concern that you'll forget anyone.

To send an e-mail message to a distribution list:

1. Click the **New Mail Message** button [New] on the Standard toolbar to open a Message window.

2. Click the **To** button to open the Select Names dialog box, click the **Show names from the** list arrow, and then click your name. The names and distribution list you created appear in the left list box.

3. Click **Suppliers** in the list box, and then click the **To** button. The distribution list moves into the Message Recipient list box. You want to copy Alan on this notice.

4. Click **Alan Gregory** in the list box, and then click the **Cc** button. See Figure 1-22.

Figure 1-22	SELECT NAMES DIALOG BOX

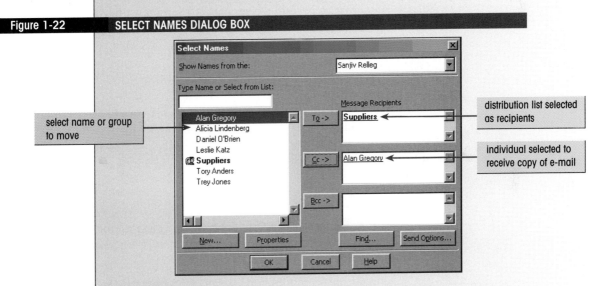

select name or group to move

distribution list selected as recipients

individual selected to receive copy of e-mail

5. Click the **OK** button. The recipients you selected appear in the To and Cc boxes.

6. Click in the **Subject** text box, and then type **The Express Lane Warehouse Holiday Closings** in the Subject box.

7. Click in the message body, type **Our warehouse is closed for delivery on the following days: New Year's Day, Memorial Day, Independence Day, Labor Day, and Christmas. Please reschedule deliveries for these dates on the previous or next business day. Thank you.**, press the **Enter** key twice, and then type your name. See Figure 1-23.

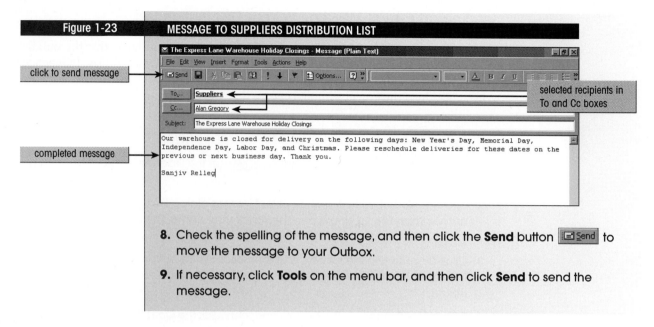

| Figure 1-23 | MESSAGE TO SUPPLIERS DISTRIBUTION LIST |

8. Check the spelling of the message, and then click the **Send** button to move the message to your Outbox.

9. If necessary, click **Tools** on the menu bar, and then click **Send** to send the message.

Alan suggests that you create a personal distribution list for different types of suppliers, such as the produce suppliers, the dry goods suppliers, meat suppliers, and so forth. You decide to delete the current list and create the other lists later.

Deleting a Personal Distribution List

When you delete a distribution list, you remove the list you created from the Address Book. The individual addresses that made up that list remain unaffected in your Address Book. Therefore, when you delete the Suppliers distribution list, the individual suppliers on that list still appear in the Address Book.

To delete a personal distribution list:

1. Click the **Address Book** button on the Standard toolbar to open the Address Book, click the **Show Names from the** list arrow, and then click your name.

2. Click the **Suppliers** distribution list, and then click the **Delete** button on the Address Book toolbar.

3. Click the **Yes** button to confirm that you want to permanently delete this list from your Address Book. The distribution list is removed.

4. Close the Address Book.

You have started and set up Outlook to deliver Plain Text messages. You've created a Personal Address Book that contains all the suppliers' e-mail addresses and set up a personal distribution list. In addition, you have created and sent out a variety of e-mail messages. In Session 1.2, you'll retrieve and respond to those messages.

Session 1.1 QUICK CHECK

1. What is the difference between an item and a folder?

2. Explain what a profile is.

3. Define e-mail and list two benefits of using it.

4. What is the host name in the e-mail address: "alan@expresslane.com"?

5. Why would you select Plain Text as your message format default?

6. List three netiquette guidelines you should follow when writing e-mail.

7. What is a Personal Address Book?

8. What are two advantages of using a personal distribution list?

SESSION 1.2

In this session, you'll receive, read, reply to, forward, and print e-mail messages. You'll work with adding and reading attachments to e-mail messages. You'll learn how to customize your messages with signatures and stationary. Finally you'll learn how to get help in Outlook.

Receiving and Responding to E-mail

When someone sends you an e-mail message, whether your network server or your ISP's server receives it, depends on your setup. In most cases, messages are moved automatically from your mailbox on your network server into your Inbox. If you are using a dial-up-connection, you check manually for new e-mail messages at any time day or night and as often as you like. Some people retrieve their messages once or twice each day, whereas others check periodically throughout the day. How often you check for incoming messages will depend on your needs and preferences.

In addition to messages from other people, you also may receive notice from a system administrator that a message you sent is undeliverable. This could occur for a variety of reasons—you may have typed the recipient's e-mail address incorrectly, or your server, the recipient's server, or something in between is not working properly. Read the message from the system administrator; sometimes delivery attempts will continue for several days, other times you will need to resend the message after verifying the e-mail address.

Downloading Messages

You check manually for new e-mail messages by clicking the Send/Receive button on the Standard toolbar in any of the mail folders. Outlook connects to your e-mail server, sends any messages in the Outbox, and downloads any incoming messages that have arrived since you last checked. New messages are delivered into the Inbox. These messages may be removed from your mail server and stored on the computer you are using.

You'll switch to the Inbox and download the messages you sent earlier.

To retrieve e-mail messages manually:

1. If you took a break after the previous session, make sure Outlook is running and the **Inbox** is displayed in the Information viewer.

2. Click the **Send/Receive** button [Send/Receive] on the Standard toolbar. If necessary, enter your password in the dialog box that opens.

3. Watch for the new messages to appear in the Inbox. The number of new, unread messages you receive appears within parentheses next to the Inbox icon on the Outlook Bar. See Figure 1-24. Your Inbox might contain additional e-mail messages.

| Figure 1-24 | INBOX WITH NEW MESSAGES |

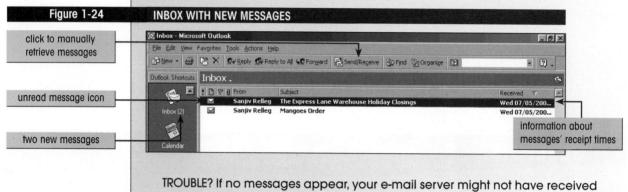

click to manually retrieve messages

unread message icon

two new messages

information about messages' receipt times

TROUBLE? If no messages appear, your e-mail server might not have received your messages yet. Wait a few minutes and then repeat Steps 2 and 3.

Reading Messages

The Inbox Information viewer is divided into two panes. The upper pane, called the Message pane, displays a list of all e-mail messages that you have received, along with columns of information about the message. These columns include From (the sender's name) the message subject, and the date and time that the message was received, as well as icons that indicate the message's status. For example, the two leftmost icons indicate whether the message has an importance level of high ❗ or low ↓ and specify whether the message has been unread ✉ or read ✉. You can change any column width by dragging the border of any column header with the double-headed arrow ↔ that appears when you position the pointer between columns.

To help you locate new messages easily, messages are ordered in the Inbox from newest to oldest. At times, you may want to reorder the messages alphabetically by their sender or subject. You can change the default order by clicking the column heading by which you want to order messages. Clicking a heading a second time reverses the order of messages, such as from oldest to newest.

The lower pane, called the preview pane, displays the contents of the selected message. At the top of the preview pane is the message header, which indicates the sender, all recipients, and the subject. You can resize the panes by dragging the border above the message header up or down.

To read a message:

1. In the message list, click the **Mangoes Order** message to display its contents in the preview pane. See Figure 1-25.

Figure 1-25	READING A MESSAGE

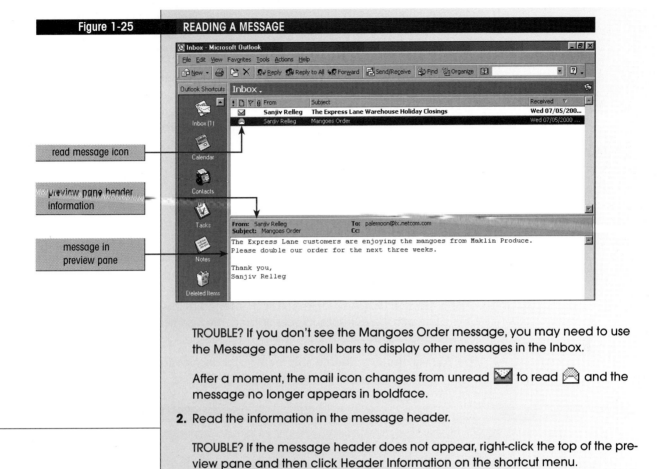

read message icon

preview pane header information

message in preview pane

TROUBLE? If you don't see the Mangoes Order message, you may need to use the Message pane scroll bars to display other messages in the Inbox.

After a moment, the mail icon changes from unread ✉ to read 📭 and the message no longer appears in boldface.

2. Read the information in the message header.

TROUBLE? If the message header does not appear, right-click the top of the preview pane and then click Header Information on the shortcut menu.

3. Read the message. If a message extends beyond the Preview pane, scroll bars appear along the edge of the pane. Use these to bring the rest of the message into view.

After you read a message, you have several options—you can leave the message in the Inbox and deal with it later, reply to the message, forward the message to others, print the message, or delete it. As with paper mail you receive, it's best to respond to messages as you receive them rather than letting them collect in your Inbox.

Replying to and Forwarding Mail

Many messages you receive require some sort of response—for example, confirmation you received the information, the answer to a question, or sending the message to another person. The quickest way to respond to messages is to use the Reply, Reply to All, and Forward features. The **Reply** feature responds to the sender, whereas the **Reply to All** feature responds to the sender and all recipients; Outlook inserts their e-mail addresses into the appropriate boxes. The **Forward** feature sends a copy of the message to one or more recipients you specify.

With both the Reply and Forward features, the original message is included for reference (unless you change the default settings), separated from your new message by the text "Original Message" and the original message header information. Your response is added at the top of the message body above the original message. This makes it simpler for recipients to read your message because they don't have to scroll through earlier message text to find the new text.

If you're responding to a very long message (or several replies have been exchanged), you might want to delete text that is no longer relevant or necessary to the current discussion to keep the message smaller. However, if you delete too much material and send only your response, recipients might no longer recall the context of the message. For example, the message, "We'll change your order as requested," leaves doubt as to what changes will occur because the request for the mangoes order to be doubled for the next three weeks is no longer included as reference. In addition, the same netiquette guidelines apply for message replies. Responses also use the same format as the original message, unless you specify otherwise. In other words, if you receive a message in HTML format, your response is in HTML format; if you receive a message in Plain Text format, your response is in Plain Text format.

You'll reply to the Mangoes Order message. In reality, you would respond to someone other than yourself.

To reply to a message:

1. Make sure the Mangoes Order message is selected in the Inbox, and then click the **Reply** button ⟨Reply⟩ on the Standard toolbar. A Message window opens with the original sender's name or e-mail address in the To box (in this case, your name) and RE: (short for Regarding) inserted at the beginning of the Subject line with the current subject still listed. The insertion point is in the body of the message ready for you to type.

2. Type **You will receive double shipments of mangoes for the next three weeks. Thank you for your order.** See Figure 1-26.

Figure 1-26	REPLYING TO A MESSAGE

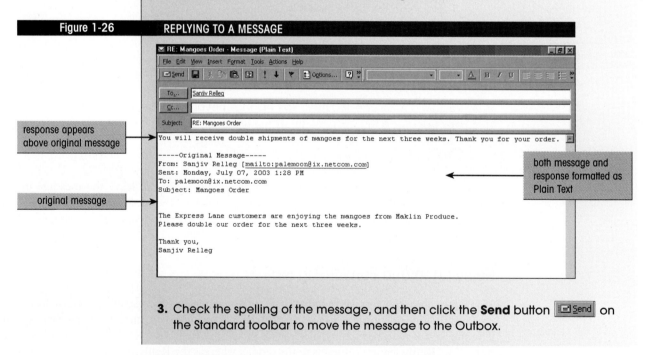

response appears above original message

original message

both message and response formatted as Plain Text

3. Check the spelling of the message, and then click the **Send** button ⟨Send⟩ on the Standard toolbar to move the message to the Outbox.

Next, you'll forward the message to Leslie Katz, the manager at Foods Naturally. Because her e-mail address is in the Personal Address Book, you can address the message to her quickly.

To forward a message:

1. Make sure that the Mangoes Order message is selected in the Inbox, and then click the **Forward** button [Forward] on the Standard toolbar. This time, the insertion point is in the empty To box and FW: (for Forward) precedes the Subject line.

2. Click the **To** button, switch to your Address Book, double-click **Leslie Katz**, and then click the **OK** button.

   Outlook checks the name against the names in your Personal Address Book. When Outlook recognizes that the name matches one in your Personal Address Book, it underlines the name. It adds a red, wavy underline if multiple names in your Address Book match the name you typed. In that case, right-click the name to select from the list of names found.

   TROUBLE? If the recipient name is not underlined, automatic name checking may not be turned on. Click Tools on the Outlook menu bar, click Options, click the Preferences tab, click the E-mail Options button in the Options dialog box, click the Advanced E-mail Options button in the E-mail Options dialog box, click the Automatic name checking check box to insert a check mark in the Advanced E-mail Options dialog box, and then click the OK button in each dialog box.

3. Press the **Tab** key until the insertion point is at the top of the message body, and then type **Please update The Express Lane account**. (including the period).

4. Check the spelling, and then click the **Send** button [Send] on the Standard toolbar.

5. If necessary, click the **Send/Receive** button [Send/Receive] on the Inbox Standard toolbar to send both messages to their recipients.

Printing Messages

Although e-mail eliminates the need for paper messages, sometimes you'll want a printed copy of a message to file or distribute. You can use the Print button on the Standard toolbar to print a selected message with the default settings, or you can use the Print command from the File menu to verify and change settings before you print. You'll verify the settings and then print the Mangoes Order message in your Inbox.

To verify settings and print a message:

1. If necessary, select the Mangoes Order message in the Inbox.

2. Click **File** on the menu bar, and then click **Print**. The Print dialog box opens, as shown in Figure 1-27.

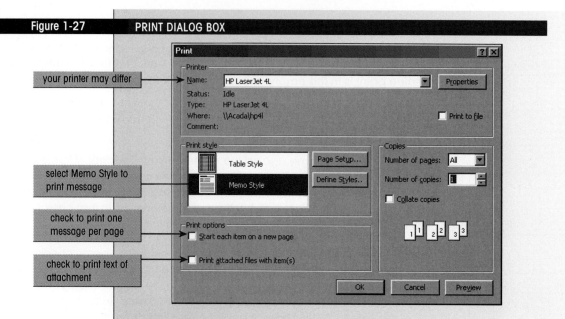

Figure 1-27   PRINT DIALOG BOX

your printer may differ

select Memo Style to print message

check to print one message per page

check to print text of attachment

3. Make sure that the correct printer for your system appears in the Name list box.

4. If necessary, click **Memo Style** in the Print style section to select it. Memo style prints the contents of the selected item—in this case, the e-mail message. Table Style prints the view of the selected folder—in this case, the Inbox folder. Other folders have different print style options.

5. Click the **OK** button. The message prints.

6. Repeat Steps 1 through 5 to print The Express Lane Warehouse Holiday Closings message.

7. Press and hold the **Ctrl** key, click the **FW: Mangoes Order** message and the **RE: Mangoes Order** message, and then release the **Ctrl** key.

8. Click **File** on the menu bar, click **Print**, and then print both messages on the same page.

Alan asks you to file the printed messages for future reference. Notice that the printouts appear in the format of a memo.

Customizing Messages

There are several ways to enhance e-mail messages that you send from Outlook. First, you can specify that specific text appear on every e-mail you send. In addition, you can change default font and style, colors, and backgrounds used in your messages. Formatting options you decide to use will be visible only to those recipients who can view messages in HTML or Outlook Rich Text. Rather than change the default message format to HTML, you'll set it for specific messages.

Creating a Signature

A **signature** is text that is automatically added to every e-mail message you send. For example, you might create a signature with your name, job title, company name, and phone number. In addition, you can create more than one signature and then use the Signature button on the Standard toolbar to select which one you want to include in a particular message. For example, The Express Lane might create one signature that contains a paragraph about how to order groceries for e-mail messages to customers and a second signature that includes the warehouse information for e-mail messages to vendors and suppliers. Although you can attach a signature to a message in any format, the HTML and Outlook Rich Text formats enable you to apply font and paragraph formatting. For now, you'll create an unformatted signature that includes your name and the company name.

To create a signature:

1. Click **Tools** on the menu bar, click **Options**, and then click the **Mail Format** tab in the Options dialog box.

2. Click the **Signature Picker** button, and then click the **New** button in the Signature Picker dialog box.

3. Type your name in the Enter a name for your new signature text box, click the **Start with a blank signature** option button if necessary, and then click the **Next** button.

4. Type your name in the Signature text box, press the **Enter** key, and then type **The Express Lane**. See Figure 1-28.

| Figure 1-28 | EDIT SIGNATURE DIALOG BOX |

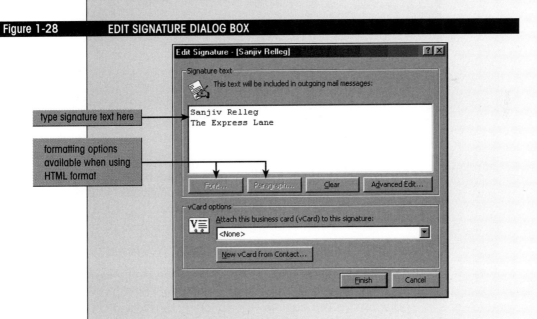

If you wanted to add formatting, you could select the text to format, and then click the Font button and change the font and style or click the Paragraph button to change the alignment and spacing. Because you plan to use this signature for both Plain Text and HTML messages, you don't add any formatting.

5. Click the **Finish** button, preview your signature in the Signature Picker dialog box, and then click the **OK** button to return to the Options dialog box.

6. Make sure that the signature with your name appears in the Use this Signature by default list box.

You want the signature to appear on only new messages that you create.

7. If necessary, click the **Don't use when replying or forwarding** check box to insert a check mark.

8. Click the **OK** button.

Whenever you start a new e-mail message, your signature will appear at the end of the message.

Using Stationery

When you send e-mail, you can select a special look for your message, much as you would select special letterhead paper for your business correspondence. **Stationery templates** are HTML files that include complementary fonts, background colors, and images for your outgoing e-mail messages. The stationery templates that come with Outlook include announcements, invitations, greetings, and other designs. You also can design your own stationery. Be aware that stationery increases the size of messages, so they take longer to send and receive. When you create a message using stationery, Outlook changes the message format for that e-mail to HTML. Remember that the recipient must be able to read HTML e-mail to view the special formatting.

REFERENCE WINDOW   **RW**

Creating an E-mail with Stationery

- Click Actions on the menu bar, point to New Mail Message Using, and then click More Stationery.
- Select the stationery you want to use.
- Click the OK button.
- Complete the To, Cc, Bcc, Subject, and message body as usual.
- Format the text in the message body as desired, using buttons on the Formatting toolbar.

Alan asks you to send an e-mail message to Daniel O'Brien, inviting him to lunch as a thank you for the quality of his produce and the timeliness of his shipments. You'll use stationery to give the message a more celebratory look.

To create an e-mail message with stationery:

1. Click **Actions** on the menu bar, point to **New Mail Message Using**, and then click **More Stationery**. The Select a Stationery dialog box opens with the available designs. You can preview stationery by clicking its name in the Stationery list box. Stationery is listed in alphabetical order, and you can press the first letter of the one you want to move quickly through the list.

2. Type **r**, and then click **Running Birthday** in the Stationery list box. See Figure 1-29.

Figure 1-29	SELECT A STATIONERY DIALOG BOX

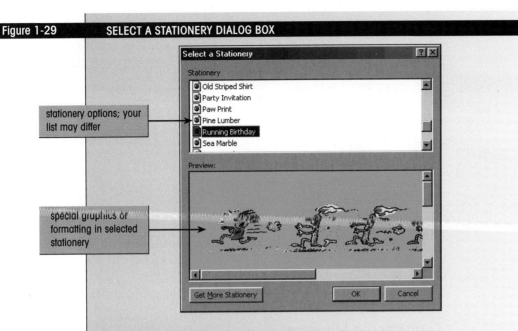

stationery options; your
list may differ

special graphics or
formatting in selected
stationery

TROUBLE? If the Running Birthday stationery doesn't appear, select another
design of your choice.

3. Type **j**, and then click **Jungle** in the Stationery list box.

   TROUBLE? If the Jungle stationery doesn't appear, select another design of
   your choice.

4. Click the **OK** button. The new mail message window opens with the stationery
   and your signature.

   You want to send this message to Daniel O'Brien and copy Alan Gregory.

5. Complete the To and Cc fields getting the addresses from your Personal
   Address Book, type **Thank you** in the Subject box, press the **Tab** key, type
   Daniel, press the **Enter** key twice, and then type **I would like to express the
   appreciation of the entire team here at The Express Lane for your company's commitment to high-quality produce and timely shipments. Please
   join Alan for lunch on Friday, July 27 to celebrate our two successful years
   of working together.** to create the e-mail message shown in Figure 1-30.

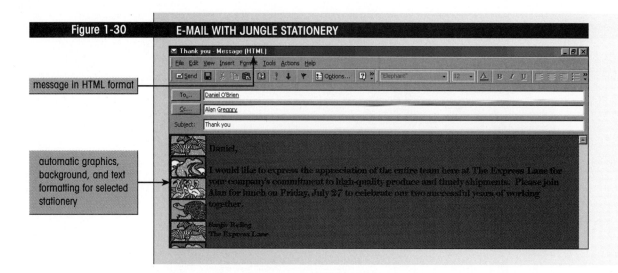

Figure 1-30   E-MAIL WITH JUNGLE STATIONERY

message in HTML format

automatic graphics, background, and text formatting for selected stationery

Before sending this message, however, you want to modify some of the text formatting.

Formatting a Message

You can format e-mail text much as you would format text in a Word document. In fact, many of the buttons and commands are the same. For example, you can set bold, underline, and italics; change the font, font size, and font color; align and indent text; create a bulleted or numbered list; and even apply paragraph styles.

To format text in an e-mail message:

1. Select **The Express Lane** in the message body. You'll make this text italic and yellow.

2. Click the **Italic** button ☐ on the Formatting toolbar.

   TROUBLE? If you don't see the Italic button, click the More Buttons list arrow, and then click the Italic button.

3. Click the **Font Color** button ☐ on the Formatting toolbar, and then click the **Yellow** tile in the palette that opens.

   TROUBLE? If you don't see the Font Color button, click the More Buttons list arrow, and then click the Font Color button.

   TROUBLE? If the Stationery that you selected has a yellow background, select another color so that the text is visible.

4. Select **Friday, July 27** and change it to yellow.

5. Click to the left of your name in the signature, click **Insert** on the menu bar, and then click **Horizontal Line**. Your message should match Figure 1-31.

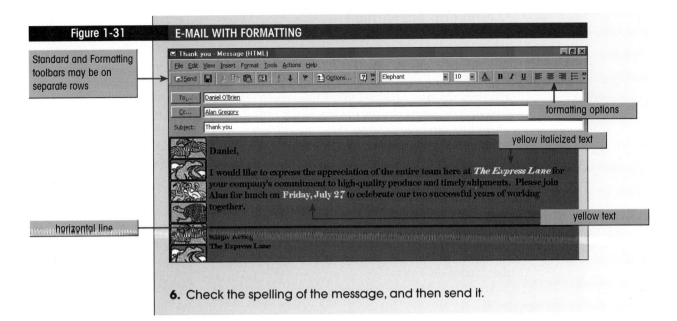

Figure 1-31 E-MAIL WITH FORMATTING

Standard and Formatting toolbars may be on separate rows

formatting options

yellow italicized text

yellow text

horizontal line

6. Check the spelling of the message, and then send it.

You could add more formatting, but a little goes a long way. Try to be judicious in your use of text formatting. Use it to enhance your message rather than overwhelm it.

To read and print the formatted HTML message:

1. If necessary, download your messages.

2. Open the **Thank you** message, read the message, and then close the window.

   TROUBLE? If you don't see the HTML formatting and you are using Lotus Notes or cc:Mail, you can complete the following steps to be able to use HTML formatting. If your mail server cannot accept messages formatted in HTML, just continue with the tutorial. Click Tools on the menu bar, click Services, click MS Outlook support for cc:Mail in the list box, and then click the Properties button. On the Delivery tab, click the Send using Microsoft Exchange rich text format option button, and then click the OK button in each dialog box. Print the **Thank you** message.

E-mail with judicious formatting can really jazz up a message.

Working with Attachments

Attachments to e-mail are a great way to share information. An **attachment** is a file that you send with an e-mail message. Attachments can be any type of file, including documents (such as a Word document, Excel workbook, or PowerPoint slide presentation), images, sounds, and programs. For example, you might send an attachment containing The Express Lane's latest sales figures to Alan for his review. The recipients can then save and open the file; for document files, the recipients must have the original program or a program that can read the file. For example, if Alan receives a Lotus 1-2-3 spreadsheet, he can open and save it with Excel.

Sending an Attachment

When you attach a file to your message, Outlook makes a copy of the original file to include with the message rather than creating a link between the attached copy and the original. If you edit the original file after attaching a copy to an e-mail message, the changes do not appear in the copy attached to the message. When you send attachments, be aware of message size; the larger the file the longer the time it takes to send and receive. Image files and sound files can be very large. If the attachment is a very large program or document, use a program, such as WinZip, to compress it. Unfortunately, WinZip doesn't do much to compress Graphic Image files or sound files. Also, be aware of the recipients' e-mail limitations. Some e-mail and online services don't allow recipients to receive attachments; others accept only one file attachment at a time. In addition, there may a size limit for an incoming message. Also, it is a good idea to include a reference to the attachment in your message. Many times people write a message and forget to attach the document or file they intended. If the attachment is referenced in the message, then the recipients know that you intended to include a file. If they do not receive an attachment with the e-mail, they can reply, asking for the attachment.

You'll send Alan the latest sales figures, which are in an Excel file, as an attachment.

To attach a file to an e-mail:

1. Click the **New Mail Message** button [New] on the Standard toolbar in the Inbox. Notice that your signature appears in the body of the message.

2. Enter **Alan Gregory** in the To box.

3. Type **Latest Sales** in the Subject box.

4. In the message area, type **The attached Excel workbook contains the latest sales figures. Looks like we're on track for this quarter. Let me know if you have any comments.** Next you'll add the attachment.

5. Insert your Data Disk in the appropriate disk drive.

    TROUBLE? If you don't have a Data Disk, you need to get one before you can proceed. You instructor or technical support person will either give you one or ask you to make your own by following the instructions on the "Read This Before You Begin" page preceding this tutorial. See you instructor or technical support person for more information.

6. Click the **Insert File** button [📎] on the Standard toolbar. The Insert File dialog box appears and functions like the Open dialog box.

7. Click the **Look in** list arrow and change the Look in list box to the **Tutorial** folder within the **Tutorial.01** folder on your Data Disk.

8. Double-click the **Sales** document to insert it as an attachment to your e-mail message, as well as close the Insert File dialog box. See Figure 1-32. The attachment appears as an icon below the message area in the attachment pane. The message is ready to send.

Figure 1-32	MESSAGE WINDOW WITH ATTACHMENT

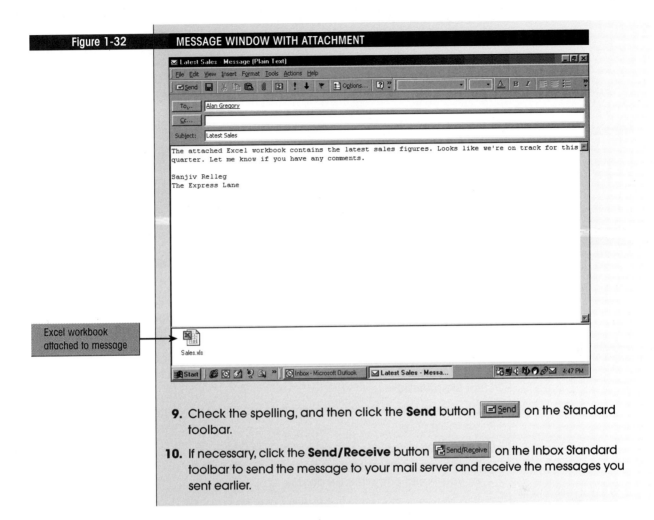

Excel workbook
attached to message

9. Check the spelling, and then click the **Send** button [Send] on the Standard toolbar.

10. If necessary, click the **Send/Receive** button [Send/Receive] on the Inbox Standard toolbar to send the message to your mail server and receive the messages you sent earlier.

A message with an attachment may take a bit longer to send because it's larger than an e-mail message without an attachment.

Receiving and Saving an Attachment

Although attachments are a great convenience, they are also one of the greatest sources of computer viruses. A **virus** is a program that attaches itself to a file and then corrupts and/or damages data on your computer, displays annoying messages, or makes your computer operate improperly. When you receive an attachment, be aware of who sent the message. Is the attachment from someone you know and trust? If not, consider deleting the attachment without opening it. **Antivirus software**, a program that examines files for viruses and disinfects them, provides another way to protect your computer from virus infections.

Messages with attached files display a paper clip icon in the message list. If the appropriate program is installed on your computer, you can open the attached file from the message itself. You can also save the attachment to your computer and then open, edit, and move it like any other file on your computer. Although you can reply to or forward a message with an attachment, the attachment is included with only the forwarded message because you will rarely, if ever, want to return the same file to the sender.

After you receive the message with the attachment, you'll save the attachment and then view it from within the message.

To save and view the message attachment:

1. If necessary, click the **Send/Receive** button [Send/Receive] on the Standard toolbar to download your messages. Again, it might take a bit longer than usual to download the message with the attachment. See Figure 1-33.

Figure 1-33   RECEIVED MESSAGES IN INBOX

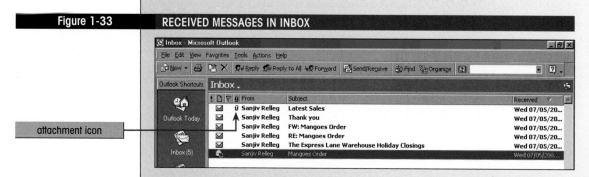

attachment icon

2. Double-click the **Latest Sales** message in the message list to open the message in a new window. Notice that the attachment appears as an icon at the bottom of the window, similar to when you created the message.

3. Right-click the **Sales** icon, and then click **Save As** on the shortcut menu. The Save Attachment dialog box appears, enabling you to select the save location for the message.

4. Change the Save in list box to the **Tutorial** folder within the **Tutorial.01** folder on your Data Disk.

5. Change the filename to **Second Quarter Sales.xls**, and then click the **Save** button to save the attached file to your Data Disk. You can work with this file just as you would any other file on disk.

   You also can view the attached file right from the Message window.

6. Double-click the **Sales** icon in the message window to open Excel and display the attached file. You can read, edit, format, and save the file just as you would any other Excel workbook.

   TROUBLE? If the file opens in a spreadsheet program other than Excel, your computer might be configured to associate the file extension .xls with spreadsheet programs other than Excel. Just continue with Step 7.

7. Review the sales figures, and then click the **Close** button [X] in the title bar to close the workbook and then exit Excel.

8. Click the **Close** button [X] in the Latest Sales - Message (Plain Text) title bar to close the Message window.

   TROUBLE? If the Office Assistant or a dialog box appears, asking whether you want to save changes, click the No button.

9. Print the **Latest Sales** message and its attachment.

As you work in Outlook, there are times when you'll want more information about certain features.

Getting **Help** in Outlook

Like other Microsoft programs, Outlook has an extensive Help system. For quick reference, you can point to a button on a toolbar and see its name in a **ScreenTip**, a yellow box with the button's name. The **What's This?** command on the Help menu changes the pointer to. When you click this pointer on a menu command, dialog box option, or anything else on your screen, a brief description appears. If you need more in-depth help, you can turn to the **Office Assistant**, an animated character that acts as an interactive guide for finding information from the Outlook Help system. You simply type a question using everyday language, and the Office Assistant searches the Help system and supplies an answer in easy-to-understand language. The answer might consist of step-by-step instructions to guide you through a feature or a clear explanation of a particular concept.

You decide to find more information about the different icons used in the Inbox.

To use the Office Assistant and Outlook Help:

1. Click the **Microsoft Outlook Help** button on the Standard toolbar. The Office Assistant opens, offering help on topics related to the task you most recently performed.

   TROUBLE? If the Office Assistant does not open, click Help on the menu bar, and then click Show Office Assistant.

2. Type **What icons are used in the Inbox?**, and then click the **Search** button. The Office Assistant balloon displays Help topics related to icons. See Figure 1-34.

| Figure 1-34 | OFFICE ASSISTANT |

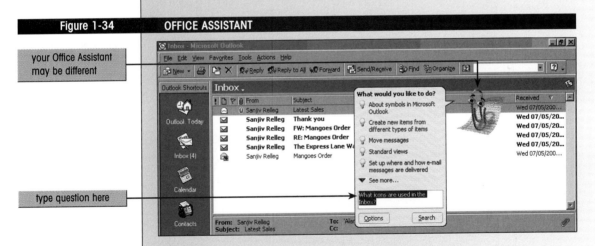

your Office Assistant may be different

type question here

TROUBLE? If the list in your balloon varies, don't worry. Just continue with Step 3.

3. Click **About symbols in Microsoft Outlook**.

   The Microsoft Outlook Help window opens with underlined hyperlinks that further narrow the search topic.

4. Maximize the Help window, and then click **Symbols in Inbox** to open a related Help screen.

5. Click the **Show** button 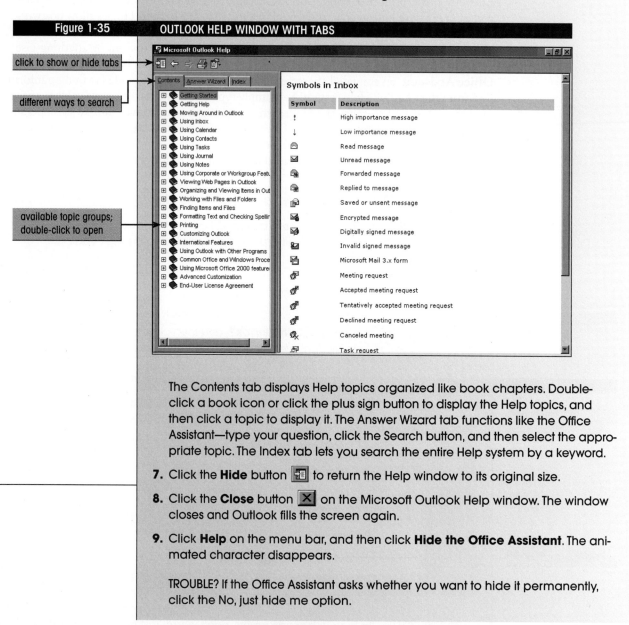. Additional Help window tabs appear.

6. Click the **Contents** tab, as shown in Figure 1-35.

| Figure 1-35 | OUTLOOK HELP WINDOW WITH TABS |

click to show or hide tabs

different ways to search

available topic groups;
double-click to open

Symbols in Inbox

Symbol	Description
!	High importance message
↓	Low importance message
	Read message
	Unread message
	Forwarded message
	Replied to message
	Saved or unsent message
	Encrypted message
	Digitally signed message
	Invalid signed message
	Microsoft Mail 3.x form
	Meeting request
	Accepted meeting request
	Tentatively accepted meeting request
	Declined meeting request
	Canceled meeting
	Task request

The Contents tab displays Help topics organized like book chapters. Double-click a book icon or click the plus sign button to display the Help topics, and then click a topic to display it. The Answer Wizard tab functions like the Office Assistant—type your question, click the Search button, and then select the appropriate topic. The Index tab lets you search the entire Help system by a keyword.

7. Click the **Hide** button 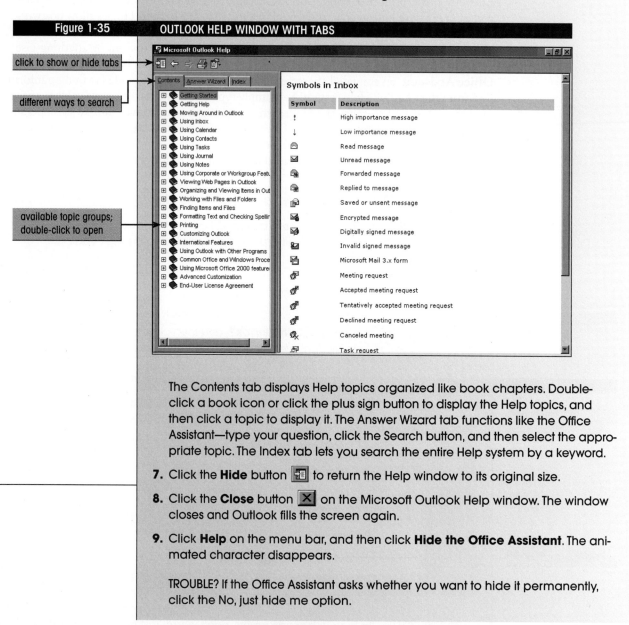 to return the Help window to its original size.

8. Click the **Close** button ⊠ on the Microsoft Outlook Help window. The window closes and Outlook fills the screen again.

9. Click **Help** on the menu bar, and then click **Hide the Office Assistant**. The animated character disappears.

TROUBLE? If the Office Assistant asks whether you want to hide it permanently, click the No, just hide me option.

When you no longer need messages or other items, you should delete them to keep your Inbox clear and Outlook streamlined.

Deleting Items and Exiting Outlook

When you finish using Outlook, you should **exit** (or close) the program. Unlike with other programs, you don't need to save or close any other files. Before you exit, however, you'll delete each of the items you created in this tutorial. When you delete items, they move to the Deleted Items folder. This folder acts like the Recycle Bin in Windows. Items you delete stay in this folder until you empty it.

To delete items and exit Outlook:

1. Click the **Mangoes Order** message in the Message pane of the Inbox to select it, press and hold the **Ctrl** key, and then click each of the other messages you created.

2. Click the **Delete** button ☒ on the Standard toolbar to move these selected messages to the Deleted Items folder.

3. Click the **Address Book** button 📖 on the Standard toolbar, show your Personal Address Book, click the first name in the list, press and hold the **Shift** key as you click the last name in the list, click ☒, and then click the **Yes** button to confirm that you want to permanently delete these entries.

4. Close the Address Book.

   Next you'll remove the signature you created.

5. Click **Tools** on the menu bar, click **Options**, and then click the **Mail Format** tab in the Options dialog box.

6. Click the **Signature Picker** button, click the name of your signature in the Signature box, and then click the **Remove** button.

7. Click the **Yes** button to confirm that you want to permanently remove this signature, and then click the **OK** button in each dialog box.

   Next you'll remove the items from the Deleted Items folder to empty it.

8. If necessary, scroll the Outlook Shortcuts group so you can see the Deleted Items folder, right-click the **Deleted Items** folder, and then click **Empty 'Deleted Items' Folder** on the shortcut menu. A dialog box opens, asking you to confirm the deletion.

9. Click the **Yes** button in the dialog box to empty the Deleted Items folder.

   Now you're ready to exit Outlook.

10. Click the **Close** button ☒ in the title bar to exit Outlook.

Alan thanks you for your help. The Express Lane can now fill all of its customers' orders for mangoes until the end of the season. As the first quarter numbers show, a happy customer means a profitable business.

Session 1.2 QUICK CHECK

1. Describe the purposes of the Inbox and the Outbox.
2. **What is the difference between the Preview pane and the Message pane in the Inbox?**
3. Explain the difference between the Reply button and the Reply to All button?
4. True or False: When you forward a message, the sender's e-mail address appears in the To box.
5. What is a signature?
6. What are two ways to enhance the look of your e-mail messages?
7. What are two potential problems of attachments?
8. True or False: You can save a file attached to a message, but you cannot open it from Outlook.

REVIEW ASSIGNMENTS

Lora Shaw focuses on the customer end of the business, which includes finding new customers, responding to customer comments, and processing customer payments. She asks you to help her with customer communication for The Express Lane.

1. Start Outlook and, if necessary, switch to the Inbox.

2. Create a new e-mail message to yourself with the subject "Increase Customer Base" and the message "The Express Lane's goal is to double its customer base by the end of the year. I can think of several ways to accomplish this, including: (1) increase our advertising in traditional media, (2) offer a rebate or other incentive to current customers who refer friends and family, and (3) enroll all customers who spend at least $100 in a drawing for an all-expenses-paid vacation. Let me know what you think of these ideas." Sign the e-mail with your name.

3. Check the spelling, send the e-mail to the Outbox, and then if necessary to your mail server.

4. In your Personal Address Book, create an entry for Lora Shaw using your e-mail address, and then create entries for the following customers using your e-mail address: Cicely Browne, Juan Ruiz, Kara Newton, Paula Dexter, Mark Tonelli, and Rick Lon.

5. Create a new e-mail message addressed to Lora Shaw with the subject "Tea Health Benefits?" and the message "I've heard that drinking tea has health benefits. Do you have any information about this?" Sign the e-mail message with your name. Check the spelling, and then send the e-mail message.

6. Create a personal distribution list called "Customers" for all the names you entered in your Personal Address Book except Lora Shaw.

7. Create a new e-mail message to the Customers personal distribution list with the subject "Welcome New Customer" and the message "Welcome to The Express Lane. We're sure you'll find our grocery delivery service more convenient and cheaper than your local grocery store, not to mention more healthful, because all our foods are certified organic. If you have any questions or comments, feel free to e-mail us." Sign the e-mail message with your name. Check the spelling, and then send the e-mail message.

Explore ▶ 8. Create a signature that uses your name on one line and the title "Customer Service Representative" on the next line. Use the signature with all e-mail messages. (*Hint: Clear the Don't use when replying or forwarding check box.*)

9. Download your new messages. If the Tea Health Benefits message hasn't arrived, wait a few minutes and try again.

10. Reply to the Tea Health Benefits message with the text "In addition to being the world's second favorite drink to water, there is growing evidence of a link between tea and disease prevention, particularly cancer and heart disease. Check out The Express Lane's large selection of black, oolong, and green teas. The attached file has some information about teas. I hope this information is helpful."

Explore ▶ 11. Change the message format to HTML by clicking Format on the menu bar, and then clicking HTML.

12. Format the text of your e-mail message in 12-point Times New Roman, and then format "The Express Lane" in bold and green.

13. Attach the **Tea** document located in the **Review** folder within the **Tutorial.01** folder on your Data Disk.

14. Check the spelling, and then send the message.

15. Forward the Increase Customer Base message to Lora Shaw with the message "Let's meet next week to talk about implementing some of these ideas."

16. Check the spelling, and then send the message.

17. If necessary, download your messages.

Explore   18. Sort the messages by subject by clicking the Subject column header in the Inbox and then sort the messages by date of receipt by clicking the Received column header.

19. Save the attachment in the Tea Health Benefits message as **Tea Health Benefits** to the **Review** folder within the **Tutorial.01** folder on your Data Disk.

20. Print the reply to the Tea Health Benefits message and its attachment. (*Hint:* In the Print dialog box, select the Print attached files with item[s] check box.)

Explore   21. Print the FW: Increase Customer Base and Welcome New Customer messages. (*Hint:* Select both messages before opening the Print dialog box, and then clear the Start each item on a new page check box.)

22. Delete each Outlook item you created, including all signatures, messages, and address book entries, empty the Deleted Items folder, and then exit Outlook.

CASE PROBLEMS

Case 1. Green Streets   Green Streets is a nonprofit organization in Chicago that plants trees along city sidewalks, improving the streets' appearance and providing a bit of nature among the concrete blocks. The organization works with private homeowners, neighborhood groups, and local government to encourage them to participate in and support the program. Peter Washington is in charge of responding to all inquiries.

1. Start Outlook and, if necessary, switch to the Inbox.

2. Create a new e-mail message addressed to yourself with the subject "Free Trees" and the message "How can you improve your building's appearance, enhance your property values, and please residents and tenants without any cost to yourself? Participate in the urban forestry project with Green Streets. You provide the neighborhood. We provide the trees and the labor and even the city permits. Everyone wins. To find out more about our program, reply to this message." Sign the message with your name.

Explore   3. Switch the message to HTML format, if necessary, by clicking Format on the menu bar, and then clicking HTML.

4. Change the message text to 10-point, bold Arial, and then format the entire text in green.

5. Check the spelling, and then send the message. If necessary, download the message.

6. Reply to the message with the text "Wow. This sounds great. Can I select the type of trees planted in front of my building?" Check the spelling, and then send the message.

7. Forward the message to your e-mail address and include the text "Pat, have you heard of this program? It sounds too good to be true. I'm requesting more information. When it arrives, would you like to get together to review it?" Sign your name.

8. Check the spelling, and then send the message.

9. If necessary, retrieve your messages. You may need to wait a few moments.

10. Forward the FW: Free Trees message to Peter using your e-mail address and the following text, "Peter—Please respond to this inquiry with our basic information package and the answer to the question. Thank you."

Explore 11. Check the spelling, and then print the message. (*Hint:* Click File on the message window's menu bar, and then click Print.)

Explore 12. Delete the message without sending, saving, or closing it. Click File on the message window's menu bar, and then click Delete. Click the Yes button to confirm the deletion.

Explore 13. Save each message as a file in the **Cases** folder within the **Tutorial.01** folder on your Data Disk. Select the first message in the message list, click File on the menu bar, and then click Save As. Change the Save in location to your Data Disk, but leave the subject as the filename and the file type as HTML. (If the messages did not retain HTML formatting, then save the messages as .txt files.) Click the Save button.

14. Delete all the items you created in Outlook, including the messages and address book entries.

15. Empty the Deleted Items folder.

16. Exit Outlook.

Case 2. Answers Anytime   Answers Anytime is a unique tutoring service. Students can e-mail specific questions and problem areas to subject experts and receive quick answers. The subject experts reply to students within two hours, either by e-mail message or e-mail message with an attachment.

1. Start Outlook and, if necessary, switch to the Inbox.

2. Change the message format default to HTML.

3. Create an e-mail message to your e-mail address with the subject "History Questions" and the message "Please send information about the following: What is the Bill of Rights? When did women receive the right to vote? How does Rachel Carson fit into the environmental movement?" Press the Enter key after each question to place it on its own line. Type your name at the end of the message.

Explore 4. Format the questions as a numbered list. (*Hint:* Click the Numbering button on the Formatting toolbar in the Message window.)

5. Check the spelling, and then send the message.

6. In your Personal Address Book, create entries for the following names using your e-mail address: Larry Inktamo, Erin Lawsen, Mei Hom, Vic Lopez, Cara Findley, and Stu Panell.

7. Create a personal distribution list called "Students" for all the names you entered in your Personal Address Book except Erin Lawsen and Stu Panell.

8. If necessary, download the History Questions message and then reply to it, using the following text formatted as a numbered list:

    1. See the attached document for information about the Bill of Rights.

    2. On August 26, 1920, Tennessee delivered the last needed vote and the Nineteenth Amendment was added to the Constitution. It stated that "the right of citizens of the United States to vote shall not be denied by the United States or by any State on account of sex."

3. I've forwarded this question to Stu Panell, our resident expert on the environmental movement.

9. Attach the **Amendments** document, which is located in the **Cases** folder within the **Tutorial.01** folder on your Data Disk, to the e-mail message. Check the spelling, and then send the message.

10. Forward the student's original message to Stu. Add the text "Hi Stu. Question 3 is yours. Thanks."

Explore ▶ 11. Add a flag to the message. Flags mark a message or contact so as to remind you or the recipient to follow up. You can also set a reminder. When you send a message with a flag, the recipient sees a comment with the purpose of the flag in a banner at the top of the message. If you set a reminder, a date will appear as well. Click the Flag for Follow Up button on the Standard toolbar. You can choose flag text from the Flag to list or type your own in the box. Make sure that "Follow up" appears in the Flag to box. Leave the Due by date as None. Click OK. The flag message banner appears near the top of the Message window.

12. Check the spelling, and then send the message.

13. Download your messages. Notice the red flag that appears in the Flag column of the message list next to the message you forwarded to Stu. (If you don't see the message flag, don't worry. Flagged messages may not retain their flag information when sent over the Internet via an ISP.)

14. Use the Office Assistant to find out more about flags and the process of changing a flag to complete. Follow the steps in the Office Assistant to change the flag to complete.

Explore ▶ 15. Save each message as a file in the **Cases** folder within the **Tutorial.01** folder on your Data Disk. Select the first message in the message list, click File on the menu bar, and then click Save As. Change the Save in location to your Data Disk, but leave the subject as the filename and the file type as HTML. (If the messages did not retain HTML formatting, save the messages as .txt files.) Click the Save button.

16. Print the three messages and the attachment.

17. Delete all the items you created in Outlook, including messages and Address Book entries.

18. Empty the Deleted Items folder.

19. Exit Outlook.

Case 3. Healthy Smiles Dentistry   Dr. Louise Schwartz and Dr. Randy Brasiele are partners who practice general dentistry in Montgomery, Alabama. They encourage all patients to come in for check ups and cleanings every six months. Patients schedule their next appointment as they pay for their current appointment. Because patients forget the appointments they made so far in advance, Mollie, the office receptionist, contacts patients a few days before to remind them of their scheduled visit. Mollie wants to use Outlook to send e-mail to patients to confirm their upcoming appointments and to communicate with the doctors' colleagues. You'll help her get started.

1. Start Outlook and, if necessary, switch to the Inbox.

2. Change the message format default to HTML.

3. Create an e-mail with the subject "Appointment Reminder" as the subject and the message "You have an appointment scheduled for tomorrow at Healthy Smiles Dentistry. If you need to reschedule your appointment for any reason, please contact us. Thank you."

4. Use the Office Assistant to find out how to save a draft of an e-mail message.

Explore 5. Save the message as a draft, and then close the message. All unfinished messages are saved in the Drafts folder.

6. Create a signature with your name and class section on one line and Healthy Smiles Dentistry on a second line. Do not use the signature when replying or forwarding.

Explore 7. Format your signature by selecting your name, clicking the Font button, changing the Style to Bold Italic and the Color to Purple, and then clicking the OK button.

8. In your Personal Address Book, create entries for the following names using your e-mail: Abbie Kin, Charles Forest, Chloe Specker, and Chris Hasan.

9. Create a personal distribution list called "Patients" that includes all the entries you created.

Explore 10. Edit the Patient distribution list by removing Abbie Kin from the group. (*Hint:* Double-click the distribution list to open it, click the Add/Remove Members button, click the name you want to remove in the Personal Distribution List box, press the Delete key, and then click the OK button in both dialog boxes.)

Explore 11. Create a message addressed to Abbie Kin directly from the Address Book. Select Abbie's name, and then click the New Message button on the Address Book toolbar. The Message window opens with Abbie's name in the To box. (If the Check Names dialog box opens, click the Show More Names button, click Abbie Kin in the Address Book dialog box, and then click the OK button.)

12. Type "Referral" as the subject and "Dr. Randy Brasiele is referring patient Timmy Larson to you for possible orthodontia work. He has a severe overbite that could be corrected with braces." Check the spelling, and then send the message.

13. Close the Address Book.

Explore 14. Switch to the Drafts folder in the My Shortcuts group, and double-click the Appointment Reminder message to open the saved draft in its own window.

15. Check the spelling of the message, and then address the e-mail to the Patients distribution list.

Explore 16. Insert the signature you created on its own line after the message. Click at the end of the message, press the Enter key twice, click the Signature button on the Standard toolbar, and then click your signature.

17. Format the message by changing the word "tomorrow" to boldface and both instances of Healthy Smiles Dentistry to blue. Print the message, and then send the message.

18. Download your messages, if necessary, and then reply to the Referral message with the text "Thank you for your referral. I'll be seeing Timmy next week and will update you then."

Explore 19. Save your reply message as a file in the **Cases** folder within the **Tutorial.01** folder on your Data Disk. Click File on the menu bar, and then click Save As. Change the Save in location to your Data Disk, leave the subject as the filename, and change the file type to .txt so you can read the messages in Word or WordPad. Click the Save button.

20. Close the message, saving the changes.

21. Switch to the Drafts folder, and then print the RE: Referral message.

22. Delete all the items you created in Outlook, including any messages, Address Book entries, and signatures.

23. Empty the Deleted Items folder.

24. Exit Outlook.

Case 4. Party Planners Jace Moran plans events ranging from company picnics to children's birthday parties to weddings. Right now, she is working on a graduation party. The client has given Jace the e-mail addresses for the entire guest list so that Jace can send the invitations using Outlook.

1. Start Outlook and, if necessary, switch to the Inbox.

Explore 2. Send an e-mail message to yourself with "Graduation Party" as the subject, using an Excel worksheet as the message body. From the Inbox, click Actions on the menu bar, point to New Mail Message Using, point to Microsoft Office, and then click Microsoft Excel Worksheet. In column A, enter a list of foods for the party. In column B, enter the probable cost for the food. Total the cost column by clicking the AutoSum button on the toolbar. Send the e-mail message. Close Excel without saving the worksheet.

3. Create entries in your Personal Address Book for yourself, Jace Moran, and at least three guests, using your own e-mail address.

4. Create a personal distribution list called "Guests" for the guests.

5. Create a second personal distribution list called "Organizers" for yourself and Jace, as the party organizers.

6. Close the Address Book.

7. Use Balloon Party Invitation stationery to create the party invitation.

8. Address the invitation to the guests distribution list with a copy to the party organizers distribution list. Type "Celebrate" as the subject.

Explore 9. Fill in the Day, Time, and Place. (*Hint:* Click after the text heading and then enter the appropriate information.)

Explore 10. Modify the format of the stationery; try changing the font or color or size of existing text or moving the balloons.

11. Check the spelling, and then send the message.

12. If necessary, download your messages.

13. Read the food cost e-mail, and then reply to the message, approving the budget. Check the spelling, and then send the message.

14. Download your messages, if necessary, and then read them.

15. Print the Celebrate and RE: Graduation Party messages.

Explore 16. Save the messages in the Inbox to the **Cases** folder within the **Tutorial.01** folder on your Data Disk. Select a message in the message list, click File on the menu bar, and then click Save As. Change the Save in location to your Data Disk, but leave the subject as the filename and the file type as HTML. (If the message did not retain HTML formatting, then save the messages as .txt files.) Click the Save button.

17. Delete all the Outlook items you created, including the messages and Address Book entries.

18. Empty the Deleted Items folder.

19. Exit Outlook.

QUICK | CHECK ANSWERS

Session 1.1

1. An item is a basic element that holds information in Outlook, such as an e-mail message. A folder is the space where these items are stored in Outlook.

2. A profile is a group of settings that specify how Outlook is set up for a user.

3. E-mail is the electronic transfer of messages between computers. It's inexpensive for communicating with others, whether nearby or faraway. You can send and read messages at your convenience.

4. expresslane.com

5. Use Plain Text when you want to ensure that all recipients can read your messages.

6. Three of the following: reread your messages; be concise; use standard capitalization; check spelling and grammar; avoid sarcasm; don't send confidential information.

7. The Personal Address Book is a custom address book you create to store e-mail addresses you use frequently.

8. A personal distribution list saves time and insures you don't inadvertently leave out someone when sending a message to a group.

Session 1.2

1. The Inbox stores e-mail messages you have received. The Outbox stores e-mail messages you have written but not yet sent.

2. The Message pane displays a list of the e-mail messages you have received; whereas the Preview pane displays the contents of the message selected in the Message pane.

3. Reply responds only to the sender of the e-mail message; Reply to All responds to the sender and any other recipients of the e-mail message.

4. False. The Senders e-mail appears in the From box.

5. A signature is text that is automatically added to every e-mail message you send.

6. You can format the message text or use stationery.

7. Any two of the following: The message size may make the e-mail take longer to send and receive. Some e-mail recipients cannot receive attachments or have a size limit for incoming messages. Attachments may contain viruses.

8. False. You can save the file to view later or you can open it directly from Outlook.

OBJECTIVES

In this tutorial you will:

- Create, customize, organize, and print notes

- Create a task list with one-time and recurring tasks

- Organize tasks by categories and views

- Assign a task to someone else

- Schedule appointments and events in the Calendar

- Plan a meeting

- Save your calendar as a Web page

- Delete notes, tasks, categories, appointments, events, and meetings

SCHEDULING IN OUTLOOK

Planning a Meeting for Wertheimer Accounting's Web Site

CASE

Wertheimer Accounting

Wertheimer Accounting is an accounting firm in Austin, Texas, that provides tax preparation as well as bookkeeping, payroll, and financial consulting to local businesses. Established in 1998 by Lisa Wertheimer, the firm has established a reputation as being a dependable, affordable, and reliable firm, dedicated to working with smaller businesses. Lisa and her four associates prepare their client's business and individual income tax returns; record, analyze, and verify financial documents for their clients; and provide advice about the tax advantages and disadvantages of certain business decisions.

Computers have changed the nature of accounting work. Lisa's firm uses special software packages to summarize transactions for financial records and organize data for financial analysis. These accounting packages greatly reduce the amount of tedious manual work associated with data and record keeping. In addition, all members of the firm use Outlook to communicate with clients, create their to-do lists, coordinate their schedules, and plan meetings to ensure that clients' needs are met in a timely way.

Lisa wants to expand the firm's client list. She plans to create a company Web site as a way to communicate with current clients and to attract new clients. She wants the site to include background about the firm—its history and goals, its services, and its staff—as well as business tax-related content, such as a monthly Tax Tips section, a Latest Laws section, important tax dates, and other useful information. She intends to have a staff meeting to discuss the content.

In this tutorial, you'll jot down notes about the Web site and other tasks, update and organize a to-do list, and delegate a task. Then you'll schedule time to complete tasks and make appointments in the calendar. Finally, you'll plan a meeting to discuss the Web site.

SESSION 2.1

In this session, you'll jot down and then customize notes on the Outlook notepad. Then you'll create a to-do list with both one-time and recurring tasks. Finally you'll organize your tasks by adding categories and changing the Tasks view.

Taking Notes

Outlook comes with a never-ending electronic pad, called **Notes**. Rather than plaster your desk and monitor with colored squares of paper, Notes enables you to easily jot down and organize your ideas, questions, and reminders. You can leave a note open on the screen as you work or you can close it, knowing that it will never get buried under a file or inadvertently tossed in the garbage. Like other Outlook items, notes are saved automatically.

Jotting Down a Note

The New button on the Standard toolbar creates the most logical item for the open folder. For example, clicking the New button in the Inbox folder creates a new e-mail message, but clicking it in the Notes folder creates a new note. The button's icon and the ScreenTip remind you which item it will create. You can use the button's list arrow to select any new Outlook item, regardless of which folder is displayed. In this way, you can create a note when the idea hits, without a lot of extra mouse clicks, no matter which folder you are working with at the time. You'll create several notes to remind you of the items for your calendar.

To create a note:

1. Start Outlook and, if necessary, display the Outlook Bar and hide the Folder List, using View on the menu bar.

2. Click the **New** button list arrow 🗋 New on the Standard toolbar, and then click **Note**. A square, yellow note appears, labeled with the current date and time.

   TROUBLE? If your note is not yellow or the date and time don't appear, then the Notes settings are different on your computer. Click the Close button in the upper-right corner of the note to close it. Click Tools on the menu bar, click Options, click the Preferences tab, and then click the Note Options button. If necessary, change the color to Yellow, the size to Medium, the font to Comic Sans MS, and then click the OK button. Click the Other tab, click the Advanced Options button, click the When viewing Notes, show time and date check box in the Appearance options area to insert a check mark, and then click the OK button in each dialog box. Repeat Step 2.

3. Type **Web site ideas: tax preparation tips and little-known deductions** as the note text. As you type, text wraps within the note's width. If you enter a long note, the text would scroll vertically. See Figure 2-1.

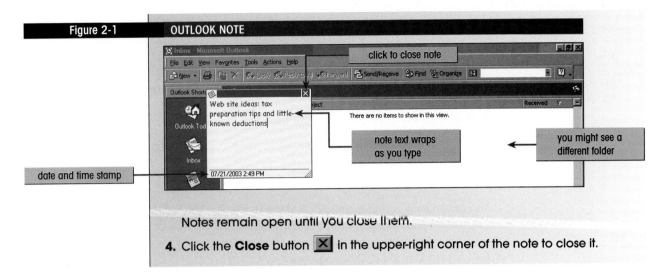

Figure 2-1 — OUTLOOK NOTE

Notes remain open until you close them.

4. Click the **Close** button ☒ in the upper-right corner of the note to close it.

The Notes Information viewer displays an icon for each note you create along with the first few words of the note. It is helpful to type a few key words in the first line of the note, such as "Web site ideas", so that you can know the note's content without having to open it.

To create additional notes from the Notes folder:

1. Click **Notes** in the Outlook Shortcuts group on the Outlook Bar to switch to the Notes Information viewer. You can see the icon for the note you created. See Figure 2-2.

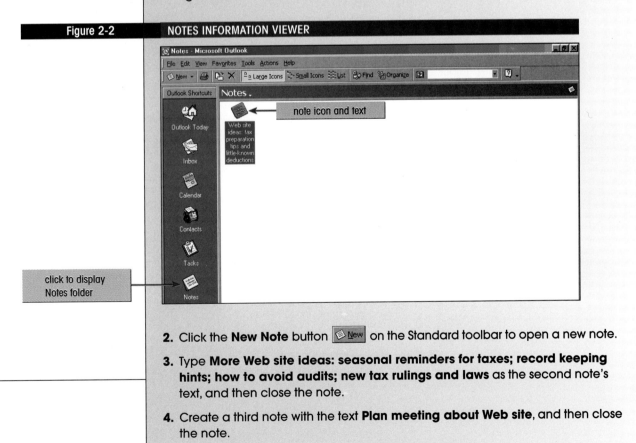

Figure 2-2 — NOTES INFORMATION VIEWER

2. Click the **New Note** button 📝 New on the Standard toolbar to open a new note.

3. Type **More Web site ideas: seasonal reminders for taxes; record keeping hints; how to avoid audits; new tax rulings and laws** as the second note's text, and then close the note.

4. Create a third note with the text **Plan meeting about Web site**, and then close the note.

The Notes Information viewer shows icons for the three notes you created. Sometimes you might want to revise a note. You can edit the text in an open note, just as you can edit the text in any document.

To open and edit a note:

1. Double-click the **More Web site ideas** note to open it.

2. Double-click **taxes** to select the word, and then type **estimated payments**. The new text replaces the old.

You can edit any text in the note. Unlike with a paper pad and pen, the changes remain neat and legible. In addition, you can customize the look of your Outlook notes.

Customizing the Look of Notes

You can customize your notes by changing their font, color, and size. Different colors are helpful for organizing your notes. For example, you'll leave task notes as yellow and change informational notes to blue. Resizing notes enables you to display all the text in a large note or eliminate the excess space in a short note.

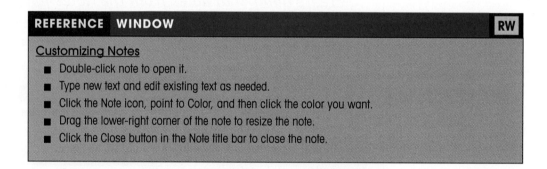

REFERENCE WINDOW   **RW**

<u>Customizing Notes</u>
- Double-click note to open it.
- Type new text and edit existing text as needed.
- Click the Note icon, point to Color, and then click the color you want.
- Drag the lower-right corner of the note to resize the note.
- Click the Close button in the Note title bar to close the note.

You'll change the background color of the notes you created.

To change the color of notes:

1. Click the **Note** icon 🎨 in the upper-left corner of the note, point to **Color**. The shortcut menu lists the five colors you can use for your notes—blue, green, pink, yellow, or white. See Figure 2-3.

Figure 2-3	NOTES SHORTCUT MENU

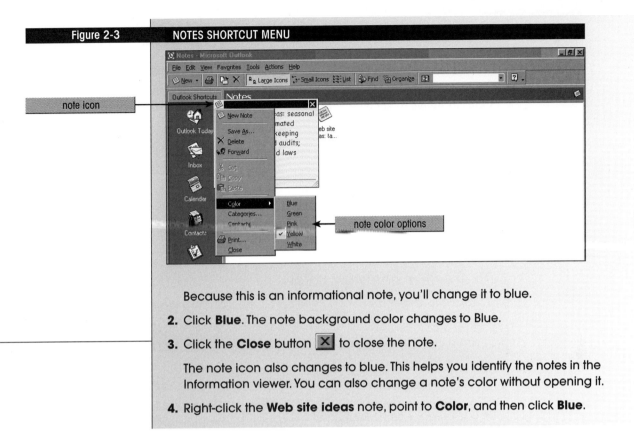

note icon

note color options

Because this is an informational note, you'll change it to blue.

2. Click **Blue**. The note background color changes to Blue.

3. Click the **Close** button ☒ to close the note.

The note icon also changes to blue. This helps you identify the notes in the Information viewer. You can also change a note's color without opening it.

4. Right-click the **Web site ideas** note, point to **Color**, and then click **Blue**.

You can resize any open note by dragging from any border. The top and bottom edges change a note's height, whereas the left and right edges change a note's width. If you want to change both the height and width at once, you can drag the lower-right corner.

To resize a note:

1. Double-click the **Plan meeting** note to open it.

2. Point to the lower-right corner of the open note until the pointer changes to ↖.

3. Drag diagonally outward about two inches to expand the note height and width, and then drag diagonally inward approximately three inches, as shown in Figure 2-4, to reduce the height and width, but do not release the mouse button.

Figure 2-4	RESIZING A NOTE

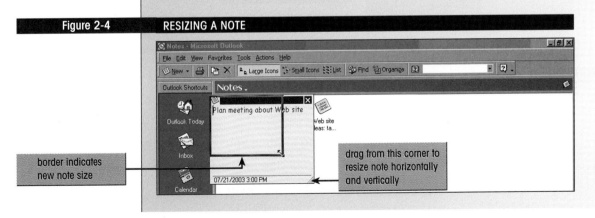

border indicates new note size

drag from this corner to resize note horizontally and vertically

4. Release the mouse button to resize the note.

5. Click the **Close** button ☒ to close the note.

One advantage to keeping your notes in Outlook is that you can organize them to meet your needs.

Organizing Notes

From the Notes folder, you can organize the notes in a variety of views. One view shows all notes arranged by icons, the other views provide various list options. For example, you can view notes organized in a list by color or date. You can change views using the View menu or the Organize button.

To organize and view notes:

1. Click the **Organize** button 🔠 Organize on the Standard toolbar in the Notes Information viewer.

   From the Organize pane that opens, you can quickly organize your notes by using views.

2. Click **Using Views**, and then click **By Color** in the Change your view list box.

   The existing notes become grouped by the note color—in this case, blue and yellow. The Expand buttons indicate that the groups contain items.

3. Click the top **Expand** button ⊞ to display the blue notes. The Expand button changes to a Collapse button ⊟ to indicate that all items are visible. See Figure 2-5.

Figure 2-5   NOTES ORGANIZED BY COLOR

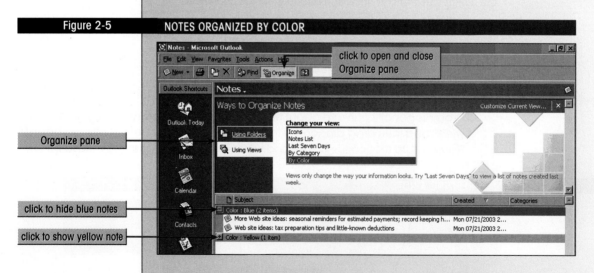

4. Click **Last Seven Days** in the Change your view list box. The notes appear in descending order according to when you created them.

5. Click **Icons** in the Change your view list box to arrange the notes by icons.

6. Click 🔠 Organize to close the Organize pane.

There may be times when you'll want to pass a note to someone else.

Passing Notes to Others

One of the most convenient features of Outlook is the ability to integrate the various features. Some notes you'll want or need to pass along to someone else. Rather than retyping your note in an e-mail message, you can include the note as the message body or an attachment.

To create an e-mail with the note in the message body, drag the note to the Inbox folder on the Outlook Bar. The note appears in the message body preceded by its date and time stamp, and the Subject line is filled in with the note's first line. You need only address the e-mail and enter any additional text you want.

To create an e-mail and include the note as an attachment, just right-click the note, and then click Forward. A Message window opens with the note included as an attachment and the Subject line completed. Again, you need only address the e-mail and enter the text you want.

Printing Notes

Although the advantage of Outlook notes is that they don't clutter your desk with scraps of paper, sometimes you might want to print one or more notes. You can print all notes in the Notes folder using the Print command. Or you can print selected notes. Click one note to select it; to select two or more notes, press and hold the Ctrl key while you click the notes you want. These are the same selection techniques as are used in My Computer, Windows Explorer, and other Office programs. When you print, you have the option of printing all the notes on one page or on separate pages. You'll print the notes that refer to the Web site.

To print notes:

1. Click the **Web site ideas** note to select it, press and hold the **Ctrl** key, click the **More Web site ideas** note, and then release the **Ctrl** key. Both messages are selected.

2. Click the **Print** button on Standard toolbar to open the Print dialog box. See Figure 2-6.

Figure 2-6   PRINT DIALOG BOX FOR NOTES

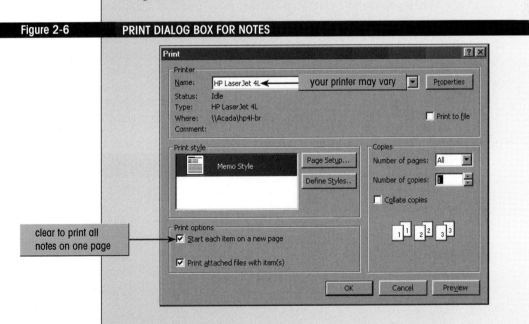

clear to print all notes on one page

3. Click the **Start each item on a new page** check box to remove the check mark. This way, both notes will print on the same page.

> TROUBLE? If the Start each item on a new page check box is grayed out, then you cannot change this option. When you click the OK button in Step 4, each note will print on a separate page.
>
> **4.** Verify that the correct printer appears in the Name text box, and then click the **OK** button. Notice that the printout includes the text of both notes along with your name and the dates and times you created or edited them.

Notes are great as short-term reminders or storage, but you'll want to act on them promptly. Otherwise, your notes will collect into an unmanageable pile rather quickly. Some notes, such as the "Plan meeting" note, you'll want to move onto your to-do list.

Compiling a To-Do List

A to-do list is an effective way to remember all the tasks you need to accomplish. A **task** is any item on your to-do list that you want to track. When you track a task you follow its progress so you know how much you completed and when you completed it. A task can occur once, such as returning a phone call to plan a meeting; or, it can occur repeatedly (called a **recurring task**), such as sending a monthly status report. Your tasks can simply list the things you need to complete, or you can include more details, such as a due date, start date, status, priority, percentage complete, and other notes.

Creating a Task List

You can create a task from scratch or from an existing Outlook item. When you create a task from scratch, you must enter a subject—a short description of a task, such as "Organize Web site ideas." If you want to include more descriptive information, such as additional notes, a starting date, a due date, and a priority, you need to open the task window.

When you create a task from another item, much of the information is transferred to the appropriate fields for you. Fields appear as text boxes or check boxes in the dialog box. The **AutoCreate** feature generates a new item when you drag an item from one folder to another. For example, dragging a note icon from the Notes Information viewer into the Tasks folder creates a task and dragging an e-mail message from the Inbox Message pane into the Calendar folder creates an appointment. Outlook inserts relevant information from the original item into the appropriate fields such as subject and date text boxes and places the contents of the original item in the text box. You can enter additional information in the open window.

REFERENCE WINDOW   **RW**

<u>Creating a Task</u>
- Click the New button list arrow, and then click Task to display a blank Task window (*or* drag a note to the Tasks folder).
- Enter a task subject; select the due date and priority, if necessary; and enter other task details you want to record.
- Click the Save and Close button on the Standard toolbar.
  or
- Switch to Tasks folder, and select the view with the task details you want to record.
- Click in each text box and enter the appropriate information, such as a task subject or due date.

You'll use AutoCreate to set up a task by moving the yellow note from the Notes folder to the Tasks folder.

To create a task from a note:

1. Drag the yellow **Plan meeting** note to Tasks in the Outlook Shortcuts group on the Outlook Bar. When you release the mouse button, a Task window with information from the note opens; the first line of the note is entered in the Subject text box.

2. Click the **Due date** list arrow. A calendar opens below the Due date field. Today's date is surrounded by a red border and shaded in gray.

3. Click tomorrow's date to assign a deadline for the task.

4. Click the **Priority** list arrow, and then click **High** to change the task's urgency level. Figure 2-7 shows the completed Task window.

Figure 2-7	COMPLETED TASK WINDOW

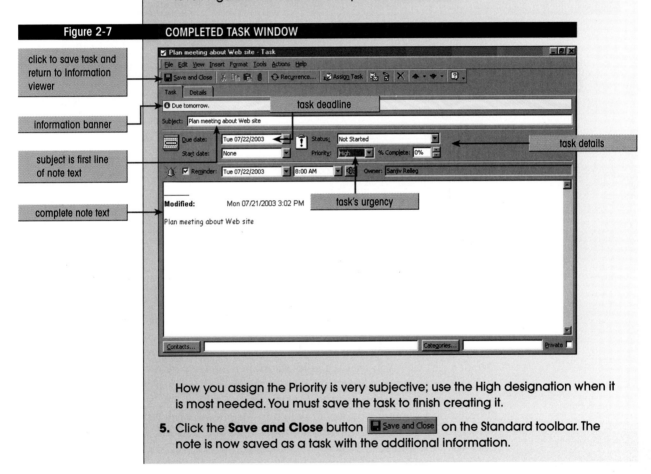

click to save task and return to Information viewer

information banner

subject is first line of note text

complete note text

task deadline

task details

task's urgency

How you assign the Priority is very subjective; use the High designation when it is most needed. You must save the task to finish creating it.

5. Click the **Save and Close** button 🔲 Save and Close on the Standard toolbar. The note is now saved as a task with the additional information.

Because you no longer need the note you converted to a task, you'll delete it.

To delete a note:

1. Click the yellow **Plan meeting** note to select it, if it is not already selected.

2. Click the **Delete** button ☒ on the Standard toolbar. The note is moved to the Deleted Items folder.

The Deleted Items folder acts like the Windows Recycle Bin—items remain in the folder until you empty the folder. You will work with the Deleted Items folder later in this tutorial.

Next, you'll switch to the Tasks folder to view the new task and create additional tasks. The Tasks folder displays all the tasks you created, and provides a task list to which you can add new tasks.

To create a one-time task from the Tasks folder:

1. Click **Tasks** in the Outlook Shortcuts group on the Outlook Bar to display the Tasks Information viewer.

   You want to switch to the view that displays a list of task subjects and due dates.

2. Click **View** on the menu bar, point to **Current View**, and then click **Simple List**. See Figure 2-8.

Figure 2-8	TASKS IN SIMPLE LIST VIEW

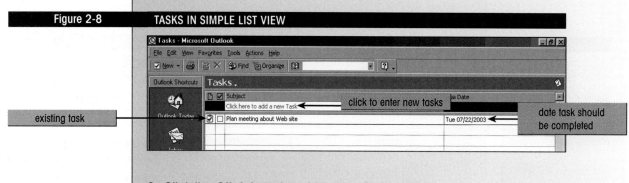

existing task

click to enter new tasks

date task should be completed

3. Click the **Click here to add a new Task** text box.

4. Type **Organize Web site ideas** as the subject of the task. You can now enter a due date.

5. Click the **Due Date** text box, click the **Due Date** list arrow to display the calendar, select the date for next Tuesday, and then press the **Enter** key. The task is added to the list of tasks above the Plan meeting task.

The Simple List view shows only a few fields of information; other views, however, display more fields. If you want to see information not displayed in the current view, you can change to another view. For example, when you switch from the Simple List view to the Detailed List view, you see each task's status, percentage complete, and assigned categories.

A task can be updated from any view in the Tasks folder. To change a task's information, you can type data into the appropriate text box. For example, if you wanted to enter status information for a task, you would switch to Detailed List view, click that task's Status text box, and then select from the list of options that are displayed, which include Not Started, In Progress, Completed, Waiting on someone else, and Deferred. You could also enter any necessary data in the Task window, which contains all the fields. You open the Task window for any task by double-clicking its name in the task list.

Creating and Updating a Recurring Task

When a specific task must be repeated at some regular interval, you can set up a recurrence pattern for it rather than create a new task each time. You might set a recurring task for getting a haircut, putting together monthly reports, or planning quarterly staff meetings. You can set a recurrence pattern for an existing task or a new one. The recurrence pattern tells Outlook when the task is active and due.

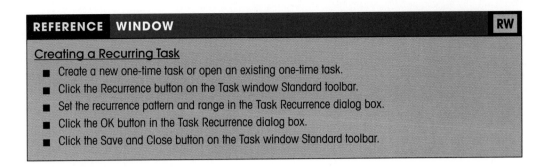

REFERENCE WINDOW   RW

Creating a Recurring Task
- Create a new one-time task or open an existing one-time task.
- Click the Recurrence button on the Task window Standard toolbar.
- Set the recurrence pattern and range in the Task Recurrence dialog box.
- Click the OK button in the Task Recurrence dialog box.
- Click the Save and Close button on the Task window Standard toolbar.

You want to have the Tax Tips section updated on a regular basis. This is a recurring task. You'll create a new task that reminds you each time you need to write the update for the Tax Tips section of the Web site.

To create a recurring task:

1. Click the **New Task** button ☑ New on the Tasks Standard toolbar to open a new Task window.

2. Type **Write Tax Tips for Web site** as the task subject.

3. Click the **Recurrence** button ↻ Recurrence... on the Task window Standard toolbar. The Task Recurrence dialog box opens.

You can determine how you want a task to recur—how often you want the task to recur, and whether it should recur on a certain date or day in each time period or after a specified interval after the last occurrence. In addition, you can determine when the recurrence starts and ends.

You'll set the recurrence pattern to be monthly on the last Monday of every month.

To set the recurrence pattern:

1. Click the **Monthly** option button in the left column of the Recurrence pattern area.

   The right column of the Recurrence pattern area changes to reflect options for monthly recurrences. You fill in the options and click the list arrows to create a sentence that describes your recurrence pattern.

2. Click the middle option button to the left of the word **The** in the right column of the Recurrence pattern area.

3. Click the first list arrow in the line, click **last**, click the next list arrow, and then click **Monday**. The Recurrence pattern line should read "The last Monday of every 1 month."

   Next, you'll set the range of recurrence to begin next Monday and end after 6 occurrences.

4. Click the **Start** list arrow to display a calendar, and then click the date for next Monday.

5. Click the **End after** option button, press the **Tab** key to select 10, and then type **6**. Your dialog box should match Figure 2-9.

Figure 2-9   COMPLETED TASK RECURRENCE DIALOG BOX

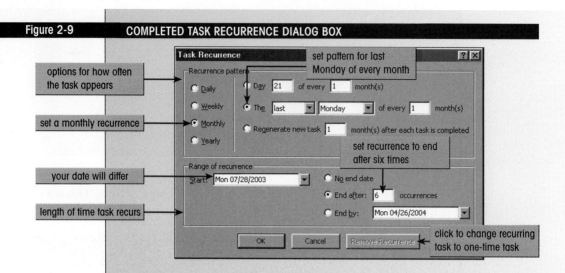

options for how often
the task appears

set a monthly recurrence

your date will differ

length of time task recurs

set pattern for last
Monday of every month

set recurrence to end
after six times

click to change recurring
task to one-time task

The task will occur monthly on the last Monday of each month, beginning next Monday and continuing for the next six months.

6. Click the **OK** button to return to the Task window. The information banner indicates the due date of the first occurrence and the recurrence pattern. See Figure 2-10.

Figure 2-10   TASK WINDOW WITH RECURRENCE SET

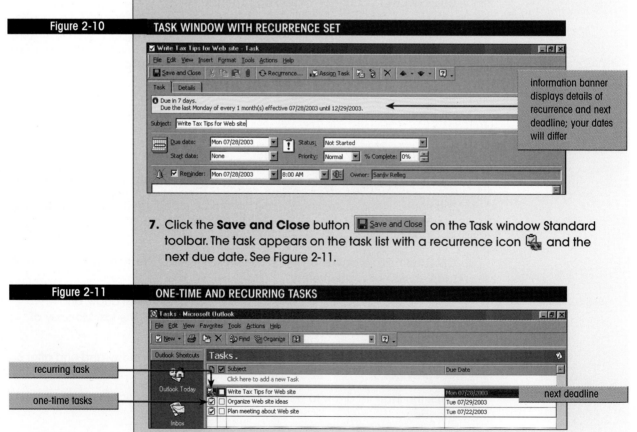

information banner
displays details of
recurrence and next
deadline; your dates
will differ

7. Click the **Save and Close** button on the Task window Standard toolbar. The task appears on the task list with a recurrence icon and the next due date. See Figure 2-11.

Figure 2-11   ONE-TIME AND RECURRING TASKS

recurring task

one-time tasks

next deadline

You can choose to skip any occurrence of a recurring task by opening the task, clicking Actions on the task window menu bar, and then clicking Skip Occurrence. Outlook sets the due date to the next scheduled occurrence.

Organizing Your Tasks

A benefit of listing your tasks in Outlook is that you can arrange them in a variety of ways without rewriting the list. Just like you changed the color of different types of notes, you can distinguish tasks in a variety of ways—by categories, by due dates, by subject.

Assigning Categories to Tasks

One way to classify your tasks (as well as all other Outlook items) is to assign each one to a category. A **category** is a keyword or phrase that you assign to an item to help organize and later locate and group related items, regardless of whether they are stored in the same folder. You can assign items to 20 general categories from the Master Category List, such as Business and Personal, or to more specific categories that you add to the master list, such as Web Site and Payroll and project or client names. You can assign as many categories as you like to an item. Using categories appropriately are the key to staying organized in Outlook.

REFERENCE WINDOW   **RW**

Assigning a Category

- Right-click the item, and then click Categories (*or* double-click the item to open it, and then click the Categories button).
- Click one or more categories in the available category list of the Categories dialog box.
- To add a new category, click the Master Category List button, type the category name in the New category text box, click the Add button, and then click the OK button (*or* type the category name in the top text box of the Categories dialog box, and then press the Enter key).
- Click the OK button.
- If necessary, save and close the item.

You'll assign a category from the built-in Master Category List to the Organize Web site ideas task.

To assign a category to a task:

1. Double-click the **Organize Web site ideas** task to open its Task window.

2. Click the **Categories** button at the bottom of the window. The Categories dialog box opens, showing all the categories available in the Master Category List.

3. Click the **Ideas** check box to add that category to the task. See Figure 2-12. The top text box shows all the categories assigned to the selected item.

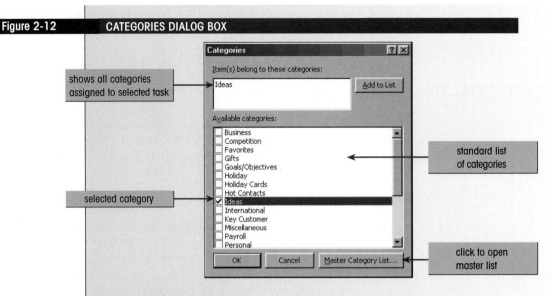

Figure 2-12 CATEGORIES DIALOG BOX

shows all categories assigned to selected task

standard list of categories

selected category

click to open master list

TROUBLE? If your list shows additional categories, then someone has added categories to the master list. Just continue with Step 4.

4. Click the **OK** button. The category appears in the Category text box at the bottom of the Task window.

Although the category you just added to the task is accurate, it may be too general to help you organize your tasks effectively.

Adding Categories to the Master Category List

The categories that come with Outlook are fairly broad and not specific to any industry. As a result, you will often want to add more precise categories that reflect your work. For example, you might create categories for each client or project that you work with, or each type of business contact, or each department in your organization. If you consistently assign client categories to all Outlook items, you can quickly find everything associated with a specific client.

Because you want to be able to organize your Outlook items related to the new Web site, you will create a category called "Web Site" and assign it to any notes, tasks, contacts, e-mail messages, and meetings related to creating and maintaining the company's Web site.

To add a new category to the master list:

1. Click the **Categories** button in the Organize Web site ideas Task window. The Categories dialog box opens.

2. Click the **Master Category List** button. The Master Category List dialog box that opens shows the list of available categories.

   Because "Web Site" is not on the default list, you'll create it now.

3. Type **Web Site** in the New category text box, and then click the **Add** button to enter this category in the list.

Be aware that categories are case sensitive, which means that capitalization counts and Outlook sees "Web Site," "web site," and "WEB SITE" as different categories.

4. Scroll down to view the new category in the list. See Figure 2-13.

Figure 2-13 **MASTER CATEGORY LIST DIALOG BOX**

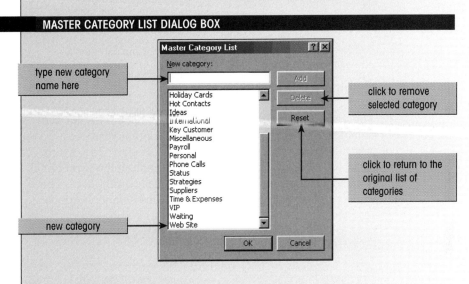

type new category name here

new category

click to remove selected category

click to return to the original list of categories

5. Click the **OK** button to return to the Categories dialog box.

You can add categories to an item from the Categories dialog box, the item's window, or a shortcut menu. You can remove a category from an item in these same locations.

To add and remove categories for an item:

1. Click the **Web Site** check box in the Available categories list, and then click the **OK** button. The Categories text box shows the selected categories separated by a comma.

Although you could leave both categories, the Web Site category is much more appropriate. You'll delete the Ideas category from the task.

2. Drag to select **Ideas,** (including the comma and the following space) in the Categories text box. See Figure 2-14.

Figure 2-14 **CATEGORIES ASSIGNED TO A TASK**

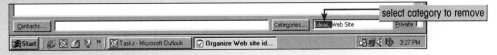

select category to remove

3. Press the **Delete** key. The Ideas category is removed from the task, but remains in the Master Category List.

4. Click the **Save and Close** button 🖫 Save and Close on the Standard toolbar to close the task. The task is saved with only the Web Site category assigned.

5. Right-click the **Plan meeting about Web site** task, and then click **Categories** on the shortcut menu. Even though you did not open the item, you will assign a category.

6. Click the **Web Site** check box in the Categories dialog box, and then click the **OK** button.

The two tasks are now assigned to the same category.

Viewing for Tasks by Category

The Tasks folder is in Simple List view, which does not show all details of the tasks. You should select the view that best meets your current need. If you want to group items by a particular heading, for example, the By Category view organizes tasks by category. No matter which view you use, Outlook provides flexibility: you can click a column header to sort or arrange the items, such as chronologically by due date. This is similar to the way columns work in Windows Explorer and other Microsoft applications.

To view tasks by categories:

1. Click **View** on the menu bar, point to **Current View**, and then click **Detailed List**. Notice the additional details about your tasks, including the High priority icon ! next to the Plan meeting task.

2. Click **View** on the menu bar, point to **Current View**, and then click **By Category**.

3. Click the **Expand** button ⊞ next to each category to display the tasks included in those categories. See Figure 2-15.

| Figure 2-15 | TASKS GROUPED BY CATEGORY |

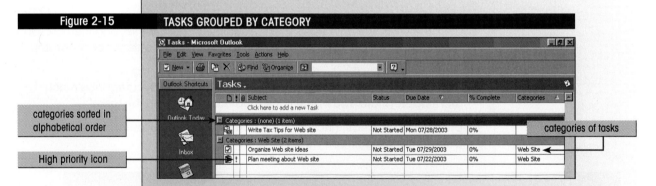

If you had left the Ideas category in the Organize Web site ideas task, there would have been a third category listed in the view and the task would have appeared in two categories.

4. Click the **Subject** column header to sort the tasks alphabetically within each category.

5. Click the **Due Date** column header to sort the tasks by due date within each category, and then click the column header again to reverse the order. The direction of the arrow in the column header indicates ascending or descending order.

6. Click **View** on the menu bar, point to **Current View**, and then click **Simple List**.

You can assign one or more categories to any Outlook item. You can then use the Find command to locate all items associated with a specific category.

Assigning a Task

So far, you own all of the tasks you created, which means that you are responsible for completing them. Sometimes, however, you'll want someone else to complete a task. When you **assign** a task, you delegate it to someone else. For example, you'll assign a task to design the company Web site to Antonio Delgado, the newly hired Webmaster. Each assigned task involves two people—one to send a **task request** (an e-mail message with details about the task to be assigned) and one to respond to the task request. The person who sends the task request transfers ownership of the task to the recipient once that person accepts the task, although the original owner can keep an updated copy of the task in his or her task list and receive status reports.

Task requests are always sent in RTF format, even if you have your mail format set as Plain Text or HTML. This means that to keep the task request intact as it travels over the Internet, you need to make sure that RTF format is enabled for the recipient. You can make this change for any recipient you add to your Personal Address Book or the Contacts folder, or you can set this when you create the task request. If the RTF format is not enabled, then the recipient won't be able to respond to the task request.

REFERENCE WINDOW **RW**

Assigning a Task

- Create a new task or open an existing task.
- Click the Assign Task button on the Task window Standard toolbar.
- Check or uncheck the check boxes to determine whether or not you keep a copy of the task and receive a status report.
- Type an e-mail address in the To box (or click the To button and select a name from your address book).
- Right-click the e-mail address in the To box, click Properties, click the Always send to this recipient in Microsoft Outlook rich-text format check box to insert a check mark, and then click the OK button.
- Click the Send button on the Task window Standard toolbar, click OK to turn off the task reminder, and then if necessary click the Send/Receive button on the Inbox or Outbox Standard toolbar.

You cannot assign a task to yourself. To complete the steps in this section, the Responding to a Task Request section, and the Receiving a Response to a Task Request section, you'll need a classmate's e-mail address. If you don't have a classmate's e-mail address, ask your instructor for one. Otherwise, you should read but not complete these sections.

To assign a task to another person:

1. Click the **New Task** button ☑ New on the Standard toolbar. A blank Task window opens.

2. Type **Web site design** in the Subject text box.

3. Click the **Due date** list arrow to display a calendar, click the right scroll arrow twice to advance the months, and then click the same date number as today to select a due date two months from today.

4. Click the **Priority** list arrow, and then click **High**.

5. Click the **Categories** button, click the **Web Site** check box, and then click the **OK** button.

6. Click the **Assign Task** button [Assign Task] on the Task window Standard toolbar. The Task window changes to include a To box, in which you can specify the task recipient. See Figure 2-16.

| Figure 2-16 | TASK WINDOW FOR ASSIGNMENT |

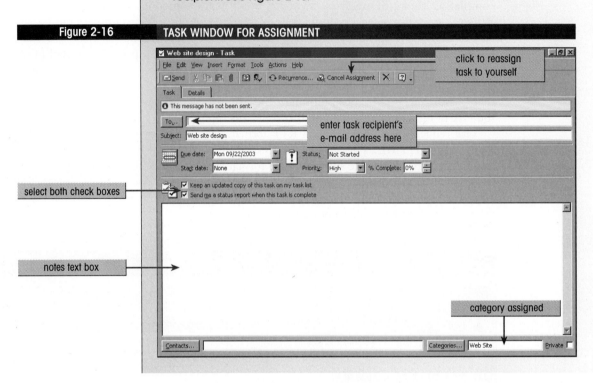

Notice the two new check boxes in the Task window. The Keep an updated copy of this task on my task list check box creates a copy of the task in the original owner's task list. The original owner receives updates when the assigned owner changes the task. The Send me a status report when this task is complete check box specifies that the original owner receive a message indicating that the task is complete when the new owner finishes it.

To send the task assignment:

1. Type a classmate's e-mail address in the To box, and then press the **Tab** key. You could address the task to anyone in the Address Book, just as you would address an e-mail message.

   TROUBLE? If you don't have a classmate's e-mail address, you'll need to get one from your instructor. Otherwise, read but do not complete the steps in this section.

2. Right-click the e-mail address in the To box, and then click **Properties**. The Properties dialog box opens for the address.

3. Click the **Always send to this recipient in Microsoft Outlook rich-text format** check box to insert a check mark, and then click the **OK** button.

4. Click the **Send** button [Send] on the Standard toolbar.

A dialog box or the Office Assistant will open to remind you that the task reminder has been turned off because you are no longer the owner of the task.

5. Click the **OK** button to confirm that the task reminder is turned off. The task icon changes to 🔌 to indicate that it has been assigned.

6. If necessary, click the **Send/Receive** button ⌨ Send/Receive on the Inbox Standard toolbar to send the message.

Before a task is assigned to another person, that person must receive and respond to the task request.

Responding to a Task Request

The task request appears as an e-mail message in the recipient's Inbox. The person who receives the task request can accept, reject, or reassign the task. Note that to process a task request, both the sender and receiver must be using Outlook for e-mail. By accepting the task, the receiver becomes the new owner and the only person who can update the task. If the receiver declines the task, it returns to the original owner. Receivers who assign the task to someone else can no longer change the task, but they can keep it in their task list and receive status reports, giving them the same rights and control over the task as the original owner. To assign a task to someone else, you must use the Assign Task button and not the Forward button.

Only the current task owner can update a task. If the task was assigned to other people before the current task owner, every change that the owner makes to the task is automatically copied to the task in the previous owners' task lists if they kept a copy of the task. When the current owner completes the task, the previous owners receive a status report if they requested one.

The next set of steps assumes that you have received a task request from someone else. If you have not received a task request, you can read but not complete the next set of steps.

To accept a task request:

1. Switch to the **Inbox**, retrieve your messages if necessary, and then click the task request e-mail that someone else sent you. The basic information about the task request appears in the Message pane, and a special icon indicates the task request. See Figure 2-17.

| Figure 2-17 | RECEIVED TASK REQUEST |

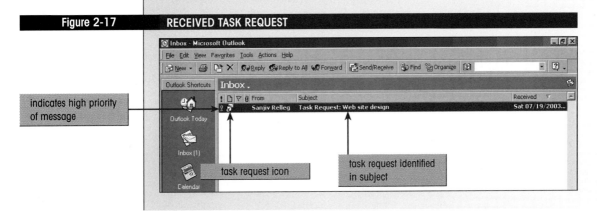

> **TROUBLE?** If the message does not yet appear, wait a few minutes and then try again.

2. Open the task request message. The information banner shows the name of the person who assigned the task and the date on which it was assigned. See Figure 2-18.

| Figure 2-18 | TASK REQUEST MESSAGE |

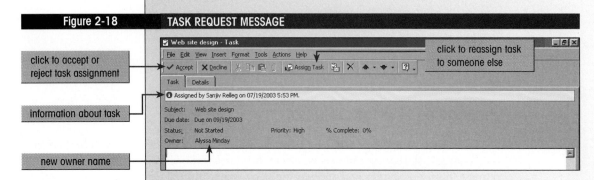

click to accept or reject task assignment

information about task

new owner name

click to reassign task to someone else

The Standard toolbar of the task request message has two additional buttons—the Accept button and the Decline button. You'll click the Accept button to take on the task. If you wanted to reject the request, you would click the Decline button.

3. Click the **Accept** button ✔ Accept on the Standard toolbar to accept the request. The Accepting Task dialog box shown in Figure 2-19 opens.

| Figure 2-19 | ACCEPTING TASK DIALOG BOX |

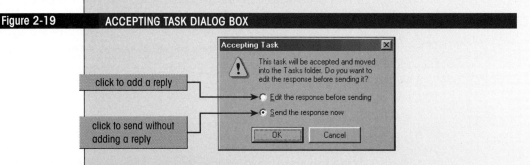

click to add a reply

click to send without adding a reply

4. Click the **Edit the response before sending** option button, and then type **I'd be happy to complete this task.** in the Task window's text box. Your acceptance appears in the information banner.

5. Send the message.

Outlook sends your acceptance reply, adds the task to your Tasks folder, and makes you owner of the task. As owner, you have full access to the task and can update information about that task.

Receiving a Response to a Task Request

When you receive a response to a task you assigned, it appears in your Inbox with your other e-mail messages. The task response message in the Inbox displays a message header, which indicates whether the recipient accepted or declined the task. To view any more detailed replies, you must open the message. If you opted to keep a copy of the task, the task remains in your task list and includes a reminder of the new task owner—the only person who can update or change the task. If you did not keep a copy, Outlook removes the task from your list.

To receive a task request response:

1. Download the task request response message. The message icon 🗒 and subject both indicate the acceptance of the task request.

2. Open and read the message. The information banner indicates the message is accepted and owned by another person. See Figure 2-20.

Figure 2-20	ACCEPTED TASK REQUEST MESSAGE

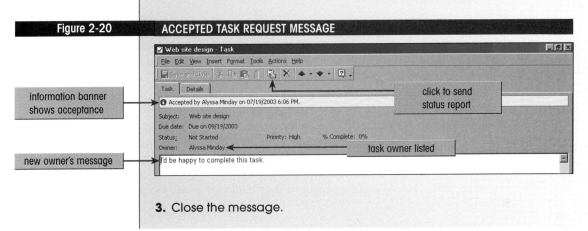

information banner shows acceptance

new owner's message

click to send status report

task owner listed

3. Close the message.

When the task owner updates the task, everyone who is keeping a copy of the task receives a status report via e-mail and Outlook updates the task in his or her task list. When the task has been completed, Outlook sends a status report to any original owners who requested one. The current task owner can see the names of everyone who will receive updates and status reports in the Updated List box on the Details tab in the Task window.

So far you have jotted down notes and created tasks. To ensure that you complete all of your tasks in a timely manner, you can schedule time to work on them using your calendar. You'll do this in the next session.

Session 2.1 QUICK CHECK

1. What are notes?
2. Explain the difference between a task and a recurring task.
3. What happens when you drag a note to the Tasks folder?
4. What is the purpose of a category?

5. Why would you add categories to the Master Category List?

6. How many categories can you add to each item?

7. What is a task request?

8. How many people does it take to assign a task? Are there any special requirements for them?

SESSION 2.2

In this session, you'll learn how to use the Calendar to set up and view your schedule. You'll schedule appointments and events, and then print your calendar. Next you'll plan a meeting and send e-mail invitations to invitees. Finally you'll convert your calendar to a Web page.

Scheduling in Calendar

The **Calendar** is a scheduling tool for planning and recording your upcoming appointments, events, and meetings. Each of these terms has a special meaning in Outlook. An **appointment** is an activity with a specific start and end time that you schedule in your calendar but that does not involve other people or resources. For example, Antonio might schedule an appointment in his calendar to block out time to design the company Web page or attend a class on HTML programming. An **event** is a one-time or annual activity that lasts 24 hours or more, such as a seminar, trade show, or vacation. An **annual event** occurs each year on a specific date, such as a holiday, birthday, or anniversary. A **meeting** is an appointment to which you invite people or for which you reserve resources, including conference rooms and projection equipment. Meetings can take place either face-to-face or online. You can send meeting requests only if all parties use Outlook for e-mail.

Viewing the Calendar

The Calendar Information viewer can be arranged in a variety of views that resemble traditional planner books. The most familiar looking view—Day/Week/Month—provides space for recording events, appointments, and meetings and usually includes a **TaskPad**, a summary list of the Tasks folder. You can select the time span shown in this view, depending on your needs and preferences. There are additional table views available on the View menu, which show lists of active appointments, recurring meetings, events, and so on.

You'll switch between the various Calendar views.

To navigate within the Calendar:

1. If you took a break after the previous session, make sure Outlook is running.

2. Click **Calendar** in the Outlook Shortcuts groups on the Outlook Bar.

3. Click **View** on the menu bar, point to **Current View**, and then click **Day/Week/Month**. The Standard toolbar contains a variety of buttons that change the way you view the Calendar—as a daily, weekly, or monthly planner.

4. Click the **Day** button [1 Day] on the Standard toolbar if it is not already selected to display the Calendar as a daily planner. See Figure 2-21.

Figure 2-21	CALENDAR IN DAY VIEW

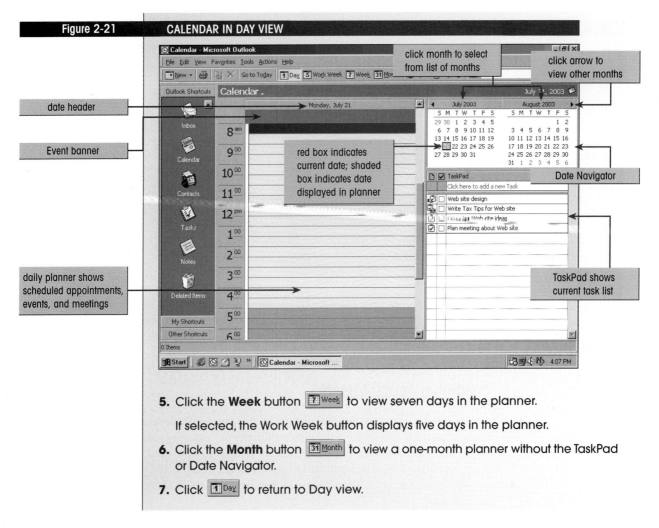

5. Click the **Week** button 📅 Week to view seven days in the planner.

   If selected, the Work Week button displays five days in the planner.

6. Click the **Month** button 📅 Month to view a one-month planner without the TaskPad or Date Navigator.

7. Click 📅 Day to return to Day view.

Another way to move around your calendar is with the Date Navigator. The Date Navigator enables you to quickly display any month or date in the planner. A shaded box indicates which day or days appear in the planner. A red box surrounds today's date. You can click any date on the Date Navigator calendar to display its planner. If you want to see the planner for a day that isn't visible in the Date Navigator calendar, then you can use the arrows and month names to bring the calendars for other months into view.

You'll display different days in the planner using the Date Navigator.

To move around the Calendar with the Date Navigator:

1. Click the date for next Monday on the Date Navigator. The planner changes to show that day's schedule.

2. Click the scroll arrow to the right of the Date Navigator to move to the next month's calendar.

3. Click the right month name in the Date Navigator to display shortcuts to the three months before or after that month. See Figure 2-22.

Figure 2-22   DATE NAVIGATOR SHORTCUTS

click for shortcut to three months before or after selected month

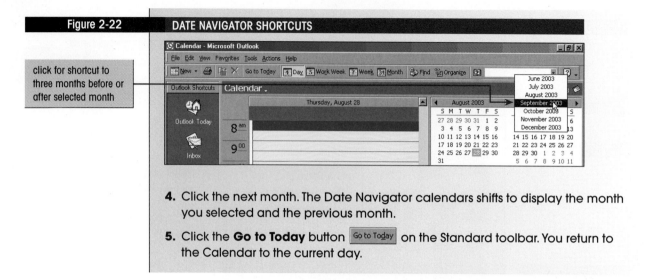

4. Click the next month. The Date Navigator calendars shifts to display the month you selected and the previous month.

5. Click the **Go to Today** button [Go to Today] on the Standard toolbar. You return to the Calendar to the current day.

You can customize your calendar by changing the fields visible on the screen or the font and size of the text. To do so, you would click View on the menu bar, point to Current View, and then click Customize Current View. The View Summary dialog box contains buttons that enable you to modify the view settings.

Scheduling Appointments

You can schedule and change appointments in your own calendar, and you can give others permission to do the same. Likewise, other people can give you permission to make and modify schedules in their calendars. To let people know about your availability, you can specify how time is blocked out for an appointment, as indicated in Figure 2-23. Other people cannot see an appointment marked as private, even if they have permission to access your calendar.

Figure 2-23   APPOINTMENT AVAILABILITY CODES

TIME SHOWN AS	BACKGROUND COLOR	AVAILABILITY TO OTHERS
Busy	blue	unavailable
Free	clear	available
Tentative	light blue	available
Out of office	purple	unavailable

Although you can create an appointment using the New Appointment button on the Standard toolbar, you can also schedule an appointment by dragging a task from the Tasks folder to the Calendar folder or from the Calendar TaskPad to the planner.

REFERENCE WINDOW **RW**

Scheduling an Appointment
- Drag a task or other item to the Calendar folder or planner (*or* click the New button list arrow, and then click Appointment).
- If necessary, enter an appointment subject, type or select a location, select start and end times, turn on or off the reminder, and then select how the time appears in your calendar.
- To create a recurring appointment, click the Recurrence button on the Appointment window Standard toolbar, set a recurrence pattern and duration in the Appointment Recurrence dialog box, and then click the OK button.
- Click the Save and Close button.
  or
- Drag to select the appointment duration on the calendar planner, type the appointment subject, and then press the Enter key.
- To add more details or a recurrence, double-click the appointment to open its window.

You'll use drag a task to schedule an appointment for completing the "Plan meeting about Web site ideas" task.

To schedule an appointment from a task:

1. Click the **Plan meeting about Web site** icon to select the task in the TaskPad.

2. Drag the **Plan meeting about Web site** task from the TaskPad onto the planner. The Appointment window opens.

   The subject is already filled in from the task subject. You can see the Due Date and Priority (High), Status, Percent Complete, Total and Actual work, and Owner in the appointment's notes text box. All this information is entered from the Task window.

3. If necessary, maximize the window.

4. Type **Conference Room** in the Location box. This box records the place where the appointment occurs. Outlook remembers all locations you enter, so next time you could choose this location from the list.

   The appointment time is the same as the date and time you created the task, which is in the past, as indicated in the Information banner. You'll schedule the appointment for the future.

5. Press the **Tab** key twice to move to the date Start time text box.

Next you'll enter the block of time during which you plan to work on the task. You could type specific dates and times in the Start time and End time text boxes or select from the calendar that opens when you click the Start time and End time list arrows. However, we often think of dates and times in reference to where we are right now.

The **AutoDate feature** converts natural-language date and time descriptions, such as "one week from today" and "noon", into the numerical format that represents the month, day, and year or time, respectively. You can also type abbreviations, such as "Wed" or "Feb", and holiday names with or without punctuation, such as "New Year's Day". To remove a date or time, just type "none" in the text box.

You'll enter the start and end times for the appointment.

To schedule the appointment's start and end times:

1. Type **next Tuesday** in the date Start time text box, and then press the **Tab** key. The correct date for next Tuesday appears in the Start time text box, the banner that said that the appointment was in the past is removed, and the insertion point is in the time Start time text box.

2. Type **ten** in the time Start time text box, and then press the **Tab** key twice. The end time is already set to next Tuesday's date because the end time cannot precede the start time.

3. Click the time **End time** list arrow, and then click **11:00 AM (1 hour)** to enter the time you think you'll be finished with the meeting plan.

The reminder is set by default when you schedule a new appointment (unless the default settings for Outlook were changed). Fifteen minutes before the scheduled appointment, a sound will play to alert you to the upcoming appointment. You can turn off the reminder for a meeting by clearing the Reminder check box. Or, you can change the amount of time for the reminder by selecting a time from the list or typing a new time in the text box.

You'll set the reminder, and then save the appointment.

To set the reminder and finish the appointment:

1. If necessary, click the **Reminder** check box to insert a check mark.

2. Click the **Reminder** list arrow, and then click **5 minutes**.

The only other item you need to change for this appointment is how you show this time on your calendar. You can set the appointment time as unavailable (Out of Office or Busy) or available (Free or Tentative) to others. People who have access to your calendar then know when you're occupied.

3. Click the **Show time as** list arrow, and then click **Tentative**. See Figure 2-24.

Figure 2-24	COMPLETED APPOINTMENT WINDOW

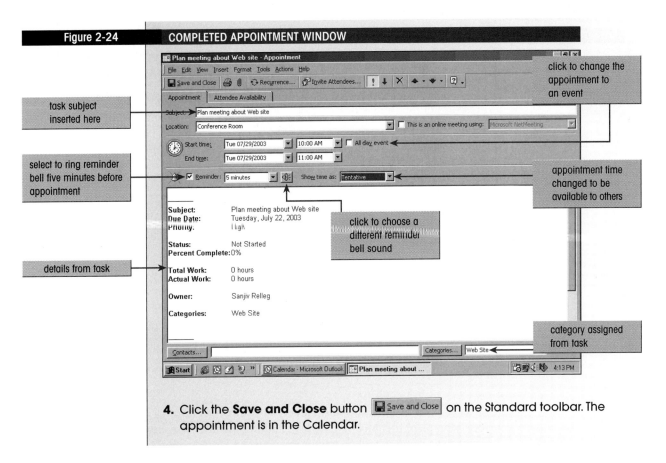

task subject inserted here

select to ring reminder bell five minutes before appointment

details from task

click to change the appointment to an event

appointment time changed to be available to others

click to choose a different reminder bell sound

category assigned from task

4. Click the **Save and Close** button [Save and Close] on the Standard toolbar. The appointment is in the Calendar.

Next Tuesday's date appears in boldface in the Date Navigator, indicating that you have an appointment scheduled on that day.

You can also schedule appointments by selecting the date and time in the planner and then typing the appointment subject. You'll schedule a second appointment for next Tuesday.

To schedule an appointment by selecting the date and time:

1. Click next Tuesday's date in the Date Navigator.

The Plan meeting appointment spans the one-hour block from 10 AM to 11 AM. The appointment border is light blue to remind you that the time is scheduled as Tentative.

2. Click **2:00** in the planner to select the 2:00 to 2:30 block, and then drag to select the next half-hour block as well. The 2:00 to 3:00 block of time changes to dark blue to indicate that it's selected.

3. Type **Create meeting agenda**. As you begin to type, a white text box opens in the time block. The text box has a dark blue border, which indicates that the appointment is shown as Busy in your calendar. See Figure 2-25.

Figure 2-25   CALENDAR WITH APPOINTMENTS

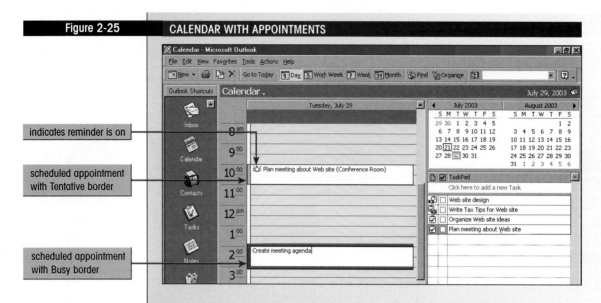

indicates reminder is on

scheduled appointment with Tentative border

scheduled appointment with Busy border

4. Press the **Enter** key. The second appointment is saved in your calendar.

The reminder bell icon ⚠ indicates that the Reminder is set to the default 15 minutes.

After looking at both appointments, you realize you need to create the meeting agenda before you plan the meeting. You could reschedule the appointment by opening its Appointment window and changing the times. A simpler method is to move the appointment by selecting it and then dragging it to a new location on the planner.

To reschedule an appointment by dragging:

1. Click the **Create meeting agenda** appointment to select it.

2. Point to the leftmost border of the appointment. A move pointer ✥ indicates that you can drag the appointment to a new location. See Figure 2-26.

Figure 2-26   SELECTED APPOINTMENT

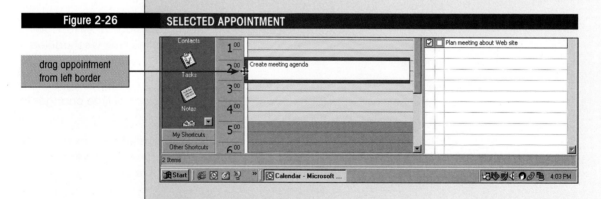

drag appointment from left border

3. Drag the **Create meeting agenda** appointment up by its left border so that it occurs from 9:00 AM to 10:00 AM. The two appointments occur one right after the other and each span a one hour block.

TROUBLE? If you resized the time, making the appointment longer or shorter, then you dragged the top or bottom border rather than dragging the appointment block to a new time slot. Drag the top or bottom border until the appointment spans 1 hour, and then repeat Steps 1 through 3, being careful to drag from the appointment's left border.

As you can see, with Outlook you can quickly reschedule any meeting as well as have a visual image of how the appointments are scheduled for your day.

Scheduling a Recurring Appointment

The plan is to schedule a meeting every week for the next month to discuss the Wertheimer & Associates Web site and you must create an agenda for each meeting. Rather than schedule the same appointment for each of the next three weeks, you decide to make this appointment recurring. A **recurring appointment** repeats on a regular basis, such as weekly or on the third Tuesday of the month. To schedule a new recurring appointment, you can click the Actions menu, click New Recurring Appointment, and then enter the recurrence information as well as the appointment information. If the appointment already exists, you can change it to a recurring appointment.

To schedule a recurring appointment:

1. Double-click the **Create meeting agenda** appointment to open its Appointment window.

2. Click the **Recurrence** button ⟳ Recurrence... on the Standard toolbar. The Appointment Recurrence dialog box opens. See Figure 2-27.

| Figure 2-27 | APPOINTMENT RECURRENCE DIALOG BOX |

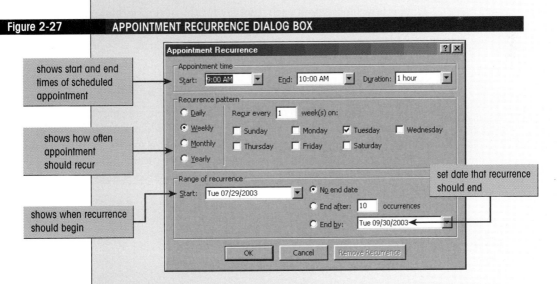

shows start and end times of scheduled appointment

shows how often appointment should recur

shows when recurrence should begin

set date that recurrence should end

3. In the Recurrence pattern area, click the **Weekly** option button if it is not already selected, and make sure that this appointment is set to Recur every **1 week(s)** on **Tuesday**.

4. In the Range of recurrence section, make sure that the Start list box shows next Tuesday's date, click the **End by** option button, press the **Tab** key twice, and then type **one month** in the text box.

5. Click the **OK** button. The Appointment window changes to reflect the recurrence and displays a reminder. The information banner reminds you of the recurrence pattern. See Figure 2-28.

| Figure 2-28 | RECURRING APPOINTMENT WINDOW |

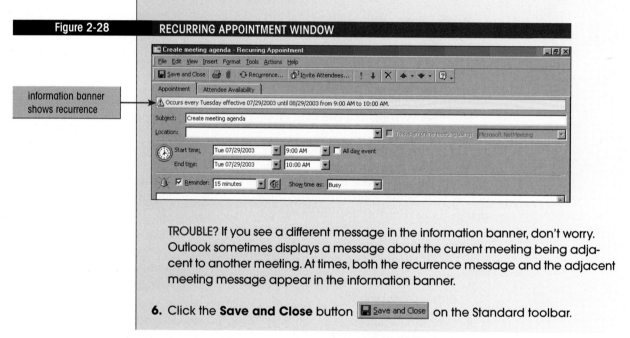

TROUBLE? If you see a different message in the information banner, don't worry. Outlook sometimes displays a message about the current meeting being adjacent to another meeting. At times, both the recurrence message and the adjacent meeting message appear in the information banner.

6. Click the **Save and Close** button [Save and Close] on the Standard toolbar.

Time is now blocked out each Tuesday for the next month to plan the meeting agenda, as indicated by the bold dates in the Date Navigator. Also, notice that the recurrence icon appears below the reminder bell in the appointment.

Scheduling Events

Events last from midnight to midnight. They can occur for one or more days, such as a one-day training seminar or a three-day health fair. Unlike appointments, events are always scheduled as free time in your calendar. To block out a specific time to attend an event, you must create an appointment. You schedule a one-day event and a multi-day event in similar fashion. In Day/Week/Month view, you can quickly create an event by double-clicking the date heading of the day of the event.

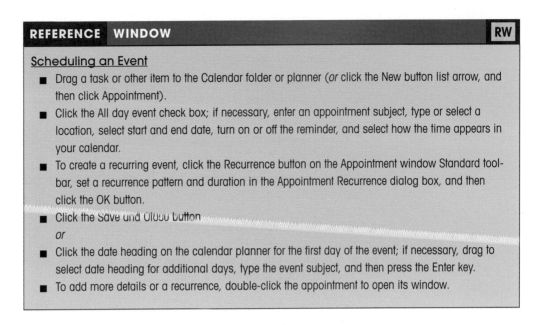

REFERENCE WINDOW RW

Scheduling an Event

- Drag a task or other item to the Calendar folder or planner (*or* click the New button list arrow, and then click Appointment).
- Click the All day event check box; if necessary, enter an appointment subject, type or select a location, select start and end date, turn on or off the reminder, and select how the time appears in your calendar.
- To create a recurring event, click the Recurrence button on the Appointment window Standard toolbar, set a recurrence pattern and duration in the Appointment Recurrence dialog box, and then click the OK button.
- Click the Save and Close button

  or
- Click the date heading on the calendar planner for the first day of the event; if necessary, drag to select date heading for additional days, type the event subject, and then press the Enter key.
- To add more details or a recurrence, double-click the appointment to open its window.

Wertheimer & Associates has planned a seminar for next week to review the latest changes to the tax code. You'll add this two-day event to your calendar.

To schedule an event:

1. Click the **Work Week** button [Work Week] on the Standard toolbar to display the five workdays for next week in the calendar.

2. Click the date heading for next Wednesday. The box below the date changes to white, indicating that you can type in it.

   This action would create a one-day event. Instead, you want to create a two-day event.

3. Drag to select the date headings for Wednesday and Thursday. Both boxes are white when selected.

4. Type **Tax Code Seminar** as the event subject. See Figure 2-29.

Figure 2-29 **CALENDAR IN WORK WEEK VIEW**

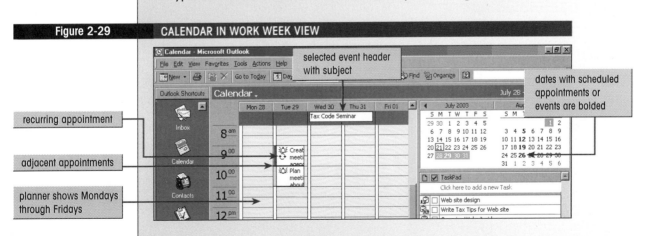

5. Press the **Enter** key. The default reminder is applied to the event; you can see the icon. You want to change the reminder option and add a location for the event.

6. Double-click the **Tax Code Seminar** event heading. The Event window opens.

Because the All day event check box is selected, the window does not provide options to set starting and ending times.

7. Click the **Location** list arrow, and then select **Conference Room**. Outlook remembered the room location you entered earlier.

8. Click the **Reminder** check box to remove the check mark and turn off the reminder.

9. Click the **Save and Close** button 🖫 Save and Close on the Standard toolbar.

Like tasks, you can add categories to your appointments to help you organize them. If you assign categories to all your Outlook items, you can use the Find command to locate all items associated with a specific category. Now that you've scheduled some appointments and an event, you'll print your calendar.

Printing a Calendar

A printed calendar is helpful when you need to leave your office and want to take your schedule along. Outlook provides a variety of printing styles you can choose for your calendar. You can print each day, each week, or each month on a separate page, or you can choose other memo or list styles. You decide to print next week's calendar. Outlook changes the print specifications to match the Calendar view you are showing.

To print your calendar:

1. Click the **Print** button 🖨 on the Standard toolbar. The Print dialog box opens. See Figure 2-30.

| Figure 2-30 | CALENDAR PRINT DIALOG BOX |

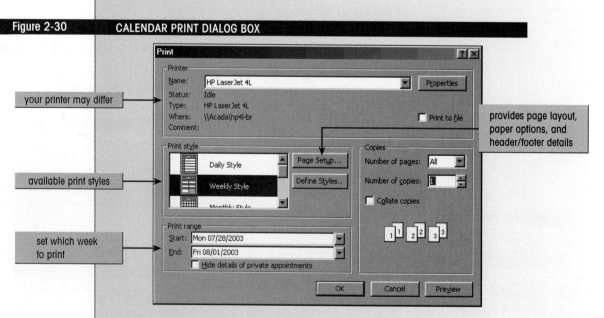

your printer may differ

provides page layout, paper options, and header/footer details

available print styles

set which week to print

2. Click **Weekly Style** in the Print style list, if it is not already selected.

3. Click the **Start** list arrow and select next Monday's date, if necessary. Monday is the first day you want to print.

You also can use AutoDate to set the start and end dates.

4. Press the **Tab** key, type **next Friday** in the End text box, and then press the **Tab** key.

Outlook changes the date to display next Friday's date, the last day that you want to print.

5. Click the **Preview** button to see the calendar as it will print on paper. See Figure 2-31.

| Figure 2-31 | CALENDAR IN PRINT PREVIEW |

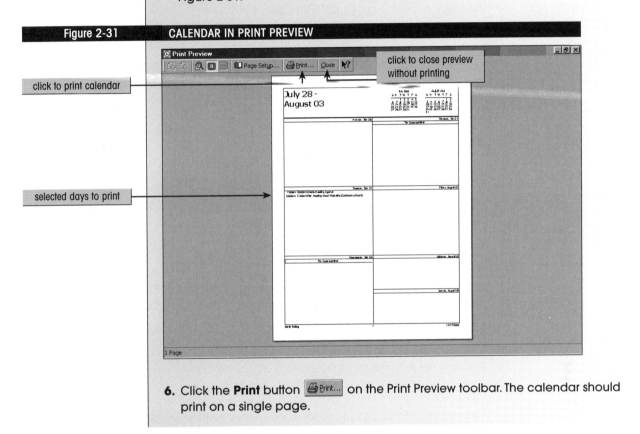

click to print calendar

selected days to print

click to close preview without printing

6. Click the **Print** button 🖨 Print... on the Print Preview toolbar. The calendar should print on a single page.

Now you're ready to schedule the meeting to discuss the Web site.

Planning a Meeting

Recall that a meeting differs from an appointment in that it includes other people and resources. A meeting can take place face-to-face or online (such as a NetMeeting). When planning a meeting, you specify the people who should attend and the resources to be reserved; you also pick a date and time for the meeting. All invitees should be using Outlook. Each invitee and resource receives an e-mail message with the meeting request. You receive e-mail replies when they respond to the request, which enables you to easily track who can attend and what resources are reserved.

Selecting Meeting Attendees and Resources

Meeting attendees are the people you invite to a meeting. You can select attendees from your Address Book or enter other names. Anyone who has an e-mail address will receive an e-mail meeting request. If you have access to their calendars, Outlook will display their free and busy times and you can find a meeting time that is most convenient to all invitees.

Like task requests, meeting requests are always sent in RTF format. Again, you must make sure that RTF is enabled for the recipients, otherwise they won't be able to use respond to the meeting request. You can check each address as you send the meeting request, or you can specify the format when you enter the person in your Address Book.

You'll add a few names to your Personal Address Book, and enable them to receive RTF, so you can plan the meeting.

To add names to your Personal Address Book:

1. Click the **Address Book** button 📖 on the Standard toolbar.

TROUBLE? If the Address Book is not available, you may need to add it to your profile. Click Tools on the menu bar, click Service, click the Add button, click Personal Address Book, and then click the OK button. Click the Browse button and select the location for the Address Book, and then click the Open button. Click the OK button in each dialog box. Click File on the menu bar, click Exit and Log Off, and then restart Outlook.

2. Click the **New Entry** button 🔲 on the Standard toolbar of the Address Book window.

3. Select your Personal Address Book in the Put this entry In the list, click **Internet Mail Address**, and then click the **OK** button.

4. Type **Lisa Wertheimer** in the Display name text box, type your e-mail address in the E-mail address text box.

5. Click the **Always send to this recipient in Microsoft Exchange rich-text format** check box to insert a check mark, and then click the **OK** button.

6. Repeat Steps 2 through 5 to create an entry for **Antonio Delgado**, using your e-mail address.

7. Close the Address Book window.

Meeting **resources** include conference rooms, audiovisual equipment, and other company available materials. Before you can reserve a resource, it must have its own mailbox on your server. The resource then becomes self-sufficient, accepting and rejecting meeting requests automatically. It accepts any invitation when it is available, and the meeting is automatically entered in the resource's calendar. The resource administrator can restrict the ability to schedule the resource. For example, if only managers are allowed to book certain conference rooms, permissions can be set so that requests from managers are accepted and requests from nonmanagers are declined. To schedule a resource, you must have adequate permissions to reserve the resource.

Sending a Meeting Request

Before sending meeting requests, you need to plan the details of your meeting. Consider who you are inviting, what resources you need, when the meeting will occur, and where the meeting will take place. Once you know this information, you're ready to create the meeting. You can create meetings in several ways: (1) A New Meeting Request enables you to specify the meeting details and attendees, and then check their schedules if they are on the same network. (2) Plan a Meeting enables you to select meeting attendees and resources, and then specify a meeting time and place or have Outlook find one for you. (3) Invite Attendees adds people to an existing appointment or event, which changes the item to a meeting.

REFERENCE WINDOW   RW

Planning a Meeting

- Click Actions on the Calendar menu bar, and then click Plan a Meeting.
- Click the Invite Others button to open the Select Attendees and Resource dialog box.
- Display the appropriate address book, click each name you want to invite, and click the Required or Optional or Resource button, and then click the OK button when you're done.
- Right-click each e-mail address, click Properties on the shortcut menu, click the Always send to this recipient in Microsoft Exchange rich-text format check box to insert a check mark, and then click the OK button.
- Click the AutoPick button or enter a date and time for the meeting, and then click the Make Meeting button.
- Enter a subject, location, category, notes, and other details as needed.
- Click the Send button on the Meeting window Standard toolbar, click the Close button in the Plan a Meeting dialog box, and if necessary click the Send/Receive button on the Inbox or Outbox Standard toolbar.

  or

- Click the New button list arrow, and then click Meeting Request (*or* open an existing appointment and click the Invite Attendees button on the Appointment Standard toolbar).
- Click the To button, display the appropriate address book, click each name you want to invite and click the Required or Optional or Resource button, and then click the OK button when you're done.
- Right-click each e-mail address, click Properties on the shortcut menu, click the Always send to this recipient in Microsoft Exchange rich-text format check box to insert a check mark, and then click the OK button.
- Enter a subject, location, start and end times, category, notes, and other details as needed.
- Click the Send button on the Standard toolbar and if necessary click the Send/Receive button on the Inbox or Outbox Standard toolbar.

You'll schedule the meeting to discuss the company's Web site.

To schedule a meeting:

1. Click **Actions** on the Calendar menu bar, and then click **Plan a Meeting**. The Plan a Meeting dialog box opens. See Figure 2-32.

Figure 2-32   PLAN A MEETING DIALOG BOX

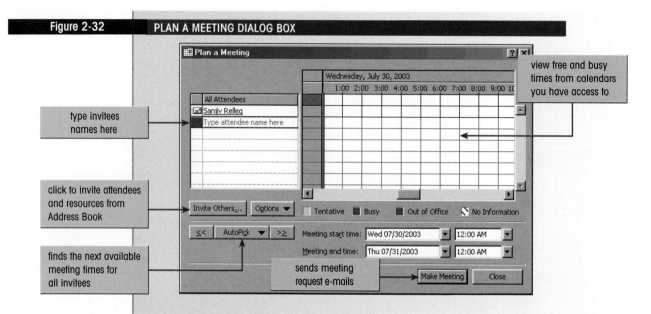

type invitees names here

click to invite attendees and resources from Address Book

finds the next available meeting times for all invitees

sends meeting request e-mails

view free and busy times from calendars you have access to

2. Click the **Invite Others** button. The Select Attendees and Resources dialog box opens. See Figure 2-33.

Figure 2-33   SELECT ATTENDEES AND RESOURCES DIALOG BOX

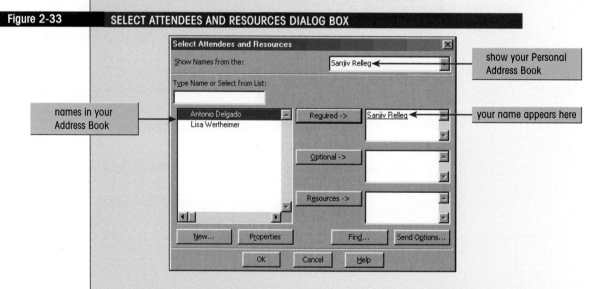

show your Personal Address Book

names in your Address Book

your name appears here

TROUBLE? If the Select Attendees and Resources dialog box doesn't display the names you entered, make sure the Show Names from the list box shows your Personal Address Book.

3. Click **Antonio Delgado** in the names list, and then click the **Required** button.

    Required and Optional attendees appear in the To box. You are listed in the Required list by default.

4. Click **Lisa Wertheimer** in the names list, and then click the **Optional** button to invite Lisa as an optional attendee.

5. Click the **OK** button. Each invitee appears in the All Attendees list in the Plan a Meeting dialog box. If you have access to their calendars, Outlook will display their free and busy times.

6. Scroll through the free/busy times. Your schedule includes Tentative and Busy indications.

   If you have access to others' schedules, AutoPick is a great way to select the best time for all invitees.

7. Click the **AutoPick** button, and then click **All People and Resources**. A vertical bar selects the next available free time for all invitees. See Figure 2-34.

| Figure 2-34 | MEETING TIME SELECTED BY AUTOPICK |

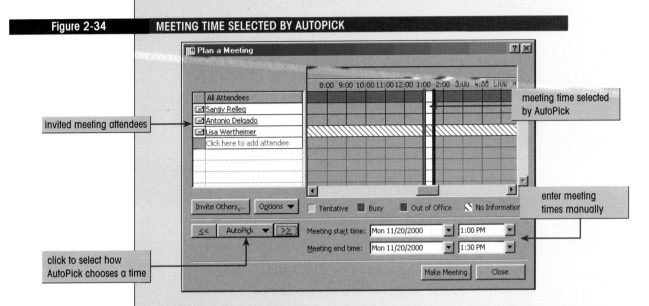

invited meeting attendees

meeting time selected by AutoPick

enter meeting times manually

click to select how AutoPick chooses a time

You can use the left scroll arrow to find the first available free time for the selected AutoPick option or the right scroll arrow to find the next available free time. Because you don't have access to Lisa's or Antonio's schedules, you'll enter a convenient date and time.

8. Pressing the **Tab** key to move from field to field, set the Meeting start time for **next Wednesday** at **10 am** and the Meeting end time for **next Wednesday** at **1 pm**.

9. Click the **Make Meeting** button. The Meeting window opens. See Figure 2-35.

| Figure 2-35 | MEETING WINDOW |

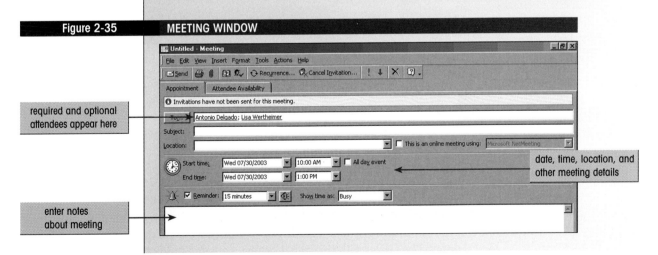

required and optional attendees appear here

date, time, location, and other meeting details

enter notes about meeting

As with an appointment, you must specify the meeting subject, location, and so forth. Invitees appear in the To box.

To create the meeting invitation:

1. Type **Company Web Site** as the Subject.

2. Select **Conference Room** as the location.

3. Click the **Categories** button, select **Web Site** as the category, and then click the **OK** button.

Next, you'll insert the notes you jotted down earlier into the meeting invitation.

Inserting Notes into the Meeting Request

You can insert any item into another as text, an attachment, or as a shortcut. For example, if you wanted to include an agenda, meeting minutes, or other information that invitees should review before the meeting, you could attach a file to your meeting request, just as you would attach a file to any other e-mail message.

To insert notes text into a meeting request:

1. Click **Insert** on the menu bar, and then click **Item**.

2. Click **Notes** in the Look in list box, press and hold the **Ctrl** key as you click each blue note to select it, and then click the **Text only** option button. See Figure 2-36.

Figure 2-36	INSERT ITEM DIALOG BOX

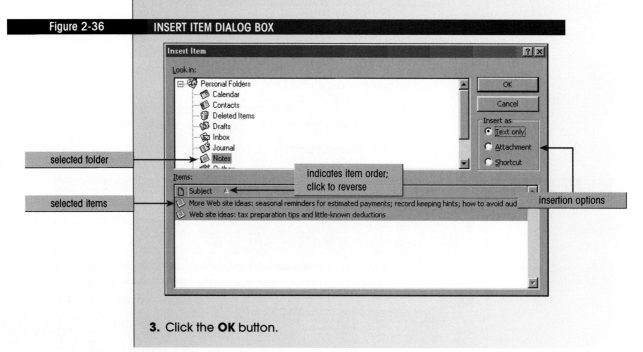

3. Click the **OK** button.

The notes' text and dates appear in the text box of the meeting request. Because they are difficult to read this way, you'll use the Office Clipboard to rearrange the text into a more logical order. The **Office Clipboard** is a storage area that holds a maximum of 12 items you have collected by cutting or copying. You can paste a single stored item or you can paste all stored items at once.

To collect and paste the notes' text:

1. Right-click the **Standard toolbar**, and then click **Clipboard**. The Clipboard toolbar opens.

2. Select the text **Web site ideas:** from the inserted notes' text, and then click the **Copy** button 📋 on the Clipboard toolbar. An icon appears for the copied phrase.

   Your Clipboard toolbar might contain other icons, depending on whether you or another user cut or copied items before you started this tutorial. The toolbar may also contain icons for other Office programs, such as Word or Excel.

3. Select the text **tax preparation tips**, and then click 📋 to place that phrase on the Clipboard.

4. Copy the text **and little-known deductions** to the Clipboard.

5. Copy the text **seasonal reminders for taxes; record keeping hints; how to avoid audits; new tax rulings and laws** to the Clipboard.

6. Place the mouse pointer over each icon, one at a time, to see its contents in a ScreenTip. See Figure 2-37.

Figure 2-37	OFFICE CLIPBOARD TOOLBAR

Once you collect all the pieces of text that you want to copy, you can paste them into the notes text box.

To paste text from the Clipboard:

1. Select all the text in the notes text box. When you paste the first selection from the Clipboard, the selected text will be replaced.

2. Click the **Web site ideas** icon. The text replaces the selected notes text.

3. Press the **Enter** key, click the **tax preparation tips** icon, type **;** (a semicolon), and then press the **spacebar**.

4. Click the **seasonal reminders for taxes; record keeping...** icon, type **;** (a semicolon), and then press the **spacebar**.

5. Click the **and little-known deductions** icon to paste the last item. The text appears in a more logical order that is easy to read in the notes area. See Figure 2-38.

Figure 2-38   **PASTED NOTES TEXT**

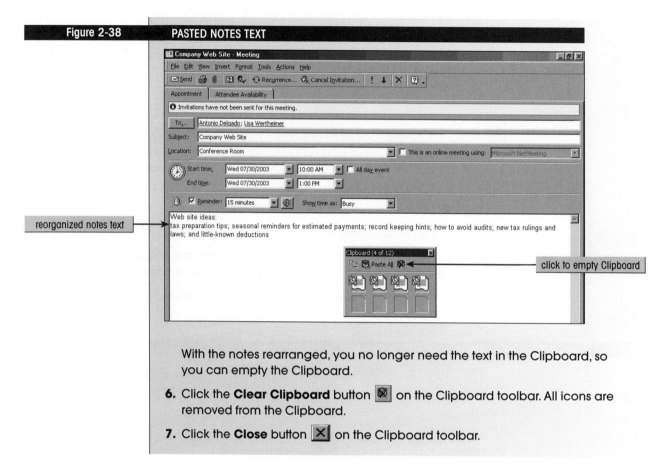

reorganized notes text

click to empty Clipboard

With the notes rearranged, you no longer need the text in the Clipboard, so you can empty the Clipboard.

6. Click the **Clear Clipboard** button 🔳 on the Clipboard toolbar. All icons are removed from the Clipboard.

7. Click the **Close** button 🔳 on the Clipboard toolbar.

Now that the note text is easier to read, you can finish scheduling the meeting by sending the meeting request and closing the meeting dialog box.

To finish scheduling the meeting:

1. Click the **Send** button [✉ Send] to send the meeting request. You can see the time listed as busy for the invitees in the Plan a Meeting dialog box.

2. Click the **Close** button in the Plan a Meeting dialog box. The scheduled meeting appears in your calendar. The meeting icon 🈁 distinguishes this entry from an appointment.

You receive and respond to a meeting request similarly to how you respond to a task request. The e-mail message each meeting invitee receives displays a meeting request icon 🈁. You have to open the e-mail message in its own window. You then indicate whether you can definitely, possibly, or cannot attend the meeting by clicking the Accept, Tentative, or Decline button. If you'd like, first check your schedule by clicking the Calendar button. When you send a reply, you have the option of adding comments to the return message. Once you reply, Outlook updates your calendar accordingly.

Reviewing and Changing Meeting Details

As the meeting organizer receives replies, Outlook compiles the responses. You can see a summary of responses and view attendees availability from the Meeting window. The Appointment tab in the Meeting window summarizes the responses you received; for example, "2 attendees accepted, 0 tentatively accepted, 0 declined." The Attendee Availability tab lists the people who are invited and, depending on the option you choose, their free/busy times or their attendance status. Invited participants can also see these details about all the other participants.

To review attendee availability:

1. Double-click the **Company Web Site** meeting in your calendar to open it.

2. Review the information banner on the Appointment tab. So far no responses have been received for this meeting.

3. Click the **Attendee Availability** tab in the Meeting window. You see the current status of the invited attendees. See Figure 2-39.

Figure 2-39	ATTENDEE AVAILABILITY TAB IN MEETING WINDOW

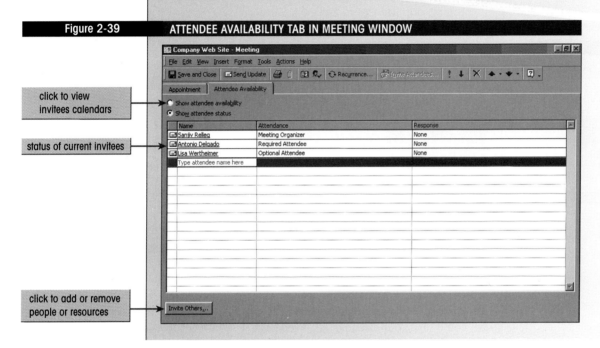

click to view invitees calendars

status of current invitees

click to add or remove people or resources

After you review the attendees' status, you may need to make changes to the meeting. You can add or remove meeting attendees and resources from this window.

To add or remove attendees:

1. Click the **Invite Others** button. The Select Attendees and Resources dialog box opens.

   You can add attendees or resources by selecting them, and then clicking the Required, Optional, or Resources button. You can remove an attendee or resource by clicking its name in the Required, Optional, or Resources box, and then pressing the Delete key.

   You don't need to make any changes, so you'll close the dialog box without updating the meeting.

2. Click the **Cancel** button.

3. Close the Meeting window.

Checking Off Completed Tasks

One of the most satisfying aspects of a to-do list is crossing off completed items. You can do this from either the Tasks folder or the Calendar TaskPad. Because you have finished a task on your task list—planning a meeting—you can mark it as completed.

To check off a completed task:

1. If necessary, switch to the Calendar.

2. Click the check box in the completed column for the "Plan meeting about Web site" task in the TaskPad. A check mark appears in the box, and the task is crossed out. See Figure 2-40.

Figure 2-40	CALENDAR WITH APPOINTMENTS AND MEETINGS

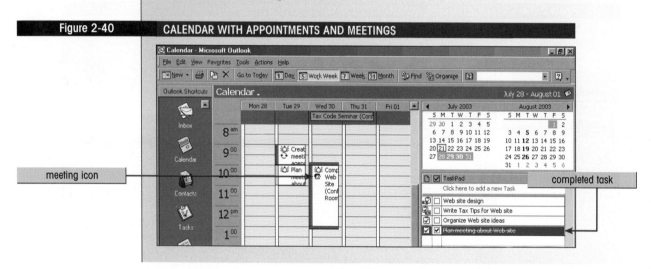

meeting icon

completed task

If you check off a task inadvertently, just click it again to return to the task in progress. Next, you'll save your calendar as a Web page.

Saving a Calendar as a Web Page

You can save a calendar as a Web page and then share it with others. For example, Lisa might post a calendar with important client dates as a page on the company intranet, or she might include a calendar of tax form and payment due dates on the company's Web site. Client dates and other information would appear on the calendar as appointments. When you save a calendar as a Web page, you specify the start and end dates that should display, and you indicate whether to include appointment details from the text box in the Appointment window.

You can refer others to the calendar by distributing its **Uniform Resource Locator (URL)**, an address for a file or HTML document on the Internet. A URL includes the protocol that a Web browser uses to access the file (such as "http://" for a Web page), the name of the server where the file resides, and perhaps the path to the file. For example, Lisa's company could use the URL http://www.wertheimeraccounting.com/calendar/duedates.html to indicate the location of its calendar of due dates for filing tax forms and submitting payments on its Web site.

REFERENCE   WINDOW   RW

Saving a Calendar as a Web Page
- Display the calendar, click File on the menu bar, and then click Save as Web Page.
- Enter the dates to include on the Web page in the Start date and End date list boxes.
- Clear or select the Include appointment details check box and the Open saved web page in browser check box.
- Type your name in the Calendar title text box, and then browse for or enter the path and filename for save location.
- Click the Save button.

You'll save next week's calendar as a Web page to see how this process works.

To save a calendar as a Web page:

1. Click **File** on the menu bar, and then click **Save as Web Page**. The Save as Web Page dialog box opens. See Figure 2-41.

Figure 2-41   SAVE AS WEB PAGE DIALOG BOX

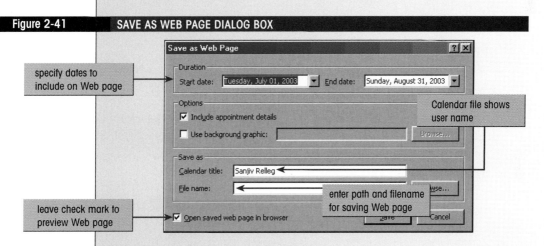

specify dates to
include on Web page

Calendar file shows
user name

enter path and filename
for saving Web page

leave check mark to
preview Web page

2. Type **next Monday** in the Start date list box.

3. Press the **Tab** key to move to the End date list box, and then type **next Friday**.

4. Make sure that the **Include appointment details** check box contains a check mark. This option saves the details contained in the notes box on your calendar item, such as details about appointment or meeting times.

5. Type your name in the Calendar title text box if it is not already there.

   This information becomes the name of the calendar Web page. If you do not enter a title, the user name for your computer becomes the title.

6. Click the **Browse** button, switch to the **Tutorial** folder within the **Tutorial.02** folder on your Data Disk, type **Calendar** in the File name text box, and then click the **Select** button.

7. Make sure that the **Open saved web page in browser** check box contains a check mark. After Outlook saves the calendar as a Web page, the Web page calendar will open in your browser so that you can preview it.

8. Click the **Save** button. After a few moments, the saved Web page calendar opens in your browser. See Figure 2-42.

Figure 2-42	WEB PAGE CALENDAR IN BROWSER

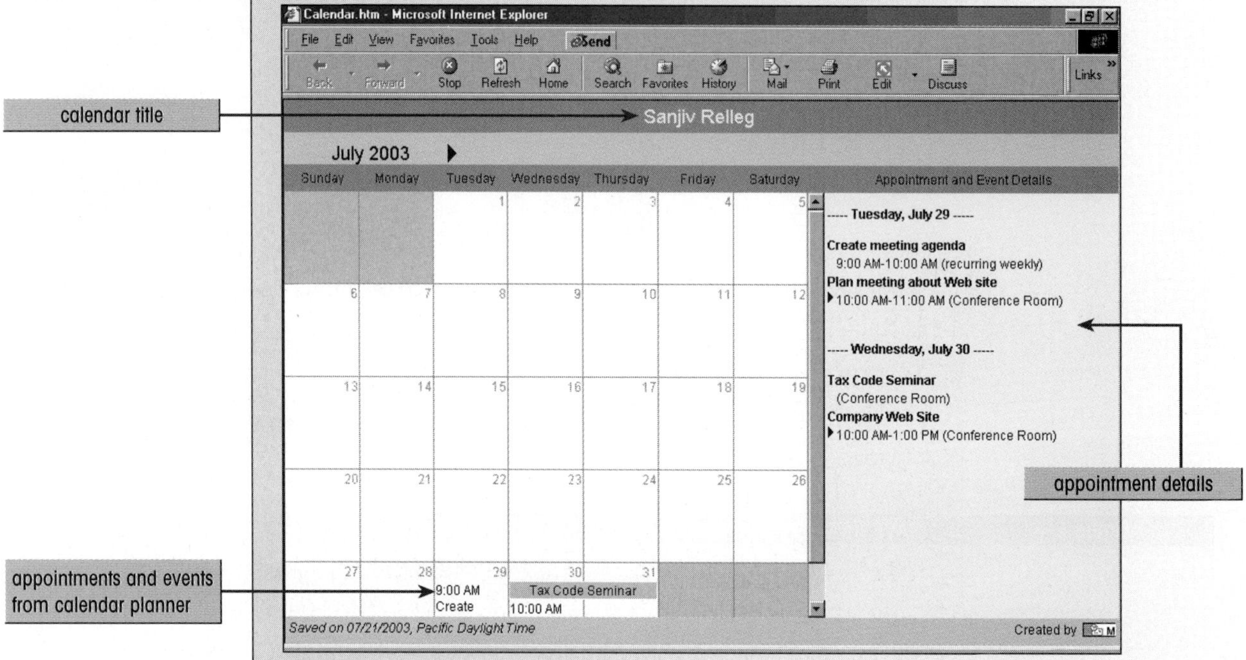

calendar title

appointment details

appointments and events from calendar planner

You may have Internet Explorer or Netscape Navigator as your default browser. The Web page will display in both but with some slight differences.

9. Click **File** on the browser's menu bar, click **Print**, and then click the **OK** button to print the calendar.

10. Close the Web page and then close the browser.

Before you finish for the day, you'll delete any Outlook items you created.

Deleting **Outlook Items**

You can delete any Outlook items that you are finished with and don't want to store. For example, most notes are used as reminders or temporary storage. After you act on them, these notes have no value except to create electronic clutter and use up storage. Other items, such as your calendar appointments, events, and meetings, you might want to archive (store in a compressed storage file) for later reference. For now, you'll delete all the Notes, Tasks, Categories, Appointments, Events, and Meetings you created.

You'll start by removing the Web Site category you added to the Master Category List. When you remove a category, it still appears in the existing items, although it is not available to add to new items.

To delete a category:

1. From the Inbox, click **Edit** on the menu bar, and then click **Categories**. The Categories dialog box opens.

2. Click the **Master Category List** button. The Master Category dialog box opens.

3. Click **Web Site** in the list, and then click the **Delete** button to remove the category.

4. Click the **OK** button in the Master Category dialog box.

5. Click the **OK** button in the Categories dialog box.

Next you'll remove the Calendar items you created. Remember that you can use the Ctrl key to select multiple items to delete at one time.

To delete Calendar items:

1. In the Calendar, press and hold the **Ctrl** key, click the **Plan Meeting** appointment, click the **Create meeting agenda** appointment, click the **Tax Code Seminar** event, click the **Company Web Site** meeting, and then release the **Ctrl** key. The four items are selected.

2. Click the **Delete** button ☒ on the Standard toolbar. All one-time items are removed and a dialog box opens, asking whether you want to delete one or all occurrences of the recurring appointment.

3. Click the **Delete all occurrences** option button, and then click the **OK** button. The appointment is removed, and a second dialog box opens, asking whether you want to send a meeting cancellation message.

4. Click the **Delete without sending a cancellation** option button, and then click the **OK** button. The meeting is removed.

Next, you'll delete all the tasks you created.

To delete Task items:

1. Press and hold the **Shift** key, click the **Web site design** task at the top of the list, click the last task in the TaskPad, and then release the **Shift** key.

2. Press the **Delete** key.

3. Click the **Delete all** option button in the dialog box, and then click the **OK** button. All the tasks disappear from the TaskPad. Your calendar should have no items left on it.

   TROUBLE? If your calendar still has items that you created in this tutorial, click each item and then press the Delete key to remove them.

Finally you'll delete the messages and notes you created.

To delete e-mails and notes:

1. Delete any messages from the Inbox, Outbox, and Sent Items folders that you created in this tutorial, including task requests, task responses, and meeting invitations.

2. Switch to **Notes**, and then delete both blue notes.

All the items you deleted are moved to the Deleted Items folder. They remain in the Deleted Items folder until you empty the folder. This way, you can selectively restore items you may not have wanted to delete, unless you've already emptied the folder.

To work with the Deleted Items folder:

1. Click the **Deleted Items** folder in the **Outlook Shortcut** group on the Outlook Bar. The Information viewer shows all the items you deleted from the other folders. You can change the views of the Deleted Items Information viewer just like the other folders' Information viewers.

2. Drag the **Organize Web site ideas** task from the Deleted Items Information viewer to the Tasks folder on the Outlook Bar. The task moves back to the Tasks folder.

3. Switch to the **Tasks** folder. The item is restored to its original location.

4. Drag the task from the **Tasks** folder to the **Deleted Items** folder. Once again the item is moved.

   All the items remain in the Deleted Items folder until you empty it. Once you empty this folder, the items can no longer be retrieved.

5. Right-click the **Deleted Items** folder on the Outlook Bar, and then click **Empty "Deleted Items" Folder** on the shortcut menu.

6. Click the **Yes** button to confirm that you want to permanently delete these items. The folder text should indicate that there are no items to show in this view.

Lisa is looking forward to the meeting you planned with her and Antonio to talk about the content and design of the new company Web site. Outlook makes it simple and convenient to plan schedules and coordinate meetings.

Session 2.2 QUICK CHECK

1. Explain the difference between an appointment, an event, and a meeting.
2. What is the TaskPad?
3. What happens if you drag a task from the Tasks folder to the Calendar folder?
4. Explain the purpose of AutoDate and how it works?
5. What is a meeting request?
6. How does AutoPick work?
7. What is the maximum number of items that the Office Clipboard can store?
8. Describe what happens when you delete an appointment from Outlook.

REVIEW ASSIGNMENTS

Assad Fahid handles the payroll for Wertheimer Accounting's clients. He asks you to work with him to help prepare his task list and schedule for the next few months. He needs to prepare the payroll for two clients—Beau Foods, an independent corner grocery store, and Photos & More, a film developer and framing company. He also asks you to set up a meeting with a potential client—Best Cleaners, a small dry-cleaning company that uses using environmentally safe dry-cleaning methods. You'll create a schedule for the coming days and plan a meeting with Assad and Chris Newson of Best Cleaners.

1. Start Outlook and, if necessary, hide the Folder List and display the Outlook Bar.

2. Create a green note with the text "Plan meeting with Best Cleaners", and then close it.

3. Create a pink note with the text "Prepare payroll for Beau Foods", and then close it.

Explore 4. Assign the Payroll category to the green note. (*Hint:* You might need to create an entry in the Master Category List.)

5. Create a task from the green note with a due date of tomorrow, and then delete the green note.

6. Create a new green note with the text, "talk about advantages of outsourcing payroll; mention reliability and accuracy of our firm; and offer Beau Foods as reference", and then close it.

Explore 7. Assign the Payroll category to the pink and green notes. (*Hint:* Right-click the closed note, and then click Categories on the shortcut menu to open the Categories dialog box.)

Explore 8. Create a pink note with the text "Purchase more laser checks", assign the Supplies and Payroll categories to the note, and then close the note. (*Hint:* You might need to create an entry in the Master Category List.)

Explore 9. View the notes by color, expand all colors, and then print in Table Style the notes in all rows.

10. Create a task with the subject "Prepare Photos & More payroll" and a due date of next Friday. Assign the task to the Payroll category.

11. View the tasks by category.

12. Schedule an appointment for the Prepare Photos & More payroll task for next Tuesday morning between 10 and 10:15. Do not enter a location. Turn off the reminder, if necessary.

Explore 13. Schedule an appointment from the Prepare payroll for Beau Foods note for next Thursday between 1:30 PM and 2:30 PM. (*Hint:* Drag the note from the Notes folder to the Calendar icon on the Outlook Bar to open a new Appointment window.)

14. Create a two-day event with the subject "Health Fair" that begins next Wednesday.

15. Create a recurring appointment to attend the event on both days between 10 AM and 1 PM. Show the time as Tentative.

Explore 16. Change the start time for the Prepare payroll for Beau Foods appointment to 2 PM by dragging the appointment start time. (*Hint:* Click the appointment to select it, drag the top border of the appointment down to the 2 mark.)

17. Preview and print your calendar for next week in Weekly Style.

18. Add yourself, Lisa Wertheimer, Assad Fahid, and Chris Newson to your Personal Address Book, using your e-mail address.

19. Schedule a two-hour meeting for next Tuesday starting at 1 PM with Assad and Chris as required attendees, the subject "Best Cleaners payroll," and the location "Assad's Office". Show the time in your calendar as Busy. (Do NOT send the meeting request yet.)

Explore 20. Insert the green note as an attachment in the text area of the meeting request.

21. Send the meeting request.

Explore   22. Add Lisa as an optional attendee. Double-click the meeting in the planner, click Actions on the menu bar, and then click Add or Remove Attendees. Show names from your Personal Address Book, click Lisa's name, click the Optional button, and then click the OK button. Click the Send Update button and send updates only to added or deleted attendees.

23. Check off the Plan meeting with Best Cleaners task as completed.

24. Save your calendar for next week as a Web page. Use the filename **Schedule** and save it to the **Review** folder within the **Tutorial.02** folder on your Data Disk.

25. Print the Web page, close the Web page, and then close the browser.

26. Delete all of the items, Personal Address Book entries, and categories (Payroll, Supplies) that you created in these assignments.

27. Exit Outlook.

CASE PROBLEMS

Case 1. Movie Madness Movie Madness is a video store chain that rents videos and DVDs of current and classic movies to walk-in customers and shows films in its stores. The stores are open 24 hours a day, 7 days a week, so that customers can rent videos or watch a movie no matter what the day or time. Renna Lisant, manager of Movie Madness, organizes the staff and movie schedules using Outlook Calendar, saves the calendar as a Web page, and then posts the schedule on the company intranet. This week, the stores are showing their customers' favorite 100 movies, based on customers' rental history.

1. Start Outlook, create a yellow note with the text "Prepare list of top 100 movies"; then press the Enter key twice to double space and type "Create this list from the customer database. Find out which 100 movies were rented most frequently in the last 24 months." Close the note.

Explore   2. Create an e-mail message from the note by dragging the note to the Inbox icon on the Outlook Bar. Address the e-mail to yourself. Notice that the subject is the first line of the note.

3. Send message, and then download it, if necessary.

Explore   4. Create a task from the e-mail by dragging the e-mail message from the Inbox to the Tasks icon on the Outlook Bar. Set a due date of this Friday, set the priority to High, and turn off the reminder.

Explore   5. Assign the task to yourself. Send the task request. Click the OK button in the dialog box, informing you that you cannot assign a task to yourself. Click the Cancel Assignment button.

6. Create a second task with the subject "Set up next week's staff schedule" and a due date of four hours from now. Assign the task to the new category called "Schedule". Save and close the task.

7. Change the Calendar to Work Week view.

8. Schedule the staff for next Monday through Friday by creating a new appointment for each shift. Each shift lasts eight hours and recurs every two days. End each recurrence next Friday. One staff member works each shift. Enter the staff member's name as the appointment's sub-ject; do not enter a location. Show the time as Free. The staff includes you, Lydia Jiminez, Frank Zapata, Chris Soto, Corrie Beppu, and Maurice Singleton. (*Hint:* You will have three appointments for Monday and three appointments for Tuesday. The Monday appointments will recur on Wednesday and Friday; the Tuesday appointment will recur on Thursday.

9. Check off the Set up next week's staff schedule task as completed.

10. Create an event for each day next week with a different movie title of your choice for the subject; these are the movies that will be shown that day. Turn off the reminders.

Explore 11. Plan a meeting for next Tuesday from 10 AM to 11 AM in the Conference Room with the entire staff of Movie Madness except the staff member whom you assigned to work that shift; use "Staff Meeting" as the subject. Do not send e-mail meeting requests. (*Hint:* Open the Plan a Meeting dialog box. Type the names of attendees in the All Attendees list by clicking the Click here to add attendee text box and typing a name. Click the envelope icon next to each name, and then click the Don't send meeting to this attendee option. Click the Make Meeting button, enter the subject and location, click the Send button on the Standard toolbar, and then click the Yes button to save and close the meeting.)

Explore 12. Preview next week's calendar in the Tri-fold Style, and then print it. (*Hint:* Select the print style, click the Preview button in the Print dialog box, and then click the Print button on the Print Preview toolbar.)

13. Save next week's calendar as a Web page with the filename **Movie Schedule** to the **Cases** folder within the **Tutorial.02** folder on your Data Disk. Print the Web page.

14. Delete any Outlook items, including notes, tasks, appointments, events, and meetings (without sending a cancellation notice), and the category (Schedule) that you created in this case, and then empty the Deleted Items folder.

Case 2. Velez Studio Bruce Velez runs a music studio housed with the latest recording, mixing, and editing equipment. Musicians rent the studio by the half hour to record their music. Bruce uses Outlook to track the tasks he needs to complete to keep the studio running and to organize the studio rental schedule.

1. Create a white note with the text "Check speaker connections", and then close it.

2. Create a yellow note with the text "Buy new microphone", assign the Suppliers category to the note, and then close it.

Explore 3. Copy the yellow note onto the desktop so that it is visible even when Outlook is closed or minimized. You can either drag the note to the desktop or select the yellow note, press the Ctrl+C keys to copy the note to the Clipboard, minimize Outlook to display the desktop, and then press the Ctrl+V keys to paste the note. You can open, close, and print the note just as you would from within Outlook.

4. Maximize the Outlook window, and verify that the original note still exists in Outlook.

5. Minimize the Outlook window, and then double-click the note to open it.

6. Close the note, click the note to select it if necessary, press the Delete key to move the item to the Recycle Bin, and then click the Yes button to confirm the deletion.

7. Maximize the Outlook window, and verify that the original note still appears in the Notes folder.

8. Create tasks from both notes, assigning them to the category "Equipment" that you add to the Master Category List. Do not assign a due date or priority.

9. Create a task with the subject "Calibrate equipment" that recurs daily every weekday starting next Monday and ending after 5 occurrences. Set the priority to Low and the reminder for 9 AM. Save and close the task.

10. View the tasks by category, and then click the Expand button for each category to display the tasks. Notice that the Buy new microphone task appears in two category groups.

Explore 11. Change the Calibrate equipment task priority to High. (*Hint:* Click the Priority text box, and then click High.)

Explore 12. Print all rows of the task list in Table Style.

13. Switch to the Calendar and set the view to Work Week.

14. Create an appointment for Leslie Gorman (Subject) in the Studio for next Monday between 10 AM and 1 PM and no reminder. Type "Need to hook up harp to recording equipment" in the notes text box. Assign the appointment to the Key Customer category. Save and close the appointment.

Explore ▸ 15. Copy the appointment to Wednesday starting at 1 PM. Click the Monday appointment to select it, press and hold the Ctrl key, drag the appointment to Wednesday between 1 PM and 4 PM, and then release the Ctrl key.

16. Create appointments for Wes Carpenter (Subject) in the Studio for next Tuesday between 11:30 AM and 4:30 PM and for next Thursday between 1 PM and 5 PM. Turn off the reminders.

17. Create appointments for Rick Anders (Subject) in the Studio for next Wednesday and next Thursday between 9 AM and noon. Turn off the reminders.

18. Create an event for next Thursday with the subject "Local Battle of the Bands" and turn off the reminder.

Explore ▸ 19. Create a task from the event with the subject "Distribute studio brochure at battle of the bands." (*Hint:* Drag the event to the TaskPad. Modify the subject in the Task window.)

20. Print your calendar in Calendar Details Style.

21. Delete all the Outlook items (notes, tasks, appointments, and events) and the category (Equipment) you created in this case, empty the Deleted Items folder, and then exit Outlook.

Case 3. Balloon Creations   Wendy and Matthew Connors, as Balloon Creations, entertain at private parties and corporate events by fashioning animals and other objects out of balloons. They are hired to practice their craft at birthday parties, fundraisers, grand openings, and other special events. In addition, they offer classes where they teach others how to create objects from balloons. They use Outlook to organize their schedule.

1. Start Outlook, create a pink note with the text "Buy supplies" on one line, press the Enter key twice to double space, and then type "balloons, markers, helium" on another line. Close the note.

2. Create a yellow note with the text "Meet Randy for lunch on Tuesday" and then close it.

3. Open the pink note, edit the list to "colored balloons, black markers, refill helium tank", and then close the note.

4. Create a task from the pink note with a due date of next Wednesday, no reminder, and a High priority.

5. Create a task with the subject "Confirm Thursday's party with Helen Olynciew", a due date of next Tuesday, and no reminder.

Explore ▸ 6. Create an appointment from the yellow note by dragging the note to the Calendar icon on the Outlook Bar. Set the appointment at Bob's Diner for next Tuesday between 11:30 AM to 1 PM. Set a reminder for 1 hour before the appointment. Show the time as Out of Office.

Explore ▸ 7. Create an appointment from the Confirm Thursday's party task for Monday at 3 PM to 3:30 PM. Set a reminder for 10 minutes before the appointment. Show the time as Free.

8. Create appointments for the following with no locations, using the default appointment reminder, and show time as Busy:

DAY	TIME	SUBJECT
Monday	Noon to 3 PM	Advanced Animals Class
Tuesday	1:30 PM to 4:30 PM	Jeremy Gottleib's 5th Birthday Party
Thursday	11:30 AM to 3:30 PM	Helen Olynciew's Sweet 16
Friday	1 PM to 6 PM	Public Radio Benefit Party
Saturday and Sunday	10 AM to 3 PM	Firefighter Carnival

9. Change the Advanced Animals Class to a recurring appointment that recurs every 2 weeks on Mondays for the next month.

Explore 10. Change the Firefighter Carnival on both days to all-day events. Show the time as Busy and turn off the reminder. (*Hint:* Open the Appointment window, and then click the All day event check box to insert a check mark.)

11. Preview your calendar in Daily Style and then print it.

12. Delete all the Outlook items (notes, tasks, appointments, events) you created in this case, and then empty the Deleted Items folder.

Case 4. Family Services Family Services is a nonprofit organization that provides aid to needy families. They provide clothing, household goods (such as dishes, vacuum cleaners, and furniture), and even money to pay for rent, food, and necessary items that the organization cannot get donated. Ada Cox, the director of Family Services, is planning the annual fundraiser to encourage community members to donate goods and money. Ada asks you to jot down ideas for the fundraiser's theme, create a task list, and then schedule time to complete those tasks. The fundraiser will take place three weeks from this Friday.

1. Create at least three notes with ideas for the fundraiser, and then close them. For example, one note might suggest possible themes, and another might include a reminder to send directions to party guests.

2. Color code the notes, using at least two colors.

3. Add a new category called "Fundraiser" to the Master Category List.

Explore 4. Assign the Fundraiser category to the three notes. (*Hint:* Select the three notes, right-click the selected notes, and then click Categories to open the Categories dialog box.)

5. Print all the Fundraiser notes on one page.

6. Create a task list of at least four activities that Ada must complete before the fundraiser. For example, she might need to finalize the number of guests and provide that information to a caterer.

7. Assign all tasks to the Fundraiser category.

8. Schedule appointments to complete each task during the week before the party.

Explore 9. Create a new task request to yourself with the subject "Create raffle drawing", a due date of the Monday before the party, and assigned to the Fundraiser category. (*Hint:* Click the New button list arrow, and then click New Task Request to open a Task Request window without first creating a task.)

Explore 10. Click the Cancel Assignment button on the Task Request Standard toolbar to change the task assignment to a regular task.

Explore 11. In the notes text box, type "To raise additional money during the fundraiser, arrange a raffle drawing. Ask local businesses to donate an item or service ranging in value from $10 to $150. We'll sell tickets for the drawing and give away the donations as prizes."

12. Plan a final meeting with Ada with the subject "Finalize plans" for the Thursday before the fundraiser between 3 PM and 4 PM and the category Fundraiser.

13. Don't send a meeting request to either yourself or Ada. (*Hint:* Click the e-mail icon to the left of each name, and then click Don't send meeting to this attendee.)

14. Insert any appropriate notes as attachments into the notes text box of the Meeting window.

Explore 15. Insert the Create raffle drawing task as an attachment into the text box area of the Meeting window.

16. Send the meeting request, and then click the Yes button to save and close the meeting.

17. Preview and print the calendar for the week of the party. Use the Daily Style.

18. Save your calendar as a Web page, using the filename **Fundraiser Calendar** in the **Cases** folder within the **Tutorial.02** folder on your Data Disk.

Explore ▷ 19. Find all Outlook items that are assigned to the Fundraiser category. (*Hint:* Click Tools on the menu bar, and then click Advanced Find to open the Advanced Find dialog box. Select Any type of Outlook item in the Look for list. Click the More Choices tab, click the Categories button, click the Fundraiser category, and then click the OK button. Click the Find Now button.)

Explore ▷ 20. Select all the items and then press the Delete key. Click the Yes button to confirm that you want to delete all the items. (*Hint:* To select all the items, click the first item, press and hold the Shift key, click the last item, and then release the Shift key.)

21. Click the Close button in the title bar of the Advanced Find dialog box to close the dialog box.

22. Delete the category that you created in this case, and then empty the Deleted Items folder.

QUICK | CHECK ANSWERS

Session 2.1

1. A never-ending electronic notepad in Outlook to jot down ideas, reminders, and other thoughts.

2. A task is a one-time item on your to-do list that you want to perform. A recurring task occurs repeatedly.

3. The AutoCreate feature converts the note to a task.

4. A category is a way to assign items a keyword or phrase that you can then use to organize and locate related items.

5. You would add categories to the master list to create precise categories that reflect your specific needs.

6. You can assign as many categories as you'd like to any item.

7. A task request is an e-mail message with details about the task to be assigned.

8. You need two people to assign a task—one to send the task request and one to respond to the task request. Both must be using Outlook.

Session 2.2

1. An appointment is an activity that does not involve other people or resources. An event is an activity that lasts one or more full days. A meeting is an appointment with other people or resources.

2. A summary list of the Tasks folder that appears in the Day/Week/Month view of the Calendar.

3. Outlook schedules an appointment using the task's subject, notes, and categories.

4. An Outlook feature that converts natural-language date and time descriptions—such as "one week from today" and "noon"—into the numerical format that represents the month, day, and year or time, respectively.

5. An e-mail message that each invited attendee and resource receives and responds to.

6. If you have access to others' calendars, AutoPick selects the next available free time for all invited people and resources.

7. 12

8. The appointment is moved the Deleted Items folder.

OBJECTIVES

In this tutorial you will:

- Add the Outlook Address Book to your profile

- Enter and edit contact information

- Send an e-mail message, write a letter, and schedule an appointment with contacts

- Send and receive contact information and vCards

- Organize contacts by categories

- Flag contacts for follow-up

- Filter and sort a contact list

- Merge a form letter with contacts

- Delete contacts and other Outlook items

MANAGING CONTACTS

Communicating with LinkUp's Members

CASE

LinkUp

LinkUp is a car sharing company located in Philadelphia, Pennsylvania. Felicia Rogers founded it in the year 2000. For urban dwellers that drive fewer than 10,000 miles per year, car sharing is becoming an increasingly popular alternative to owning a car. LinkUp currently has about 200 members who prefer to share a fleet of 40 vehicles, rather than spending thousands of dollars on personal automobiles and all the associated expenses. These numbers are growing dramatically each month. LinkUp's cars are located throughout the city's neighborhoods, close to members' homes and workplaces. Members pay for only the hours and miles they drive. LinkUp charges a $120 annual fee as well nominal fees for the actual hours and miles driven, $2.50 and $0.50, respectively. Insurance, gasoline, and maintenance are included in the rates. Members reserve a car by phone or online for immediate or future use. At their reserved time, members use their access keys to unlock the closest available car, usually within five blocks of their location, and drive away. They return the car to the same location and lock it. LinkUp bills their credit card every month for actual usage.

LinkUp uses Outlook to keep track of its members and service providers, such as garages, cleaning companies, insurance company, and so forth. Once all the identifying contact information is compiled in the Contacts folder, it is available throughout Outlook. For example, LinkUp can send e-mail messages to specific contacts, write them letters, assign them tasks, and even schedule meetings or appointments with them.

In this tutorial, you will compile and organize LinkUp's contact list. Then you will send an e-mail message and write a letter to individual members. Finally you will create a personalized form letter to send to LinkUp's members informing them of the latest cars being added to the company's fleet.

SESSION 3.1

In this session, you will create and edit contacts. Then you will display the contacts in different views, print your contact list, and group similar contacts into a distribution list. Finally you will forward and receive contact information by e-mail.

Setting Up Contact Information

Most of our lives, both business and personal, involve interacting with people—writing them letters, calling them on the phone, sending them e-mail messages. Communication options seem to be expanding daily, so that most people have a variety of street addresses, telephone numbers, and e-mail addresses. With so much contact information available for each person, a paper address book can become bulky and inconvenient. In fact, a paper address book can become downright messy and difficult to use as people change addresses, get new area codes, or sign up for additional e-mail addresses. Paper address books often do not provide the space to jot down personal details such as birthdays or children's names.

You can save as much or as little information about people as you like in Outlook. No matter what particulars you want to record about friends, family, coworkers, and business associates, Contacts provides the place to do so. **Contacts** is the Outlook folder that stores detailed information about the people and businesses with whom you communicate. Each person or organization is called a **contact**. You can store business-related information about each contact, including job titles, phone numbers, postal and e-mail addresses, and assistants' names, as well as more personal information, such as notes, birthdays, anniversaries, and children's names.

Adding the Outlook Address Book Information Service to Your Profile

The Contacts folder is included in the Address Book as the Outlook Address Book. Recall that the Address Book is the collection of address books that you use to store names, e-mail addresses, fax numbers, and distribution lists. The Outlook Address Book is created from your Contacts folder and is updated whenever you update your contact list. In addition to the Outlook Address Book, the Address Book also may contain a customizable Personal Address Book in a file format you can copy to disk and a Global Address List for an organization that is created and modified only by a network administrator.

You can keep your personal contacts in either the Personal Address Book or the Contacts folder. The Contacts folder provides more options and flexibility in Outlook than the Personal Address Book. For example, the Contacts folder enables you to store many phone numbers, birthdays, anniversaries, and other custom information with your contacts. You can also choose how to sort, filter, and view your contacts, such as by last name first or by postal code. In addition, you can print your Contacts folder in a variety of formats by changing the view.

You'll check what information services are included in your profile, and if the Outlook Address Book information service is not already installed, you'll add it to your profile.

To add the Outlook Address Book information service:

1. Start Outlook, click **Tools** on the menu bar, and then click **Services**. The Services dialog box opens, listing services set up for your profile.

2. Look for **Outlook Address Book** in the list on the Services tab. If you see the entry, then the Outlook Address Book is already installed; click the **Cancel** button and skip the rest of these steps. If the entry doesn't appear, you need to add it; continue with step 3.

3. Click the **Add** button to open the Add Service to Profile dialog box.

4. Click **Outlook Address Book**, and then click the **OK** button.

   A dialog box opens, reminding you that you must exit and restart Outlook to make the new service available.

5. Click the **OK** button in the dialog box, and then click the **OK** button in the Services dialog box.

6. Click **File** on the menu bar, and then click **Exit and Log Off** to close Outlook.

7. Restart Outlook, selecting your profile, if necessary.

Next, you want to verify that the Contacts folder is displayed in the Address Book. This way you can be sure that when you address e-mail messages, Outlook looks up the name or address in the Contacts folder.

To verify that the Contacts folder is available as an e-mail address book:

1. Right-click **Contacts** in the Outlook Shortcuts group on the Outlook Bar, and then click **Properties**. The Contacts Properties dialog box opens.

2. Click the **Outlook Address Book** tab. See Figure 3-1.

| Figure 3-1 | CONTACTS PROPERTIES DIALOG BOX |

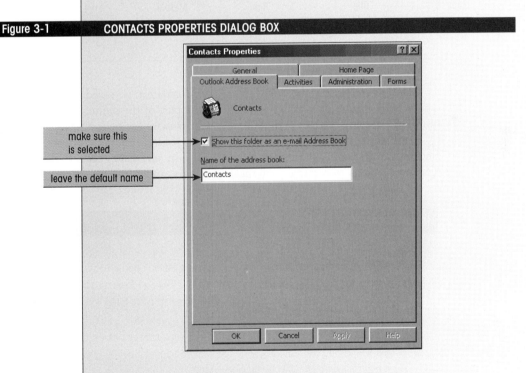

make sure this is selected

leave the default name

3. Click the **Show this folder as an e-mail Address Book** check box to insert a check mark if it is not already checked. This enables you to address your e-mails using the Contacts folder.

   You'll leave the default name for the folder as Contacts.

4. Click the **OK** button to close the dialog box.

Now you can use your Contacts folder to address e-mail messages to any contact.

Creating Contacts

In today's connected world, most people have a lot of contact information. Consider Felicia. She has different mailing addresses for home and work. She has phone numbers for her home, main office, direct line, cell phone, pager, home fax, business fax, and assistant. She also has several e-mail addresses for personal and business use. A written record of all this information would require a full page in a paper address book; Outlook stores up to three addresses, nineteen phone numbers, three e-mail addresses, and one Web page URL, plus related information on one contact card.

When you create a contact, you open a blank contact card and then enter all necessary information. Information you enter about a contact is actually individual units of data, called **fields**. For example, a complete contact name is actually comprised of several fields, as shown in Figure 3-2.

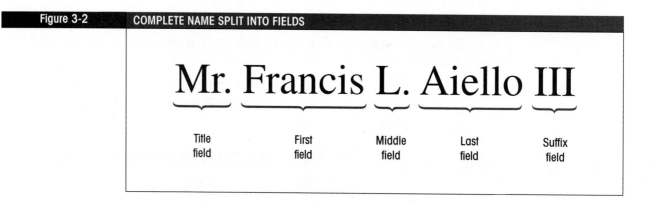

Figure 3-2   COMPLETE NAME SPLIT INTO FIELDS

Mr. Francis L. Aiello III

| Title field | First field | Middle field | Last field | Suffix field |

The field's name or label identifies what information is stored in that field. Fields enable you to sort, group, or look up contacts by any part of the name. Without fields, you could not find a specific contact or alphabetize your contact list by last name.

Outlook uses fields to organize data in all its folders. You have already worked with fields such as Subject, Due Date, Start Time, Location, and Categories in the Inbox, Tasks, and Calendar folders to create e-mail messages, tasks, appointments, events, and meetings.

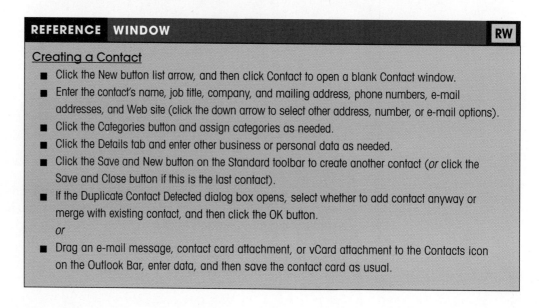

REFERENCE WINDOW   **RW**

Creating a Contact

- Click the New button list arrow, and then click Contact to open a blank Contact window.
- Enter the contact's name, job title, company, and mailing address, phone numbers, e-mail addresses, and Web site (click the down arrow to select other address, number, or e-mail options).
- Click the Categories button and assign categories as needed.
- Click the Details tab and enter other business or personal data as needed.
- Click the Save and New button on the Standard toolbar to create another contact (or click the Save and Close button if this is the last contact).
- If the Duplicate Contact Detected dialog box opens, select whether to add contact anyway or merge with existing contact, and then click the OK button.
  or
- Drag an e-mail message, contact card attachment, or vCard attachment to the Contacts icon on the Outlook Bar, enter data, and then save the contact card as usual.

LinkUp stores information about its members and service providers in the Contacts folder. Felicia asks you to create new contact cards for several members. You could start a new contact from any folder by clicking the New button list arrow and then clicking New Contact. Instead, you'll switch to the Contacts folder.

To create a contact:

1. Click **Contacts** on the Outlook Bar. The New button reflects the most likely item you'll want to create from this folder. See Figure 3-3.

| Figure 3-3 | CONTACTS FOLDER |

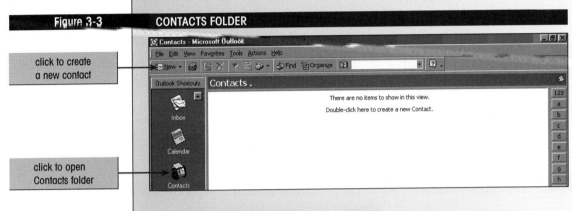

click to create a new contact

click to open Contacts folder

2. Click the **New Contact** button [New ▾] on the Standard toolbar. A new, untitled Contact window opens, displaying text boxes in which you enter the contact information. See Figure 3-4.

| Figure 3-4 | BLANK CONTACT WINDOW |

stores more personal details

stores most commonly used information

name and company

e-mail addresses

mailing addresses

phone numbers

URL

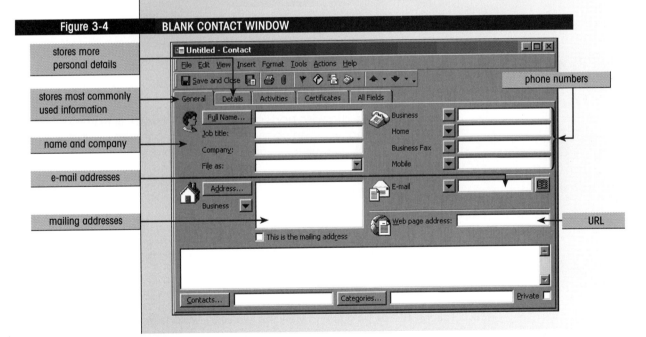

Contact information is entered on two tabs. The General tab stores the most pertinent information about a contact, including the contact's name, job title and company, phone numbers, and addresses. The Details tab contains less frequently needed information, such as the names of the contact's manager, assistant, spouse, as well as the contact's birthday, anniversary, and nickname.

You can create contacts for people or organizations. If a contact is a person, then you type his or her name in the Full Name text box; the Job title and Company text boxes are optional for people. If the contact is an organization, you type a name in the Company text box, and leave the Full Name and Job title text boxes empty.

The File as text box shows how your contacts are ordered in the Contacts Information viewer. By default, Outlook alphabetizes contacts by last names. If you enter a name and a company for a contact, Outlook suggests a variety of ways to display that contact in the contact list. It is best to use the same File as option for all your contacts so that the contact list is organized consistently.

You'll begin by entering the contact's name, job title, and organization.

To enter a contact's name and company:

1. Type **Mr. Francis L. Aiello III** in the Full Name text box, and then press the **Enter** key. The insertion point moves to the next text box. The contact name appears last name first in the File as text box.

2. Click the **Full Name** button to open the Check Full Name dialog box. Although you entered the contact name in one text box, Outlook stores each part of the name as a separate field. See Figure 3-5.

Figure 3-5	CHECK FULL NAME DIALOG BOX

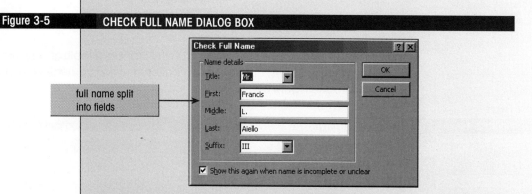

full name split into fields

If Outlook cannot distinguish parts of a name, the Check Full Name dialog box will open so that you can correct the fields. You can also open the dialog box to confirm that Outlook recognized the name properly.

3. Click the **Cancel** button to close the Check Full Name dialog box without making any changes.

4. Type **Project Manager** in the Job title text box, and then press the **Tab** key. The insertion point moves to the Company text box

5. Type **Levinson Systems** in the Company text box, and then press the **Tab** key.

   You want all the contacts filed last name, first name, but you'll look at the other options.

6. Click the **File as** list arrow to view the five filing options. See Figure 3-6.

| Figure 3-6 | CONTACT CARD WITH NAME AND JOB INFORMATION |

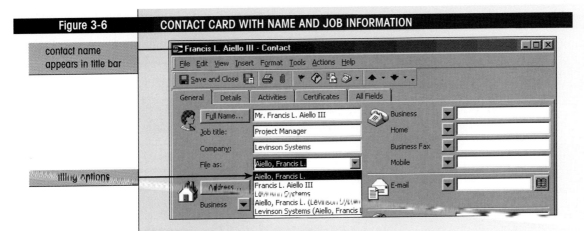

contact name appears in title bar

filing options

If two contacts had the same name, you might file these contacts last name, first name (company name) to distinguish them.

7. If necessary, click **Aiello, Francis L.**

Next, you'll enter the contact's phone numbers. You can enter as many as 19 phone numbers per contact. No matter how you enter phone numbers—with or without spaces, hyphens, or parentheses—Outlook formats them consistently, for example, (215) 555-3492. Be sure to enter area codes for all numbers outside your area; if you leave out the area code, Outlook inserts your local area code. Enter international phone numbers with the three-digit country code, such as 021. You can also include additional text after a number, such as the contact's extension "x385".

Outlook can automatically dial the phone numbers for your contacts if you have a modem installed on your computer. If you use Outlook to dial your calls, it dials all the numbers until it reaches a letter, in this case "x". Otherwise, Outlook dials the additional numbers; although most telephone systems ignore any extra dialed numbers.

The contact card displays four phone numbers at once—Business, Home, Business Fax, and Mobile phone fields by default. You can enter phone numbers in any or all of the four displayed phone fields as needed, leaving the phone field blank if appropriate. You can also change the field labels to access any of the other 15 available phone fields or change the order that phone numbers appear on the card. It is possible to display any of the phone fields two, three, or even four times on a contact card. Be aware that you are looking at the multiple displays of the same stored field. Any changes you make to the number in one field will appear in all displays.

For more information about phone numbers in Outlook, visit the Slipstick Systems Web site: **www.slipstick.com/config/olphone.htm**.

Next you'll enter Francis's business, pager, and home phone numbers.

To enter a contact's phone numbers:

1. Click in the **Business** text box, type **215 555 9753**, and then press the **Tab** key. Outlook formats the phone number with parentheses around the area code and a hyphen after the prefix, even though you didn't type them. It underlines the number when it recognizes it as a valid phone number.

2. Click the **Home down arrow** button ▼. The check mark next to Business indicates that there is a number entered for that field. See Figure 3-7.

Figure 3-7   SELECTING A PHONE NUMBER FIELD

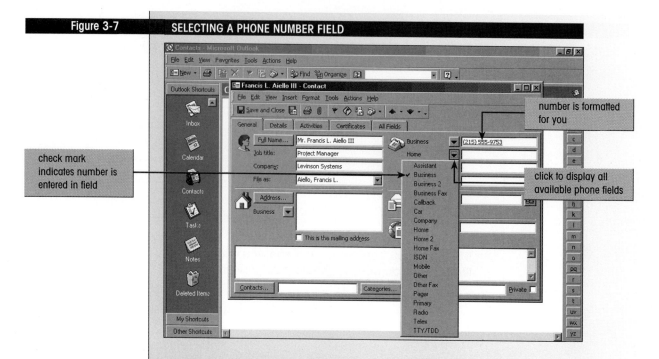

check mark indicates number is entered in field

number is formatted for you

click to display all available phone fields

You can select which number you want to enter and display in the next text box. In this case, you'll enter Francis's pager phone number.

3. Click **Pager** to change the field label, type **215 555 9752**, and then press the **Tab** key.

4. Change the Business Fax field label to **Home**, and then enter **215 555 6441** as the Home number.

You need to enter the extension for Francis's business line. You can do that by editing the existing number.

5. Click in the **Business** text box to the right of the phone number, press the **spacebar**, type **x384**, and then press the **Tab** key.

If Outlook is unsure how to distinguish parts of a number, it may open the Check Phone Number dialog box. You can also open this dialog box for any number to confirm that Outlook recognized the number properly.

6. Double-click the **Business** phone number. The Check Phone Number dialog box opens so you can verify the number. See Figure 3-8.

Figure 3-8   CHECK PHONE NUMBER DIALOG BOX

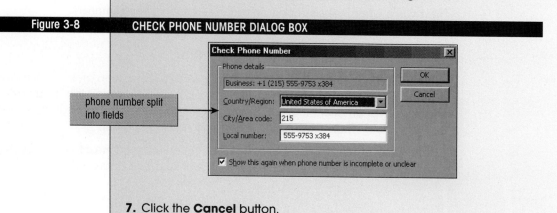

phone number split into fields

7. Click the **Cancel** button.

You can enter as many as three postal addresses for each contact: Business, Home, and Other. By default, Outlook is set for you to enter a Business address. If you want to enter another type of address, as with most of LinkUp's members, you can set the mailing address to Home or Other. Outlook assumes that you want to send printed correspondence to whichever address you enter first, although you can change this at any time. Only one address can be marked as the mailing address.

You enter addresses by typing in the Address text box and pressing the Enter key between lines, so that the address follows the standard postal addressing. Outlook organizes the address into its appropriate fields, such as Home Address Street, Home Address City, and Home Address State. Outlook may open the Check Address dialog box so you can confirm that Outlook recognized this address properly. If an address is complex, you might want to click the Address button to open the Check Address dialog box and enter the address parts in their appropriate text boxes.

You'll enter Francis's home address and specify that it is the mailing address.

To enter a contact's home mailing address:

1. Click the **Business down arrow** button ▼, and then click **Home**. The insertion point is in the Address text box, ready for you to enter the home address.

2. Type **12 Haymarket Blvd.**, and then press the **Enter** key. The insertion point moves to a new line.

3. Type **Philadelphia, PA 19107**.

   You'll verify that Outlook recorded the address in the correct fields although you don't usually need to do so for a simple address.

4. Click the **Address** button. The Check Address dialog box opens. See Figure 3-9.

| Figure 3-9 | VERIFYING THE MAILING ADDRESS |

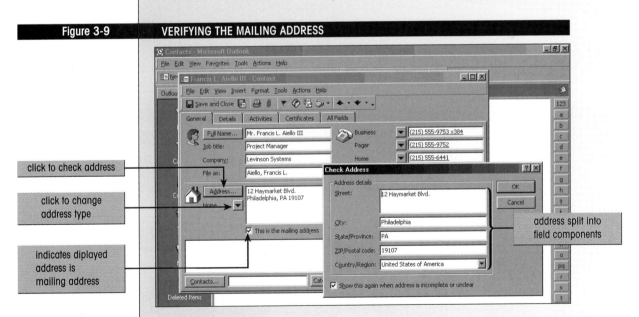

5. Click the **Cancel** button to close the dialog box.

   This is the mailing address check box is checked. Outlook assumes that the first address you enter for a contact is the mailing address. You could enter additional addresses and specify any one of them as the mailing address.

Today many people have a variety of e-mail addresses for business and personal use. Outlook accepts three e-mail addresses for each contact, which are labeled E-mail, E-mail 2, and E-mail 3. You should enter the primary address you plan to use in the E-mail field, so you don't need to think about which address to select.

In most cases, each contact would have a unique e-mail address to which you would send e-mail messages. For this tutorial, you will use your own e-mail address.

To enter a contact's e-mail address:

1. Click in the **E-mail** text box, and then type your e-mail address.

2. Press the **Enter** key. Outlook underlines the address when it recognizes it as a valid e-mail address.

Categories provide a great way to organize and group all your Outlook items, as you have seen when you assigned categories to tasks. By consistently assigning categories, you can always find all related items. For example, LinkUp assigns each contact the category of "Key Customer" or "Suppliers" or "Business" to distinguish member contacts from vendor contacts from employee contacts. You'll assign the Key Customer category to this contact card because Francis is a member of LinkUp.

To assign a category to a contact:

1. Click the **Categories** button to open the Categories dialog box.

2. Click **Key Customer** in the Available categories list.

3. Click the **OK** button to assign the category. Key Customer appears in the Categories text box; if you assigned more than one category, commas would separate them.

   You have entered all of the general contact information for Francis, as shown in Figure 3-10.

| Figure 3-10 | COMPLETED GENERAL TAB FOR CONTACT |

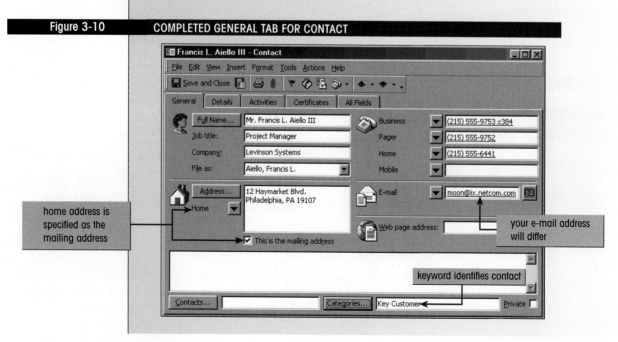

home address is specified as the mailing address

your e-mail address will differ

keyword identifies contact

In addition to contact information, most people have other information that is helpful to record. The Details tab provides a place to enter additional information. You can record business details, such as the contact's department, profession, manager, or assistant, or you can record personal details, such as a contact's nickname, spouse, birthday, or anniversary.

When you enter a birthday or an anniversary date, Outlook requires that you include a year. If you enter only a month and day, Outlook adds the current year to the date. You might use 1900 (rather than the current year) when you don't know the year to insure that you don't inadvertently assume the incorrect age or anniversary year. Once you save the contact, Outlook adds a recurring appointment to your calendar for those dates.

You'll enter some of these details for Francis.

To enter information on the Details tab and close a contact:

1. Click the **Details** tab. Notice the different types of information you can enter. See Figure 3-11.

Figure 3-11	DETAILS TAB

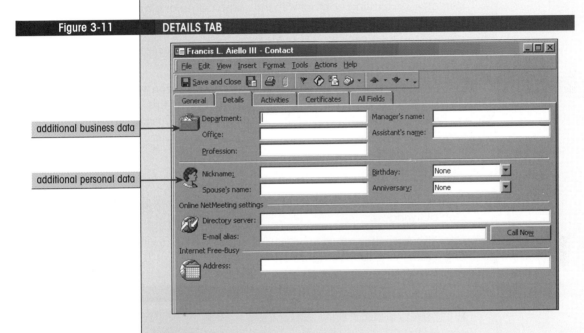

You'll enter Francis's nickname and birthday.

2. Click in the **Nickname** text box, and then type **Frank**.

You can enter a birthday or anniversary by typing a date or selecting a day from a calendar.

3. Press the **Tab** key to select the Birthday text box, and then type **8/20/1969**, press the **Tab** key to enter the date.

4. Click the **OK** button to confirm that you want to save the date information.

TROUBLE? If a dialog box opens, asking "Do you want to designate this contact as a Small Business Customer Manager contact?" click the No button.

You have entered all the contact information for Francis, so you can save and close the Contact window.

5. Click the **Save and Close** button [Save and Close] on the Standard toolbar. The contact card appears in the Contacts Information viewer. See Figure 3-12.

Figure 3-12	CONTACTS INFORMATION VIEWER WITH CONTACT CARD

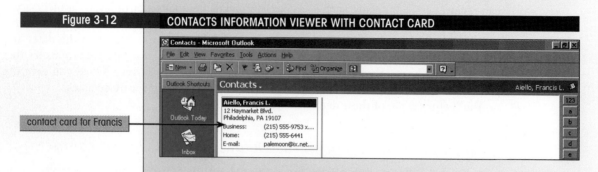

contact card for Francis

TROUBLE? If the Duplicate Contact Detected dialog box opens, then Outlook detected an existing contact with the same name or e-mail address as the contact you're entering. Click the Add this as a new contact anyway option button, and then click the OK button.

Francis's contact card appears in the Contacts Information viewer, and his birthday is added to the Calendar as a recurring event. You could verify this from the calendar; another way is to look on the Activities tab in the Contact window. This tab shows all Outlook items related to the open contact.

To view a contact's activities:

1. Double-click Francis's contact card in the Information viewer to open its Contact window.

2. Click the **Activities** tab in the Contact window. His birthday appears as a recurring event in the list. See Figure 3-13.

Figure 3-13	DETAILS TAB OF CONTACT WINDOW

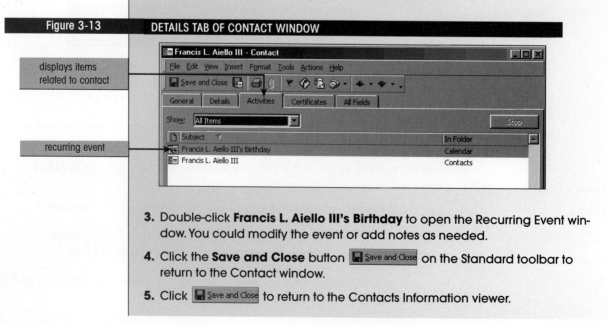

displays items related to contact

recurring event

3. Double-click **Francis L. Aiello III's Birthday** to open the Recurring Event window. You could modify the event or add notes as needed.

4. Click the **Save and Close** button [Save and Close] on the Standard toolbar to return to the Contact window.

5. Click [Save and Close] to return to the Contacts Information viewer.

You can also see the recurring event in the Calendar.

To view the recurring event in the Calendar:

1. Click **Calendar** in the **Outlook Shortcuts** group on the Outlook Bar.

2. In the Date Navigator, click the month scroll arrows to display **August** and then click **20** on the calendar. Francis L. Aiello's birthday is listed as a recurring event. See Figure 3-14.

| Figure 3-14 | RECURRING EVENT IN CALENDAR |

event banner shows recurring event

event is private and hidden from anyone with access to your calendar

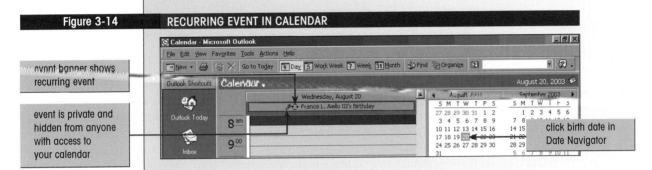

click birth date in Date Navigator

3. Click **Contacts** in the **Outlook Shortcuts** group on the Outlook Bar.

Next, you'll enter additional contacts for Felicia.

To enter additional contacts:

1. Click the **New Contact** button on the Standard toolbar to open a new, blank contact card.

2. Enter the following contact: name **Jill E. White**, home phone **215-555-1224**, home fax **215-555-4331**, address type **Home**, home mailing address **19 Hillcrest Way, Philadelphia, PA 19107**, category **Key Customer**, spouse **Karl**.

When you need to enter multiple contacts, you can save and close one contact card and open a new contact card in the same step.

3. Click the **Save and New** button on the Standard toolbar. Jill's contact information is saved and Outlook opens a new, blank contact card.

TROUBLE? If a dialog box opens, asking "Do you want to designate this contact as a Small Business Customer Manager contact?" click the No button.

4. Enter the following contact: name **Michael Lang**, home phone **215-555-0785**, address type **Home**, home mailing address **2938 Catherine Street, Philadelphia, PA 19102**, category **Key Customer**, nickname **Mike**.

5. Click to save Mike's contact information and open a new, blank contact card.

TROUBLE? If a dialog box opens, asking "Do you want to designate this contact as a Small Business Customer Manager contact?" click the No button.

6. Enter the following contact: name **Felicia Rogers**, title **President**, company **LinkUp**, business phone **215-555-9797**, business fax **215-555-9701**, pager **215-555-2157**, address type **Business**, business mailing address **2932 12th Street**, **Philadelphia, PA 19102**, Web page **www.linkupcarsharing.com**, category **Business**.

7. Click 🖫.

TROUBLE? If a dialog box opens, asking "Do you want to designate this contact as a Small Business Customer Manager contact?" click the No button.

If you enter an address as the wrong address type, you can use the Office Clipboard to move the address to the correct text box. Select the address in the text box, press Ctrl+X to cut the address to the Clipboard, switch to the Business, Home, or Other address text box as needed, click in the address text box, and then press Ctrl+V to paste the address.

As your contact list grows, you may inadvertently try to reenter an existing contact or you may encounter two or more contacts with the same name. Outlook helps prevent the former and informs you of the latter by checking new names against those already in your contact list. If Outlook detects that another contact already has the same name as the current contact, it opens the Duplicate Contact Detected dialog box so you can decide whether to add the contact anyway or combine it with an existing contact. Outlook also searches for duplicate e-mail addresses, and provides the same options if it encounters one.

The next contact you'll enter, a vendor for LinkUp, has the same name as a LinkUp customer.

To enter a contact with a duplicate name:

1. Enter the following business contact: name **Michael Lang**, job title **mechanic**, company **Aldrich Garage**, business phone **215-555-8715**, mobile phone **215-555-2145**, address type **Business**, business mailing address **78 Carpenter Street**, **Philadelphia, PA 19109**, category **Suppliers**, and nickname **Mike**.

2. Click the **Save and Close** button 🖫 Save and Close on the Standard toolbar. The Duplicate Contact Detected dialog box opens. See Figure 3-15.

Figure 3-15	DUPLICATE CONTACT DETECTED DIALOG BOX

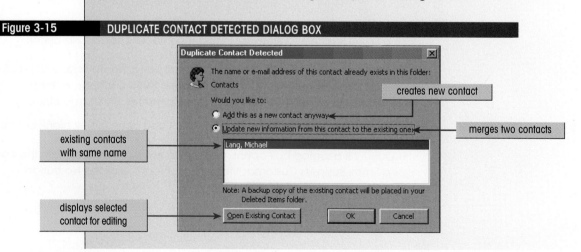

You decide to change the File as name to help distinguish the two Michael Langs.

3. Click the **Cancel** button in the dialog box to return to the contact.

 TROUBLE? If you click the Open Existing Contact button the original Michael Lang contact card opens for editing. You want to return to the new Michael Lang contact card instead. Click the Close button in the contact card title bar to close the Contact window, and then continue with Step 4.

4. Click the **File as** list arrow on the General tab, and then click **Lang, Michael (Aldrich Garage)**. Now each Michael Lang will appear differently in the contact list so you can distinguish the two.

5. Click 💾 Save and Close to reopen the Duplicate Contact Detected dialog box.

6. Click the **Add this as a new contact anyway** option button, and then click the **OK** button.

 TROUBLE? If a dialog box opens, asking "Do you want to designate this contact as a Small Business Customer Manager contact?" click the No button.

The Contacts Information viewer displays each of the five contacts you entered.

Using Different Contact Views

There are a variety of ways to look at the information in the Contacts folder. **Views** specify how information in a folder is organized and which details are visible. For example, Address Cards view displays names and mailing addresses in blocks. Phone List view displays details about your contacts, such as name, job title, and telephone numbers, in columns. Each Outlook folder has a set of standard views from which you can choose.

To change the contact view:

1. Click **View** on the menu bar, point to **Current View**, and then click **Detailed Address Cards**. Your contacts appear in alphabetical order by last name as specified in the File as text box and much of the information you entered is visible. See Figure 3-16.

Figure 3-16   DETAILED ADDRESS CARDS VIEW

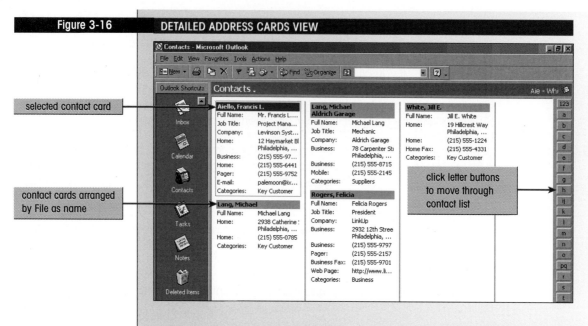

selected contact card

contact cards arranged by File as name

click letter buttons to move through contact list

When you have many contacts, you can click a letter button on the right side of the screen to display contacts filed under that letter, and then scroll to find the specific contact you want.

2. Click **View** on the menu bar, point to **Current View**, and then click **Phone List**. Contacts' names, companies, phone numbers, and other information appear in table columns.

3. Click **View** on the menu bar, point to **Current View**, and then click **By Company**. Contacts appear grouped by the company names you entered earlier.

4. If necessary, click the **Expand** button ⊞ to display the names in each group.

5. Click **View** on the menu bar, point to **Current View**, and then click **By Category**. The contacts you created earlier are grouped in three categories: Business, Suppliers, and Key Customer.

6. If necessary, click ⊞ to display the names in each group. See Figure 3-17.

Figure 3-17   CONTACTS GROUPED BY CATEGORY

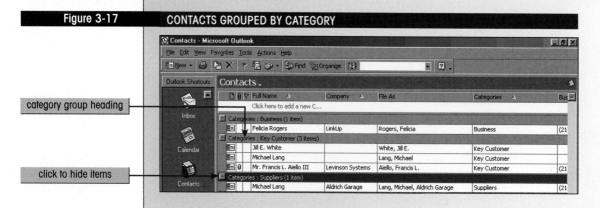

category group heading

click to hide items

7. Click **View** on the menu bar, point to **Current View**, and then click **Detailed Address Cards**.

You can change the way you view your contacts at any time, depending on the task you need to accomplish.

Editing Contacts

Any aspect of a contact's information may change over time. A person or company may move to a new street address, or be assigned a new area code. A person may change jobs periodically. You may discover that you entered information incorrectly. Rather than deleting the card with the wrong information and starting over, you can update the existing contact card as needed by double-clicking the contact to open the Contact window and edit the information. You also can make changes directly in the Contacts Information viewer from the Address Card or Detailed Address Card view.

Felicia tells you Jill White has moved recently to 27 Hamilton Street. You'll make this correction directly in the Information viewer.

To edit a contact:

1. If necessary, click the **WX** button along the right side of the Information viewer, and use the scroll bars to display Jill White's contact information.

   TROUBLE? If you don't have a WX button, then click the W button on the right side of the Information viewer.

2. Click to the left of the street address in Jill's contact card to display the insertion point.

   TROUBLE? If the insertion point doesn't appear, then again click to the left of the street address.

3. Drag to select **19 Hillcrest Way**. The entire street address is selected. See Figure 3-18.

Figure 3-18	EDITING A CONTACT CARD

4. Type **27 Hamilton Street** to revise the address.

5. Click anywhere outside Jill's contact card. Outlook saves the changes.

Just this one simple change demonstrates an advantage of Outlook over a paper system. No matter how small or in-depth the edits you need to make are, your contact list remains neat and legible.

Printing a Contact List

Although most of the time you'll work with your contacts within Outlook, sometimes a printed list is helpful, such as when you need to hand out group members contact information at a meeting. Outlook provides a variety of printing styles for your contacts; the available options differ depending on whether a card or table view is selected. The card views can be printed as successive blocks of information, in memo format on separate pages, or as a phone list with select information. The table views enable you to print only the actual list format you see. In either case, the printout can include all your contacts or only selected contacts.

You'll print your entire contact list.

To print your contact list:

1. Click the **Print** button 🖨 on the Standard toolbar. The Print dialog box opens.

2. Click **Card Style** in the Print style area, if it is not already selected.

3. Click the **All items** option button in the Print range area, if necessary, to indicate that you want to print the five contacts you created earlier. See Figure 3-19.

Figure 3-19	PRINT DIALOG BOX

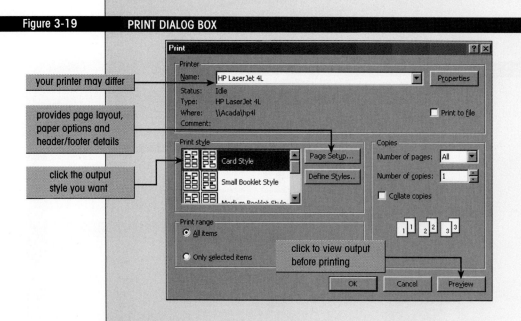

TROUBLE? If your contact list has more than five contacts, your printout will include all the contacts visible in the Information viewer.

4. Click the **Page Setup** button. The Page Setup: Card Style dialog box opens. You can change the layout and look of the printout from here.

5. In the Options area, click the **Blank forms at end** list arrow, and then click **None**. This ensures that you do not print any extra forms for jotting down information about new contacts.

6. Click the **OK** button to return to the Print dialog box.

7. Click the **OK** button to send the contact list to the printer.

The contact list prints without blank forms.

Creating a Contacts Distribution List

Recall that a distribution list stores the names of a related group of contacts as one entry. When you want to send an e-mail, write a letter, or schedule time to all members of that group, you select the group name from the Contacts list in the Address Book.

REFERENCE WINDOW RW

Creating a Distribution List
- Click Actions on the menu bar, and then click New Distribution List.
- Click the Select Members button near the top of the Distribution List window.
- Click the Show names from the list arrow, and then click Contacts.
- Double-click the names you want to add to the distribution list, and then click the OK button.
- Click in the Name text box, and then type a contact name for the distribution list.
- Click the Save and Close button on the Standard toolbar.

You'll create a distribution list that includes all of LinkUp's customers.

To create a contacts distribution list:

1. Click **Actions** on the menu bar, and then click **New Distribution List**. The Distribution List window opens.

2. Type **LinkUp Members** in the Name text box. This is the contact name for the distribution list.

3. Click the **Select Members** button below the Name text box. The Select Members dialog box opens.

4. Click the **Show Names from the** list arrow, and then click **Contacts**. A contact appears in the left list box once for each e-mail address and fax number. See Figure 3-20.

Figure 3-20   **SELECT MEMBERS DIALOG BOX**

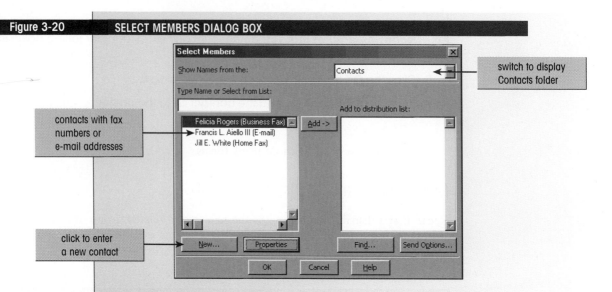

contacts with fax numbers or e-mail addresses

switch to display Contacts folder

click to enter a new contact

You'll move the two members into the distribution list.

5. Double-click **Francis L. Aiello III (E-mail)** to move the contact to the Add to distribution list box. Double-clicking the name is the same as clicking the name and then clicking the Add button.

6. Move **Jill E. White (E-mail)** to the Add to distribution list box, and then click the **OK** button.

7. Click the **Categories** button, click **Key Customer** in the Categories dialog box, and then click the **OK** button. See Figure 3-21.

Figure 3-21   **COMPLETED DISTRIBUTION LIST WINDOW**

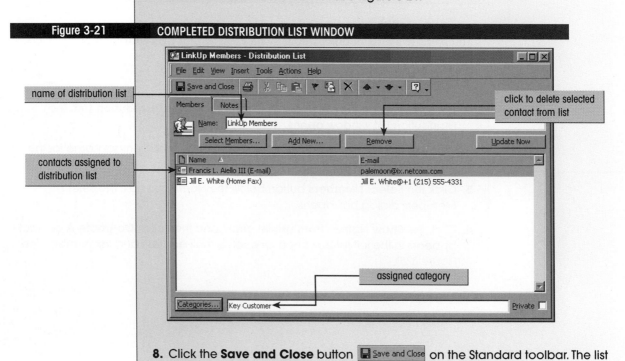

name of distribution list

click to delete selected contact from list

contacts assigned to distribution list

assigned category

8. Click the **Save and Close** button [Save and Close] on the Standard toolbar. The list appears in the Contacts Information viewer with the group name displayed, as shown in Figure 3-22.

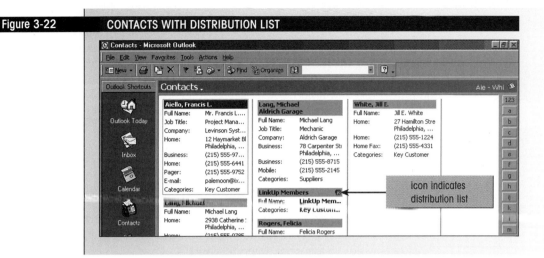

Figure 3-22   **CONTACTS WITH DISTRIBUTION LIST**

You can use the LinkUp Members distribution list contact just as you would any one-person contact.

Sending Contact Information to Others

Whatever reason you may need to send some of your contacts to others, you can do so quickly. When you forward contacts to a colleague or friend, or receive contacts from them, you can pass along or enter the information without retyping or copying and pasting the information. When you forward contact information as an Outlook Contact window, it contains the same data contained in your Contacts folder. Alternatively, you can send contact information as a vCard. A **vCard** is a file that contains a contact's personal information, such as the contact's name, mailing address, phone numbers, and e-mail address. The vCard files are compatible with other popular communication and information manager programs, including Lotus Organizer, Netscape Communicator, and Sidekick. You also can use vCards to exchange contact information with handheld personal digital assistants (PDAs) such as PalmPilot.

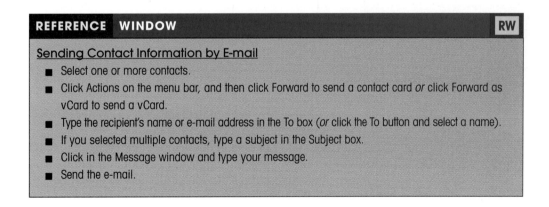

REFERENCE WINDOW   **RW**

Sending Contact Information by E-mail

- Select one or more contacts.
- Click Actions on the menu bar, and then click Forward to send a contact card *or* click Forward as vCard to send a vCard.
- Type the recipient's name or e-mail address in the To box (*or* click the To button and select a name).
- If you selected multiple contacts, type a subject in the Subject box.
- Click in the Message window and type your message.
- Send the e-mail.

You'll send contact information as a contact card and a vCard by e-mail.

Sending Contact Information by E-mail

If the recipient uses Outlook, you probably want to send the entire contact card. Not only are you sending the most complete information, but also the recipient can quickly drag the contact into their own Contacts folder. You can send one or more contact cards by e-mail at one time. Press and hold the Ctrl key as you click contacts to select nonadjacent entries; click the first contact and press and hold the Shift key as you click the last contact to select consecutive entries.

To forward contact information:

1. Click **Lang, Michael Aldrich Garage** to select that contact.

2. Click **Actions** on the menu bar, and then click **Forward**. A Message window opens, with an icon for the selected contact. The subject lists the selected contact name—in this case, Michael Lang.

3. Type **Francis L. Aiello** in the To box.

4. Click in the message body and type **Michael is LinkUp's ace mechanic. I highly recommend him. His contact information is attached.**, press the **Enter** key twice, and then type your name. See Figure 3-23.

Figure 3-23	E-MAIL WITH FORWARDED CONTACT CARD

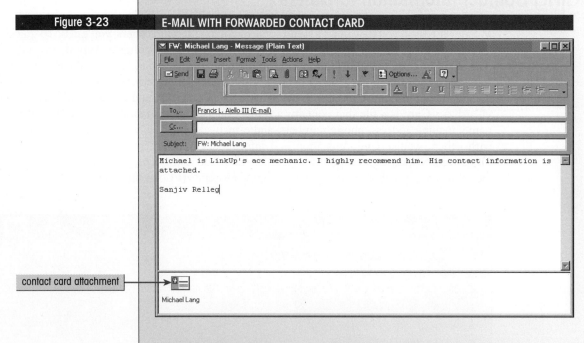

contact card attachment

TROUBLE? If your e-mail message is in a different font, Outlook is probably set up for Rich Text or HTML format rather than Plain Text. The process of creating a message works the same; just continue with Step 5.

5. Send the e-mail.

The process for sending a vCard is similar.

TUTORIAL 3 MANAGING CONTACTS**OUT** 3.23   OUTLOOK

Sending a vCard by E-mail

A vCard is appropriate to send when the recipient is not using Outlook. There are two methods for creating a vCard. One saves the vCard file, and the other does not. If you want to save the file, you can use the Save As command on the File menu to create a vCard for a selected contact. If you don't need to save the file, you can create a vCard for a contact and start an e-mail message in one step.

To forward contact information:

1. Click **Rogers, Felicia** to select that contact.

2. Click **Actions** on the menu bar, and then click **Forward as vCard**. A Message window opens, with an icon for the contact you selected. The subject lists the contact name.

3. Type **Francis L. Aiello** in the To box.

4. Click in the message body and type **LinkUp tries to distribute its cars evenly among its members. If you feel that your neighborhood has a high enough demand to justify an additional car, you might consider contacting Felicia Rogers. Her contact information is attached.**, press the **Enter** key twice, and then type your name. See Figure 3-24.

| Figure 3-24 | E-MAIL WITH FORWARDED VCARD |

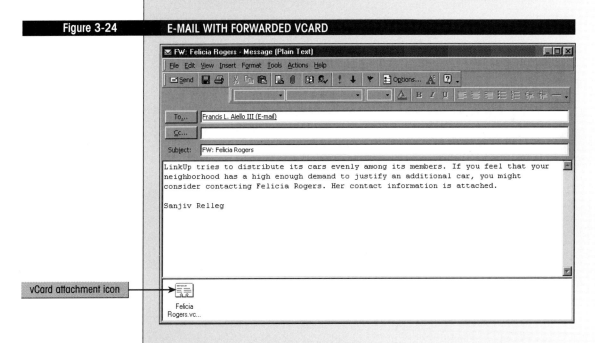

vCard attachment icon

TROUBLE? If your e-mail message is in a different font, Outlook is probably set up for Rich Text or HTML format rather than Plain Text. The process works the same; just continue with Step 5.

5. Send the e-mail.

You can also attach vCard files that you created earlier and saved to e-mail messages.

Receiving a Contact and vCard

Sometimes you'll be the recipient of forwarded contact information. Whether you receive a contact card or a vCard, you can add the contact information you receive by e-mail to your Contacts folder without retyping information. The process is the same for contact cards or vCards.

You'll download the messages you sent, and enter the vCard as a new contact.

To download and read your messages:

1. Switch to the **Inbox**, and then download your e-mail messages, if necessary.

2. Double-click the **Michael Lang** message to open it in its own window, read the message, and then double-click the **Michael Lang (Aldrich Garage)** attachment icon at the bottom of the window to open the file.

   TROUBLE? If the only HTML attachment received was the body of the e-mail message, not the contact fields, and you are using Lotus Notes or cc:Mail, you can complete the following steps to be able to send and receive contact information: (1) Click Tools on the menu bar, click Services. (2) Click MS Outlook support of cc:Mail in the list box, and then click the Properties button. (3) On the Delivery tab, click the Send using Microsoft Exchange rich text format option button. (4) Click the OK button in each dialog box. If your mail server cannot accept messages formatted in HTML, just continue with the tutorial.

3. Review the contact information, close the file, and then close the message.

4. Open the **Felicia Rogers** message, read it, and then double-click the **Felicia Rogers** attachment icon to open the file.

5. If necessary, click the **Open it** option button in the Opening Mail Attachment dialog box, and then click the **OK** button.

6. Review the information in the vCard, and then click the **Cancel** button to close it.

Next, you'll create a new contact card for Felicia Rogers from the vCard.

To create a new contact card from a vCard:

1. Drag the **Felicia Rogers** icon from the Message window to the **Outlook** button on the taskbar, pause over the button until the main Outlook window opens, and then drag the icon over the **Contacts** folder on the Outlook Bar. See Figure 3-25.

| Figure 3-25 | DRAGGING VCARD ICON TO CONTACTS FOLDER |

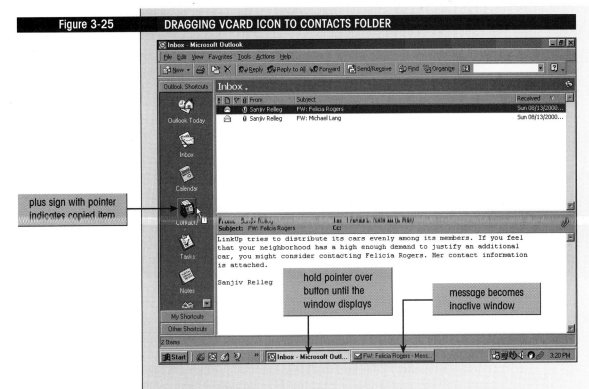

plus sign with pointer
indicates copied item

hold pointer over
button until the
window displays

message becomes
inactive window

2. Release the mouse button. A new Contact window opens with all the information entered from the vCard.

3. Review the information on the General tab, and then click the **Save and Close** button ![Save and Close] on the Standard toolbar.

   Because Felicia Rogers' information already appears in your contact list, the Duplicate Contact Detected dialog box opens. This time, you'll combine the two contacts.

4. Click **Update new information from this contact to the existing one** option button, and then click the **OK** button.

5. Close the Message window.

6. Switch to the **Contacts** folder.

You have created, edited, and printed a contact list of some of LinkUp's members, vendors, and employees, and then exchanged specific contact's information by e-mail. In Session 3.2, you will work with this list by communicating with specific contacts by e-mail and letter. Then you will send a form letter to only the LinkUp members, informing them of the latest cars being added to the LinkUp fleet.

Session 3.1 QUICK CHECK

1. True or False: In Outlook, a contact is a person, but not an organization.

2. What is the purpose of the File As name?

3. Why should you assign categories to contacts?

4. What happens if you try to enter a contact with the same name or e-mail address as an existing contact?

5. Explain the purpose of views in Outlook.

6. What is a vCard?

7. Describe the process for selecting nonadjacent contacts.

8. How do you add the information from a vCard into your contact list?

SESSION 3.2

In this session, you will learn how to work with your contact list. You'll communicate with your contacts by sending an e-mail and writing a letter to a contact. Next you will organize your contacts by categories, filter the contacts to view only LinkUp members, and change the sort order of the filtered list. Then you'll merge the filtered contact list and letter Felicia wrote to create personalized form letters. Finally you'll remove the filter and sort and delete contacts.

Working with Contacts

Once you have set up a contact list, there are many ways to work with it. You can access contacts from any folder and integrate them with other Outlook items. You can associate a contact with any Outlook item much as you would assign a category to the item. For example, you can link an appointment, meeting, and task to a contact by opening that item's window, clicking the Contacts button at the bottom of the window, and then selecting the contact. You can also connect one contact to another. This is helpful in keeping related contacts associated. In addition, a contact list enables you to more easily perform a variety of daily activities, including:

- Sending an e-mail to a contact
- Creating a printed letter to a contact
- Scheduling an appointment or a meeting with a contact
- Assigning a task to a contact
- Dialing a contact's phone number from Outlook (as long as you have a modem installed on your computer and the computer is connected to a phone line)

These are probably the most common actions you'll perform. You can do any of these activities for a single contact or any of the first four for a distribution list.

Sending an E-mail to a Contact

Sending an e-mail message to one or more contacts follows the same process as sending a message to someone in your Personal Address Book. You can quickly set up and send a message to anyone in the Contacts folder, as long as the contact has an e-mail address.

Felicia asks you to send Francis an e-mail message reminding him to use the LinkUp credit card to pay for refilling a car.

To send an e-mail message to a contact:

1. If you took a break after the previous session, make sure Outlook is running, the Contacts folder is displayed, and the Information viewer is set to Detailed Address Cards.

2. Click **Aiello, Francis L.** in the Contacts information viewer to select that contact.

3. Click the **New Message to Contact** button 🖼 on the Standard toolbar. A Message window opens addressed to Francis (your e-mail address) in the To box.

   You enter a subject and message and any attachments just as you would any other e-mail message.

4. Create an e-mail with the subject **Paying for gas** and the message **Please use the LinkUp credit card you received with your membership package to purchase any gas you put into LinkUp automobiles. We cannot reimburse you for any gas charges billed to your personal credit card. Thank you.**

5. Press the **Enter** key twice and type your name. See Figure 3-26.

Figure 3-26	E-MAIL TO CONTACT

your message may be in HTML

e-mail address entered by Outlook; yours will be different

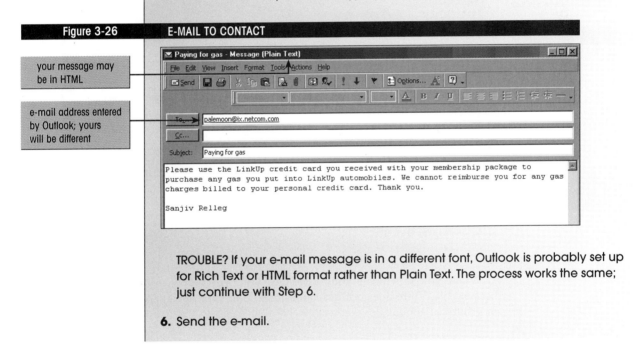

TROUBLE? If your e-mail message is in a different font, Outlook is probably set up for Rich Text or HTML format rather than Plain Text. The process works the same; just continue with Step 6.

6. Send the e-mail.

You send an e-mail to a distribution list using the same steps, except you select the group name in the Contacts folder instead of an individual contact. Everyone on the list receives the same message. If someone doesn't have an e-mail address, their name is entered in the To box as a reminder to enter the address.

Sending personal e-mails to groups of family and friends or sending commercial e-mails to people who request them are acceptable uses of distribution lists. Sending an unsolicited commercial e-mail, such as an advertisement, to a distribution list is an unacceptable use. For more information about unsolicited commercial e-mail, you can visit the Coalition Against Unsolicited Commercial Email Web site at **www.cauce.org**, the Internet Mail Consortium Web site at **www.imc.org/imc-spam**, or the Federal Trade Commission Web site at **www.ftc.gov** and search for **unsolicited commercial e-mail**.

To send an e-mail to a distribution list:

1. Click **LinkUp Members** in the Contacts information viewer to select the distribution list.

2. Click the **New Message to Contact** button 🖼 on the Standard toolbar. A Message window opens addressed to the LinkUp Members distribution list in the To box.

3. Create an e-mail with the subject **Monthly billing** and the message **LinkUp will charge members' credit cards for their previous month's usage on the third business day of each month. The new billing date goes into effect next month. Thank you.**

4. Press the **Enter** key twice and type your name. See Figure 3-27.

| Figure 3-27 | MESSAGE TO DISTRIBUTION LIST |

your message may be in HTML

distribution list

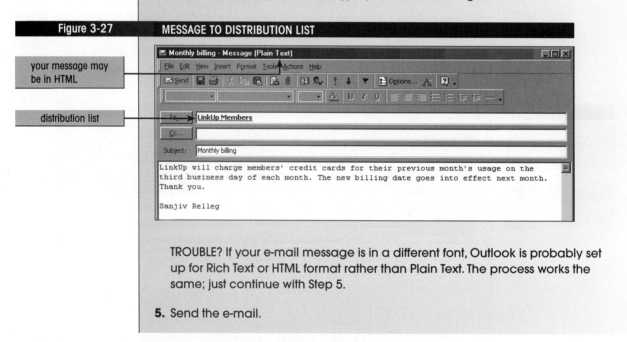

TROUBLE? If your e-mail message is in a different font, Outlook is probably set up for Rich Text or HTML format rather than Plain Text. The process works the same; just continue with Step 5.

5. Send the e-mail.

When you download your messages you will receive one undeliverable message because Jill White does not have an e-mail address. You can also write letters to contacts or groups of contacts.

Writing a Letter to a Contact or Distribution List

Although e-mail is handy for sending quick messages, you may need to create a printed letter that you can fax or mail to a contact. When you write a letter to a distribution list contact, every contact receives the same letter. Outlook uses the Word Letter Wizard to help you create the letter. The **Letter Wizard** is a tool that takes you step by step through the letter-writing process in Word. In the wizard, you select the look and format of the letter, verify the recipient's name and mailing address and your sender information, and then select a salutation and closing. The letter document then opens, ready for you to type the letter body.

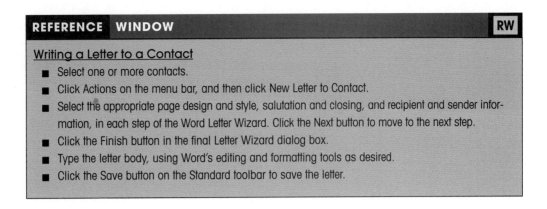

REFERENCE WINDOW **RW**

Writing a Letter to a Contact
- Select one or more contacts.
- Click Actions on the menu bar, and then click New Letter to Contact.
- Select the appropriate page design and style, salutation and closing, and recipient and sender information, in each step of the Word Letter Wizard. Click the Next button to move to the next step.
- Click the Finish button in the final Letter Wizard dialog box.
- Type the letter body, using Word's editing and formatting tools as desired.
- Click the Save button on the Standard toolbar to save the letter.

You'll write a letter to Jill White, welcoming her as a new LinkUp member.

To write a letter to a contact:

1. Click **White, Jill E.** to select that contact.

2. Click **Actions** on the menu bar, and then click **New Letter to Contact**. A blank document opens in Word and the Letter Wizard appears. See Figure 3-28.

Figure 3-28 | LETTER WIZARD—STEP 1 OF 4 DIALOG BOX

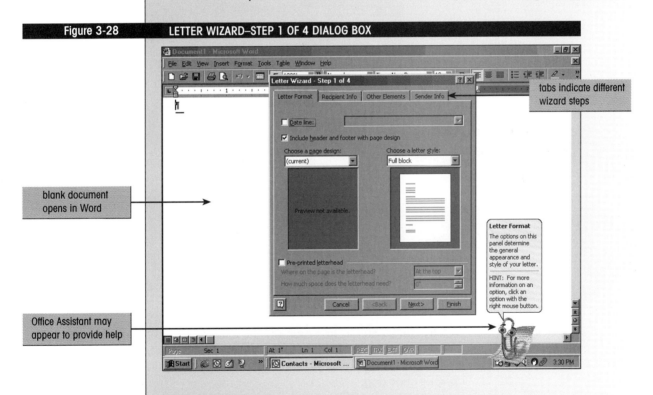

blank document opens in Word

Office Assistant may appear to provide help

3. Click the **Choose a page design** list arrow, and then click **Contemporary Letter**.

4. Verify that **Full block** appears in the Choose a letter style list box, and then click the **Next** button.

The name and mailing address of the contact you selected in Outlook appears as the recipient information. You need only to select the letter salutation. Word provides several options in each category or you can enter your own.

5. Click the **Business** option button. The standard business salutation "Dear Jill E. White:" appears in the list box.

The next step provides opportunities to enter other information, such as a reference line, subject line, or courtesy copy information. You don't need to enter any of this, so you'll skip right to the last step.

6. Click the **Sender Info** tab. Your name and address already appear, so you need only specify the letter's closing.

TROUBLE? If your name and address don't appear, then you didn't enter complete personal contact information when you set up your Outlook profile. Type your name in the Sender's name text box and type your address in the Return address text box, pressing the Enter key to place the street on its own line.

7. Click the **Complimentary closing** list arrow, and then click **Sincerely yours,**.

8. Type **Membership Services** in the Job title text box, and then type **LinkUp** in the Company text box. See Figure 3-29.

Figure 3-29	LETTER WIZARD–STEP 4 OF 4 DIALOG BOX

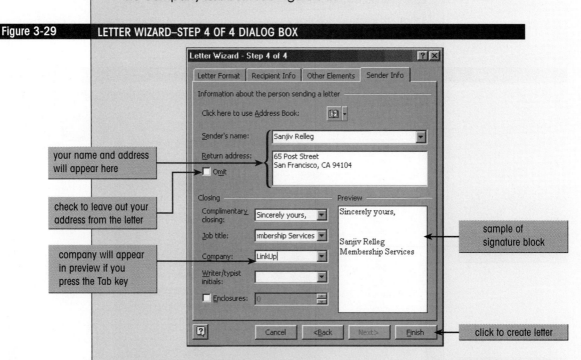

your name and address will appear here

check to leave out your address from the letter

company will appear in preview if you press the Tab key

sample of signature block

click to create letter

9. Click the **Finish** button. In a moment the letter opens, with placeholder text in the body selected so you can begin typing. When you type the letter in Word, you have access to all of Word's word processing and formatting tools, including spell checking.

To type the letter:

1. Type **Welcome to LinkUp! Our insurance company has approved your driving record at the standard rate. This means that your annual membership is $120, or just $10 per month. As a member, you'll have access to our entire fleet of cars. Just visit our reservation Web site to reserve a vehicle near you. Rental fees are calculated on an hourly rate of $2.50 and $0.50 per mile. Remember that these fees include insurance and gasoline. If the gas tank dips below the 1/4 mark, please fill up the car and use your LinkUp credit card to pay. You will receive your LinkUp credit card in a separate mailing.**

2. Press the **Enter** key, and then type **If you have any questions, please do not hesitate to contact me. Thank you.** See Figure 3-30.

Figure 3-30	FINISHED LETTER TO CONTACT

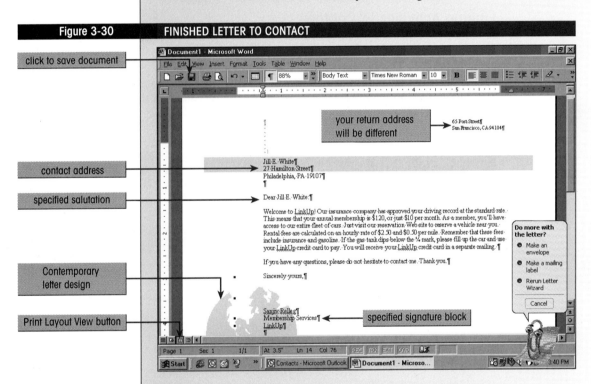

click to save document

your return address will be different

contact address

specified salutation

Contemporary letter design

Print Layout View button

specified signature block

TROUBLE? If you do not see the shaded bar and graphic, then Word is displaying the letter in Normal view. Click the Print Layout View button.

3. If the Office Assistant is open, click the **Cancel** button in the Office Assistant to close it.

4. Click the **Save** button on the Standard toolbar, and then save the letter as **Jill White Letter** in the **Tutorial** folder within the **Tutorial.03** folder on your Data Disk.

5. Click the **Print** button on the Standard toolbar to print the letter.

6. Click the **Close** button in the Word title bar to close the letter and exit Word.

You can use any or all of the features and tools in Word to format and enhance your letter.

Scheduling an Appointment or a Meeting with a Contact

Contacts can help simplify the management of your calendar. Whenever you need to set aside time for someone in your contact list, you can quickly schedule an appointment or meeting by dragging that contact from the Contacts Information viewer to the Calendar icon on the Outlook Bar or by clicking New Meeting Request or New Appointment on the Actions menu. A blank Appointment window opens, with the contact name in the Contacts text box at the bottom of the window. You complete the window with the relevant information.

The process for assigning a task to a contact works similarly. Select the contact to whom you want to assign the task, and then click New Task for Contact on the Actions menu. You can also drag the contact to the Tasks icon on the Outlook bar. The task request opens, and you complete the window with the appropriate information.

Linking Activities to Contacts

One way to track tasks, appointments, e-mail, notes, or documents related to a contact is to **link**, or connect, them to the contact. When you create an Outlook item, such as a task, you can link it to the related contact by entering the contact's name in the Contacts text box. You also can link any existing item to a contact. Then you can open the contact from any linked item just by clicking the contact's name in the Contacts text box.

REFERENCE WINDOW   **RW**

Linking an Activity to a Contact

- Open the contact to which you want to link an item.
- Click Actions on the menu bar, point to Link, and then click Items.
- Click the folder that contains the items you want to link in the Look in list box, and then click one or more items in the Items list.
- Click the OK button.

When you entered Francis Aiello's birthday in his contact card, Outlook linked the recurring event with his contact.

To view an event linked to a contact:

1. Double-click **Francis Aiello's** contact card in the Contacts Information viewer to open it.

2. Click the **Activities** tab in the Contact window.

3. Double-click **Francis L. Aiello III's Birthday** in the list. The Recurring Event window opens. See Figure 3-31.

Figure 3-31	EVENT WINDOW FOR FRANCIS L. AIELLO III'S BIRTHDAY

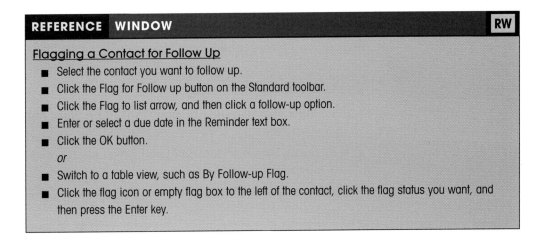

event linked to contact

Contacts... | Mr. Francis L. Aiello III | Categories... | | Private ☑

4. Click the **Close** button ☒ on the title bar of the Recurring Event window to close it.

5. Click the **Close** button ☒ on the title bar of the Contact window to close it.

Flagging a Contact for Follow Up

At times, you need to remember to perform some activity related to a contact, such as calling that person to confirm a lunch appointment or verifying the status of a project. Rather than jotting yourself a reminder note, you draw attention to the contact by flagging the contact for follow up. The standard flags are: Follow up, Call, Arrange Meeting, Send E-mail, and Send Letter. After you determine the action, you can set a reminder due date by which to complete the follow up. As with your schedule, you can select a due date from a calendar or enter a descriptive natural language date, such as "next Tuesday". If a due date passes without the flag being changed to completed, then the contact becomes red as a visual reminder of the missed deadline.

REFERENCE WINDOW   **RW**

__Flagging a Contact for Follow Up__
- Select the contact you want to follow up.
- Click the Flag for Follow up button on the Standard toolbar.
- Click the Flag to list arrow, and then click a follow-up option.
- Enter or select a due date in the Reminder text box.
- Click the OK button.
  or
- Switch to a table view, such as By Follow-up Flag.
- Click the flag icon or empty flag box to the left of the contact, click the flag status you want, and then press the Enter key.

You'll flag the contact card for Jill to send her a letter.

To flag a contact for follow up:

1. Select the **Jill White** contact card in the Contacts Information viewer.

2. Click the **Flag for Follow Up** button ⚑ on the Standard toolbar. The Flag for Follow Up dialog box opens. See Figure 3-32.

Figure 3-32   **FLAG FOR FOLLOW UP DIALOG BOX**

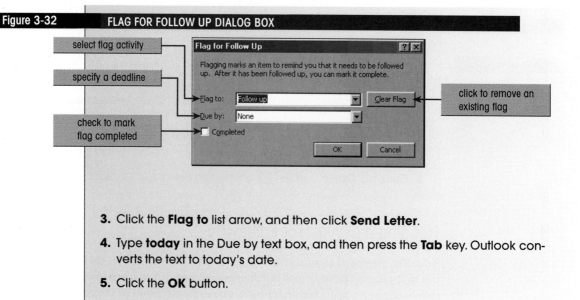

3. Click the **Flag to** list arrow, and then click **Send Letter**.

4. Type **today** in the Due by text box, and then press the **Tab** key. Outlook converts the text to today's date.

5. Click the **OK** button.

The Address Cards view and the Detailed Address Cards view both display the follow-up reminder as the first line of the contact card. It also appears in the information banner of the open contact card.

You can change the view to display all the contacts flagged for follow up in one group. This enables you to look at activities you need to complete. You can then plan your schedule, by dragging flagged contacts to the Notes, Tasks, or Calendar folder to create notes, set up tasks, or schedule appointments to complete your follow ups. You can also check off completed follow-up activities, clear flags that are no longer necessary, or add flags to other contacts.

Because you already sent the letter to Jill, you'll change the flag to complete.

To view contacts by flags:

1. Click **View** on the menu bar, point to **Current View**, and then click **By Follow-up Flag**.

2. If necessary, click the **Expand** button [+] for each category to display the hidden contacts.

3. Click the **flag** icon ⚑ to the left of Jill's contact. A list box appears. See Figure 3-33.

Figure 3-33   **FLAGGING A CONTACT FROM THE INFORMATION VIEWER**

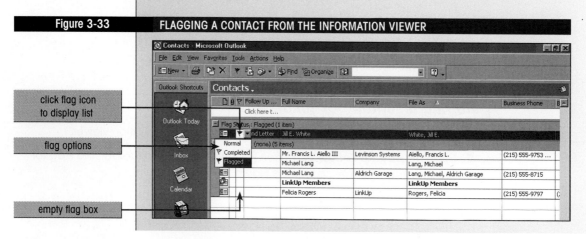

4. Click **Completed**, and then press the **Enter** key. Outlook changes that contact's flag status and moves it into the appropriate group.

5. Click the flag box for Francis, click **Flagged**, and then press the **Enter** key. Again, Outlook changes the flag status and moves the contact into the appropriate group.

   The contacts are organized into three possible groups: contacts that have outstanding flags (red flag icon), contacts that have completed flags (gray flag icon), and contacts that have no flags (called cleared or normal). If you want to add a deadline or assign an activity other than follow up, you must open the Flag for Follow Up dialog box for that contact.

6. Click the **Francis L. Aiello** contact to select it.

7. Click the **Flag for Follow Up** button 🏳 on the Standard toolbar, type **yesterday** in the Due by text box, and then click the **OK** button.

8. Click the **OK** button in the dialog box to confirm that the day and time are in the past and no reminder will be set.

9. Click another contact to deselect Francis's contact. Francis's contact is now red, indicating it is past due. See Figure 3-34.

| Figure 3-34 | **CONTACTS WITH FLAGS** |

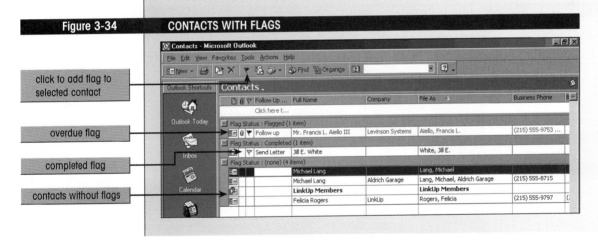

click to add flag to selected contact

overdue flag

completed flag

contacts without flags

The flags provide one way to organize your contacts. There are many other ways to arrange them.

Organizing Contacts

The ability to organize and reorganize contacts quickly and cleanly is one of the most obvious advantages of Outlook over a paper address book. For example, you might arrange your contacts in groups by their assigned categories. You might display and hide certain contacts based on criteria that you set, such as contacts that reside in a certain city. You can choose what order you want displayed contacts to appear in the Information viewer, such as alphabetically by last name. For even greater contact management, you can combine any or all of these organization methods to create the exact presentation of your contacts that you want. This kind of flexibility is simply not available with paper address books.

Organizing Contacts by Category

The list of contacts you created earlier includes more than just members. Because each contact has been assigned a category, you can organize all the contacts by category by changing the view. The Organize pane provides a quick way to switch between views.

To organize contacts by category:

1. Click the **Organize** button ![Organize] on the Standard toolbar. The Organize pane opens, providing several ways to arrange your contacts—by folders, categories, or views.

2. Click **Using Views**. All the available views appear in the list box.

3. Click **By Category** in the Change your view list box. The contacts are organized into three categories—Business (staff), Key Customer (customers), and Suppliers (vendors). Any contact that has more than one category assigned appears in multiple groups.

4. If necessary, click the **Expand** button ![+] for each category to display the contacts. See Figure 3-35.

| Figure 3-35 | CONTACTS ORGANIZED BY CATEGORY |

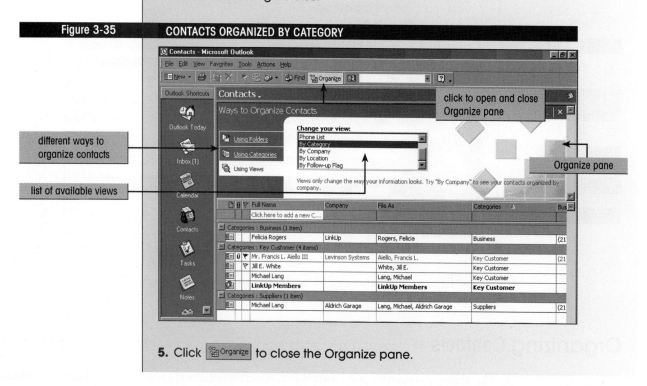

5. Click ![Organize] to close the Organize pane.

Arranging the contacts by category, follow-up flags, company, or other available views is helpful in separating all the contacts into groups. However, sometimes, you'll want to work with only a subset of your contacts (or other Outlook items) and temporarily hide the ones you don't need.

Filtering a View

Felicia wants to see the contact cards for all the LinkUp members. You can display items in a folder that match a certain criteria by setting a **filter**. In this case, you'll filter the contacts to display only the ones assigned to the Key Customer category. The other contacts remain in the folder but are not visible until you remove the filter. A filter applies only to the current view. So if you set a filter in one view, and then switch views, you'll see all the available contacts, not the set of filtered contacts, in the new view.

REFERENCE WINDOW   **RW**

Filtering a View
- Click View on the menu bar, point to Current View, click Customize Current View, and then click the Filter button in the View Summary dialog box (*or* right-click the Information viewer, and then click Filter).
- Set the filter options you want in the Filter dialog box (*or* click the Clear All button to remove an existing filter).
- Click the OK button in the Filter dialog box.
- Click the OK button in the View Summary dialog box, if necessary.

You'll filter the LinkUp contacts to display only the members in the Key Customers field.

To apply a filter:

1. Click **View** on the menu bar, point to **Current View**, and then click **Customize Current View**. The View Summary dialog box opens.

2. Click the **Filter** button. The Filter dialog box opens, offering criteria you can set to filter the contacts, such as by keyword or by e-mail address.

3. Click the **More Choices** tab, which provides additional filter options. See Figure 3-36.

Figure 3-36	FILTER DIALOG BOX

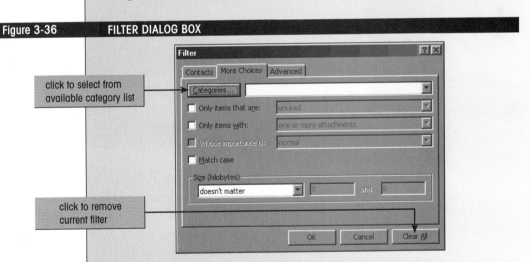

click to select from available category list

click to remove current filter

4. Click the **Categories** button to open the Categories dialog box, click **Key Customer** in the Available Categories list, and then click the **OK** button.

5. Click the **OK** button to return to the View Summary dialog box. Notice the filter settings in the View Summary dialog box. See Figure 3-37.

Figure 3-37 **VIEW SUMMARY DIALOG BOX**

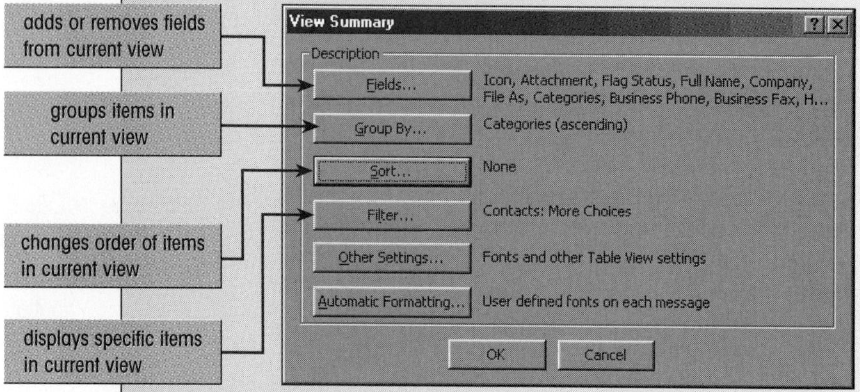

adds or removes fields from current view

groups items in current view

changes order of items in current view

displays specific items in current view

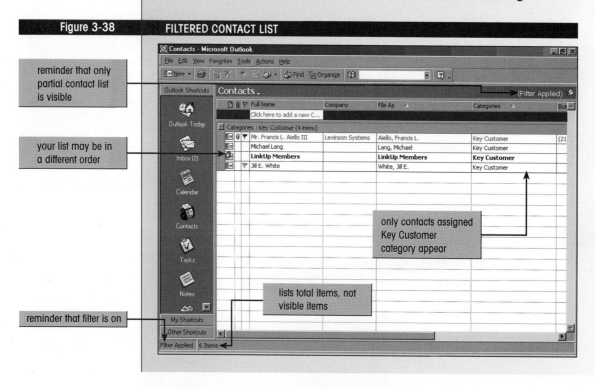

6. Click the **OK** button to return to the Information viewer. See Figure 3-38.

Figure 3-38 **FILTERED CONTACT LIST**

reminder that only partial contact list is visible

your list may be in a different order

reminder that filter is on

only contacts assigned Key Customer category appear

lists total items, not visible items

Only the contacts that match your filter appear in the folder. As a reminder, the words "Filter Applied" appear in the status bar and on the Folder Banner until you remove the filter from the view.

Sorting Contacts by Field

As you work with a filtered list of contacts, you might want to further organize them by changing their display order. Although Outlook often sorts contacts alphabetically by the File As field, you can re-sort contacts at any time. If you're using a table view, such as By Category, the quickest way to sort information is by clicking the appropriate column header. If you're in a card view, then you'll need to use the Sort dialog box.

The Sort dialog box enables you to select up to four fields by which to sort. Each subsequent sort field is applied to the subset of the sort. For example, if you sort contacts by company and then by name, Outlook first arranges the contacts by company and then arranges the contacts by name within each company. You can also specify the order of each sort: ascending or descending. **Ascending order** arranges items alphabetically (A to Z), chronologically (earliest to latest), or numerically (lowest to highest). **Descending order** reverses the ascending sort order—Z to A, latest to earliest, or highest to lowest.

REFERENCE WINDOW   **RW**

Sorting by Field

- Switch to the Information viewer in the view you want to sort.
- Click View on the menu bar, point to Current View, click Customize Current View, and then click the Sort button in the View Summary dialog box (or right-click the Information viewer, and then click Sort).
- Click the Select available fields from list arrow, and then click a subset of fields.
- Click the Sort items by list arrow, click a field name, and then click the Ascending or Descending option button.
- If necessary, change the available fields option, click the top Then by list arrow, click a field name, and then click the Ascending or Descending option button. Repeat for the bottom Then by list arrow.
- Click the OK button in the Sort dialog box.
- Click the OK button in the View Summary dialog box, if necessary.

Felicia wants to organize the contacts first by their ZIP code and then by their File As name.

To sort contacts using the Sort dialog box:

1. Click **View** on the menu bar, point to **Current View**, and then click **Customize Current View**. The View Summary dialog box opens.%

2. Click the **Sort** button. The Sort dialog box opens.

   Because there are such a variety of fields available by which to sort contacts, you can select a subset of fields to more easily find the field you want.

3. Click the **Select available fields from** list arrow, and then click **Address fields**.

4. Click the **Sort items by** list arrow, press **Z** to quickly move down the list, click **ZIP/Postal Code**, and then click the **Descending** option button.

5. Click the **Select available fields from** list arrow, click **Name fields**, click the active **Then by** list arrow, and then click **File As**. Your Sort dialog box should match Figure 3-39.

Figure 3-39   SORT DIALOG BOX

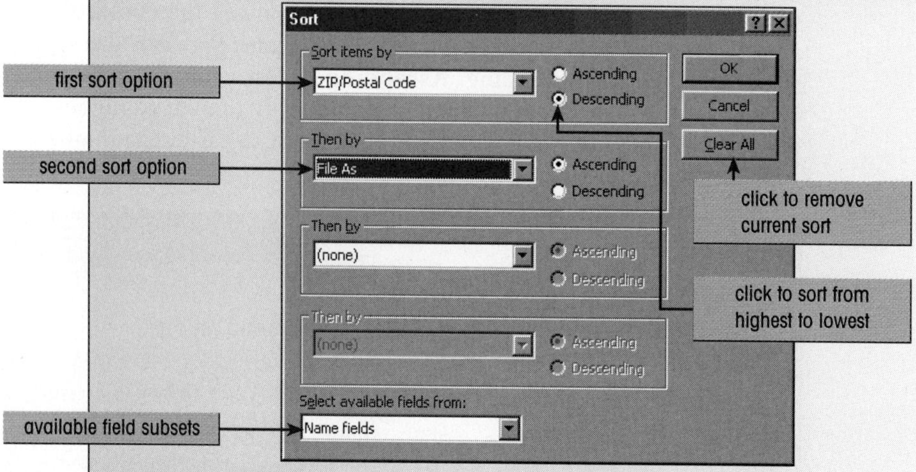

first sort option

second sort option

click to remove
current sort

click to sort from
highest to lowest

available field subsets

6. Click the **OK** button. Because you selected a field that is not visible in the current view, Outlook gives you the option of customizing the view by adding the ZIP/Postal Code field.

7. Click the **No** button. The group by, filter, and sort settings in the View Summary dialog box show how the contacts will be organized.

8. Click the **OK** button. Only the contacts assigned to the Key Customer category appear in the folder, in descending order by ZIP code (even though you can't see the ZIP fields), and then alphabetical order by the File As name.

Felicia asks you to send a letter to all the LinkUp members, informing them of the latest automobiles being added to the fleet. Because you want to send the letter to only the members, you can use the filtered view. The sort order you selected will enable you to more easily match the printed letters to their prepared envelopes. You'll create the letter with Word.

Creating a Word Mail Merge from Outlook

One of the most common activities businesses perform is to create one message and then send it to a large group of people by mail, fax, or e-mail. The trick to making people read these messages is to include a bit of personal information in each. If you send the message to your contacts or a distribution list, each person would receive the same message without any unique information. If you want to personalize each copy, you need to perform a mail merge.

What Is Mail Merge?

Mail merge is the process of combining a document file with a data file. A **document file** is the file that contains the standard text, such as the body of a letter in a Word document. A **data file** is the list of variable information, such as recipient names and addresses in an Outlook contact list. To specify what information to include in the document file from the data file, you insert **merge fields**, special codes that identify the variable information that should appear in that location. The letter you will create for Felicia will combine a standard message in a Word document with variable name and address information in your contact list.

REFERENCE WINDOW   **RW**

Merging Outlook Contacts and a Word Document
- Sort and filter, or select the contacts you want to use.
- Click Tools on the menu bar, and then click Mail Merge.
- Click the All contacts in current view option button, and then click the All contact fields option button.
- Browse for an existing document file or create a new one.
- Click the Document type list arrow, and then click the document option you want.
- Click the Merge to list arrow and click the output option you want.
- Click the OK button in the Mail Merge Contacts dialog box.
- Type the standard text as needed in the Word document, using Word's editing and formatting features.
- Click the Insert Mail Merge Field button on the Mail Merge toolbar, and then click the merge field you want to insert at the location of the insertion point in the Word document.
- Click the Save button on the Standard toolbar to save the document file.
- If necessary, click the View Merged Data button to preview the final letters.
- Click the Merge to New Document button on the Mail Merge toolbar (or click the Merge to Printer button or click the Merge button, select Electronic Message, and then click the OK button).
- Click the Save button to save the merged documents.

You'll start to create the letter to LinkUp members by specifying the mail merge document file, data file, document type, and output option.

Creating the Form Letter

When you start the mail merge process from Outlook, you determine whether to include every contact field available in Outlook or only those visible in the current view. You also choose which contacts to include in the merge—all contacts in the current view, selected contacts in the current view, or a filtered contact list. For the LinkUp letter, you'll use the filtered contact list as the data file so that you include only members, not vendors or LinkUp employees.

After you indicate which contacts to use for the data file, then you specify whether you want to create a new document for the mail merge or use an existing one. In this case, Felicia already created the letter.

Next, you select the type of document you want to create and the final output. The main document types—form letters, mailing labels, envelopes, and catalog—and the output options—new document, printer, and e-mail—are the same as those available in Word. Each document type creates a different format: Form letters combine standard text with merge fields to create correspondence. Mailing labels accesses Word templates for standard adhesive labels sold by Avery and other companies. Envelopes lets you select from standard mailing envelopes sizes. Catalog provides a way to create lists of certain data, such as a list of names and fax numbers. The output options provide the option of creating a file, hard copy, or message.

To create a mail merge form letter:

1. Click **Tools** on the menu bar, and then click **Mail Merge**. The Mail Merge Contacts dialog box opens. See Figure 3-40.

Figure 3-40	MAIL MERGE CONTACTS DIALOG BOX

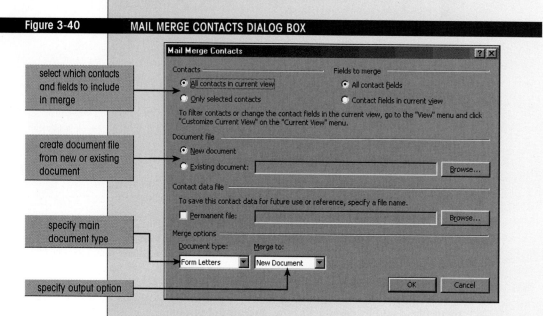

select which contacts and fields to include in merge

create document file from new or existing document

specify main document type

specify output option

The data file for this mail merge is the filtered contact list with access to all the available fields for each contact.

2. Click the **All contacts in current view** option button if it is not already selected, and then click the **All contact fields** option button.

   For this mail merge, you'll edit the letter that Felicia started rather than creating a new letter.

3. Click the **Existing document** option button, and click the **Browse** button.

4. Open the **LinkUp Letter** document in the **Tutorial** folder within the **Tutorial.03** folder on your Data Disk. Outlook opens and verifies the document.

   You want a form letter that you will save to a file.

5. If necessary, select **Form Letters** in the Document type list box in the Merge options area, and then select **New Document** in the Merge to list box.

6. Click the **OK** button. Because a distribution list cannot be used in a merge, a dialog box opens, indicating that the LinkUp Members distribution list will not be included.

7. Click the **OK** button in the dialog box. Word opens so you can finish the form letter.

   TROUBLE? If the Office Assistant opens, click the Edit MailMerge document option, right-click the Assistant, and then click Hide.

Once the document file opens in Word, you can enter the appropriate merge fields where you want to insert variable information. The current date should appear on the letter below the Word Art logo for LinkUp. The Mail Merge toolbar in Word provides all the tools you need to finish the form letter. As you insert merge fields, you also type any punctuation and spaces that should appear between fields, such as a comma and space between the city and state merge fields.

To insert merge fields:

1. Click in the second blank line below the date, click the **Insert Merge Field** button on the Mail Merge toolbar to display the list of available fields. See Figure 3-41.

Figure 3-41   MAIL MERGE FIELDS AVAILABLE IN WORD

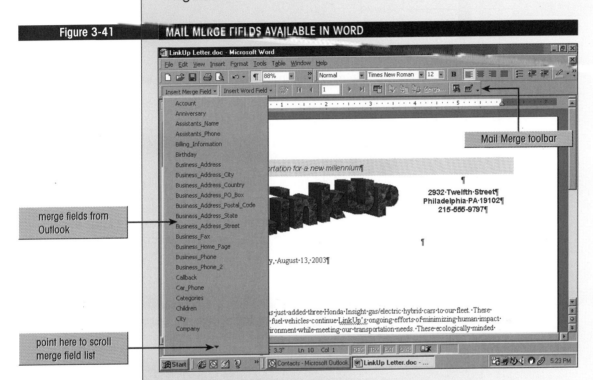

merge fields from Outlook

point here to scroll merge field list

TROUBLE? If you do not see the characters between words or paragraph markers, as shown in Figure 3-41, the nonprinting characters are hidden. If you would like to display them, click the Show/Hide button on the Word Standard toolbar. However, displaying these characters is a matter of preference and will not affect your work.

2. Click **Full_Name** (you may need to scroll through the fields in the drop-down list). The merge field is entered in the letter surrounded by brackets, which indicates that this is a field rather than regular text. See Figure 3-42.

Figure 3-42 | **LETTER WITH ONE MERGE FIELD**

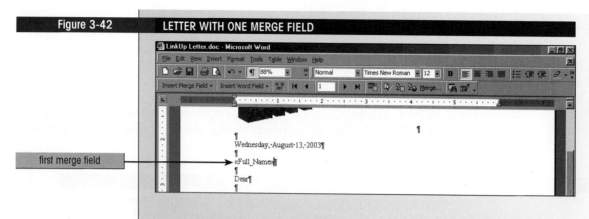

first merge field

3. Press the **Enter** key to move the insertion point to a new line.

4. Click the **Insert Merge Field** button on the Mail Merge toolbar, click **Street_Address**, and then press the **Enter** key.

5. Click the **Insert Merge Field** button on the Mail Merge toolbar, click **City**, type **,** (a comma), and then press the **spacebar**.

6. Insert the **State** merge field, press the **spacebar**, and then insert the **ZIPPostal_Code** merge field.

7. Click to the right of the word Dear in the salutation, press the **spacebar**, insert the **First_Name** merge field, and then type **:** (a colon). You have inserted the proper fields for the inside address and salutation of a business letter as shown in Figure 3-43.

Figure 3-43 | **LETTER WITH ALL MERGE FIELDS**

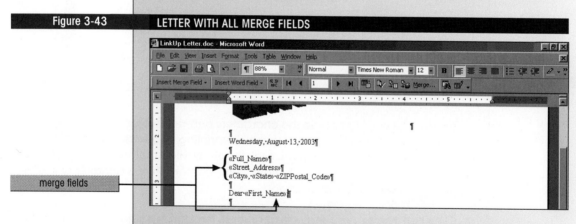

merge fields

8. Press and hold the **Ctrl** key, press the **End** key, and then release both keys to quickly go to the end of the letter, press the **Up arrow** key to place the insertion point in the blank line above Membership Services, and then type your name.

9. Click **File** on the menu bar, click **Save As** to open the Save As dialog box, and then save the document file with the filename **New Cars Document File** to the **Tutorial** folder within the **Tutorial.03** folder on your Data Disk.

With the data file specified and the document file saved, you're ready to merge the two.

Merging the Letter and Contacts

Although you already specified the merge option as new document in Outlook, you have a chance to change when you actually merge the letter and contacts. With buttons on the Word Mail Merge toolbar, you can select to merge to a new document, to the printer, or to e-mail. You want to leave the merge option as new document.

Before you actually merge the document file and the data file, you can preview how the letters will look. It is a good idea to view the merged data and document to ensure that all the contact information appears in the letters as you expected. Of course, if you have an extremely large data file, you may want to spot check the letters rather than viewing each one.

To merge the letter and contacts:

1. Click the **View Merged Data** button 〈〈 〉〉 on the Mail Merge toolbar. The merge fields are replaced by actual data. See Figure 3-44.

| Figure 3-44 | PREVIEWING THE MERGE |

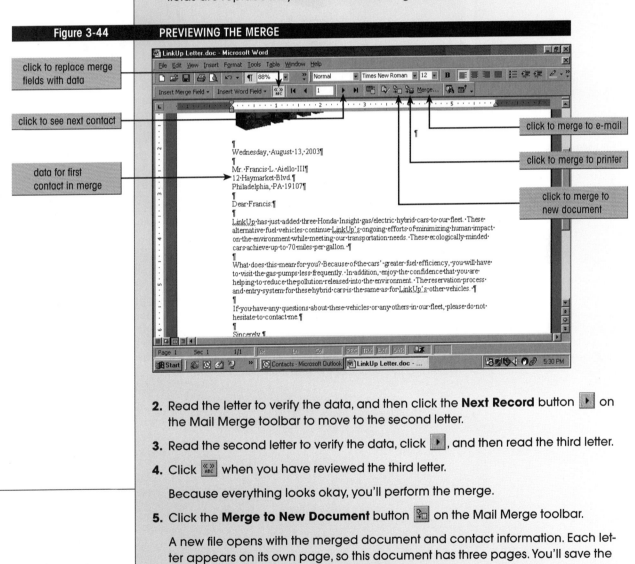

click to replace merge fields with data

click to see next contact

data for first contact in merge

click to merge to e-mail

click to merge to printer

click to merge to new document

2. Read the letter to verify the data, and then click the **Next Record** button ▶ on the Mail Merge toolbar to move to the second letter.

3. Read the second letter to verify the data, click ▶, and then read the third letter.

4. Click 〈〈 〉〉 when you have reviewed the third letter.

   Because everything looks okay, you'll perform the merge.

5. Click the **Merge to New Document** button 🔢 on the Mail Merge toolbar.

   A new file opens with the merged document and contact information. Each letter appears on its own page, so this document has three pages. You'll save the letters, and then preview and print them.

6. Click the **Save** button 🖫 on the Standard toolbar and then save the merged document as **New Cars Letters** in the **Tutorial** folder within the **Tutorial.03** folder on your Data Disk.

7. Click the **Print Preview** button 🔍 on the Standard toolbar to view the letters before printing them. See Figure 3-45.

Figure 3-45   MERGED LETTERS IN PRINT PREVIEW

click to display one page

letter is first of three

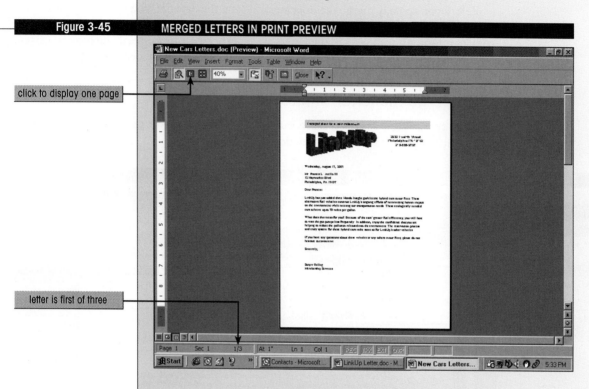

TROUBLE? If you see more than one letter, print preview is set to display multiple pages of a document. Click the One Page button on the Print Preview toolbar.

8. Scroll through all the letters, and then click the **Print** button 🖨 on the Print Preview toolbar to print all the letters.

9. Click the **Close** button on the Print Preview toolbar, click the **Close** button ✕ on the Word title bar to close Word, saving changes to the **New Cars Letters** document and the **New Cars Document File** document.

As you can see, writing a letter to one contact or many is a fairly simple task.

Cleaning Up

Once you're done with a particular organization or modified view, it is a good practice to return that view to its default. This ensures that you see all the available items each time. Also, you should remove any contacts that are outdated and that you no longer need. This keeps your contact list current and relevant.

Removing a Filter and Sort

Now that you've created the letters for the contacts in the Key Customers category, you can remove the filter to redisplay all the contacts and reset the default sort for the view.

To remove a filter and a sort:

1. Click **View** on the menu bar, point to **Current View**, and then click **Customize Current View**. The View Summary dialog box opens.

2. Click the **Filter** button to open the Filter dialog box, click the **Clear All** button, and then click the **OK** button.

3. Click the **Sort** button to open the Sort dialog box, click the **Clear All** button, and then click the **OK** button.

4. Click the **OK** button. Outlook returns the view to its default sort and filter settings.

5. Click **View** on the menu bar, point to **Current View**, and then click **Address Cards** to return to the default Contacts view.

Before finishing, you must delete any items you have created and stored in Outlook.

Deleting Contacts and Other Outlook Items

Before you finish up, you'll remove any contacts, calendar items, and e-mail messages you created while working in Outlook. Remember to use the Ctrl key or the Shift key to select multiple items.

To delete contacts and other Outlook items:

1. Select the six contact cards you created in this tutorial, press the **Delete** key.

2. Display the **Inbox**, select the three e-mails you created, press the **Delete** key, and then click the **Yes** button in the dialog box to confirm that you want to move the contacts to the Deleted Items folder.

3. Display the **Calendar**, switch to the **By Category** view, delete the recurring appointment for **Francis L. Aiello**, and then return to the **Day/Week/Month** view.

4. Display the **Sent Items** folder, and then delete the three messages you sent.

5. Right-click the **Deleted Items** folder on the Outlook Bar, click **Empty "Deleted Items" Folder**, and then click the **Yes** button to confirm the permanent deletion.

You have created, edited, and organized LinkUp contacts, as well as communicated with the contacts by sending individual e-mails and letters and personalized form letters. Felicia appreciates your help in keeping LinkUp members and vendors current and informed.

Session 3.2 QUICK CHECK

1. List three common activities you can perform with contacts.

2. What is the Letter Wizard?

3. What does a red flag icon next to a contact name indicate?

4. Describe what happens when you a filter a view.

5. Explain the difference between ascending and descending order in a sort?

6. What happens when you send a letter to a distribution list versus when you create a mail merge letter?

7. Explain the difference between a document file and a data file in a Mail Merge.

8. Define merge fields.

REVIEW ASSIGNMENTS

Felicia Rogers, founder and president of LinkUp, asks you to compile a contact list of the vendors the Philadelphia-based car sharing company uses. After creating the contacts, you'll write a letter to Felicia informing her of your status in locating a new mechanic. Then you'll create a form letter to all the current vendors, asking them for referrals.

1. Start Outlook, click the New button list arrow, and then click Contact to open a blank Contact window.

2. Enter the following contact: name "Joe Standingtree"; job title "Mechanic"; company name "Ace Engine Care"; business phone "215-555-8700 x12"; business fax "215-555-8763"; business mailing address "17 University Ave., Philadelphia PA 19287"; category "Suppliers"; Assistant name "Charley Boyd"; click the Save and New button.

3. Enter the following contact: name "Freida Cohn"; job title "Agent"; company name "A Plus Insurance"; business phone "215-555-3100 x645"; business fax "215-555-3101"; business mailing address "2949 Broad St., Philadelphia PA 19157"; category "Suppliers"; Manager's name "Eva Lorenson"; click the Save and New button.

4. Enter the following contact: name "Walt Camden"; company name "Shiny Cars Detailing"; business phone "215-555-6741"; business mailing address "841 Carpenter St., Philadelphia PA 19102"; category "Suppliers"; click the Save and New button.

5. Enter the following contact: name "Marya Little"; job title "Agent"; company name "Best Tires"; business phone "215-555-4150"; business fax "215-555-4157"; business mailing address "Callow Hill Blvd., Philadelphia PA 19107"; category "Suppliers"; click the Save and New button.

6. Enter the following contact: name "Michael Lang"; job title "Mechanic"; company name "Aldrich Garage"; business phone "215-555-8715"; business fax "215-555-2145"; business mailing address "78 Carpenter St., Philadelphia PA 19109"; category "Suppliers"; nickname "Mike"; click the Save and New button.

7. Enter the following contact: name "Felicia Rogers"; job title "President"; company name "LinkUp"; business phone "215-555-9797"; business fax "215-555-9701"; pager "215-555-2157"; business mailing address "2932 12th St., Philadelphia PA 19102"; your e-mail address; category "Business"; click the Save and Close button.

8. View the contacts as Detailed Address Cards in the Contacts Information viewer.

Explore 9. Edit Marya Little's contact to add "215-555-6110" as her Mobile phone number. (*Hint:* Double-click the contact card to open it and enter the new information.)

Explore 10. Create a distribution list called "LinkUp Suppliers" that includes all suppliers with a fax number. Assign the category "Suppliers" to the distribution list.

11. Print the entire contact list in Card Style.

Explore 12. Send a new e-mail message to Felicia Rogers with the subject "Frieda Cohn's vCard" and no message; attach the vCard file **Frieda Cohn.vcf** located in the **Review** folder within the **Tutorial.03** folder on your Data Disk. (*Hint:* Click the Attachment button on the Standard toolbar.)

13. Download the message, and then open the message in its own window.

14. Drag the Freida Cohn vCard attachment icon to the Contacts icon on the Outlook Bar, save and close the new contact card, and add as a new contact anyway.

15. Close the Message window.

16. Write a new letter to Felicia Rogers, using the Letter Wizard in Outlook, with the Elegant Letter page design with a Modified block letter style. Include a date line in the format of August 24, 2003. Select the informal salutation "Dear Felicia,". Make sure your name and address appear as the sender. The signature block should include your name and "LinkUp" as the company.

17. Type the following as the letter body: "I have been researching garages that service the new hybrid cars to add to our vendor pool. As you suggested, I will be sending out a letter to our current vendors asking for referrals. I expect that we should find someone within the next few weeks."

18. Save the document as **Felicia Rogers Letter** in the **Review** folder within the **Tutorial.03** folder on your Data Disk, and then print and close it. Exit Word.

19. Filter the contact list to display only the Suppliers category.

20. Sort the list in ascending order by Business Address Postal Code selecting the available field from the Address fields, and then in descending order by File As selected from the Frequently-used fields. Do not add any fields to the current view.

Explore 21. Select all the contacts except the distribution list. (*Hint:* Press the Ctrl+A keys to select all the contacts, press and hold the Ctrl key, and then click the LinkUp Suppliers contact to deselect it.)

Explore 22. Start the mail merge process. Set up the mail merge to use only selected contacts and all contact fields. Use the existing document **Supplier Letter** located in the **Review** folder within the **Tutorial.03** folder on your Data Disk as the document file. Create form letters that merge to a new document. Click Edit MailMerge document in the Office Assistant if it opens, then hide the Office Assistant.

Explore   23. Click in the second blank line below the date, insert the Full_Name merge field, and then press the Enter key. Insert the Business_Address merge field. (The Business Address merge field includes the street address, city, state, and ZIP code.) Insert the First_Name merge field after "Dear" followed by a colon. Type your name above "Vendor Services" at the end of the letter.

24. Use the Save As command on the File menu to save the document file as **Supplier Referral Document File** in the **Review** folder within the **Tutorial.03** folder on your Data Disk.

25. Click the View Merged Data button on the Mail Merge toolbar to verify that the business address and name for each contact appears correctly.

26. Merge the letters to a new document, save the document as **Supplier Referral Letters** in the **Review** folder within the **Tutorial.03** folder on your Data Disk.

27. Preview and print the letters, and then close Word, saving changes as needed.

28. Remove the filter and sort from the current view.

29. Delete all the contacts and messages you created in these assignments, empty the Deleted Items folder, and then exit Outlook.

CASE PROBLEMS

Case 1. Ulvang Corporation The director of human resources at Ulvang Corporation manages all employee communication with Outlook. The director has asked you to enter additional employees as contacts in Outlook, and then send a letter to one employee informing him of an earned comp day. The director also asks you to prepare mailing labels for all the employees in preparation of mailing them the updated company employee manual.

1. Start Outlook, and then switch to the Contacts Information viewer.

Explore   2. Double-click the Contacts Information viewer to open a blank Contact window.

Explore   3. Create the following contact: name "Cicely Tivo"; job title "Sales Rep"; company name "Ulvang Corporation"; business phone "203-555-9000 x12"; business fax "203-555-9701"; business mailing address "9 Main St., Norwalk CT 06851"; your e-mail address; category "Business"; click File on the menu bar and then click Save to save the contact and leave it open.

Explore   4. Click Actions on the menu bar, and then click New Contact from Same Company. A new contact card opens with duplicate information except the name, title, and categories fields.

5. Enter "Jack Lipson" as the name, "Sales Rep" as the job title, change the phone extension to "x13", and assign "Business" as the category; save the contact but leave the card open. (*Hint:* Press Ctrl+S to save the contact card without closing it.)

6. Create the following new contacts from the same company, and then save and close any open contact cards:

   - your name, Sales Rep, x38, Business
   - Erin Gleason, Sales Rep, x45, Business
   - Lyle Nobless, Sales Rep, x47, Business
   - Parker Karlen, Sales Rep, x32, Business
   - Ross Bookland, Customer Rep, x22, Business
   - Pamela Treemont, Customer Rep, x17, Business

7. Use the Letter Wizard in Outlook to write a letter to Ross, informing him that the overtime he worked during the latest product launch entitles him to a comp day. Use the date line, page design and letter style, salutation, and closing of your choice. Use your information as the sender name and address.

8. Save the letter as **Ross Letter** in the **Cases** folder within the **Tutorial.03** folder on your Data Disk, print the letter, and then exit Word.

Explore → 9. Schedule a half-hour appointment to meet with Pamela next Tuesday at 10 AM to arrange her maternity leave; assign the category "Personal" to the appointment. (*Hint:* Select Pamela's contact card, click Actions on the menu bar, and then click New Appointment with Contact. Set up the appointment as usual.)

10. Add a completed flag to follow up to Lyle's contact.

Explore → 11. Organize the contacts by category, and then filter the view to display only the sales reps (*Hint:* On the Contacts tab, search for "Sales Rep" in the Frequently-used text fields.)

Explore → 12. Create a mail merge using all contacts in current view and all contact fields. Create a new document, set the document type as Mailing Labels, and merge to a new document.

Explore → 13. Click the Complete Setup option in the Office Assistant to open Word's Mail Merge Helper dialog box.

Explore → 14. Click the Setup button to open the Label Options dialog box. Select Avery standard labels, product "5160 – Address," and then click the OK button.

Explore → 15. Click the Insert Merge Field button and click Full_Name to insert the merge field, press the Enter key, insert the Business_Address merge field, and then click the OK button.

Explore → 16. Click the Merge button in the Mail Merge Helper dialog box. Make sure the Merge dialog box is set to merge to a new document, and then click the Merge button.

17. Save the labels document as **Ulvang Mailing Labels** in the **Cases** folder within the **Tutorial.03** folder on your Data Disk, and then print and close the document.

18. Save the document file as **Ulvang Document File** in the **Cases** folder within the **Tutorial.03** folder on your Data Disk, and then close the document and close Word.

19. Remove the filter you set.

Explore → 20. Switch to Detailed Address Cards view, sort the contacts by File As name.

21. Print the entire contact list in Card Style.

22. Delete all the contacts and the calendar item, empty the Deleted Items folder, and then exit Outlook.

Case 2. Wilmington Bank Wilmington Bank has many customers who reside at the same address and share a telephone number. Carey Lincoln, executive vice president, wants to create separate contact cards for each customer, but connect those that share a residence and phone. Carey asks you to enter several contacts and connect related ones.

1. Start Outlook, and then switch to the Contacts Information viewer.

2. Create the following contact: name "Natalie Thiboau"; home phone "302-555-1574"; mobile phone "302-555-7874"; home mailing address "92 Park Street, Wilmington DE 19885"; category "Personal"; spouse "Pierre"; save and close the contact.

Explore   3. Copy the contact by holding down the Ctrl key while you drag the contact card from the Contact Information viewer to the Contacts icon on the Outlook Bar, and then release the mouse button.

4. If necessary, switch to the Detailed Address Cards view.

5. Edit a contact card from within the Information viewer. Change the name on one of the Natalie Thiboau contact cards to "Pierre Thiboau"; click outside the contact card to save it.

6. Open the contact card and change the spouse name to "Natalie."

Explore   7. Assign Pierre as a contact for Natalie's card. Open Natalie's card, click the Contacts button on the General tab, click Contacts in the Look in list box, click Pierre Thiboau in the Items list, click the OK button, and then save and close Natalie's contact card.

8. Open Pierre's contact card to verify Outlook assigned Natalie as the contact for Pierre. Close the contact card.

9. Copy Pierre's contact card using the Ctrl+drag method you used in Step 3; change the name to "Channing Thiboau" and delete the spouse name from the card; save and close the contact card.

10. Create the following contact: name "Ari Finley"; home phone "302-555-8214"; home mailing address "7 Innsbruck Avenue, Wilmington DE 19885"; category "Personal"; save and close the contact.

11. Create the following contact: name "Orlando Parkes"; home phone "302-555-3659"; home mailing address "23 Great Way Blvd., Wilmington DE 19885"; category "Personal"; save and close the contact.

12. Print the entire contact list in Card Style, removing the blank contact cards forms at the end if necessary.

13. Save each contact card you created as a vCard in the **Cases** folder within the **Tutorial.03** folder on your Data Disk.

Explore   14. Filter the contacts to display only the two related to Natalie Thiboau. Use the advanced filter to set a specific criterion by which to select contacts. (*Hint:* Click the Advanced tab in the Filter dialog box, click the Field button, point to Frequently-used Fields, click Contacts, click the Condition list arrow, click is (exactly), type "Natalie Thiboau" in the Value text box, and then click the Add to List button. Click OK in each dialog box.)

Explore   15. Create a mail merge using all contacts in the current view and all contact fields. Select the existing document **Natalie** in the **Cases** folder within the **Tutorial.03** folder on your Data Disk, select the document type as Catalog, and merge to a new document.

16. On the blank line at the top of the document, insert the Full_Name merge field, press the Tab key, insert the Home_Phone merge field, and then press the Enter key.

17. View the merged data, and then merge to a new document. Type your name on a blank line below the catalog in the merged document.

18. Save the merged document as **Natalie Contacts Merged** in the **Cases** folder within the **Tutorial.03** folder on your Data Disk. Print the Natalie Contacts Merged document.

19. Save the data file as **Natalie Data File** in the **Cases** folder within the **Tutorial.03** folder on your Data Disk, and then exit Word, saving changes as needed.

20. Remove the filter from the view.

21. Delete all the contacts and other items you created in this case, empty the Deleted Items folder, and then exit Outlook.

Case 3. Mobley Collection Agency Mobley Collection Agency (MCA) is hired by other companies to track down and obtain immediate payments from delinquent accounts. MCA employees contact late payers and arrange a mutually agreeable payment schedule. MCA retains 25% of all monies it collects as the fee for the services rendered. Currently, MCA is entering contacts in Outlook for nonpaying companies.

1. Start Outlook, and then switch to the Contacts Information viewer.

2. Create the following contact: company "Wagley Group"; business phone "650-555-2600 x145"; business mailing address "3873 University Way, Palo Alto CA 94306"; category "Phone Calls"; save and close the contact.

3. Create the following contact: company "Xpert Systems"; business phone "916-555-8540 x11"; business mailing address "83 Kilander Place, Gold River CA 95670"; category "Phone Calls"; save and close the contact.

4. Create the following contact: company "Music Miracles"; business phone "415-555-6000 x35"; business mailing address "39 Blake Street, Suite 4, Mill Valley CA 94941"; category "Phone Calls"; save and close the contact.

5. Create the following contact: company "EZ Training Workshops"; business mailing address "9273 Ethelanne Street, Berkeley CA 94704"; category "Waiting"; save and close the contact.

6. Create the following contact: company "Connections"; business mailing address "56 Lake Blvd., Mill Valley CA 94941"; category "Waiting"; save and close the contact.

7. Create the following contact: company "Desktop Designs"; business mailing address "83 Delores Street, Suite 9374, San Francisco CA 94112"; category "Waiting"; save and close the contact.

Explore

8. View the contacts by category, and then print all rows of the contact list in Table Style. (*Hint:* Make sure that each category group is expanded; if the contacts are not visible onscreen, only the group heading appears on the printout.)

Explore

9. Forward all of the contacts in the Phone Calls category to your e-mail address using the subject "Phone Calls" and the message "We need to contact all these companies by telephone to encourage them to pay their outstanding bills immediately." Press the Enter key twice, and then type your name. (*Hint:* To select all the contacts in a category, click the first contact and then press and hold the Shift key as you click the last contact in the group.)

Explore

10. Forward as vCards all of the contacts in the Waiting category to your e-mail address using the subject "Waiting" and the message "We need to contact all these companies by mail to encourage them to pay their outstanding bills immediately." Press the Enter key twice. and then type your name. (*Hint:* To select all the contacts in a category, click the first contact and then press and hold the Shift key as you click the last contact in the group.)

11. Send and receive the messages as needed.

12. Flag for follow-up all the contacts in both the Phone Calls and the Waiting categories.

Explore ▶ 13. Filter the contacts to display only those with follow-up flags. (*Hint:* Click the Advanced tab in the Filter dialog box, click the Field button, point to Frequently-used fields, click Follow Up Flag, click the Condition list arrow, click is not empty, click the Add to List button, and then click the OK button.) This advanced filter enables you to set specific criteria by which to select contacts; this time you'll set a single criterion.

14. Change the follow-up flags for Wagley Group and Desktop Designs to Completed. These contacts remain visible.

15. Clear the follow-up flag for Xpert Systems and Connections by changing the flag to Normal. These contacts disappear from the filter.

Explore ▶ 16. Revise the filter to display only flagged contacts, not contacts with cleared or completed flags. (*Hint:* On the Advanced tab in the Filter dialog box, click the Remove button to move the filter criterion you set earlier to the edit boxes. Click the Field button, point to Frequently-used fields, click Flag Status, verify that equals appears in the Condition list box, click the Value list arrow, click Flagged, click the Add to List button, and then click the OK button.)

Explore ▶ 17. Add a second criterion to the filter so that only flagged contacts in the Waiting category appear. (*Hint:* Open the Filter dialog box, add the Waiting category to the filter from the More Choices tab as usual, leaving the other criterion on the Advanced tab.) Only the EZ Training Workshops contact in the Waiting category that is flagged for follow up appears in the Information viewer.

18. Remove the filter, and then return the view to Address Cards.

19. Delete all the contacts and other items you created in this case, empty the Deleted Items folder, and then exit Outlook.

Case 4. Fan Club You are president of the fan club for your favorite movie star or sports figure. The fan club usually meets in a member's home once a month. The week before each meeting, you remind members of the upcoming meeting's date, time, and location. You just learned that a meeting of all the clubs around the world is scheduled next November. Rather than wait for the next meeting, you decide to send a personal letter to all members inviting them to attend the world meeting. You'll use Outlook to compile a list of the club members and keep in touch with them.

1. Start Outlook, and create a contact card for yourself. Enter as much information about yourself as possible on the General and Details tabs. Save and close the card.

Explore ▶ 2. Save your contact information as a vCard file with your name in the **Cases** folder within the **Tutorial.03** folder on your Data Disk. (*Hint:* Select the contact, click File on the menu bar, click Save As, change the save location, type the filename, and change the Save as type to vCard Files.)

3. Create five more contacts, entering a name, mailing address, phone number, and your e-mail address for each contact. Add each as a new contact anyway.

4. Open the Organize pane, and click the Using Categories link. You'll use the Organize pane to create a new category and then assign it to each contact.

Explore 5. Type "Members" in the Create a new category called text box, and then click the Create button.

Explore 6. Select each of the contacts you created, except the one for you, and then click the Add contacts selected below to list arrow, click Members, and then click the Add button.

7. Select all the contacts you created, and then print the contact list in Memo Style. Do *not* start each contact on its own page and do *not* print attached files with items.

8. Filter the contact list to display only contacts assigned to the Members category, sorted in ascending order by the File As name.

Explore 9. Start a mail merge letter using all contacts in current view (the filtered contact list) and all contact fields. Create a new document as the document file. Select form letters as the document type and merge to a new document.

Explore 10. Create a letter to send the members of your local fan club, inviting them to the international meeting of all the fan clubs. Include the appropriate merge fields to personalize the letter. Also include a description of the international meeting as well as the dates and location. End the letter with your name.

11. Save the document file as **Fan Club Document File** in the **Cases** folder within the **Tutorial.03** folder on your Data Disk.

12. Merge the letter and the contacts to a new document, and then save the form letters as **Fan Club Letters** in the **Cases** folder within the **Tutorial.03** folder on your Data Disk.

13. Print the letters, and then exit Word, saving documents as needed.

14. Delete all the contacts and other items you created in this case, including the category, empty the Deleted Items folder, and then exit Outlook.

QUICK CHECK ANSWERS

Session 3.1

1. False

2. The file as name specifies how your contacts should be ordered in the Contacts Information viewer.

3. Categories make it simple to locate, organize, and group similar types of contacts.

4. Outlook opens the Duplicate Contact Detected dialog box, enabling you to add the contact anyway, combine the new contact with an existing contact, or open the existing contact to edit it.

5. Views change the way information is displayed in the Information viewer, such as arranged as contact cards or grouped by category.

6. A vCard is a file that contains name and address information about a contact and is compatible with other popular communication and information manager programs, including Lotus Organizer, Netscape Communicator, and Sidekick.

7. Click the first contact, press and hold the Ctrl key, and then click the additional contacts.

8. Drag the vCard attachment icon from the e-mail message to the Contacts icon on the Outlook Bar; a Contact window opens with all the information from the vCard entered. Add or edit information as needed, and then save the card as usual.

QUICK | CHECK ANSWERS

Session 3.2

1. Any three of the following: send an e-mail, write a letter, schedule an appointment or a meeting, assign a task

2. A tool that walks you through the letter-writing process in Word when you write a letter to a specific contact or distribution list.

3. A red flag indicates that the contact has been marked for follow up on some activity.

4. The Information viewer displays only those items in a folder that match certain criteria, such as contacts assigned to the Key Customer category.

5. Ascending order arranges items alphabetically (A to Z), chronologically (earliest to latest), or numerically (lowest to highest). Descending order reverses the sort ascending order—Z to A, latest to earliest, or highest to lowest.

6. The distribution list letter is the same for all contacts, whereas the mail merge letter can be personalized for each contact.

7. A document file contains the standard text and merge fields, such as a letter in Word; a data file is the list of variable information, such as an Outlook contact list.

8. Merge fields are special codes that identify the variable information that should appear in that location.

MANAGING YOUR INBOX

Arranging a Crew for Speedy Cleaning Company

CASE

Speedy Cleaning Company

Nadya Rutskoi manages the Speedy Cleaning Company, which has provided pre- and post-party cleanup services for individuals in the Washington, D.C. area since 1992. Whether clients are having an intimate wedding, a lavish New Year's Eve party, or a formal business-related gathering, the Speedy Cleaning team makes their homes spotless. Before and after an event, Nadya sends in a cleanup crew with enough people to thoroughly clean the house in four hours. A two-person crew can efficiently clean a smaller home, whereas a dozen or more people might be required for larger homes. The crew arrives with its own cleaning supplies and equipment, and each crew member has an assigned task, such as vacuuming, dusting, polishing, window washing, and so forth. Rather than hiring full-time employees, Speedy Cleaning relies on independent contractors who can accept or decline any offered job. This enables Speedy Cleaning to accommodate clients who plan events well in advance and also those who decide to throw last-minute events. Nadya uses Outlook to communicate with clients and contractors, schedule cleanup times, and arrange cleaning crews. In this tutorial, you will help Nadya prepare for an upcoming birthday party hosted by the Gormanns. You will send and receive messages with flags, voting buttons, and other tracking and delivery options. You will create subfolders in the Inbox so you can file messages both manually and with rules you create. Then you will find, sort, group, and filter messages. Next you will archive messages, and turn on a filter to detect junk e-mail messages. Finally you will learn how to set up Outlook to work remotely (when you are not connected to a mail server).

SESSION 4.1

In this session, you will send and receive messages with flags, voting buttons, delivery receipts, and specific delivery dates. Then you will create subfolders in the Inbox. Finally you will file messages both manually and by using rules.

Flagging **Messages**

Some messages you send require a specific response or action from the recipients. Although the subject should be informative and the message can provide any explicit instructions, often a more obvious reminder would better draw attention to your request. A **message flag** is an icon that appears in the message list. The message flag also includes text that appears in an information banner in the Message window. You can choose from preset flag text or create your own, such as "need cleaning crew."

Message flags can also include a deadline. You can select a specific due date or enter descriptive words such as "tomorrow" that Outlook converts to the correct date. When a recipient receives and stores a flagged message in the Inbox, Outlook displays a reminder at the appropriate time. Reminders are activated only from flagged messages in the Inbox. If the recipient moves the message to another folder, no reminders appear.

After you send a flagged message, your copy of the message in the Sent Items folder does *not* show the flag (although you can see a reference to it in the information banner if you open the message). You can add a flag to a message in this folder the same way as you would a new message. It is important to note that you will not be reminded on the specified date although the message header will change to red when the flag becomes due.

You'll create an e-mail, and then add a Need Cleaning Crew flag with a due date for one week from today to the message.

To create a message flag:

1. Start Outlook, create a new e-mail message addressed to your e-mail address with the subject **Schedule cleaning crew** and the message **Please set up a five-person cleaning crew for the Gormann event two weeks from today**, press the **Enter** key twice to double space, and then type your name.

2. Click the **Flag for Follow Up** button 🚩 on the Standard toolbar. The Flag for Follow Up dialog box opens.

3. Click the **Flag to** list arrow to display the preset flag options. Although you often may find it appropriate to select from these, in this case you want to type your own.

4. Click in the **Flag to** text box and type **Need Cleaning Crew**. See Figure 4-1.

Figure 4-1	FLAG FOR FOLLOW UP DIALOG BOX

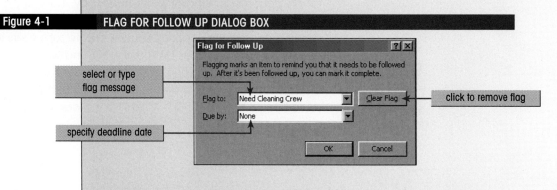

You want to add a due date to this flag for one week from today.

5. Click the **Due by** list arrow, and then click the date for one week from today.
6. Click the **OK** button. The Flag for Follow Up dialog box closes and you return to the Message window. The information banner shows the flag message. See Figure 4-2.

Figure 4-2 E-MAIL WITH FLAG MESSAGE

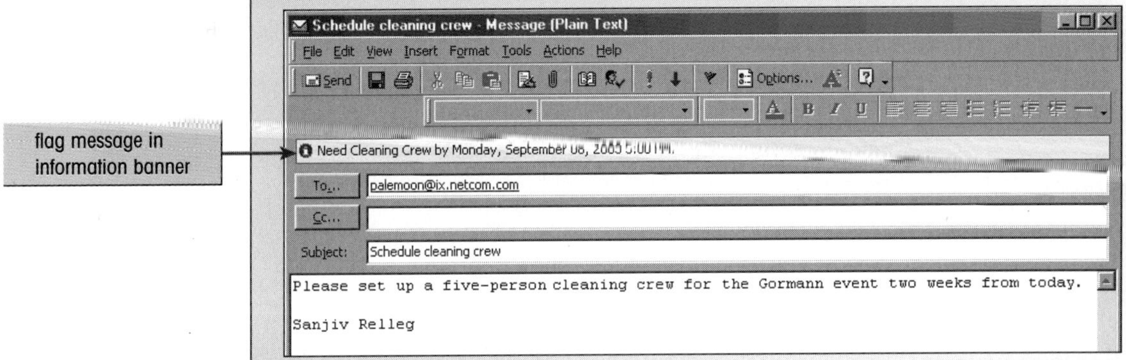

7. Send the message.

When the recipient receives the message, the message displays a red flag in the Flag status column of the Inbox Information viewer. The recipient could choose to put the request on their to-do list, create a reminder note, or schedule an appointment to respond to the message flag by dragging the message to the Tasks, Notes, or Calendar folder. Once the flag request is completed, the recipient can mark the flag completed. This can be done from the Flag for Follow Up dialog box, or right in the Inbox Information viewer.

To respond to a message flag:

1. Switch to the **Inbox** and then download your messages, if necessary. The message flag icon appears next to the Schedule cleaning crew message. You cannot see the flag text, so you'll open the message. See Figure 4-3.

Figure 4-3 RECEIVED MESSAGE WITH FLAG

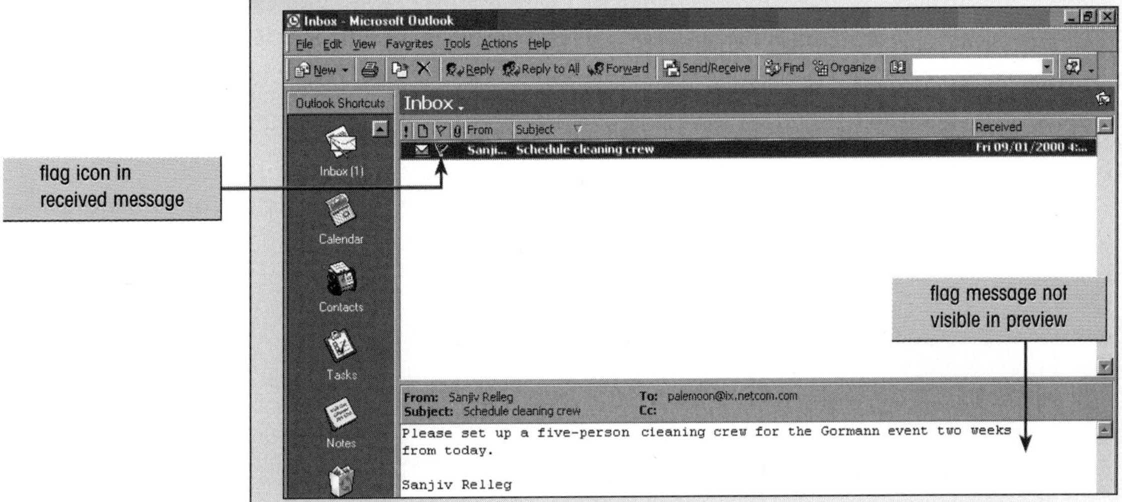

TROUBLE? If the message flag does not appear with your received message, then it was lost when the message was sent over the Internet. Your ISP may not support message flags. You will not see the flag text in Step 2 or Step 4.

2. Double-click the **Schedule cleaning crew** message in the message list to open it in a separate window. The flag text appears in the information banner. See Figure 4-4.

Figure 4-4 | RECEIVED E-MAIL WITH FLAG MESSAGE

flag message and deadline

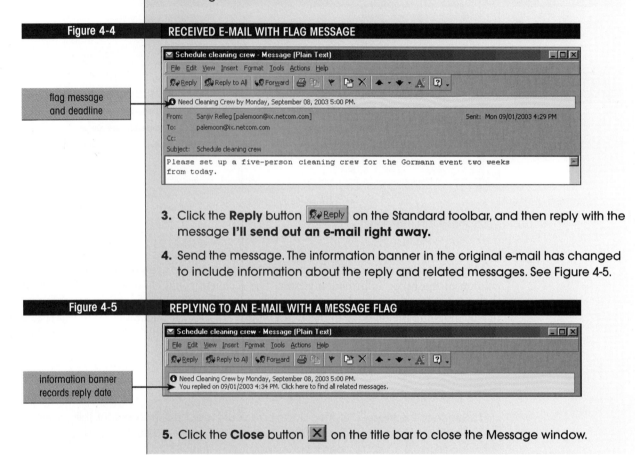

3. Click the **Reply** button on the Standard toolbar, and then reply with the message **I'll send out an e-mail right away.**

4. Send the message. The information banner in the original e-mail has changed to include information about the reply and related messages. See Figure 4-5.

Figure 4-5 | REPLYING TO AN E-MAIL WITH A MESSAGE FLAG

information banner records reply date

5. Click the **Close** button ⊠ on the title bar to close the Message window.

You will send out an e-mail message to locate team members, so you'll mark the flag complete. You could have done that with the Flag button from the open Message window, but because you already closed the message, you'll change the flag status from the Inbox.

To respond to a message flag:

1. Right-click the **flag** icon 🚩 for the Schedule cleaning crew message. The shortcut menu has options for marking the flag as complete or clearing it. See Figure 4-6.

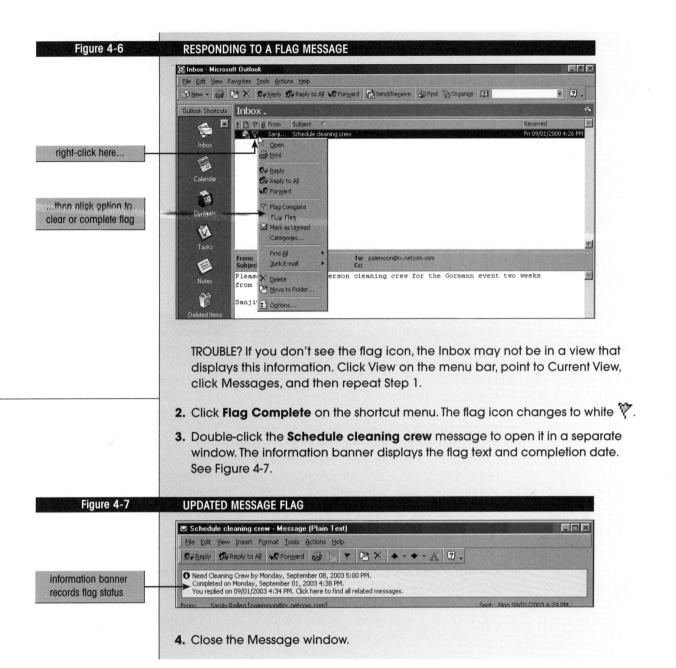

Figure 4-6 — **RESPONDING TO A FLAG MESSAGE**

right-click here...

...then click option to clear or complete flag

TROUBLE? If you don't see the flag icon, the Inbox may not be in a view that displays this information. Click View on the menu bar, point to Current View, click Messages, and then repeat Step 1.

2. Click **Flag Complete** on the shortcut menu. The flag icon changes to white 🏳.

3. Double-click the **Schedule cleaning crew** message to open it in a separate window. The information banner displays the flag text and completion date. See Figure 4-7.

Figure 4-7 — **UPDATED MESSAGE FLAG**

information banner records flag status

4. Close the Message window.

You'll send an e-mail message to ask for information about a cleaning crew member's availability.

Setting **Message Options**

Outlook sets up new messages based on the default options specified in the Options dialog box. These options include setting the priority and privacy of a message, adding voting buttons, requesting receipts, and specifying the initial and expiration delivery dates. You can override these options for specific messages using the Options button in the Message window.

The available message options vary depending on whether you are using the Corporate or Workgroup service option with Exchange Server, Microsoft Mail, or another MAPI-compliant e-mail system. If you are using an Internet mail server, check with the administrator to determine which capabilities (if any) they provide.

REFERENCE WINDOW   **RW**

Setting Message Options
- Create a new e-mail message.
- Click the Options button on the Message window Standard toolbar.
- Select appropriate options, such as voting buttons, receipts, delivery and expiration dates, and then click the OK button.
- Send the message.

The message you'll create to determine a crew member's availability will use voting buttons, delivery receipts, and an expiration date.

Specifying Votes and Message Delivery

When you want people to respond to a multiple-choice question you can ask them to cast a vote. **Voting buttons** provide a limited set of possible options from which recipients can choose one answer. Outlook has three standard sets of voting buttons: Approve or Reject; Yes or No; and Yes or No or Maybe. These work well for a variety of purposes, such as evaluating a proposal or responding to an invitation. However, not all situations can be addressed by one of these three standard voting buttons. For example, you may need to have people select a meeting day, choose a lunch entrée, or pick a team leader. In these cases you can create custom voting buttons to elicit the information you need. You can include as many buttons as you like in a set of voting buttons.

You create custom voting buttons by typing the button names separated by semicolons in the Message Options dialog box, for example: Monday;Wednesday;Friday or Pizza;Tacos or Lars;Caryl;Mac;Sophie. Do not include any spaces.

Each message can contain only one set of voting buttons, whether you use a standard set or create a custom set. The voting buttons don't appear in the Message window until after the message is sent. Outlook also adds an information banner with the text, "Please respond using the buttons above."

You and the recipients must be using the Corporate or Workgroup service option with Exchange Server or Microsoft Mail or another MAPI-compliant e-mail client to use voting buttons. In addition, the recipient's e-mail address must be set to Microsoft Exchange rich text format or Microsoft Outlook rich text format.

You'll create a message in which consultants can specify their availability by clicking a Yes, No, or Maybe voting button.

To create a message with voting buttons:

1. Create a new message to your e-mail address with the subject **Available for pre-party cleaning?** and the message **The Gormann birthday party is two weeks from today and will require pre-party cleaning from 6 AM to 10 AM. Please open this message and click a voting button to indicate whether you are available**, press the **Enter** key twice, and then type your name.

   Next you'll set your e-mail address to the Rich Text format.

2. Right-click your e-mail address in the To box, and then click **Properties** on the shortcut menu. The E-mail Properties dialog box opens.

3. Click the **Always send to this recipient in Microsoft Outlook rich-text format** check box to insert a check mark, and then click the **OK** button.

4. Click the **Options** button on the Standard toolbar. The Message Options dialog box opens.

Although you could define your own buttons, this time you will use a default set.

5. Click the **Use voting buttons** list arrow, and then click **Yes;No;Maybe**. See Figure 4-8.

Figure 4-8 MESSAGE OPTIONS DIALOG BOX

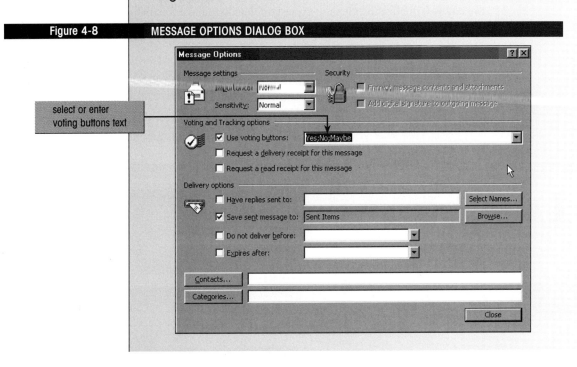

select or enter voting buttons text

You could send the message as is. However, because this message is time sensitive, you want to know when the message is received and opened.

Tracking Message Delivery

Like phone messages and letters, you cannot be sure that someone has received your e-mail message unless they reply with a confirmation receipt. However, confirming receipt of every incoming e-mail and then later crafting a more complete reply can be time-consuming for the recipient and slow down Internet traffic. Instead you can have Outlook notify you when the recipient receives the message, when the recipient opens the message, or both. You set these delivery receipts in the Message Options dialog box.

The delivery receipt and read receipt tracking options are functional when you are using the Corporate or Workgroup service option with Exchange Server or Microsoft Mail as well as with some mail servers.

To request message delivery receipts:

1. Click the **Request a delivery receipt for this message** check box to insert a check mark. You will receive a message when the recipient receives the message.

2. Click the **Request a read receipt for this message** check box to insert a check mark. You will receive a message when the recipient opens the message (although you have no guarantee that the recipient has actually read the message unless he or she replies).

With Outlook, you can determine when a message is delivered or deleted. When you delay the delivery time, Outlook stores the message in your Outbox and then delivers it on the specified delivery date. You also can set an expiration date and time for a message. Exchange deletes the message if the recipient hasn't opened it by the date and time you specified.

The delivery time limit options are functional only when you are using the Corporate or Workgroup service option with Exchange Server or with a mail server that offers these capabilities.

Because a response from the cleaning employee becomes irrelevant after next Monday, the day you finalize the cleanup crew, you decide to have the message expire next Monday at 9 AM. Because this message is time sensitive, you want to deliver it immediately.

To set delivery time limits:

1. Click the **Expires after** list arrow, and then click the date for next Monday.

2. Select the time in the Expires after text box, and then type **9 AM**. Although your dates will differ, your Message Options dialog box should look similar to Figure 4-9.

Figure 4-9	COMPLETED MESSAGE OPTIONS DIALOG BOX

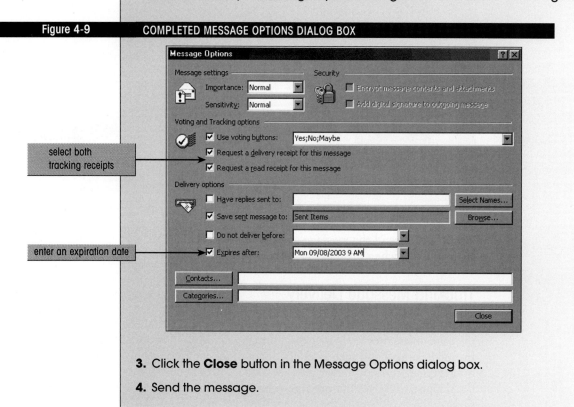

3. Click the **Close** button in the Message Options dialog box.

4. Send the message.

The message you just sent did not mention the location of the party. This information could be helpful to some potential crew members.

Recalling or Resending Messages

With the speed with which we can send e-mail messages, sometimes you may wish you could bring back or modify part of the message, such as when you type an incorrect time or date for a proposed meeting or wish to include additional details like the Gormann party location. With Outlook, you can attempt to recall or resend the message. A **recall** removes unread copies of the message from the recipient's Inbox or replaces the unread message with a corrected one. You can recall messages only if they have not been read or removed from the recipient's Inbox. This is common sense as removing these types of messages would be confusing for the recipient who has already seen the message. You must have requested a read receipt when sending the message in order for Outlook to determine whether it was read; otherwise, Outlook cannot recall the message.

If the message cannot be recalled, you might want to simply send a corrected version. To do so, click Resend This Message on the Actions menu. A Message window opens with the original message and recipients. You can modify it as needed and then send the revised message to the recipients as usual. Because the original message may still be unread in the recipient's Inbox or may have been read, you might want to add a message flag to draw attention to this newer version.

Message recall is available only when both you and the recipient have Outlook running and are logged onto Exchange, and the message remains unopened in the recipient's Inbox.

You will attempt to recall the message you just sent and add information about the party location.

To recall a message:

1. Click the **Sent Items** icon in the **My Shortcuts** group on the Outlook Bar.

2. Open the **Available for pre-party cleaning?** message.

3. Click **Actions** on the menu bar, and then click **Recall This Message**. The Recall This Message dialog box opens. See Figure 4-10.

| Figure 4-10 | RECALL THIS MESSAGE DIALOG BOX |

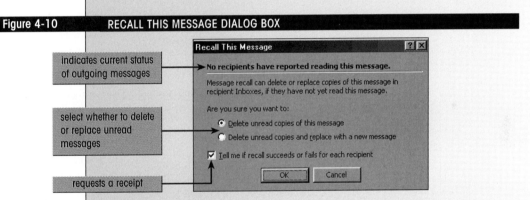

Nadya suggests that you send the directions to the Gormann house only to those who respond that they can work the party.

4. Click the **Cancel** button.

5. Close the Message window.

6. Return to the Inbox Information viewer.

If you request a message recall, you will receive messages in your Inbox informing you of the success or failure of the recall.

Casting a Vote

Messages with voting buttons and tracking options arrive the same way as any other message—in your Inbox. If you review the message in the Preview pane of the Inbox Information viewer, the voting buttons and information banner aren't visible; these appear only in an open message window. One way to ensure that recipients open the e-mail and respond using the voting buttons is to include that instruction in the message body, like you did with the Available for pre-party cleaning message.

From the open window, the recipient can click the appropriate voting button. The selection is added to the subject line and the recipient has the option of adding a note to the reply e-mail. After the reply is sent, the information banner in the original message changes to reflect the recipient's vote as well as the date and time it was made.

You'll respond to the Available for cleaning crew? message using the voting buttons.

To cast a voting response:

1. If necessary, download your messages.

2. Open the **Available for pre-party cleaning?** message. The voting buttons and information banner appear above the message header. See Figure 4-11.

Figure 4-11	MESSAGE WITH VOTING BUTTONS

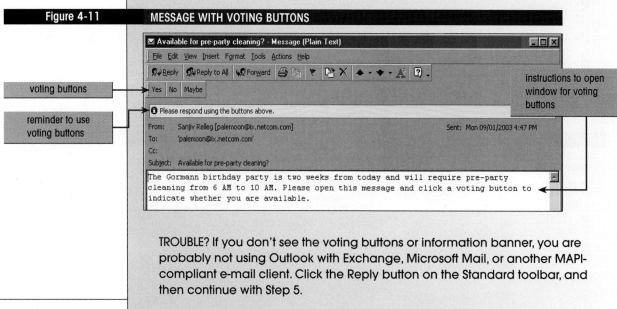

TROUBLE? If you don't see the voting buttons or information banner, you are probably not using Outlook with Exchange, Microsoft Mail, or another MAPI-compliant e-mail client. Click the Reply button on the Standard toolbar, and then continue with Step 5.

3. Click the **No** voting button. A dialog box opens confirming your response and giving you the option to add notes to your reply e-mail. The first option returns your vote to the sender. The second option opens a reply Message window so you can type a response. Either option adds the text of the voting button you selected to the subject line. See Figure 4-12.

Figure 4-12	MESSAGE DIALOG BOX

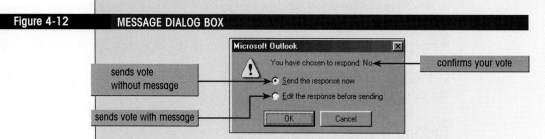

4. Click the **Edit the response before sending** option button, and then click the **OK** button. A reply Message window opens, in which you can type a response.

5. Type **I will be on vacation for that week.** in the Message window.

6. Send the message. The information banner in the original message reflects your vote and the date and time of your response.

7. Close the Available for per-party cleaning? message.

The benefit of using voting buttons rather than having recipients type their replies is that Outlook can tally the votes for you.

Tracking Votes and Message Delivery

When you receive replies, each e-mail shows the recipient's vote as well as any message that was added. You can open, view, and save those messages the same way as any other messages.

To receive voting replies:

1. Download your messages, if necessary. One messages is a read receipt and another contains the vote reply. See Figure 4-13.

| Figure 4-13 | RECEIVING READ RECEIPTS AND VOTING REPLIES |

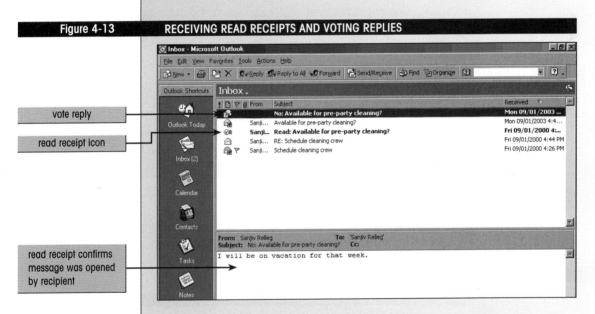

vote reply

read receipt icon

read receipt confirms message was opened by recipient

TROUBLE? If you don't see the read receipt, you are probably not using Outlook with Exchange or a mail server that offers this capability. Skip to Step 3. If your voting reply looks different from the one shown in Figure 4-13, then you were not able to use the voting buttons in the preceding set of steps. Skip Steps 2 through 4, and continue with the next section "Organizing Your Inbox."

2. Click the **Read: Available for pre-party cleaning?** message to preview it.

3. Open the **No: Available for pre-party cleaning?** message. Note the vote response in the information banner and the reply message.

4. Close the Message window.

A copy of the original message you sent with the voting buttons is stored in the Sent Items folder. This e-mail not only records your outgoing message, it also tracks the recipients' votes as well as delivery and read dates. Once you receive replies, a special icon 📧 marks the message in the Sent Items folder. When you open the message it contains two tabs—the Message tab contains your original message; the Tracking tab lists all the recipients' names and votes as well as the dates of the delivery and read receipts if requested.

To track votes and message delivery:

1. Click the **Sent Items** icon in the **My Shortcuts** group on the Outlook Bar. The icon 📧 next to the Available for pre-party cleaning? message indicates that the vote tally will be collected in this e-mail. See Figure 4-14.

Figure 4-14	SENT ITEMS FOLDER

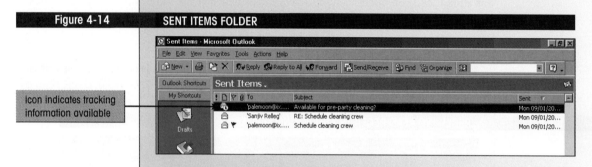

icon indicates tracking information available

2. Open the **Available for pre-party cleaning?** message. You want to review the information on the Tracking tab.

3. Click the **Tracking** tab in the Message window. See Figure 4-15.

Figure 4-15	TRACKING TAB FOR VOTING AND READ RECEIPTS

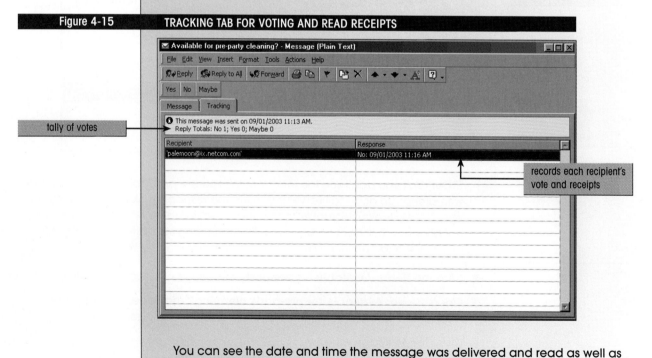

tally of votes

records each recipient's vote and receipts

You can see the date and time the message was delivered and read as well as what votes were cast. The information banner tallies the votes for the entire group of recipients.

4. Close the message.

As you work, items will begin to pile up, especially in the Inbox. To work effectively and efficiently, you'll need to "clean house" periodically by moving items from one folder to another.

Organizing Your Inbox

As you can readily see, messages can collect quickly in your Inbox. Even if you respond to each message as it arrives, all the original messages remain in your Inbox. Some messages you'll want to delete. Others you'll want to file and store, just as you would file and store paper memos in a file cabinet. In fact, the Folder List acts like an electronic file cabinet. After you create an organizational system, you create and label a series of folders, and subfolders within folders, in which to store items. For example, Nadya might create folders in which to store messages for Speedy Cleaning and for each client within the Inbox folder.

You'll display the Folder List in order to switch between folders and organize your messages. You could hide the Outlook Bar to leave more room onscreen, but you'll be using both. Moving messages with the Information viewer and the Folder List works in much the same way as Windows Explorer to manage your files.

To display the Folder List:

1. Click **View** on the menu bar, and then click **Folder List**.

2. Click the **Inbox** folder in the Folder List. The Inbox Information viewer appears. See Figure 4-16.

| Figure 4-16 | FOLDER LIST AND INBOX |

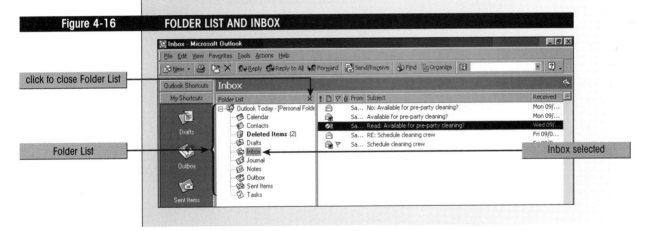

If you have used Windows Explorer, this setup should look familiar. You will see how the Folder List makes it simple to create subfolders.

Creating a Folder

You can create folders at the same level as the default folders, such as Inbox, Outbox, and Sent Items, or you can create subfolders within any main folder. Where you choose to place folders is a matter of personal preference. Some people prefer to group folders they create within the default folder of the same type (such as creating a folder within the Inbox); others prefer to keep any folders they create within the Personal Folders at the same level as the default folders. For now, you'll create two subfolders in the Inbox folder, called Speedy Cleaning and Gormann. Once you create a subfolder within another folder, either an Expand or a Collapse button precedes the main folder. Which button appears depends on whether the subfolders are displayed (Collapse button) or hidden (Expand button).

When you create a folder, you supply a name, select the type of Outlook items you want to store in it, and choose its location. Each folder can store only one type of item—appointment, contact, journal, mail, note, or task. You'll create folders to store mail messages.

To create subfolders:

1. Click the **New** button list arrow 📄 New on the Standard toolbar, and then click **Folder**. The Create New Folder dialog box opens.

   In this dialog box, you'll name the folder, select the type of items the folder will contain, and choose the folder's location.

2. Type **Speedy Cleaning** in the Name text box.

3. Click the **Folder contains** list arrow, and then view the choices. You can also create subfolders to store appointments, contacts, journal entries, notes, and tasks.

4. Click **Mail Items**, and then click **Inbox** in the Select where to place the folder list as the location for your new folder. See Figure 4-17.

Figure 4-17	CREATE NEW FOLDER DIALOG BOX

specify folder name →

subfolder stores e-mail messages →

create a subfolder within Inbox →

Create New Folder   [?][X]

Name:
Speedy Cleaning

Folder contains:
Mail Items

Select where to place the folder:

- Personal Folders
  - Calendar
  - Contacts
  - **Deleted Items** (2)
  - Drafts
  - Inbox
  - Journal
  - Notes
  - Outbox
  - Sent Items
  - Tasks

[OK]   [Cancel]

5. Click the **OK** button. The new folder appears in the Folder List.

   TROUBLE? If the Office Assistant or a dialog box appears, asking whether you want to add a shortcut for this folder to the Outlook Bar, click the No button.

6. Repeat Steps 1 through 5 to create a subfolder called **Gormann** that stores **Mail Items** in the **Inbox**.

Now you can file any messages related to Speedy Cleaning Company in its folder and any messages relating to the specific client in its own folder.

Filing Messages

The ability to move items from one folder to another helps you to keep Outlook tasks, appointments, notes, and messages organized. The simplest way to file an item is to drag it from one folder to another. When you drag an item into a folder that stores that type of item, the item is moved. When you drag an item to a folder that stores another type of item, a new window opens for that folder's item so you can enter additional information to complete that item. For example, dragging a message from the Inbox to another mail folder moves the message; but dragging a message from the Inbox to the Calendar folder opens a new Appointment window and copies the message body in the notes box. You can then enter the times, add a location, or set a reminder as needed to complete the appointment.

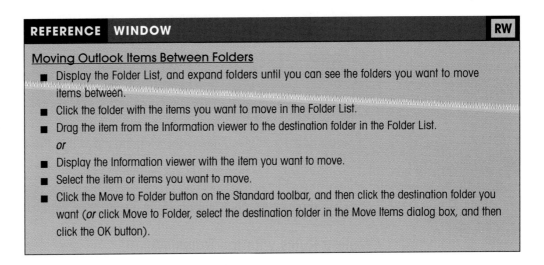

REFERENCE WINDOW   **RW**

Moving Outlook Items Between Folders
- Display the Folder List, and expand folders until you can see the folders you want to move items between.
- Click the folder with the items you want to move in the Folder List.
- Drag the item from the Information viewer to the destination folder in the Folder List.
  or
- Display the Information viewer with the item you want to move.
- Select the item or items you want to move.
- Click the Move to Folder button on the Standard toolbar, and then click the destination folder you want (*or* click Move to Folder, select the destination folder in the Move Items dialog box, and then click the OK button).

You'll file the messages you sent and received for Speedy Cleaning in its folder.

To file messages:

1. If necessary, click the **Expand** button ⊞ next to the Inbox in the Folder List to display the Gormann and Speedy Cleaning subfolders.

2. Select the **Schedule cleaning crew** message in the Inbox Information viewer. It is the first message you will move.

3. Drag the **Schedule cleaning crew** message to the **Speedy Cleaning** subfolder in the Folder List. See Figure 4-18.

| Figure 4-18 | FILING A MESSAGE FROM THE INBOX |

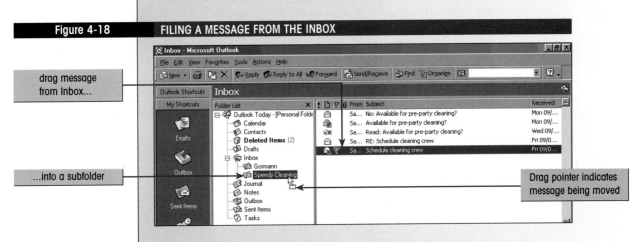

drag message from Inbox...

...into a subfolder

Drag pointer indicates message being moved

4. Release the mouse button to move the message from the Inbox into the subfolder.

You want to move all messages related to Speedy Cleaning Company into the subfolder. You could continue to move each message individually, but it's faster to move all of them at once. Remember that the Ctrl key enables you to select nonadjacent messages, whereas the Shift key enables you to select a range of adjacent messages.

To file multiple messages:

1. Click the **Re: Schedule cleaning crew** message. This is the first message you want to file.

2. Press and hold down the **Ctrl** key while you click the three **Available for pre-party cleaning?** messages that you want to move, and then release the **Ctrl** key.

   TROUBLE? If you have only two Available for pre-party cleaning? messages, the read receipt didn't arrive. Just select the two messages.

3. Drag all the selected messages from the Inbox into the **Speedy Cleaning** subfolder.

You can also have Outlook automatically file messages for you.

Creating Rules with the Rules Wizard

Rather than manually filing all your messages, you can create rules that specify how Outlook should process and organize them. For example, you can use rules to:

- Move messages to a folder based on their subject.
- Flag messages about a particular topic.
- Assign categories to sent or received messages based on their content.
- Forward messages to a person or distribution list.
- Delete messages from a specific sender.
- Delay message delivery by a specified amount of time.
- Reply automatically to certain messages using a message you've created.

Each **rule** includes three parts: the *conditions* that determine if a message is to be acted on, the *actions* that should be applied to qualifying messages, and any *exceptions* that remove a message from the qualifying group. For example, a rule might state that all messages you receive from Nadya (condition) are moved to the Speedy Cleaning folder (action) except for ones marked as high importance (exception). Outlook can apply rules to incoming, outgoing, or stored messages.

You create rules with the **Rules Wizard**, a feature that steps you through the rule-writing process. As you build a rule, you continue to refine the sentence that describes the conditions, actions, and exceptions.

If you are using Outlook with Microsoft Exchange Server, you must be online to use the Rules Wizard.

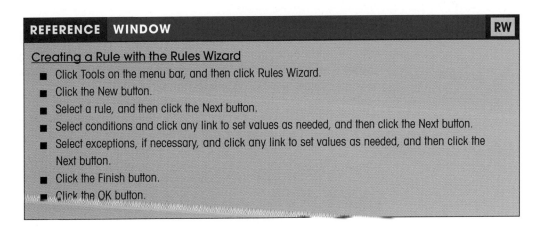

REFERENCE WINDOW **RW**

Creating a Rule with the Rules Wizard
- Click Tools on the menu bar, and then click Rules Wizard.
- Click the New button.
- Select a rule, and then click the Next button.
- Select conditions and click any link to set values as needed, and then click the Next button.
- Select exceptions, if necessary, and click any link to set values as needed, and then click the Next button.
- Click the Finish button.
- Click the OK button.

You want to create a rule to move all messages related to the Gormann birthday party to the Gormann folder. First you'll select the condition, next you'll define the actions, and then you'll add the exceptions.

To start the Rules Wizard:

1. Click **Tools** on the menu bar, and then click **Rules Wizard**. The Rules Wizard dialog box that opens lists any currently existing rules.

2. Click the **New** button. The Rules Wizard dialog box displays a list of the most common rules. See Figure 4-19.

Figure 4-19 RULES WIZARD DIALOG BOX

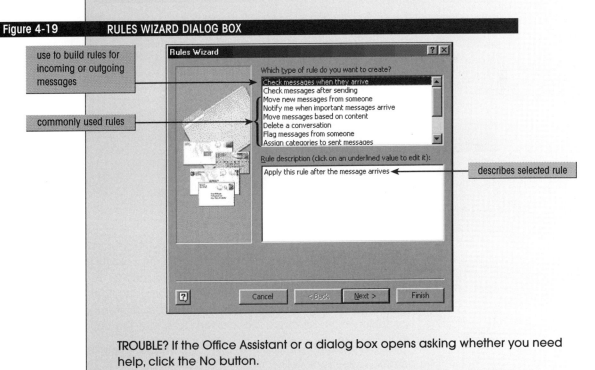

TROUBLE? If the Office Assistant or a dialog box opens asking whether you need help, click the No button.

The first two rules, Check messages when they arrive and Check messages after sending, provide access to a variety of conditions and actions that you can use to create the exact situation you want. For either of these rule types, you select the conditions and actions you want in the next dialog boxes. The other types are commonly used rules, which already include conditions and actions, which you clarify by entering the appropriate words, senders, categories, folders, and so forth, depending on the rule itself.

You'll select a rule type that already includes the appropriate condition and action—Move messages based on content. All you need to do is enter the appropriate values for the condition and for the action. You could do this by clicking the hyperlinks or by moving through the dialog box. You'll use the dialog box method this time, so you can see the other conditions and actions that are available.

To select a rule and specify a condition:

1. Click **Move messages based on content** in the Which type of rule do you want to create? list.

   The Rule description list box displays the sentence with the condition and action for the selected rule.

2. Click the **Next** button to set the conditions for the selected rule. The rule you selected already displays the appropriate condition. The colored, underlined specific words link indicates that you need to enter the words or values that will trigger the action (displayed below the condition). See Figure 4-20.

Figure 4-20	ADDING CONDITIONS TO A SELECTED RULE

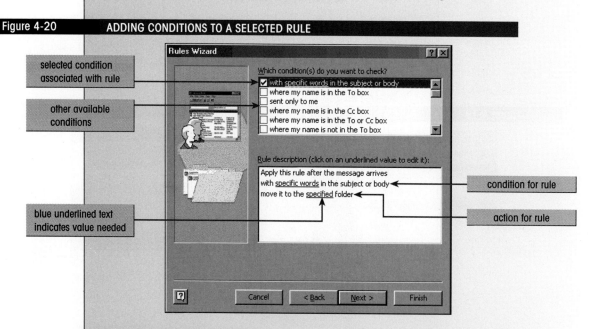

You could add and remove conditions to further clarify the rule. When you specify multiple conditions, all the conditions must be met for the action to occur. Outlook compares the message to the conditions in the order they appear in the list. If a condition in the list is met, Outlook continues to the next condition in the list. Once a condition is not met, the action will not occur.

3. Click the **specific words** link in the Rules description list box. The Search Text dialog box opens.

   You enter which keywords or phrases will trigger Outlook to move an incoming message when they appear in the subject line or message body. Outlook will search for the exact word or phrase you type, so spelling, capitalization, and spaces count.

4. Type **Gormann** in the Add new text box, and then click the **Add** button. The word appears in the Search list box surrounded by quotation marks. See Figure 4-21.

Figure 4-21   SEARCH TEXT DIALOG BOX

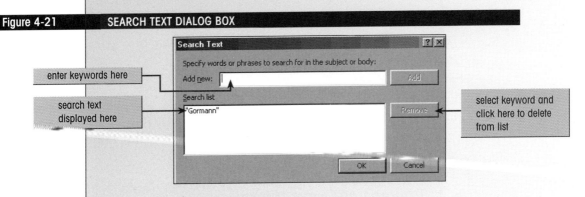

enter keywords here

search text displayed here

select keyword and click here to delete from list

5. Click the **OK** button. The link changes to black but remains underlined, so you can edit the value at anytime by clicking the link.

Next you determine the action that will occur when the rule's condition is met. The rule you selected already displays the appropriate action, but you need to enter a value. You'll advance to the next Rules Wizard dialog box so you can see the available actions.

To set the rule's action and exception:

1. Click the **Next** button in the Rules Wizard dialog box. The Rules Wizard dialog box displays a list of the available actions.

2. Click the **specified** link. A Rules Wizard dialog box opens so you can select the appropriate folder or create a new one.

3. Click the **Expand** button ⊞ next to Inbox, click the **Gormann** folder, and then click the **OK** button. The Rule description list box shows the rule you created. See Figure 4-22.

Figure 4-22   RULE WITH CONDITION AND ACTION

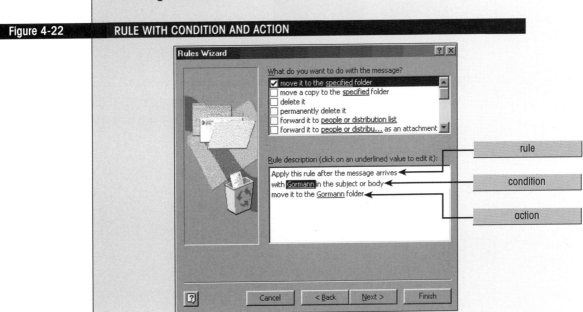

rule

condition

action

4. Click the **Next** button to advance to the Rules Wizard dialog box that lists available exceptions to add to the rule.

Because you have no exceptions, you'll move to the next Rules Wizard dialog box.

5. Click the **Next** button. The Rules Wizard dialog box has options for naming, applying, and turning on the rule.

Naming a rule enables you to turn on or off the rule and reuse it as needed. Use short descriptive names for rules so that you can identify them in the dialog box. You can also select whether you want to apply the rule to messages that already appear in the Inbox and whether you want to turn on this rule.

To name and save the rule:

1. Type **Gormann Party** in the Please specify a name for this rule text box.

2. Verify that a check mark appears only in the **Turn on this rule** check box. See Figure 4-23.

Figure 4-23	SAVING CREATED RULE WITH A NAME

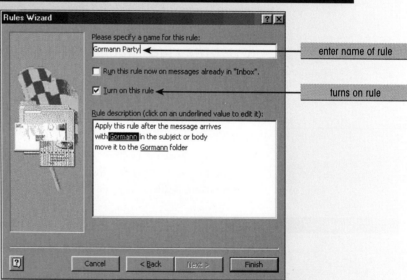

3. Click the **Finish** button to save the rule and return to the original Rules Wizard dialog box. See Figure 4-24.

Figure 4-24   ORIGINAL RULES WIZARD DIALOG BOX

check mark indicates
rule is turned on

buttons to create,
modify, duplicate,
rename, or erase
a selected rule

you may see other rules

description of
selected rule

click to run the
checked rules

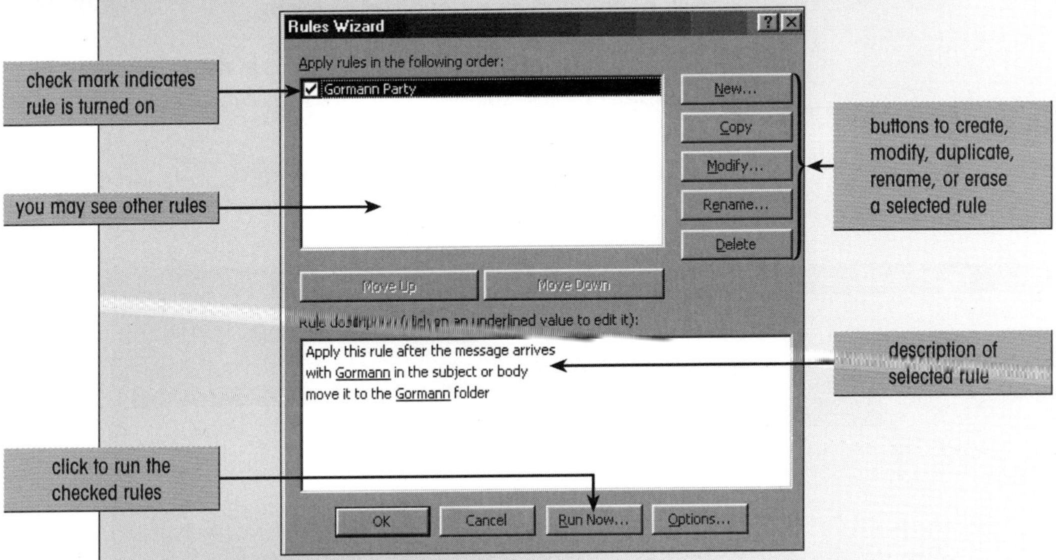

TROUBLE? If the Office Assistant or a dialog box opens and displays the message "This rule is a client-only rule, and will process only if Outlook is running," then you are set up to run Outlook with Exchange. This message appears because Outlook has determined that the rule requires access to your computer to run. Click the OK button. Outlook saves the rule and adds "(client only)" after the name of the rule in the Rules Wizard dialog box to remind you that your computer must be logged onto Exchange for the rule to be run.

The Rules Wizard dialog box enables you to manage existing rules as well as to create new ones.

Managing Rules

You can turn on or off the rules you create and change the order in which the rules are applied. Rules are turned on when a check mark appears in the check box that precedes their names. You can click the check box as needed to turn on or off a rule. For example, if the Gormann's were regular clients you might turn off the Gormann Party rule after the event to make the processing of incoming messages faster, but not delete the rule. If you have more than one rule, the rules are applied sequentially in the order they are listed. You can click the Move Up or Move Down button to rearrange the rules. In addition, you can run rules at any time.

You decide to run the Gormann Party rule now to quickly organize the messages in the Inbox and its subfolders.

To run a rule:

1. Click the **Run Now** button in the Rules Wizard dialog box. The Run Rules Now dialog box opens. Here you select the rules you want to run, in which folders to apply the rules, and what messages should be affected.

2. Click the **Gormann Party** rule check box to insert a check mark.

TROUBLE? If the Run in Folder text box does not display the Inbox, click the Browse button and then double-click Inbox.

3. Click the **Include subfolders** check box to insert a check mark. You include the subfolders to be sure that all messages are checked for the rule, not just the main folders.

4. If necessary, click the **Apply rules to** list arrow, and then click **All Messages**. See Figure 4-25.

Figure 4-25   RUN RULES NOW DIALOG BOX

check mark indicates
rule is selected

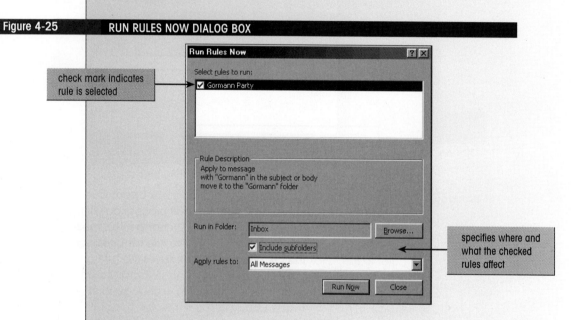

specifies where and
what the checked
rules affect

5. Click the **Run Now** button. All the messages with Gormann in the subject or body are moved to the Gormann folder.

6. Click the **Close** button in the Run Rules Now dialog box.

7. Click the **OK** button in the Rules Wizard dialog box to close it.

Rules can help keep your Inbox organized with a minimum of effort from you.

To verify the rule moved messages:

1. Click the **Speedy Cleaning** folder in the Folder List. Two messages remain in the folder; neither of these messages contain the search text "Gormann."

    TROUBLE? If you have only one message remaining in the folder, then you never received the read receipt e-mail. Just continue with Step 2.

2. Click the **Gormann** folder in the Folder List. The three messages the Rules Wizard moved all contain the search text "Gormann" in the subject or message body.

Next you'll send a message that doesn't meet the rule's criteria to see how the rule works with incoming messages. This message is noncritical, so you'll assign it a low importance level.

To send a non-rule message:

1. Create a new message to your e-mail address with subject **Client Referrals** and the text **Our clients seem very happy with our cleaning crews. I've received four inquiries this week from potential customers who were referred by current clients**, press the **Enter** key twice to double space, and then type your name.

2. Click the **Importance: Low** button ⬇ on the Standard toolbar to change the message's importance to Low.

3. Send the message and, if necessary, download the message.

4. Verify that the message remains in the Inbox.

Another helpful feature of the Rules Wizard is the ability to import and export rules. When you export rules, you save them to a file, creating a backup file that you can retrieve later or import to another computer. When you import rules, you retrieve the rules file. You'll export your rule to a backup file.

To export rules:

1. Click **Tools** on the menu bar, and then click **Rules Wizard** to open the Rules Wizard dialog box.

2. Click the **Options** button in the Rules Wizard dialog box. The Options dialog opens, enabling you to import or export the list of rules. If you are using Exchange, this dialog box also contains buttons to update the list of rules on the Exchange server.

3. Click the **Export Rules** button in the Options dialog box. The Save Exported Rules as dialog box opens, which functions like the Save As dialog box.

4. Save the rules file as **Gormann Party Rules** in the **Tutorial** folder within the **Tutorial.04** folder on your Data Disk.

5. Click the **Save** button in the Save Exported Rules as dialog box.

6. Click the **OK** button in the Options dialog box.

7. Click the **OK** button in the Rules Wizard dialog box to close it.

Now that the rule is saved on a disk you can share the rule with Nadya, who wants to import it onto her computer.

You have started to arrange a cleaning crew for an upcoming event by sending and replying to e-mails with message flags and voting options. You have also set up a rule to move specific messages into an appropriate folder. In the next session, you will find and organize messages in various ways so you can easily locate and arrange the messages. Then you will archive messages and learn to use Outlook remotely.

Session 4.1 QUICK CHECK

1. What is a message flag?

2. Explain the purpose of voting buttons.

3. Why would you request message delivery and read receipts?

4. What is one advantage of the Folder List?

5. True or False: You can create folders at the same level as the default folders or within any main folder.

6. List two ways to file messages.

7. Describe the three parts of a rule.

8. What is one reason you might export rules?

SESSION 4.2

In this session you will find, sort, and group messages to organize them in various ways. Next you will archive messages in your Inbox. Then you will turn on the junk mail filters and learn how to work remotely.

Rearranging Messages

After you place your messages in a variety of folders, you can further arrange them. Finding, sorting, grouping, and filtering provide different ways to organize your messages with a folder.

Finding Messages

As your folder structure becomes more complex and the number of stored messages increases, it might become difficult to locate a message you filed. Rather than taking the time to manually search through multiple folders, you can have Outlook find the desired message. The Find command searches for text listed in the To, Cc, or Subject box of the messages currently displayed. For example, you can search for all the cleaning crew messages in the Gormann folder. For searches of more than one criterion or multiple folders and subfolders, you must use the Advanced Find feature.

REFERENCE   WINDOW   **RW**

Finding Messages
- Open the folder you want to search.
- Click the Find button on the Standard toolbar (*or* click Tools on the menu bar, and then click Find).
- Type the search text in the Look for text box.
- Select the Search all text in the message check box if you want to search subject and message body.
- Click the Find Now button.

or
- Click Advanced Find in the Find pane (*or* click Tools on the menu bar, and then click Advanced Find).
- Select the location you want to look in.
- Specify the search criteria on the Messages, More Choices, and Advanced tabs in the Advanced Find dialog box.
- Click the Find Now button.

You'll use the Find feature with the messages you filed in the Gormann Party folder.

To find all messages related to cleaning crew:

1. If you took a break after the last session, make sure Outlook is running and the Folder List is displayed.

2. Click the **Gormann** subfolder in the Folder List to display its contents.

3. Click the **Find** button 🔍 Find on the Standard toolbar. The Find pane opens, indicating that it will find items in the open folder, in this case the Gormann folder.

4. Type **cleaning crew** in the Look for text box. This is the phrase for which you want to search.

5. Click the **Search all text in the message** check box to insert a check mark, if necessary. This option tells Outlook to search for the text in the To, Cc, and Subject boxes as well as the message body. If you clear the check box, the search is faster but not as thorough.

6. Click the **Find Now** button. After a moment, the only two messages in the Gormann folder that contain the text "cleaning crew" appear in the Information viewer, although the status bar shows that there are actually more items in the folder. See Figure 4-26.

Figure 4-26	LOCATING MESSAGES WITH THE FIND PANE

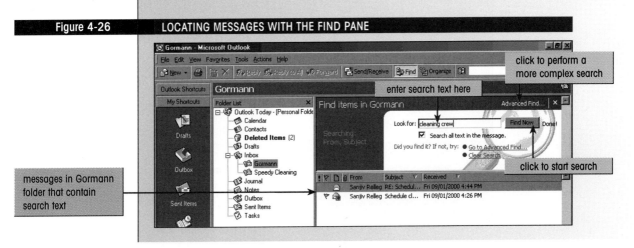

click to perform a more complex search

enter search text here

click to start search

messages in Gormann folder that contain search text

7. Click **Clear Search** in the Find pane to display all the messages again. You also could close the Find pane to redisplay all messages in that folder.

As you can see, simple searches quickly locate information within a folder based on simple text criteria. However, when you want or need to do a more complex search, you'll need to open the Advanced Find dialog box. Depending on what type of item (file, message, note, and so forth) you are looking for, the options that you can specify as search criteria in the three tabs change. For example, with message items you can search for a variety of criteria. From the Messages tab you can specify keywords, specific sender and recipient names, and dates. The More Choices tab for messages provides search access based on assigned categories, status, priority, attachments, and size. The Advanced tab for any type of item enables you to create custom criterion by specifying the field and results you want to locate, such as Flag Status equals Completed. If you want to narrow the search results to very specific items, you can specify that items match several criteria.

You'll search for any messages in all folders that include the text "Gormann" and the text "cleaning crew" in the subject or message body.

To conduct an advanced find:

1. Click **Advanced Find** in the Find pane. The Advanced Find window opens. See Figure 4-27.

Figure 4-27   ADVANCED FIND DIALOG BOX

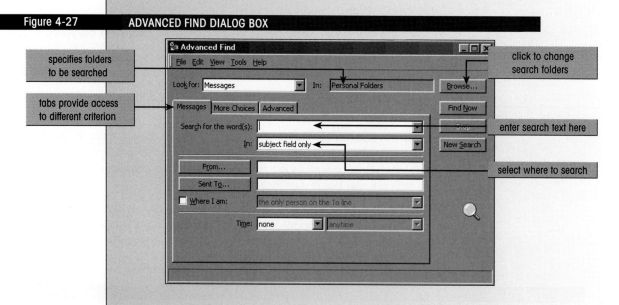

The search is already set to look for messages in Personal Folders, which will search all the folders—something you cannot do from the Find pane.

2. Type **Gormann;cleaning crew** in the Search for the word(s) text box. The semicolon separates different search criterion. Outlook will search for this text in the message subject.

3. Click the **More Choices** tab. You'll set the importance level on this tab.

4. Click the **Whose importance level is normal** check box to insert a check mark. This specifies that Outlook should find only messages that have a Normal importance.

The search text you specified on the Messages tab may appear in both the subject and the message body. You'll return to that tab and change the criterion.

5. Click the **Messages** tab, click the **In** list arrow, and then click **subject field and message body**. This specifies that Outlook should look for the search text in two places.

6. Click the **Find Now** button. Outlook searches in all folders for all messages that match your criteria and displays them in the search results table. See Figure 4-28.

Figure 4-28   COMPLETED ADVANCED FIND

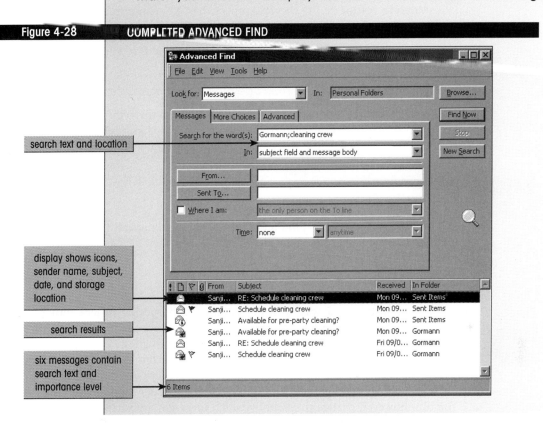

search text and location

display shows icons, sender name, subject, date, and storage location

search results

six messages contain search text and importance level

You'll perform the same search but change the importance level to Low to see how even altering one criterion can change the find results.

To perform a second advanced find:

1. Click the **More Choices** tab.

2. Click the **Whose importance level is** list arrow, and then click **low**.

3. Click the **Find Now** button. Outlook searches in all folders for all messages that match your criteria and displays them in the search results table. This time only one message in the Inbox and one message in the Sent Items folder matches your criteria.

4. Double-click the **Client Referrals** message in the Inbox folder to open that message.

5. Read the message, and then close the Message window.

If you don't find the message or messages you were expecting, check your search criteria to be sure it's not too restrictive and that you've spelled any search text correctly.

You can move, delete, or respond to messages directly from the Advanced Find window. You'll move the Client Referrals message into the Speedy Cleaning folder.

To move a message from the Advanced Find window:

1. Right-click the **Client Referrals** message that is in the Inbox, and then click **Move to Folder** on the shortcut menu. The Move Items dialog box opens, and provides access to all the folders and subfolders in Outlook.

2. Expand the Inbox if necessary, and then click the **Speedy Cleaning** folder to select it.

3. Click the **OK** button. The message moves from one folder to another.

4. Verify that the Client Referrals message has moved to the Speedy Cleaning folder by looking at the In Folder column in the Advanced Find window.

5. Close the Advanced Find window.

6. Click the **Find** button [Find] on the Standard toolbar to close the Find pane.

The Find and Advanced Find features work similarly for all Outlook folders and items. Another way to manage files is to sort them.

Sorting Messages

Recall that sorting is a way to arrange items in a specific order—either ascending or descending. Ascending order arranges messages alphabetically from A to Z, chronologically from earliest to latest, or numerically from lowest to highest. Descending order arranges messages alphabetically from Z to A, chronologically from latest to earliest, or numerically from highest to lowest.

By default, all messages are sorted in descending order by their Receive date and time. You can, however, change the field by which messages are sorted; for example, you might sort e-mail messages alphabetically by sender. Alternatively, you can sort messages by multiple fields; for example, you might sort e-mail messages alphabetically by sender and then by subject. You can sort by up to as many as four fields at one time.

The simplest way to change the sort order is to click a column heading in the Information viewer. Each time you click the heading, the column alternates between ascending order (indicated by an up triangle) and descending order (indicated by a down triangle). You can press and hold the Shift key as you click other column headings to add additional sort criteria to the view. If you click a column heading without pressing the Shift key, you replace the previous sort criterion.

You'll sort your messages first by subject, and then by date received within each subject.

To sort messages in the Gormann folder by subject:

1. If necessary, switch to the Gormann folder.

2. Click the **Subject** column heading. The sort order changes to ascending by subject, as indicated by the up arrow icon in the Subject column heading. Outlook does not include the RE: text when alphabetizing by subject.

   TROUBLE? If the arrow icon points down, then the sort order is descending. Click the Subject column heading again to sort messages in ascending order by subject.

Next you'll sort the messages within each subject in ascending order by the received date.

3. Press and hold the **Shift** key, click the **Received** column heading until the arrow icon points up, and then release the **Shift** key. See Figure 4-29.

Figure 4-29   MESSAGES SORTED IN GORMANN FOLDER

arrow icons indicate sort order

The view remains in this sort order until you change it.

4. Click the **Received** column heading until the arrow icon points down to reorder the messages in descending order by the received date.

You can sort messages in any view except Message Timeline view. Message Timeline view displays messages sorted by date. This view enables you to quickly see all your messages organized by specific date. A bar above a message indicates the amount of time that message was open.

To view the messages in Message Timeline view:

1. Be sure you are viewing the messages in the Gormann folder.

2. Click **View** on the menu bar, point to **Current View**, and then click **Message Timeline**. The messages in the Gormann folder appear on the date they were sent along a timeline.

3. Drag the horizontal scroll bar to scroll the timeline from the current date back to the previous month, and then scroll back to the current date. Because there are no other messages in the folder, the other dates are empty.

4. Click **View** on the menu bar, point to **Current View**, and then click **Messages**. The view returns to a table view of your e-mails.

If you want to sort your messages by fields that are not visible in the Information viewer, you'll need to open the Sort dialog box.

Grouping Folder Items

Grouping is a way to separate related folder items. Certain views are set up to arrange items in commonly used groups, such as By Sender or By Conversation Topic. When you switch to these views, each sender or subject becomes a different group. An Expand button indicates that a group contains the number of messages indicated; you click the Expand button to expand the grouping to display the messages. A Collapse button indicates that the grouping is expanded; you click the Collapse button to hide the messages in that group.

REFERENCE WINDOW   **RW**

<u>Grouping Messages</u>

■ Click View on the menu bar, point to Current View, and then click a grouping view, such as By
  Conversation Topic.
  or
■ Right-click a column heading to group by, and then click Group By This Field.
■ Drag additional column headings to Group By Box to create subgroups.
  or
■ Click View on the menu bar, point to Current View, and then click Customize Current View.
■ Click the Group By button in the View Summary dialog box.
■ Click the Group items by list arrow, and then click a field to group by. Select sort order as needed.
■ Click the first Then by list arrow, and then click a field.
■ Select a third and fourth grouping, if necessary.
■ Click the OK button in the Group By dialog box.
■ Click the OK button in the View Summary dialog box.

You'll arrange the messages in the Gormann folder in a variety of groups.

To group messages:

1. Click **View** on the menu bar, and then point to **Current View** to display the list
   of default views.

2. Click **By Conversation Topic**. The messages are rearranged according to the
   information in the Subject box. Each subject, or conversation topic, becomes a
   different group. The Expand button indicates that a group contains the number
   of messages indicated in parenthesis after the conversation topic.

3. Click the **Expand** button ⊞ next to **Available for pre-party cleaning?**. The
   message in that group is displayed, and a Collapse button precedes the conversation topic. See Figure 4-30.

Figure 4-30   **MESSAGES GROUPED BY CONVERSATION TOPIC**

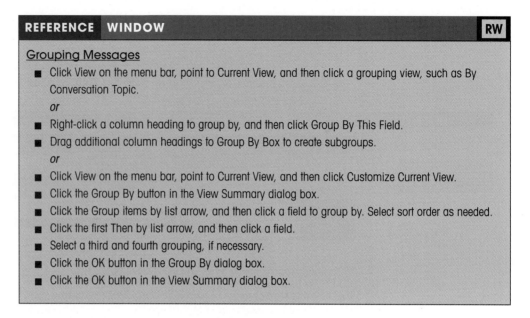

expanded group   group headings

4. Click the **Received** column heading to sort the messages within each group in
   ascending order by date.

5. Expand the **Schedule cleaning crew** group to display its sorted messages.

6. Click the **Received** column heading again to sort the messages within each
   group in descending order by date.

7. Change the current view to **Messages**, and then verify that the messages are in descending order by the Received column.

If the preset group views are not enough, you can create your own groupings using as many as four fields. When you create multilevel groups, items are grouped within groups; for example, you can group messages by sender and then group messages by subject within each sender group. If the fields by which you want to group are not visible, then you can open the Group By dialog box to create the groupings.

To create custom groups:

1. Right-click the **From** column heading, and then click **Group By This Field**. The column header moves to the Group By Box above the column headings. The messages are grouped by the sender name.

2. Click the **Expand** button ⊞ next to the group to display the messages. See Figure 4-31.

Figure 4-31	MESSAGES GROUPED BY SENDER NAME

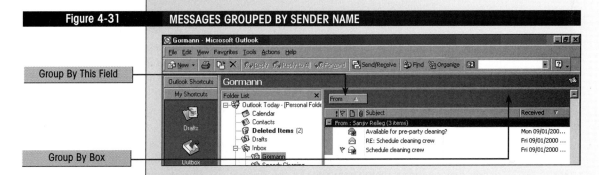

Now that the Group By Box is open, you can drag column headings to or from the Group By Box to create additional groupings or remove existing groupings.

3. Drag the **Subject** column heading to the Group By Box. Red placement arrows show where the group will be placed. Once you release the mouse button, a connecting line shows the relationship between the groups—messages are grouped by the subjects within each sender group.

4. Click the **Expand** button ⊞ next to each group to display the messages. Graphically, you can see how the groups are nested within each other.

5. Drag the **From** column heading box from the Group By Box down to the left of the Received column heading. The red placement arrows indicate the position that the column heading will be placed. See Figure 4-32.

Figure 4-32	MESSAGES GROUPED BY SENDER AND THEN BY SUBJECT

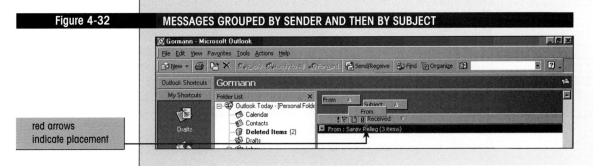

6. Release the mouse button. The messages are split into two groups based on the subject line.

You can organize the information for the messages by placing the column headings in different orders.

7. Right-click the **Subject** box and then click **Don't Group By This Field**. The Subject column is returned to the column headings to the right of the Received column.

8. Drag the **Subject** column header to its original location to the left of the Received column. The grouping is removed, but the Group By Box remains open.

9. Right-click any column heading, and then click **Group By Box** to close it.

The helpfulness of grouping becomes even more apparent when you accumulate a large number of messages (or items in other folders). You could further customize a view by removing some of the existing column headings and adding others. Another technique that helps organize items is to filter the view.

Filtering a Message View

You can filter which messages appear in a view using the same process you used to filter a contact list. Recall that a filter displays only those items in a folder that match certain criteria. Items that do not match the criteria are hidden from view, although they still appear in the folder. Filtering does not move or remove items. For example, you could filter your messages to display only the ones from Nadya. In this case, the other messages would remain in the folder but stay hidden until you remove the filter.

To apply a filter, you display the appropriate folder, click View on the menu bar, point to Current View, and then click Customize Current View. Click the Filter button. The Filter dialog box opens in which you specify the criteria for the filter. You may want to click the Clear All button so that no preexisting criteria influence the new filter criteria. Enter the filter options you want in the Filter dialog box, such as the word for which to search or the sender's name. Review your options to verify accuracy (including spelling), and then click the OK button in the Filter dialog box. The View Summary dialog box recaps your filter options. Review the settings, and then click the OK button to close the View Summary dialog box. Only the messages that match your filter will then appear in the folder. As a reminder, the words "Filter Applied" appear in the status bar until you remove the filter from the folder. To remove the filter, open the Filter dialog box again and then click the Clear All button.

Archiving Messages

Eventually, even the messages in your subfolders can become too excessive to manage easily. More often than not, you don't need immediate access to the older messages. Rather than reviewing your filed messages and moving older ones to a storage file, you can archive them. The **Archive** feature lets you manually transfer messages or other items stored in a folder to a personal folder file when the items have reached the age you specify. Recall that a personal folder file is a special storage file with a .pst extension that contains folders, messages, forms, and files; it can be viewed only in Outlook. Outlook calculates the age of an e-mail message from the date the message was sent or received, whichever is later. You can also have Outlook perform this process automatically with the **AutoArchive** feature, which moves or deletes messages or other items that have reached the age you specify each time you start Outlook. AutoArchive also can empty the Deleted Items folder.

When you create an archive, your existing folder structure from Outlook is recreated in the archive file and all the messages are moved from Outlook into the archive file. If you want to archive only a subfolder, the entire folder structure is still recreated in the archive file; however, only the messages from the selected subfolder are moved into the archive file. For example, if you archive the Gormann folder, the archive file will include both the Inbox and the Gormann subfolder, but only the message in the Gormann subfolder will be moved. Any messages in the Inbox remain in the Outlook Inbox. All folders remain in place within Outlook after archiving—even empty ones.

Archiving Messages Automatically

When you turn on AutoArchive, you have several options. AutoArchive runs only when you start Outlook; you can select whether a prompt appears before the archive process begins. You can select how often AutoArchive runs; the default for messages is every 14 days. You can also determine whether expired e-mail messages are deleted from Outlook and the Deleted Items folder after the archiving, and set the name and location of the archive file.

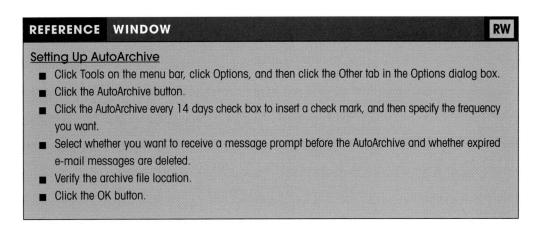

REFERENCE WINDOW **RW**

Setting Up AutoArchive
- Click Tools on the menu bar, click Options, and then click the Other tab in the Options dialog box.
- Click the AutoArchive button.
- Click the AutoArchive every 14 days check box to insert a check mark, and then specify the frequency you want.
- Select whether you want to receive a message prompt before the AutoArchive and whether expired e-mail messages are deleted.
- Verify the archive file location.
- Click the OK button.

You'll set up AutoArchive to run every 14 days, and then verify the other options and archive file location.

To set up AutoArchive:

1. Click **Tools** on the menu bar, and then click **Options**. The Options dialog box opens.

2. Click the **Other** tab, and then click the **AutoArchive** button. The AutoArchive dialog box opens.

3. Click the **AutoArchive every 14 days** check box to insert a check mark, verify that **14** appears in the text box, and then verify that the other two check boxes contain check marks. See Figure 4-33.

Figure 4-33   AUTOARCHIVE DIALOG BOX

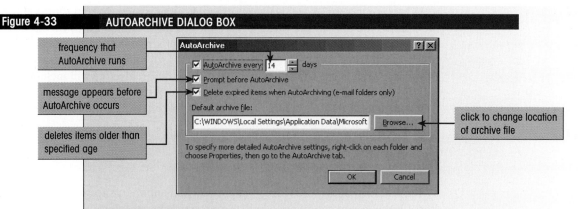

frequency that AutoArchive runs

message appears before AutoArchive occurs

deletes items older than specified age

click to change location of archive file

4. Click the **OK** button in the AutoArchive dialog box, and then click the **OK** button in the Options dialog box.

Outlook will automatically archive all the Outlook folders and subfolders (except Contacts folders) every 14 days. The items that are moved into the archive file are those that have expired, or reached a specified age. Each folder has a default expiration period for its items, as listed in Figure 4-34.

Figure 4-34   DEFAULT EXPIRATION PERIODS FOR OUTLOOK ITEMS

FOLDER	EXPIRATION PERIOD	CALCULATION METHOD
Calendar	6 months	Date started or last modified
Contacts	None	Not archived
Deleted Items	2 months	Date moved into folder
Drafts	3 months	Date created or last modified
Inbox	3 months	Date received or last modified
Journal	6 months	Date entered or last modified
Notes	3 months	Date created or last modified
Outbox	3 months	Date created or last modified
Sent Items	2 months	Date sent
Tasks	6 months	Date completed or last modified; uncompleted tasks are not archived

You'll review the AutoArchive options for the Gormann folder.

To review a folder's AutoArchive properties:

1. Right-click the **Gormann** folder in the Folder List, and then click **Properties**. The Properties dialog box for that folder opens.

2. Click the **AutoArchive** tab. See Figure 4-35.

Figure 4-35   GORMANN PROPERTIES DIALOG BOX

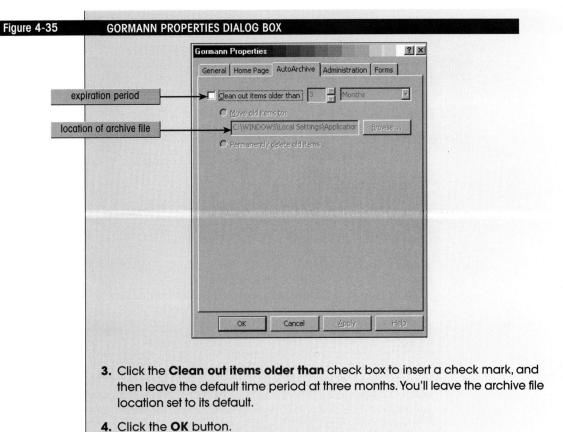

3. Click the **Clean out items older than** check box to insert a check mark, and then leave the default time period at three months. You'll leave the archive file location set to its default.

4. Click the **OK** button.

Because the messages in the Gormann folder are all recent and the AutoArchive will occur every two weeks, these messages will remain in Outlook for almost three months. Rather than wait, you can archive the folder manually.

Archiving Mail Messages Manually

You can archive a folder at any time, such as when you finish a project or event. If you have set up AutoArchive, you can use those settings for the manual archive. If you have not set up AutoArchive, you can specify which folders to archive, the age of items to archive, whether to include items excluded from AutoArchive, and the name and location of the archive file.

To manually archive a folder:

1. Click **File** on the menu bar, and then click **Archive**. The Archive dialog box opens. See Figure 4-36.

Figure 4-36   ARCHIVE DIALOG BOX

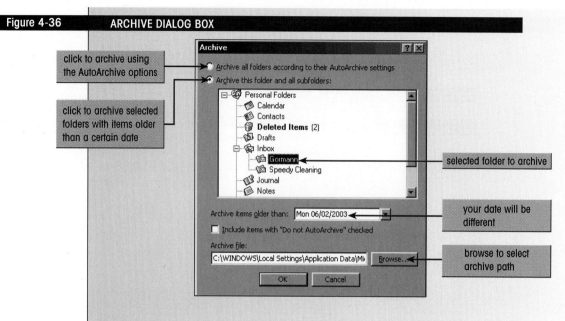

click to archive using the AutoArchive options

click to archive selected folders with items older than a certain date

selected folder to archive

your date will be different

browse to select archive path

2. If necessary, click the **Archive this folder and all subfolders** option button.

3. If necessary, click the **Expand** button ⊞ next to Inbox to display the subfolders, and then click the **Gormann** folder.

4. Type **tomorrow** in the **Archive items older than** text box, and then press the **Tab** key. Outlook will move any files dated with today's date or earlier to the archive file.

5. Click the **Browse** button. The Open Personal Folders dialog box opens.

6. Change the Save in location to the **Tutorial** folder within the **Tutorial.04** folder on your Data Disk, type **Gormann Archive** as the filename, and then click the **OK** button.

7. Click the **OK** button in the Archive dialog box.

8. Click the **Yes** button to confirm that you want to archive all the items in the folder. All of the messages in the Gormann folder are moved into the archive file you specified. The empty Gormann folder remains in the folder structure.

Archiving folder contents enables you to retrieve the items later, if necessary.

Retrieving Archived Folder Items

Archived folders let you keep the contents of your folders manageable and current while providing the security of knowing older information is available if you need access to the information. You won't need the archives unless you want access to a stored item. You can access items in your archive files several ways: You can open the file using the Open command on the File menu and then drag the items you need to a current folder, you can add the archive file to your profile, and you can restore all the items in the archive file by using the Import and Export command on the File menu.

Refusing Junk Mail

E-mail continues to increase in popularity, and a growing number of people have e-mail addresses. This trend has led to a spurt of commercial messages. Businesses, both large and small, have discovered that e-mail is an inexpensive and quick way to get a message out to many people. They are more frequently sending messages to entice you to purchase a service or product, or even to join a business. These unsolicited and unwanted messages can quickly overwhelm your Inbox, much as junk mail clutters your postal mailbox. Junk e-mail is often called **spam**. For more information about spam, visit the Junk Email Resource page at **www.junkemail.org**, the Spam Recycling Center at **www.chooseyourmail.com/spamindex.cfm**, and How to Get Rid of Junk E-mail and Spam page at **www.ecofuture.org/jmemail.html** or use a search engine to search for the keyword "spam".

Outlook can detect unsolicited messages by comparing incoming messages to a filter. A **filter** is a text file that contains words and phrases commonly used in junk e-mail along with their locations. The filter determines that messages are junk e-mail when—to list just a few examples—the From box is blank or includes "sales@"; the Subject box contains "advertisement" or "$$"; or the message body includes "money-back guarantee," "extra income," or "order today." It is important to note that Outlook will not be able to distinguish mail from a colleague that includes these words from the unsolicited mail. Figure 4-37 shows Outlook's filter for junk mail, which is stored in the Filters.txt file with the Outlook program files. There are third-party filters, which are regularly updated, that you can add to Outlook. These filters have the latest lists of commercial and adult content senders. For more information, see the Outlook Web site at **www.microsoft.com/outlook**.

Figure 4-37	JUNK MAIL FILTER

```
MICROSOFT JUNK E-MAIL FILTER README

The Junk and Adult Content filters work by looking for key words.  This file is a description
of exactly which words the filter looks for and where the filter looks for them.

Junk E-mail Filter:

From is blank
Subject contains "advertisement"
Body contains "money back "
Body contains "cards accepted"
Body contains "removal instructions"
Body contains "extra income"
Subject contains "!" AND Subject contains "$"
Subject contains "!" AND Subject contains "free"
Body contains ",000" AND Body contains "!!" AND Body contains "$"
Body contains "for free?"
Body contains "for free!"
Body contains "Guarantee" AND (Body contains "satisfaction" OR Body contains "absolute")
Body contains "more info " AND Body contains "visit " AND Body contains "$"
Body contains "SPECIAL PROMOTION"
Body contains "one-time mail"
Subject contains "$$"
Body contains "$$$"
Body contains "order today"
Body contains "order now!"
Body contains "money-back guarantee"
Body contains "100% satisfied"
To contains "friend@"
To contains "public@"
To contains "success@"
From contains "sales@"
From contains "success."
From contains "success@"
From contains "mail@"
From contains "@public"
From contains "@savvy"
From contains "profits@"
From contains "hello@"
Body contains " mlm"
Body contains "@mlm"
Body contains "///////////////"
Body contains "check or money order"
```

In addition to relying on the preset filters, you can add particular spammers whose messages might make it past the filters to a list of junk senders. This two-prong approach to unsolicited messages—filters and a junk senders list—is an effective way to control junk mail.

Turning on Junk Mail Filters

The Junk Mail filter is actually a rule with a condition, action, and exceptions. You can build this rule from scratch with the Rules Wizard or use the Organize pane to select the preset Junk Mail rule. The Organize pane provides a simpler way to rechannel the unwanted mail. The condition is already set up to compare the subject and body text of incoming messages to the keywords in the filter. You can specify what action to take for detected junk e-mail messages—color the messages to make them stand out in the Inbox or move them to another folder such as the Deleted Items folder or a Junk E-mail folder. After you specify how to handle junk e-mail, you turn on the rule.

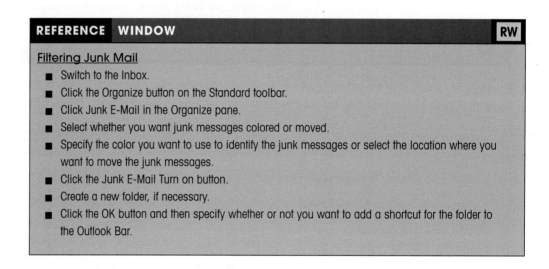

REFERENCE   WINDOW   **RW**

Filtering Junk Mail
- Switch to the Inbox.
- Click the Organize button on the Standard toolbar.
- Click Junk E-Mail in the Organize pane.
- Select whether you want junk messages colored or moved.
- Specify the color you want to use to identify the junk messages or select the location where you want to move the junk messages.
- Click the Junk E-Mail Turn on button.
- Create a new folder, if necessary.
- Click the OK button and then specify whether or not you want to add a shortcut for the folder to the Outlook Bar.

You'll set up the junk mail rule for the Inbox.

To filter junk mail:

1. Click **Inbox** in the Folder List.

2. Click the **Organize** button [Organize] on the Inbox Standard toolbar. The Organize pane opens.

3. Click **Junk E-Mail** in the Organize pane. Figure 4-38 shows the default settings for handling messages that are considered "junk" as well as messages that have "adult content."

Figure 4-38	SETTING THE JUNK MAIL FILTER

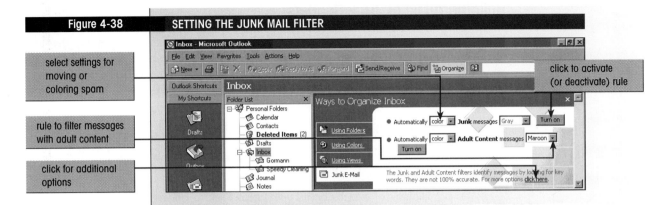

select settings for moving or coloring spam

rule to filter messages with adult content

click for additional options

click to activate (or deactivate) rule

You'll specify that "junk" messages are moved to a Junk E-Mail folder.

4. Click the **Automatically color** list arrow for Junk message, click **move** from the list box. The colors list changes to a list of available folders.

5. Click **Junk E-Mail** in the right list box. You can specify where you want to send all your mail that meets the filter conditions.

6. Click the Junk E-Mail **Turn on** button. The Create New Folder dialog box opens. You choose the location for the new folder. See Figure 4-39.

Figure 4-39	CREATE NEW FOLDER DIALOG BOX

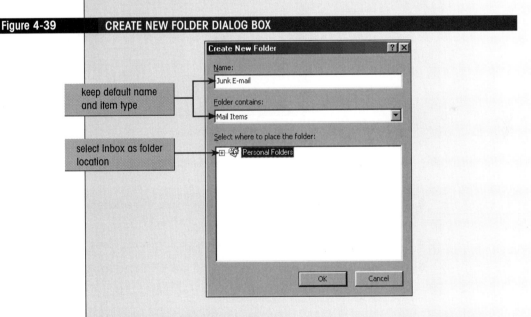

keep default name and item type

select Inbox as folder location

7. Expand the Personal Folders in the Select where to place the folder list if necessary, click **Inbox**, and then click the **OK** button.

8. Click the **No** button if you are asked whether you want to add a shortcut for the folder to the Outlook Bar. The Junk E-Mail folder is created within the Inbox.

The Organize pane shows that "New Junk messages" will be moved to "Junk E-mail." Any message that contains words from the filter will be moved into the specified folder. This is helpful in that you can quickly review the messages to ensure that nothing you wanted slipped through. When you're comfortable that only unwanted messages are being moved, you might have Outlook move the junk messages directly into the Deleted Items folder.

Building a List of Junk Senders

When you receive an unsolicited message that you consider spam, you can add that sender to the Junk Senders Content list. Any messages from these senders are then handled the same way as other junk e-mail—colored or moved to the folder you designate. In this case, the messages from the specified senders are moved to the Junk E-Mail folder.

To add someone to the Junk Senders list:

1. Click the **click here** link at the end of the message in the lower-right corner of the Organize pane.

   The pane displays a bulleted list with helpful information as well as hyperlinks to additional options and updated filters. The last bullet returns you to the previous Junk E-Mail options.

2. Click the **Edit Junk Senders** link in the second bullet. The Edit Junk Senders dialog box opens. See Figure 4-40.

| Figure 4-40 | EDIT JUNK SENDERS DIALOG BOX |

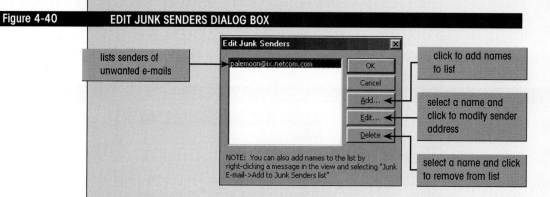

You can use this dialog box to add, edit, or remove an e-mail address from the Junk Senders list. The e-mail address of the selected message appears in the dialog box.

3. If your address appears in the list, make sure the address is selected, and then click the **Delete** button to remove it from the list.

4. Click the **OK** button. The Junk Senders dialog box closes.

5. Click the **Organize** button [Organize] on the Standard toolbar to close the Organize pane.

If you receive mail from a person or vendor and want to add them to the junk senders list, you can do so without opening the Organize pane and clicking through several options. Right-click the message header directly in the Message pane, point to Junk E-mail, and then click Add to Junk Senders list. A dialog box may open, confirming that you've added that e-mail address to the junk sender list. Click the OK button in the dialog box.

Outlook can also identify unwanted messages with adult content using a filter and a sender list. As with junk e-mail, you can then specify whether these messages should be colored or moved. The Organize pane provides similar options for turning on the Adult Content filter and adding specific senders to the Adult Content Senders list.

Cleaning Up

Before you end your Outlook session, you should delete any unnecessary rules, including the junk mail filters, and folders. You'll also delete any messages you created in this tutorial.

To delete rules:

1. Click **Tools** on the menu bar, click **Rules Wizard** to open the Rules Wizard dialog box.

2. Click **Gormann Party** in the Apply rules in the following order list, and then click the **Delete** button.

3. Click the **Yes** button to confirm the deletion.

4. Repeat Steps 2 and 3 to delete the **Junk E-mail Rule** and the **Exception List**. Note that deleting the Junk E-mail Rule turns off the junk mail filter. You can turn on the rule again to continue having Outlook filter messages.

5. Click the **OK** button to close the Rules Wizard.

Next you'll turn off AutoArchive.

To turn off AutoArchive:

1. Click **Tools** on the menu bar, click **Options**, and then click the **Other** tab in the Options dialog box.

2. Click the **AutoArchive** button. The AutoArchive dialog box opens.

3. Click the **AutoArchive every 14 days** check box to remove the check mark.

4. Click the **OK** button in the AutoArchive dialog box.

5. Click the **OK** button in the Options dialog box.

Finally you'll remove any remaining folders or messages you created in this tutorial.

To delete folders and messages:

1. Click the **Gormann** subfolder in the Inbox in the Folder List, and then press the **Delete** key.

2. Click the **Yes** button to confirm the deletion.

3. Repeat Steps 1 and 2 to delete the **Speedy Cleaning** folder and the **Junk E-Mail** folder.

4. Delete any messages you sent in the tutorial from the Inbox and Sent Items folders.

5. Empty the **Deleted Items** folder.

Nadya plans to oversee the cleaning crew at the Gormann's, yet wants to be able to check messages.

Using Remote Mail

Nadya often spends time at various locations overseeing the cleaning teams. While there, she finds it convenient to be able to use a laptop computer to send and receive messages about upcoming events. By setting up Outlook to **work offline** (disconnected from a server on a local network or a dial-up network), Nadya can have access to e-mail when at client locations or at home.

Checking Messages Remotely

Remote Mail is an alternate way to send and receive e-mail from a mail server, whether using your desktop computer or a laptop. The feature enables you to minimize the time spent online because you store finished messages in the Outbox and then send them all at one time. Sending all your written messages in a batch instead of as you finish them is helpful if your computer has a slow modem or the telephone access cost is expensive like at a hotel.

In addition, Remote Mail lets you select which messages to download to your remote computer. First you download the **message headers**, which include the Subject, From, Received, Importance, Attachment, and Size fields from a message. Then based on the message headers, you can decide whether to copy, delete, or download specific messages. You save disk space on your remote computer as well as time because you don't download unwanted or unnecessary messages. Working remotely accesses the personal folder file that stores all the Outlook information on your computer's hard disk, rather than a network server.

The basic steps for setting up Remote Mail are:

1. Set up and start Microsoft Outlook on the computer you plan to use with Remote Mail.

2. If necessary, add the Personal Folders information service to your profile.

3. Specify a mail delivery service and a dial-up connection.

4. Set messages to be delivered to your personal folder file.

The process for setting up Outlook, creating a personal folder file, and specifying a mail delivery service and dial-up connection are the same as when you set up Outlook on the non-remote computer. After you complete these steps, you need to specify where messages are sent and received on your remote computer.

To set where messages are sent and received:

1. Click **Tools** on the menu bar, and then click **Services**. The Services dialog box opens.

2. Click the **Delivery** tab.

3. Click the **Deliver new mail to the following location** list arrow, and then click **Personal Folders**.

   TROUBLE? If you don't see Personal Folders, you may have been assigned a different personal folder filename. Click your assigned personal folder filename in the Deliver new mail to the following location list.

4. Click the **OK** button.

Now that you have specified where the message headers and messages should be downloaded, you can start Outlook on the remote computer from which you want to check messages.

To check messages with Remote Mail:

1. Create a new message to your e-mail address with the subject **Remote test** and the message **This is a test to see how remote mail works.** Send the message to the Outbox.

2. Click **Tools** on the Inbox menu bar, point to **Remote Mail,** and then click **Connect.** The Remote Connection Wizard dialog box opens.

   TROUBLE? If a dialog box opens indicating that Remote Mail cannot start, click the OK button and read but do not complete the rest of the steps.

3. Click the **Internet E-mail** check box in the Connect to which information service list to select it.

   TROUBLE? If you are not using an Internet E-mail connection, click the appropriate information service in Step 3.

4. If necessary, click the **Confirm before connecting** check box to remove the check mark. If selected, the wizard provides the option to verify dialing properties, such as area code and access numbers.

5. Click the **Next** button. In the second dialog box, you choose whether to send and receive all messages, send and receive selected messages, or receive message headers.

6. If necessary, click the **Do only the following** option button, and then verify that the **Retrieve new message headers via Internet E-mail** and **Send "Remote test"** check boxes contain check marks. See Figure 4-41.

Figure 4-41	REMOTE CONNECTION WIZARD DIALOG BOX

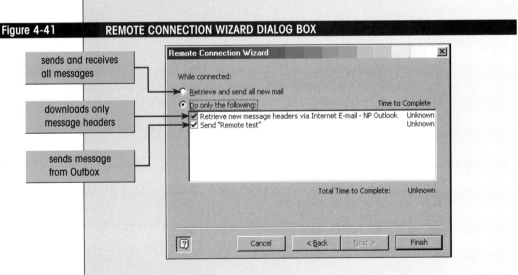

sends and receives all messages

downloads only message headers

sends message from Outbox

TROUBLE? If you are using a different connection, the option you click in Step 6 will list the information service you selected in Step 3.

7. Click the **Finish** button. Outlook connects the dial-up location.

Outlook connects to the server and displays a dialog box that indicates the progress of updating the headers. When finished, the message headers appear in the Inbox, and the Remote toolbar appears. In addition to the connecting and disconnecting buttons, the toolbar includes buttons for marking a message header to download the original message or a copy of the message, deleting selected message headers, or unmarking one or all message headers so the messages remain in their permanent location.

To work with message headers:

1. Click the **Remote test** message to select it. See Figure 4-42.

Figure 4-42	CHECKING MESSAGES REMOTELY

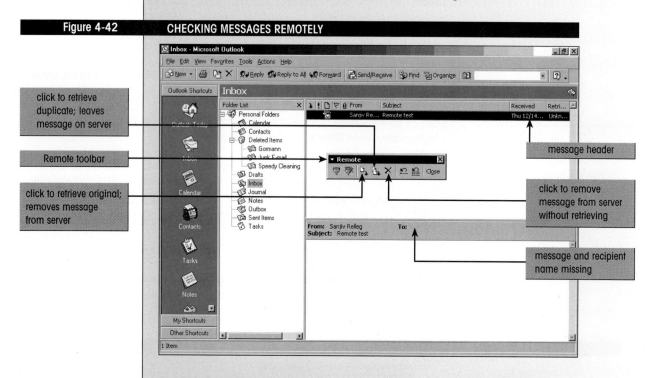

click to retrieve duplicate; leaves message on server

Remote toolbar

click to retrieve original; removes message from server

message header

click to remove message from server without retrieving

message and recipient name missing

2. Click the **Mark to Retrieve** button on the Remote toolbar. The Mark to Retrieve icon appears in the leftmost column. When you reconnect to the server, Outlook will move the complete message to the remote computer.

3. Click the **Connect** button on the Remote toolbar to reopen the Remote Connection Wizard.

4. Verify your information service, and then click the **Next** button.

The Do only the following list displays all the actions that will occur, such as downloading new message headers and downloading or deleting complete messages. You can click an action to insert or remove the check mark as needed.

5. Click the **Retrieve new message headers** check box to remove the check mark in the Do only the following list box. You won't check for new messages at this point. The Retrieve Remote test check box contains a check mark.

6. Click the **Finish** button. The complete message is downloaded and visible in the Inbox. You can work with this message just like any other message.

7. Open the message, print it, and then delete the message.

8. Click the **Disconnect** button on the Remote toolbar to end your online session.

Nadya is confident that the Gormanns will have a spotless house for their upcoming party. Your work ensures that the cleaning crews will be fully staffed and arrive on time at the correct address.

Session 4.2 QUICK CHECK

1. Discuss the difference between find and advanced find.

2. Describe the simplest process for sorting messages by two criteria.

3. What is the purpose of grouping items?

4. What is the purpose of archiving?

5. Explain the difference between Archive and AutoArchive.

6. Define spam.

7. How does Outlook detect spam?

8. When would you use Remote Mail?

REVIEW ASSIGNMENTS

Nadya Rutskoi is planning to attend a conference for professional cleaners about cleaning methods with the smallest environmental impact. The conference is next month and she needs to arrange her travel plans. In addition, she wants to host a lunch meeting for all the independent contractors who work for Speedy Cleaning Company to introduce the new methods to them.

1. Start Outlook, create a new message to your e-mail address with the subject "Eco-cleaning Conference" and the message "The conference takes place in Montreal on the 4th through the 8th of next month. Please arrange air travel and hotel for the conference." Double space and then type your name.

2. Add a message flag with the text "Make travel arrangements" and the due date of next Friday. Send the message.

3. Download the message, and then reply with the text "Liz has your plane tickets and hotel room all set up."

4. Change the importance to "High" and then send the message.

5. Change the message flag on the Eco-cleaning Conference message to complete.

6. Create a new message to your e-mail address with the subject "Lunch Meeting" and the message "Nadya Rutskoi, President of Speedy Cleaning Company, invites you to a lunch meeting to learn about the latest cleaning methods that maximize spotlessness and minimize environmental degradation. Please open this e-mail and select your lunch entrée using the voting button. If you cannot attend, click the Decline button. Thank you." Double space and then type your name.

7. Change the properties of your e-mail address to Always send to this recipient in Microsoft Outlook rich-text format.

Explore ▶ 8. Add custom voting buttons by typing "Pasta;Fish;Chicken;Decline" in the Use voting buttons text box.

9. Add a High importance to the message, and then send the message.

Explore ▶ 10. Download your messages, open the Lunch Meeting message in a separate window, and then reply by selecting a lunch entrée of your choice. Do not add a reply message. Send the message. (*Hint:* If you don't see the voting buttons, reply to the message and then type your lunch entrée preference in the message body.)

11. Download messages, open and read the Lunch Meeting reply you sent, and then close the message.

12. Open the original Lunch Meeting message in the Sent Items folder, display the Tracking tab, print the page, and then close the message. (*Hint:* If you don't have a Tracking tab, then print the original message.)

13. Display the Folder List, and then create a subfolder named "Nadya" that contains Mail Items in the Inbox. Do not add a shortcut to the Outlook Bar.

Explore ▶ 14. Create a subfolder named "Conference" that contains Mail Items in the Nadya folder. Do not add a shortcut to the Outlook Bar.

15. File all the messages in the Inbox related to Speedy Cleaning in the Nadya folder.

16. Create a rule that moves all the messages related to the conference to the Conference folder. Name the rule "Conference."

17. Run the Conference rule, and then verify the proper messages were moved.

18. Export the rule to the **Review** folder within the **Tutorial.04** folder on your Data Disk, using the filename **Conference Rule**.

19. Find all the messages with the word "environmental" or "conference" in the subject or message body.

Explore ▶ 20. Sort the messages you found in descending order by the subject. (*Hint:* Click the Subject column heading to reorder messages.)

Explore ▶ 21. Print all rows of the list of messages in the Advanced Find window in Table Style. (*Hint:* Click File on the Advanced Find menu bar, and then click Print.)

22. Click the More Choices tab, and add the criterion Whose importance is high. Print all rows of the list of messages you find in Table Style.

23. Close the Advanced Find window, and then close the Find pane.

24. Group the messages in the Conference folder using the By Conversation Topic view.

25. Expand all the groups, and then print the message list in Memo Style (do not include attachments or start each item on a new page).

26. Archive all the messages in the Conference folder as **Conference Archive** in the **Review** folder within the **Tutorial.04** folder on your Data Disk.

27. Archive all the messages in the Nadya folder as **Nadya Archive** in the **Review** folder within the **Tutorial.04** folder on your Data Disk.

Explore ▶ 28. Set up Outlook to filter junk mail and color it blue.

29. Create a new message to your e-mail with the subject "Advertisement" and the text "This advertisement message should turn blue once it goes into my Inbox." Send the message.

30. Download the message. Notice that the advertisement message changes to blue.

Explore ▶ 31. Click the Turn Off button to stop filtering junk e-mail, and then close the Organize pane.

32. Delete any rules, messages, and subfolders you created, empty the Deleted Items folder, and then exit Outlook.

CASE PROBLEMS

1. Emergency Training Group Carroll Jameson started the Emergency Training Group to provide CPR, Heimlich, and basic first aid skills training. Individuals can join a group class or organizations can arrange a training session for its members or employees. Once a year, Carroll sends out an e-mail asking attendees to rate the training session his company provided.

1. Start Outlook, create a new message to your e-mail address with the subject "Customer Feedback" and the message "It's time for our annual customer survey. Please send an e-mail message to our customers to determine their level of satisfaction with our training session." Double space and then type your name.

Explore   2. Add a message flag with the preset text "Do not Forward" and no due date. Send the message.

3. Download the message, and then reply with the text "What do you think of the following question: Please rate your level of satisfaction with the Emergency Training Group session you attended in the last 12 months, using the voting buttons in the open message window." Send the message.

4. Download the message, and then reply with the text "Use that question and include five levels on the voting buttons—completely satisfied, very satisfied, satisfied, somewhat dissatisfied, completely dissatisfied." Send the message, and then download it.

5. Create a new message to your e-mail address with the subject "Satisfaction Survey" and the message "Emergency Training Group is always striving to ensure that you are ready for any situation you encounter. Please rate your level of satisfaction with the session you attended in the last 12 months, using the voting buttons in the open message window. Thank you." Double space and then type your name.

6. Change the properties of your e-mail address to Always send to this recipient in Microsoft Outlook rich-text format.

Explore   7. Add custom voting buttons by typing "Completely Satisfied;Very Satisfied;Satisfied;Somewhat Dissatisfied;Completely Dissatisfied" in the Use voting buttons text box.

8. Request a read receipt and a delivery receipt for this message. Send the message.

9. Download the message, and open it in a separate window. Reply by selecting the Somewhat Dissatisfied voting button and adding the message "Please contact me to discuss the situation further." Double space and then type your name. Send the message.

10. Download the message, and then reply with the text "We would like to know why you are not satisfied and what we can do to improve the situation. Carroll Jameson will contact you tomorrow." Send the message.

11. Open the original Satisfaction Survey message in the Sent Items folder, display the Tracking tab, and then print the message.

12. Display the Folder List if necessary, and then create a subfolder named "Customers" that contains Mail Items in the Inbox. Don't create a shortcut to the Outlook Bar.

Explore   13. Make a copy of the Customers subfolder in the Inbox. Click the Customers subfolder to select it, press and hold the Ctrl key while you drag the folder to the Inbox, release the mouse button and the Ctrl key. The copied folder appears with the name Customers1.

Explore   14. Rename the Customers1 subfolder. Right-click the Customers1 subfolder, click Rename "Customers1", type "Carroll Jameson" as the new folder name, and then press the Enter key.

15. File all the messages related to the customer feedback survey in the Customers folder.

16. Create a rule that moves all messages that contain the name "Carroll Jameson" into the Carroll Jameson folder. Name the rule "Carroll".

17. Run the Carroll rule.

18. Export the rule to the **Cases** folder within the **Tutorial.04** folder on your Data Disk, using the filename **Carroll Rule**.

Explore 19. Use the Move to Folder button on the Standard toolbar to move the message from the Carroll Jameson subfolder back into the Customers folder. Click the message to move, click the Move to Folder button on the Standard toolbar, and then click Customers.

20. Archive all the messages in the Customers folder as **Customer Archive** in the **Cases** folder within the **Tutorial.04** folder on your Data Disk.

21. Delete any rules, messages, and subfolders you created, empty the Deleted Items folder, and then exit Outlook.

2. Getaway Havens Finding affordable vacation house rentals can be difficult for people living far from their intended destination. Getaway Havens, founded by Mindy Sterne in 1987, presents prospective vacationers with a list of prescreened rental properties throughout the United States. Properties are rated on their location, cleanliness, and prices. Mindy relies on Outlook to communicate with clients and organize messages because vacationers and property owners reside throughout the world.

1. Start Outlook, create a new message to your e-mail address with the subject "Prepare for the rush" and the message "We're heading into the high season. Get ready for an increase in customer inquiries." Press the Enter key twice to double space, and then type your name. Change the message importance to High. Send the message.

Explore 2. Create a Notify me when important messages arrive rule with the message "Open this message immediately. It's very important." and the name "Important Messages".

Explore 3. Create a Check messages when they arrive rule, with the condition "contact" or "call" in the subject or body, the action flag message for Follow up within 1 day, and the name "Follow Up". (*Hint:* Select the appropriate conditions and actions in the Rules Wizard dialog box, and then edit the values to match those in this step.)

4. Export the Important Messages and Follow Up rules to the **Cases** folder within the **Tutorial.04** folder on your Data Disk, using the filename **Getaway Rules**.

5. Delete the Important Messages and Follow Up rules from the Rules Wizard. (*Hint:* Select the two rules, click the Delete button in the Rules Wizard dialog box, and then click the Yes button to confirm the deletion.)

6. Display the Folder List if necessary, and then create a subfolder named "Follow Up" that contains Mail Items in the Personal Folders at the same level as the Contacts and Inbox folders.

Explore 7. Move the Follow Up folder to within the Inbox folder by dragging it to the Inbox.

Explore 8. Import the saved phone rules file. Click the Options button in the Rules Wizard dialog box, click the Import button in the Options dialog box, select **Getaway Rules** in the **Cases** folder within the **Tutorial.04** folder on your Data Disk, click the Open button in the Import Rules from dialog box, and then click the OK button in the Options dialog box.

Explore 9. Modify the Important Messages rule by adding a second action to move a copy of the message to the Follow Up folder. (*Hint:* Select the message in the Rules Wizard dialog box, click the Modify button, and then click the Next button until the What do you want to do with the message list appears, select the appropriate action, enter the value, and then click the Finish button.)

10. Save the modified rule as **Important Messages Modified** in the **Cases** folder within the **Tutorial.04** folder on your Data Disk.

11. Create a new message to your e-mail address with the subject "Looking for information" and the message "Please contact me with information about your rental rates for 3-bedroom houses on Martha's Vineyard in September." Double space and then type your name. Send the message.

12. Create a new message to your e-mail address with the subject "Rate increases" and the message "Note that rates will be increasing 20% for all vacation rentals between May 31 and August 31. Please be sure to include the appropriate rates in any quotes you send out. Thank you." Double space and type your name. Click the Importance: High button on the Standard toolbar to change the priority. Send the message.

13. Download your messages. Click the Open button in the New Messages of Interest dialog box. Read the Rate increase message, and then close it.

14. Click the Close button in the New Message of Interest dialog box, and then verify that a copy of the Rate increase message appears in the Follow Up folder.

Explore   15. Open the Inbox folder in its own window by right-clicking the folder, and then clicking Open in New Window.

16. Clear the message flag on the Looking for information message in the Inbox folder.

17. Print all rows of the Inbox message list in Table Style, and then close the Inbox folder window.

18. Create a new subfolder called "Getaway" that contains Mail Items within the Inbox. Do not create a shortcut to the Outlook Bar. Move all messages you created for this Case Problem and the Follow Up subfolder into it.

19. Group the messages in the Getaway folder by Importance.

20. Expand the groups, press Ctrl+A keys to select all the messages, and then print all the rows of the message list in Table Style.

21. Remove the grouping, move the Importance column heading as the leftmost column heading, and then close the Group By Box.

22. Filter the messages in the Getaway folder to show only those messages whose importance is High. (*Hint*: Right-click in the Message window, click Filter on the shortcut menu, click the More Choices tab in the Filter dialog box, and then set the filter criterion.)

23. Print all rows of the filter results in Table Style, and then clear the filter.

24. Archive the Getaway folder and all its subfolders as **Getaway Archive** in the **Cases** folder within the **Tutorial.04** folder on your Data Disk.

25. Delete any rules, messages, and subfolders you created, empty the Deleted Items folder, and then exit Outlook.

3. *Viewpoint Polls* Viewpoint Polls is hired by various organizations to take the pulse of the United States about various issues, such as gun control, civil rights, and prison reform. Right now, they are trying to determine for which political party people would vote in an upcoming election. Viewpoint Polls has begun to elicit respondents by e-mail.

1. Start Outlook, create a new message to your e-mail address with the subject "Political Party Preference" and the message "Viewpoint Polls is taking an independent survey to determine the current popularity of political parties. Please open this message and click the voting button that corresponds to the party you most affiliate with. Thank you for your time." Double space and then type your name.

2. Change the properties of your e-mail address to Always send to this recipient in Microsoft Outlook rich-text format.

Explore ▷   3. Add custom voting buttons for each of the following: Democrat, Green, Independent, Reform, Republican, Socialist, Other, and Undecided. (*Hint:* Type each button name separated by semicolons but no spaces in the Use voting buttons text box.)

4. Download the message, and then open it in a separate window. Reply by selecting the voting button of your choice. Send the reply without adding a message.

5. Download the message, open it in a separate window, and then reply by choosing the party affiliation of your choice. Send the reply without adding a message.

6. Download the message, open it, and then print the message.

7. Open the original Political Party Preference message in the Sent Items folder, display the Tracking tab, and then print the message.

8. Create a subfolder named "Viewpoint" that contains Mail Items in the Inbox. Don't create a shortcut to the folder on the Outlook Bar.

Explore ▷   9. Open the Organize pane in the Inbox, and then create a rule that moves messages from your e-mail address into the Viewpoint folder. Click the Create button.

10. Click the Yes button to run the rule on the current contents of the Inbox. Close the Organize pane.

11. Create a new message to your e-mail address with the subject "Survey results" and the message "Please create a report with all the survey results received to date as of next Friday. Thank you." Double space and then type your name.

12. Add a message flag with the text "Create survey report" and a due date of next Friday. Send the message.

13. Download the message, and then reply with the text "So far we haven't received very many replies. We should have a better response rate by next Friday." Send the message. (*Hint:* The message should be in the Viewpoint folder.)

14. Download the message, and then reply with the text "Let me know by next Wednesday if we have a response rate of less than 65%." Send the message, and then download it.

Explore ▷   15. Open the Viewpoint subfolder in its own window by right-clicking the folder, and then clicking Open in New Window.

16. Group by subject all the messages moved by the rule you created in the Organize pane. Expand each group, press the Ctrl+A keys to select all the messages, and then print all the rows of the message list in Table Style.

Explore ▷   17. Move all the messages in the Create survey report group to a new subfolder named "Survey Report" within the Viewpoint folder using the Move to Folder button on the Standard toolbar. (*Hint:* Select all the messages in the group, click the Move to Folder button on the Standard toolbar, click Move to Folder, click the New button in the Move Items dialog box, create the Survey Report subfolder, select the Viewpoint subfolder, and then click the OK button.)

18. Find all the messages with the words "survey report" or "response rate" in the subject or message body and whose importance is normal.

Explore ▷   19. Save the search as **Viewpoint Search** in the **Cases** folder within the **Tutorial.04** folder on your Data Disk. (*Hint:* Click File on the Advanced Find window menu bar, click Save Search, change the save location and filename, and then click the OK button.)

Explore ▷   20. Print in Table Style all rows of the message list in the Advanced Find window. (*Hint:* Click File on the menu bar, and then click Print.)

21. Close the Advanced Find window, and then close the Viewpoint folder window.

22. Archive the **Viewpoint** folder and all its subfolders as **Viewpoint Archive** in the **Cases** folder within the **Tutorial.04** folder on your Data Disk.

23. Delete any rules, messages, and subfolders you created, empty the Deleted Items folder, and then exit Outlook.

4. Favorite Movie Actors Discussions of favorite movie actors (male or female) are common among groups of friends. Find out who is the favorite actor among three classmates. You'll need the e-mail addresses for three classmates; if you do not have three classmates' e-mail addresses, use your own e-mail address.

1. Start Outlook, create a subfolder called "Favorite Actors" that contains Mail Items in the Inbox. Do not create a shortcut to the Outlook Bar.

Explore 2. Create a rule named "Actor" that moves all incoming messages that contain the word "actor" into the Favorite Actors subfolder. (*Hint:* Select the appropriate conditions and actions in the Rules Wizard dialog box and then edit the values to match those in this step.)

3. Export the Actor rule to the **Cases** folder within the **Tutorial.04** folder on your Data Disk, using the filename **Actor Rule**.

4. Create a new message to three classmates' e-mail addresses (or three messages to your e-mail address) with the subject "Favorite actor" and text that asks them to participate in your survey. Include your name.

5. Add a message flag that asks recipients to reply to your message today. Send the message(s).

6. Download your messages. Respond to each flagged message, letting the senders know you will participate in their surveys.

7. Change each message flag to Completed.

8. Create a new message to the same three classmates (or three messages to your e-mail address) with the subject "Vote for an actor" and a message that thanks the recipients for participating, and asks them to select one of the following actors. Include the names of five of your favorite male and/or female actors. Send the message(s).

9. Download your messages, and then reply to each Vote for an actor message with a message that indicates your favorite movie with that actor. Send the messages.

10. Download your messages, and display the Favorite Actors subfolder.

11. Group the messages by sender name, and then by subject. If necessary, expand the groups.

Explore 12. Select all the messages by pressing Ctrl+A keys, and then print all rows of the message list in Table Style. (*Hint:* Click File on the menu bar, and then click Print.)

13. Change the grouping order to subject, and then sender name. If necessary, expand the groups.

Explore 14. Print all the messages in the expanded groups.

15. Change the grouping to only by subject. If necessary, expand the groups.

16. Sort the grouped messages in descending order by subject and then in ascending order by the sender.

Explore 17. Print all rows of the Favorite Actors message list in Table Style.

18. Remove all the groupings, and then hide the Group By Box.

19. Archive the Favorite Actors folder as **Actors Archive** in the **Cases** folder within the **Tutorial.04** folder on your Data Disk.

Explore 20. Open the archive file you created. Click File on the menu bar, point to Open, and then click Personal Folders File (*.pst). The Open Personal Folders dialog box opens.

Change the Look in location to the **Cases** folder within the **Tutorial.04** folder on your Data Disk, and then double-click the **Actors Archive** file to open it.

21. In the Folder List, expand all the folders in the Archive Folders. Notice that the Inbox folder is included even though you selected only its subfolder for archiving.

Explore 22. Copy the Sent Items folder to the Actors Archive file. Press and hold the Ctrl key as you drag the Sent Items folder to the Archive Folders. Release the Ctrl key. The folder and messages are duplicated in the archive file. You could also drag the folders or file from the archive file into the Personal Folders to copy them into Outlook.

Explore 23. Close the archive file. Right-click the Archive Folders in the Folder List, and then click Close "Archive Folders" in the shortcut menu. The archive file closes and disappears from the Folder List.

24. Delete any rules, messages, and subfolders you created, empty the Deleted Items folder, and then exit Outlook.

QUICK | CHECK ANSWERS

Session 4.1

1. A message flag is an icon in the message list as well as an information banner with text and an optional due date.

2. Voting buttons provide a preset list of answers from which recipients select one; vote responses are tracked on the sender's copy of the sent message, providing a current tally.

3. A delivery receipt confirms that your message arrived in the recipient's inbox; a read receipt confirms that the message was opened (but not necessarily read).

4. The Folder List enables you to file and store messages much as if you were using Windows Explorer.

5. True

6. You can file messages manually by dragging messages from the Inbox to the appropriate subfolder or automatically by setting up rules.

7. Conditions specify which messages to act on; actions define what should happen to the qualified messages; exceptions remove messages from the qualifying group.

8. To create a backup file that you can retrieve later or import to another computer.

Session 4.2

1. Find locates messages based on one criterion in a folder; advanced find locates messages based on multiple criteria in any folder.

2. Click the column heading that is the first sort criterion, press and hold the Shift key, click the column heading that is the second sort criterion, and then release the Shift key.

3. Grouping separates related folder items, such as by subject or sender.

4. Archiving removes older messages to a storage file that you can later access.

5. Archive is the manual transfer of messages; AutoArchive is an automated process that occurs each time you start Outlook.

6. Spam is junk e-mail, unsolicited and unwanted messages.

7. After you turn on the junk mail filter, Outlook compares incoming messages to the filter (a text file with words commonly used in junk e-mail) and then colors those messages or moves them to a specified folder.

8. Remote Mail enables you to retrieve messages from your Inbox when you are away from your office.

OBJECTIVES

In this tutorial you will:

- Record activities in the Journal

- View Journal entries

- Mail Office documents

- Create Office documents from Outlook

- Import and export files

- Send and receive faxes

INTEGRATING OUTLOOK WITH OTHER PROGRAMS

Working with Homebuyers for Ace Realty

CASE

Ace Realty

Ace Realty was founded six years ago to provide an alternative, independent realtor to the residents of Omaha, Nebraska. Ace Realty provides professional real estate advice for buying and selling residential properties. The Ace team strives to help clients buy or sell their homes in the least amount of time, for the best price, and with the least amount of stress. The Ace philosophy is to put the clients' best interests first. As a result, most clients are repeat customers or referred by satisfied customers.

The Ace team consists of Khris Reilly, Ty Mumford, Cassandra Evale, and Raymond Chee. They all use Outlook to arrange their schedules, organize their tasks, and compile contact lists of buyers, sellers, lenders, and others. In addition, they rely heavily on the integration abilities of Outlook to exchange information with each other and with their clients. They frequently create e-mail messages from Office documents. They also import data from other programs into Outlook, and export their Outlook data to other file formats. As they work, they use the Journal to track their activities. You'll work with Cassandra as she helps Arlo and Nancy Kirnen find a home that meets their needs and expectations for a price they can afford.

In this tutorial, you will turn on the Journal, and then track your activities both manually and automatically. You'll use Office documents to create and send e-mail messages, and you'll create Office documents from Outlook. Then you'll import data created in other Office programs into Outlook, and export Outlook data into file formats that programs other than Outlook can use. Next you'll learn how to send and receive faxes with Outlook using Microsoft Fax. Finally you'll review the Journal to see the entries that were created.

SESSION
5.1

In this session, you will learn how to use the Journal to record your activities both automatically and manually. Then you'll learn how to send Office documents as e-mail messages and attachments, and finally how to create Office documents right from Outlook.

Recording Activities in the Journal

As you work, it's sometimes helpful to be able to look back at a timeline of your activities. You may want to find exactly when you wrote a certain letter. Or, you may want to recall exactly how you spent a particular workday. Many people write down details of their day in a paper appointment book. In Outlook, you record this information in the Journal. The **Journal** is a diary that records the date, time, and duration of your actions with Outlook items, Office documents, and other activities. The Journal can record activities automatically or you can manually record them yourself.

Cassandra at Ace Realty uses the Journal to keep records of her daily activities, including e-mail messages she sends and receives, telephone calls she makes, Office documents she works on, and so forth.

To view the Journal:

1. Start Outlook, and then click **Journal** in the **My Shortcuts** group on the Outlook Bar. The Journal opens in the Information viewer. See Figure 5-1.

| Figure 5-1 | JOURNAL INFORMATION VIEWER |

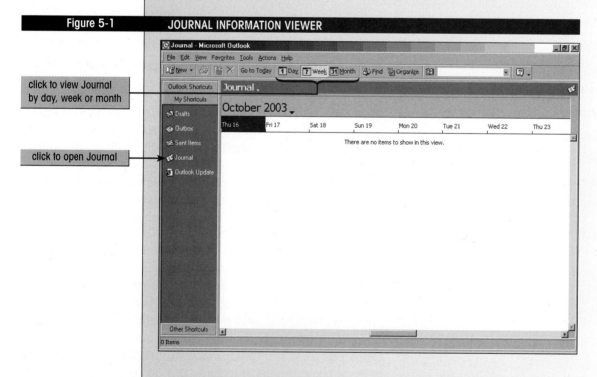

click to view Journal by day, week or month

click to open Journal

TROUBLE? If a dialog box opens, saying that the Journal can automatically track Office documents, and e-mail associated with a contact, then the Journal is not currently set to automatically track activities. Click the No button to close the dialog box and leave the Journal turned off.

Before you work with the Journal, you'll add a task to the to-do list and enter the Kirnens in the contact list.

To enter a task and a contact:

1. Create a new task with the subject **Prepare mortgage worksheet** and the due date of **next Tuesday**.

2. Create a new contact for **Arlo Kirnen**, home phone number **402-555-1574**, home fax **402-555-6789**, address type **Home**, home mailing address **17 Dodge Road, Omaha, NE 98182**, your e-mail address, and spouse **Nancy**.

You'll set up the Journal to record entries for any e-mails related to the Kirnens.

Recording Journal Entries Automatically

The Journal will record the date and time of each action for the Outlook items and the Office files you specify. You can set up the Journal to record the following Outlook items: e-mail messages; meeting requests, responses, and cancellations; and task requests and responses. Although you can check one or all the items, the Journal will record the selected items for only the contacts you specify.

Be aware that when you add entries to your contact list, you must manually select those contacts if you want to record items to or from them in the Journal. You also can have the Journal record files you create, open, close, and save in Access, Excel, PowerPoint, and Word. Outlook creates a shortcut to each Office file in the Journal, even if Outlook isn't running.

REFERENCE WINDOW	RW

Recording Journal Entries Automatically

- Click Tools on the menu bar, and then click Options.
- Click the Preferences tab, and then click the Journal Options button.
- Click the desired items' check boxes in the Automatically record these items list box.
- Click the desired contacts' check boxes in the For these contacts list box.
- Click the desired programs' check boxes in the Also record files from list box.
- Click the OK button in the Journal Options dialog box.
- Click the OK button in the Options dialog box.

Cassandra asks you to set up the Journal to record e-mail messages and Office documents related to the Kirnens. If you have other Office-compatible applications installed on your system, you can also have the Journal record any activities with those files.

To set up the Journal to record entries automatically:

1. Click **Tools** on the menu bar, and then click **Options**. The Options dialog box opens.

2. Click the **Preferences** tab, and then click the **Journal Options** button. The Journal Options dialog box opens. See Figure 5-2.

Figure 5-2	JOURNAL OPTIONS DIALOG BOX

select which Outlook items to track

lists everyone in your Contacts folder

select which Office applications to track (you may see other Office-compatible applications)

3. Click the **E-mail Message** check box in the Automatically record these items list box.

4. Click the **Arlo Kirnen** check box in the For these contacts list box.

5. Click the **Microsoft Access**, **Microsoft Excel**, **Microsoft PowerPoint**, and **Microsoft Word** check boxes in the Also record files from list box. All the Office applications and Office-compatible applications installed on your system appear in the dialog box.

6. Click the **OK** button in the Journal Options dialog box.

7. Click the **OK** button in the Options dialog box.

Although no outward change is visible in Outlook, the Journal will track any e-mail messages you send or receive as well as any Office documents you work on.

Adding Journal Entries Manually

If you don't have the Journal set up to record entries automatically, you can enter them manually. You also can manually create entries for items, files, and actions that the Journal does not record automatically. These include Outlook items such as appointments, notes, and incoming phone calls, as well as those items that you didn't check in the Journal Options dialog box; documents for non-Office programs, Office 97 programs, or Office programs not installed on your computer; and activities you've already completed, printed documents you receive, or actions such as conversations or items you purchase.

When you start a new journal entry, you must enter certain information: the date, the time, and the duration. If the duration is not significant, then just leave the default 0 minutes entry.

To record a journal entry manually:

1. Click the **New Journal Entry** button [New ▾] on the Standard toolbar. A new Journal Entry window opens. See Figure 5-3.

Figure 5-3	BLANK JOURNAL ENTRY WINDOW

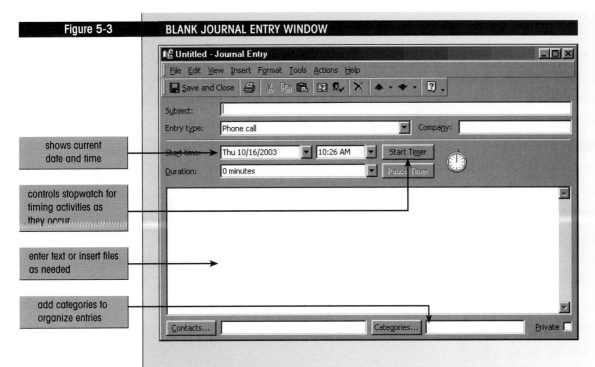

shows current date and time

controls stopwatch for timing activities as they occur

enter text or insert files as needed

add categories to organize entries

2. Type **Mortgage Worksheet for the Kirnens** in the Subject text box.

3. Click the **Entry type** list arrow, and then click **Conversation**.

4. Click the **Duration** list arrow, and then click **10 minutes**.

5. Type **Raymond talked with Arlo Kirnen. He and Nancy are sending in their list of debts for the mortgage worksheet today.** in the notes text box.

6. Type **Raymond Chee** in the Contacts text box. If Raymond had been in your Contacts list, you could have clicked the Contacts button and then selected him from the list. See Figure 5-4.

Figure 5-4	COMPLETED JOURNAL ENTRY

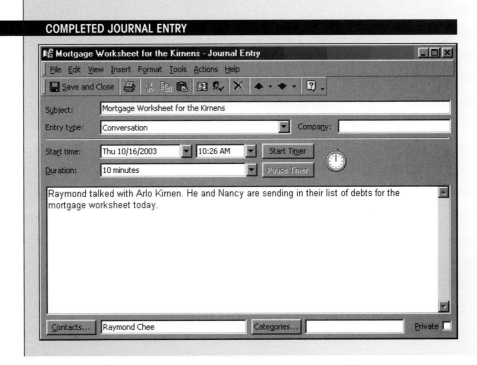

7. Click the **Save and Close** button [🖫 Save and Close] on the Standard toolbar to close the window.

The entry appears in the Journal in the By Type view.

8. Click the **Day** button [📅 Day] on the Standard toolbar, and then click the **Expand** button [➕] next to the Entry Type: Conversation. See Figure 5-5.

Figure 5-5	JOURNAL WITH CONVERSATION ENTRY

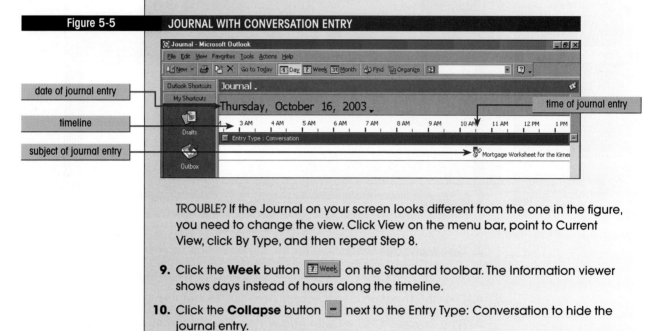

TROUBLE? If the Journal on your screen looks different from the one in the figure, you need to change the view. Click View on the menu bar, point to Current View, click By Type, and then repeat Step 8.

9. Click the **Week** button [📅 Week] on the Standard toolbar. The Information viewer shows days instead of hours along the timeline.

10. Click the **Collapse** button [➖] next to the Entry Type: Conversation to hide the journal entry.

You can use Outlook to chronicle things you do, such as a conversation, as well as significant events, such as the date a new real estate agent started working at Ace. You also can record existing items in the Journal.

Recording Existing Items in the Journal

Even if you've worked on or completed a task, held a meeting, or sent an e-mail message that was not recorded in the Journal, you can still create a Journal entry. When you create an entry that references an existing item, Outlook adds a shortcut to the item on the Journal Entry window. If you double-click the shortcut icon in the Journal, the item's window opens so you can review or modify details.

The quickest way to create a Journal entry from an existing item is to drag the item to the Journal folder. AutoCreate then starts a new journal entry using the information from the dragged item. You can modify the information as needed. If you right-drag (drag an item using the right mouse button rather than the left), a shortcut menu opens with several options, as described in Figure 5-6.

Figure 5-6	JOURNAL SHORTCUT MENU OPTIONS
SHORTCUT OPTION	**RESULTING ACTION**
Copy Here as Journal Entry with Shortcut	Starts a new Journal entry with a shortcut to the item in the notes box.
Copy Here as Journal Entry with Attachment	Starts a new Journal entry with a copy of the item attached (represented by an icon) in the notes box.
Move Here as Journal Entry with Attachment	Starts a new Journal entry with the item moved into the notes box; the item is removed from its original folder.

Earlier you added a task to the to-do list and entered the Kirnens in the contact list. These activities were not entered in the Journal, so you'll manually record them now. You'll mark down the time you've already spent working on the Prepare mortgage worksheet task you set up earlier.

To add an existing task to the Journal:

1. Switch to the **Tasks** folder in the **Outlook Shortcuts** group on the Outlook Bar.

2. If necessary, display the **Journal** folder in the **My Shortcuts** group on the Outlook Bar.

3. Right-drag the **Prepare mortgage worksheet** task to the **Journal** folder, release the right mouse button, and then click **Copy Here as Journal Entry with Shortcut**. The task's Journal Entry window opens with a shortcut to the task inserted in the notes box. See Figure 5-7.

Figure 5-7	JOURNAL ENTRY WITH SHORTCUT TO TASK

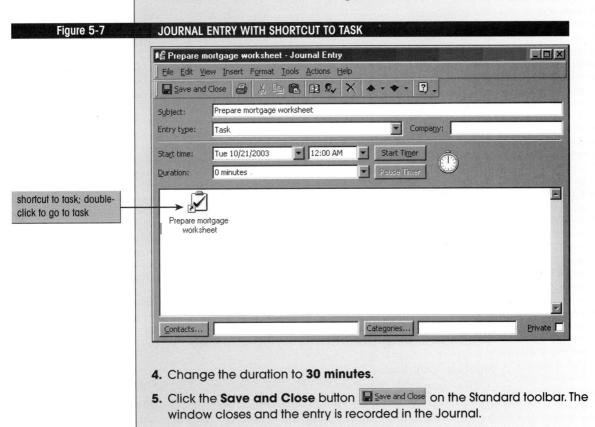

shortcut to task; double-click to go to task

4. Change the duration to **30 minutes**.

5. Click the **Save and Close** button ![Save and Close] on the Standard toolbar. The window closes and the entry is recorded in the Journal.

The ability to enter an item you completed is important if you decide to track an activity after you already invested time and effort on it. Being able to record how long you worked on various tasks or spent at appointments is helpful if you need to track your total time on a project for reporting or billing purposes. You can also record when you entered a contact into Outlook, as a reminder of the initial association.

You'll add Arlo Kirnen's contact card to the Journal with his contact card as an attachment. This way, you could print his contact card with the Journal entry at a later time.

To add an existing contact to the Journal:

1. Switch to the **Contacts** folder, and then display the **Journal** folder on the Outlook Bar.

2. Right-drag the **Arlo Kirnen** contact to the **Journal** folder, release the right mouse button, and then click **Copy Here as Journal Entry with Attachment**. The Journal Entry window for Arlo Kirnen opens with a copy of the contact item inserted in the notes box. See Figure 5-8.

Figure 5-8	JOURNAL ENTRY WITH ATTACHMENT

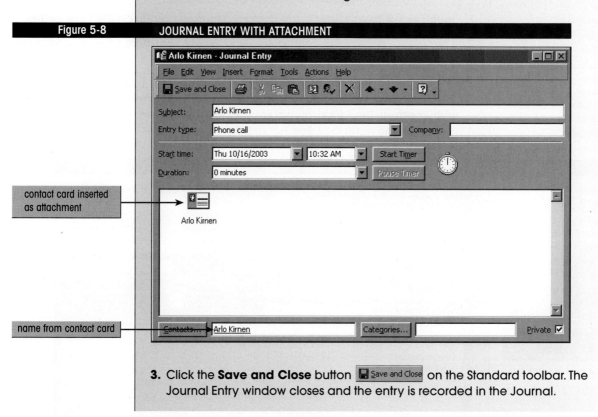

contact card inserted as attachment

name from contact card

3. Click the **Save and Close** button [Save and Close] on the Standard toolbar. The Journal Entry window closes and the entry is recorded in the Journal.

In addition to recording existing items in the Journal, you can also record files.

Adding Existing Documents to the Journal

You can add Journal entries for any file or document you've created in Office or Office-compatible programs. Why would you want to do this? Two reasons: First, it enables you to organize and track all files and items related to a specific project or task. Second, it enables you to find and open the files from Outlook, where they can be associated with a specific subject, contact, or time frame, rather than searching for them with Windows Explorer or My Computer. You choose whether to include a copy of the file in the entry or to insert an icon that you can click to open the original file.

You'll create a journal entry for the mortgage worksheet that you're developing.

To create a journal entry for an existing file:

1. Click the **New** button list arrow 📄 New and then click **Journal Entry**. A new Journal Entry window opens.

2. Type **Mortgage worksheet** in the Subject box, and then select **Microsoft Excel** from the Entry type list. As you can see, many types of entries are available in the list.

3. Click in the notes text box, type **Mortgage worksheet with categories and formulas**, and then press the **Enter** key.

4. Click **Insert** on the menu bar, and then click **Object**. The Insert Object dialog box opens. See Figure 5-9.

Figure 5-9	INSERT OBJECT DIALOG BOX FOR CREATING NEW OBJECT

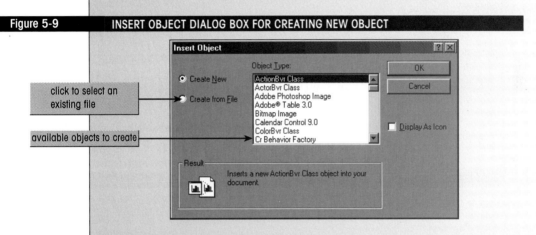

click to select an existing file

available objects to create

5. Click the **Create from File** option button.

6. Click the **Browse** button, and then double-click **Mortgage** in the **Tutorial** folder within the **Tutorial.05** folder on your Data Disk. The path to the file appears in the File text box.

7. Click the **Display As Icon** check box to insert a check mark, and verify that the Link box is unchecked. The Microsoft Excel Worksheet icon appears below the Display As Icon check box as a reminder of the selected file type. See Figure 5-10.

Figure 5-10	INSERT OBJECT DIALOG BOX FOR INSERTING FILE

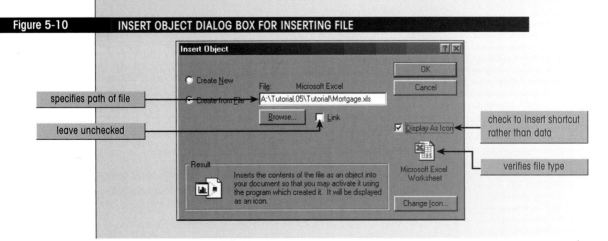

specifies path of file

leave unchecked

check to insert shortcut rather than data

verifies file type

8. Click the **OK** button. A shortcut icon to the file appears in the notes box of the Journal Entry window. See Figure 5-11.

Figure 5-11   JOURNAL ENTRY WITH SHORTCUT TO FILE

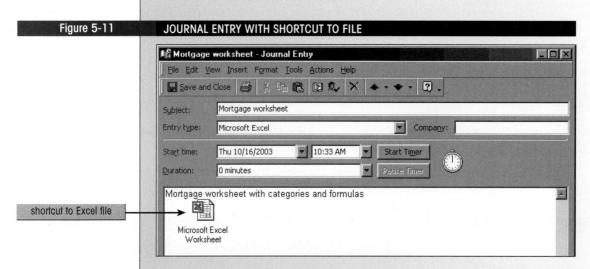

shortcut to Excel file

You can open the Excel file simply by double-clicking this shortcut icon in the Journal Entry window.

9. Double-click the **Microsoft Excel Worksheet** shortcut in the Journal Entry window. The workbook opens in Excel. See Figure 5-12.

Figure 5-12   WORKSHEET OPENED IN EXCEL

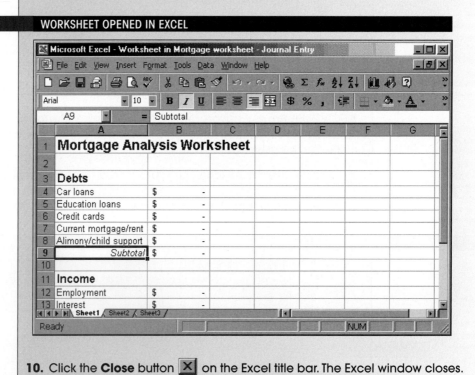

10. Click the **Close** button ⊠ on the Excel title bar. The Excel window closes.

11. Click the **Save and Close** button 🖫 Save and Close on the Standard toolbar. The window closes and the entry is recorded in the Journal.

Next you'll review the Journal entries you've created.

Viewing Journal Entries

When you switch to the Journal folder, you see a timeline with all your entries grouped by type of item, such as task, conversation, and Microsoft Excel. You can display or hide all the entries in a particular group as needed by clicking the Expand or Collapse button. After you've had the Journal on for a while, you may find it difficult to find a specific entry by scrolling. Instead, you can jump to a particular date or expand or condense the timeline to display entries for a day, a week, or a month. You also can change the view to group entries by contact or category or as a table without any groups.

To view journal entries:

1. Switch to the **Journal** folder. The Journal appears in the By Type view for the current week with today's date highlighted and four entry types. See Figure 5-13.

| Figure 5-13 | JOURNAL IN BY TYPE VIEW |

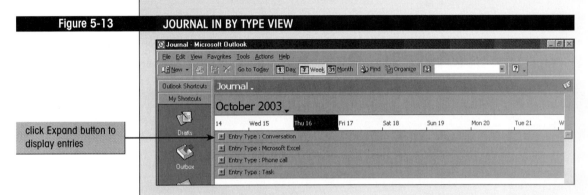

click Expand button to display entries

2. If necessary, click the **Expand** button ⊞ for each group. See Figure 5-14.

| Figure 5-14 | JOURNAL WITH ENTRY TYPE GROUPS EXPANDED |

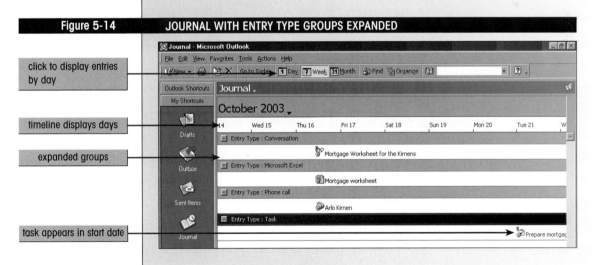

click to display entries by day

timeline displays days

expanded groups

task appears in start date

3. Click the **Day** button ⬚Day on the Standard toolbar. The Information viewer displays a timeline of the day's recorded activities. See Figure 5-15.

Figure 5-15   JOURNAL ENTRIES IN DAY VIEW

timeline displays hours

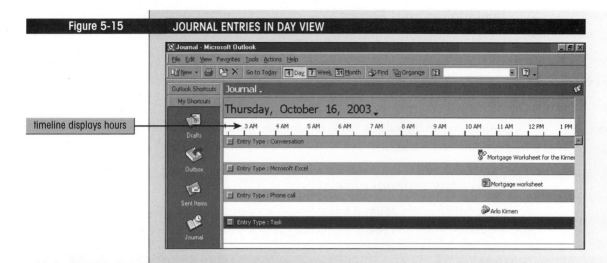

You can move to other dates in the timeline by scrolling or using a calendar.

4. Click the date in the Information viewer. A calendar opens, as shown in Figure 5-16.

Figure 5-16   CALENDAR FOR MOVING AROUND JOURNAL

click to move forward or back one month

click date to display calendar

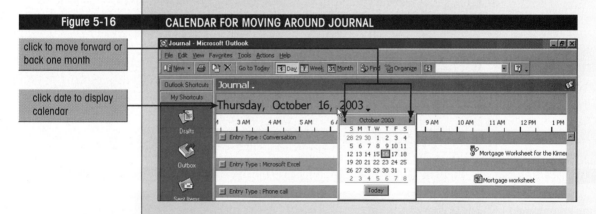

5. Click the date for next Tuesday. The Journal immediately moves to that date; notice the task you created for that day.

6. Click the **Go to Today** button [Go to Today] on the Standard toolbar. The Journal immediately returns to the current day.

All Outlook folders have a timeline view that functions similarly to the Journal timeline view.

7. Click **View** on the menu bar, point to **Current View**, and then click **Entry List**. See Figure 5-17.

Figure 5-17   JOURNAL IN ENTRY LIST VIEW

arrow indicates sort order

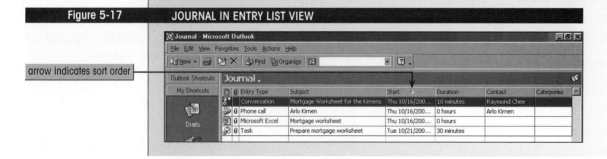

> The entries are arranged in a table view without any groupings. The sort order is currently in descending order by Start date. You can sort, group, and filter the Journal according to your needs.
>
> 8. Click the **Subject** column heading to sort the entries by that field. The arrow in the Subject column heading points up, indicating ascending order.
>
>   TROUBLE? If the arrow in the Subject column heading points down, indicating descending order, click the Subject column heading again to reverse the sort order to ascending.
>
> 9. Click the **Start** column heading to sort the entries by date in descending order.

Recall that you can press the Shift key as you press column headings to sort by more than one column. You'll leave the Journal on as you continue to work in Outlook.

Creating E-mail with Office Applications

Outlook is set up to work hand-in-hand with Office applications—Word, Excel, PowerPoint, and Access. You've already merged a Word document with Outlook contacts and written a letter in Word to a contact. You've also inserted existing Office documents as attachments to e-mail messages. There are two other ways to integrate Office applications and Outlook: (1) send a document as an e-mail message, and (2) start a new file from Outlook.

Sending Office Documents as E-mail Messages

You can create e-mail messages using a file from any Office program installed on your computer as the message body. The message header with the recipients' addresses and the subject is the same as with other messages, but the body contains a Word document, a PowerPoint slide, an Excel worksheet, or an Access Data Page (called a Data Access Page in Access). The Office program opens and its menus and toolbars give you complete access to all the selected program's features and commands. You can then create, edit, and format the message just as you would a standalone file in the program. The message is sent in HTML format. After you send the message, you can save the document, slide, worksheet, or data page as a file.

When recipients receive the message created with an Office program, the file appears as the message body, not as an attachment. Because the message is sent as HTML, all recipients can read it as long as their e-mail program can read HTML. Recipients can read and respond to the message the same as any other message. If they have the appropriate Office program installed on their computer, they can open and edit the message body in the program. If the Office program is not installed, then they can still view and edit the message body in Outlook, but they do not have access to any of the Office program's features.

For example, Cassandra can create an Excel worksheet with mortgage analysis for the Kirnens, and then send it to them as an HTML e-mail message. If the Kirnens have Excel, they can edit the entire worksheet, including the formulas. If not, they can view and edit the worksheet data like they would text in the Message window. In addition, Cassandra can save the message body as an Excel workbook and continue to work on the file. The workbook is much more convenient than saving the data in a message format because Cassandra can add worksheets, formulas, and data as the analysis develops.

REFERENCE WINDOW   RW

Mailing Office Documents

- Switch to the Inbox.
- Click Actions on the menu bar, point to New Mail Message Using, point to Microsoft Office, and then click Microsoft Word Document, Microsoft PowerPoint Slide, Microsoft Excel Worksheet, or Microsoft Access Data Page.
- Enter the recipient addresses and a subject.
- Create the document, slide, worksheet, or data access page in the message body, using the commands and features of the selected Office program.
- Click the Send a Copy, Send this Sheet, Send this Slide, or Send a Copy button, and then if necessary click the Send/Receive button on the Inbox Standard toolbar.
- If you want to save the Office file you created to your computer, click the Save button on the Office program's Standard toolbar, type a filename in the File name text box, change the Save in location as needed, and then click the Save button.
- Click the Close button in the program title bar; if necessary click the No button to close the file without saving it.

You'll e-mail an Excel worksheet with the mortgage calculation data rather than just listing the numbers in a document or message. This way, you or the Kirnens can change the numbers, and Excel will automatically recalculate the totals. No matter who updates the worksheet, you or the Kirnens, there will be accurate figures for the analysis.

To create an Excel worksheet to send by e-mail:

1. Switch to the **Inbox**, click **Actions** on the menu bar, point to **New Mail Message Using**, and then point to **Microsoft Office**.

   Microsoft Word appears in both submenus that you displayed within the Actions menu. The Microsoft Word option in the New Mail Message Using submenu includes the default mail format selected, such as Microsoft Word (Plain Text) or Microsoft Word (HTML). When you use this Microsoft Word option to create a new e-mail message, you do not have the opportunity to save the message body as a Word file. Instead, the message is saved as an Outlook item. The recipients can open, view, and edit the message, but some of the formatting may not be visible if Word is not installed on their computer.

2. Click **Microsoft Excel Worksheet**. Excel opens with a worksheet and message headers. See Figure 5-18.

Figure 5-18	EXCEL WITH WORKBOOK AND MESSAGE HEADERS

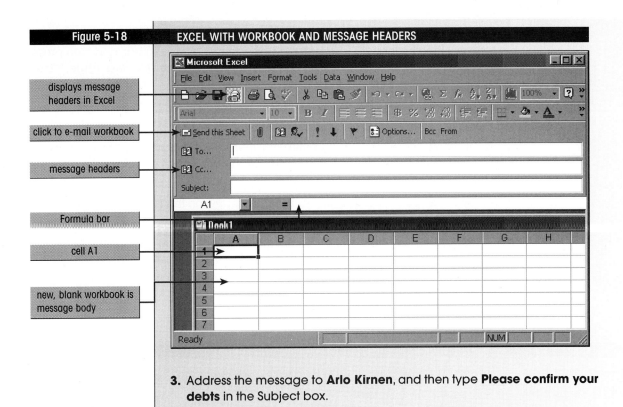

displays message headers in Excel

click to e-mail workbook

message headers

Formula bar

cell A1

new, blank workbook is message body

3. Address the message to **Arlo Kirnen**, and then type **Please confirm your debts** in the Subject box.

Next, you'll enter text, numbers, and formulas in cells within the Excel worksheet. Text creates a label for the content of cells. A formula performs a calculation and can include numbers as well as references to cells. Cells are identified by their column letter and row number; the first cell in the upper-left corner of the worksheet is cell A1.

To enter data in the Excel worksheet:

1. Click in cell **A1**, type **Debt**, press the **Tab** key to move to cell B1, type **Amount**, and then press the **Enter** key to move to cell A2.

2. Enter the following information in columns A and B. Remember to press the Tab key to move to the next cell and press the Enter key to move to the first cell in the next row. As you enter the information, don't worry if not all the text is visible in column A.

Car loan	**6000**
School loans	**15000**
Credit cards	**2000**

If all the contents of a cell are not visible, such as in column A, you can widen the column to fit the longest entry.

3. Double-click the vertical column-heading border between column headings A and B. This action widens column A to fit the longest entry in the column—School loans. All the content in that column is visible.

You'll add a formula in cell B5 to total the values in the Amount column—the range of cells B2, B3, and B4.

4. Click in cell **B5**, click the **AutoSum** button $\boxed{\Sigma}$ on the Excel Standard toolbar, verify that the formula =SUM(B2:B4) appears in the formula bar, and then press the **Enter** key. The SUM formula calculates the sum of the selected range, B2:B4. The total amount in cell B5 is 23000.

The information in the worksheet would be easier to read if the values were formatted as currency and the column headings were boldface.

5. Drag to select cells **B2** through **B5**, and then click the **Currency Style** button $\boxed{\$}$ on the Excel Formatting toolbar. The amounts are formatted with dollar signs and decimal points.

6. Select cells **A1** and **B1**, click the **Bold** button $\boxed{B}$ on the Excel Formatting toolbar. The column headings change to boldface type.

7. Select cells **A4** and **B4**, click the **Borders** button list arrow $\boxed{\Box \cdot}$ on the Excel Formatting toolbar, and then click the **Bottom Border** button $\boxed{\Box}$ on the palette. A border line separates the total line from the data above it.

8. Click in cell **A6** so you can see the changes you made. Your message should look like Figure 5-19.

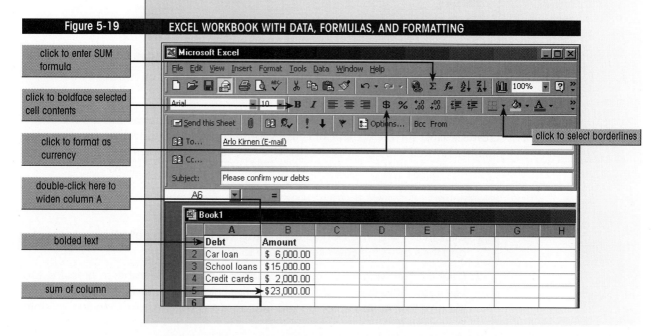

Figure 5-19   EXCEL WORKBOOK WITH DATA, FORMULAS, AND FORMATTING

Now that the worksheet contains the data, you will send the worksheet to Arlo. Once you send the message, Excel remains open so you can save the worksheet to your computer. If you don't want to keep a separate copy of the worksheet, you can close the file without saving changes. You can use the taskbar buttons to switch between Outlook and Excel.

To e-mail the worksheet and then save it:

1. Click the **Send this Sheet** button $\boxed{\text{Send this Sheet}}$ to send the message; if necessary, switch to Outlook and then send the message. Excel stays open.

2. Click the **Microsoft Excel** button on the taskbar to switch to the Excel program window.

3. Click the **Save** button 🖫 on the Excel Standard toolbar, and then save the file as **Debt Worksheet** in the **Tutorial** folder within the **Tutorial.05** folder on your Data Disk.

4. Click **File** on the Excel menu bar, and then click **Exit**. The Excel worksheet and program close.

You can open and edit the workbook file you saved in Excel at anytime.

The sent message appears in the recipients' Inbox. They can read and respond to the message like any other message. The recipients can save a message created from an Office file in its original program format (for example, as an Excel workbook, PowerPoint slide, or Access database). They can then open and edit the file in that program, as long as they have the program on their computer.

You'll download the message with the debt data, and then respond to the message as well as save the data in an Excel workbook.

To respond to and save the e-mail with the Excel data:

1. If necessary, switch to the **Inbox**, and then download your messages.

2. Double-click the message to open it, and then read the message. See Figure 5-20.

Figure 5-20	MESSAGE WITH EXCEL DATA

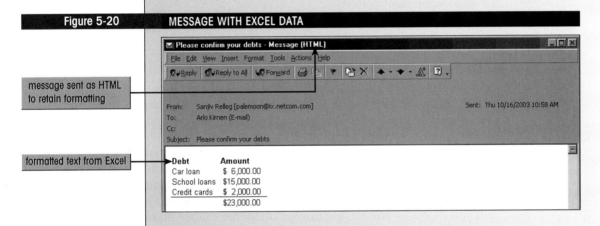

message sent as HTML to retain formatting

formatted text from Excel

You can reply to the sender and save the worksheet data in Excel.

3. Reply to the message with the text **The car loan is actually $4000. Please update your records.** above the original message.

Your reply may appear in colored type because of the HTML formatting.

4. Send the message. The information banner on the original received message marks the date and time of your reply.

The window with the original message remains open. You'll save the workbook and then update the car loan amount.

5. Right-click the message body, and then click **Edit Message** on the shortcut menu. The data from the workbook appears in an unsaved Excel workbook.

6. Click cell **B2**, type **4000**, and then press the **Enter** key. The car loan and total amounts are updated. The total becomes $21,000.

You can save the worksheet in a variety of formats, including an Excel workbook, a Web page, and formats compatible with other spreadsheet programs. The available file formats are listed in the Save as type list in the Save As dialog box.

7. Save the worksheet as a **Microsoft Excel Workbook (*.xls)** with the filename **Debt Worksheet Revised** in the **Tutorial** folder within the **Tutorial.05** folder on your Data Disk, and then close the file and Excel.

TROUBLE? If you don't see (*.xls) then your system is not set up to show file extensions.

8. If necessary, download the reply message.

Because both Cassandra and the Kirnens have access to the worksheet, either can update the information right in Excel.

Creating Office Documents from Outlook

As long as you have the specific Office program installed, you can start a new Excel worksheet or chart, Word document, or PowerPoint presentation right from Outlook. You choose whether to send the file as an attachment to an e-mail message or to save a copy to your computer. Either way, the required program opens so you can use all the program's features to create, edit, and format the file.

If you choose to send the file as an attachment, recipients can open the attachment only if they have the appropriate Office program or viewer installed on their computer. A **viewer** is a special program that enables people who don't have Office programs to see your work. Viewers are available on the Microsoft Web site at **www.microsoft.com/Office/000/viewers.htm**.

If you choose to save the file to your computer, where you start the file determines the location it is saved and stored. When you start an Office file from an Outlook folder, you save the file in that folder, which is called posting. You must be in Outlook to open a posted file. When you start a new Office file from My Computer in the Other Shortcuts group on the Outlook Bar, you have access to any template or wizard available on your computer, and you can save the file to any location on your computer or network. You then can open the file from the Office program.

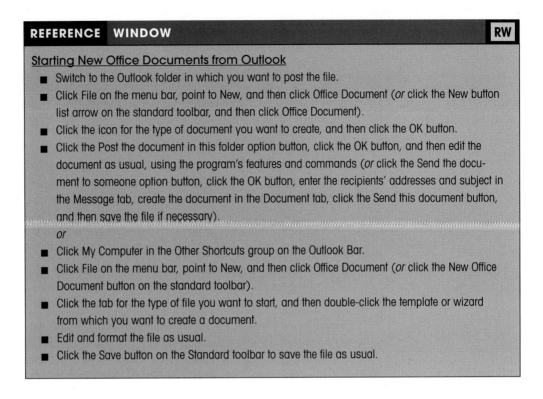

REFERENCE WINDOW — RW

Starting New Office Documents from Outlook

■ Switch to the Outlook folder in which you want to post the file.
■ Click File on the menu bar, point to New, and then click Office Document (*or* click the New button list arrow on the standard toolbar, and then click Office Document).
■ Click the icon for the type of document you want to create, and then click the OK button.
■ Click the Post the document in this folder option button, click the OK button, and then edit the document as usual, using the program's features and commands (*or* click the Send the document to someone option button, click the OK button, enter the recipients' addresses and subject in the Message tab, create the document in the Document tab, click the Send this document button, and then save the file if necessary).

or

■ Click My Computer in the Other Shortcuts group on the Outlook Bar.
■ Click File on the menu bar, point to New, and then click Office Document (*or* click the New Office Document button on the standard toolbar).
■ Click the tab for the type of file you want to start, and then double-click the template or wizard from which you want to create a document.
■ Edit and format the file as usual.
■ Click the Save button on the Standard toolbar to save the file as usual.

You'll create a new document using Word from within Outlook to send information to the Kirnens about outlining their dream house.

To start a new Word document from Outlook:

1. If necessary, switch to the Inbox.

2. Click the **New** button list arrow 🗎 New ▾, and then click **Office Document**. The New Office Document dialog box opens. See Figure 5-21.

| Figure 5-21 | NEW OFFICE DOCUMENT DIALOG BOX |

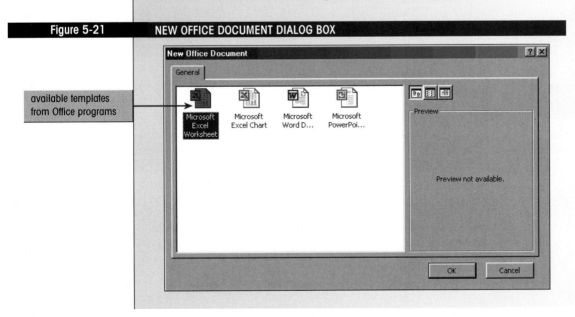

available templates from Office programs

3. Click the **Microsoft Word Document** icon, and then click the **OK** button. A dialog box opens with options for treating the document. See Figure 5-22.

Figure 5-22   POSTING OPTIONS

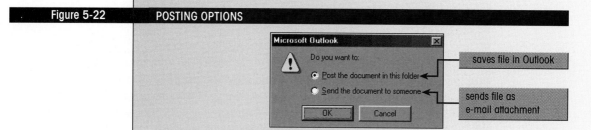

saves file in Outlook

sends file as
e-mail attachment

TROUBLE? If the Office Assistant opens, simply click Post the document in this folder.

4. Click the **Post the document in this folder** option button, and then click the **OK** button. Word opens with a new, blank document. You can enter and edit text just like in any Word document.

5. Type **Ace Realty wants to know everything you would love to have in your home. Please make a wish list that describes the home of your dreams. Start by considering the following:**, press the **Enter** key, type **Location. Where do you want to live?**, press the **Enter** key, type **Size. How much room do you need?**, press the **Enter** key, and then type **Amenities. What extras do you need?**

All the Word formatting features are available.

6. Double-click **everything** to select it, and then click the **Italic** button I on the Word Formatting toolbar. The word "everything" is formatted as italics.

7. Select the last three lines, click the **Numbering** button ☰ on the Word Formatting toolbar, and then click to deselect the text. The lines are formatted into a numbered list. See Figure 5-23.

Figure 5-23   WORD DOCUMENT WITH FORMATTED TEXT

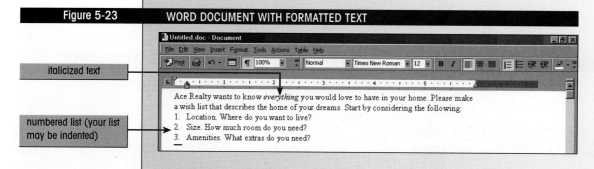

italicized text

numbered list (your list
may be indented)

TROUBLE? If you see spaces, tab characters, and paragraph marks, then Word is set to show nonprinting characters. This won't affect the document or the function of Outlook in any way. Just continue with Step 8.

8. Click the **Post** button 🖅 Post on the Word Standard toolbar. The document is saved in the Inbox as an Outlook item. See Figure 5-24.

Figure 5-24   **WORD DOCUMENT POSTED IN INBOX**

posted item

unnamed document

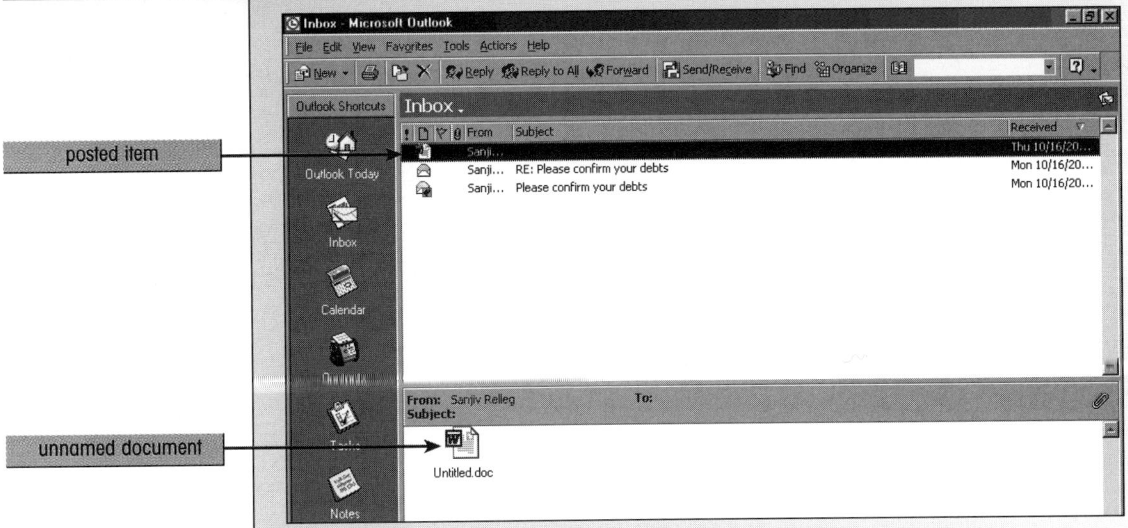

TROUBLE? If you don't see the Post button on the Standard toolbar, your setup of Word may be different. Click File on the menu bar, and then click Post.

TROUBLE? If a dialog box opens, asking whether you want to save changes, click the Yes button.

The posted document appears as an item in the Outlook folder you selected, and a short-cut icon to the Office file appears in the Preview pane. The posted document can be opened only from Outlook. When you do open the file, the appropriate Office program opens as well, so you can edit, format, and print the file as needed, using the Office program features and commands. You also can save the file to your computer or move it to another Outlook folder as needed.

You'll open the Word document posted in Inbox, and then save it to your Data Disk.

To open a document posted in Outlook:

1. Double-click the Word document item posted in the Inbox. The document opens in Word.

2. Click **File** on the menu bar, and then click **Save As**. The Save As dialog box opens.

3. Save the document as **Dream Home** in the **Tutorial** folder within the **Tutorial.05** folder on your Data Disk.

4. Close the Word document and program. The posted item remains in the Outlook Inbox.

Because you turned on the Journal to automatically record Office files, the Excel and Word documents you've created for Cassandra will appear as entries.

> *To view the entries in the Journal:*
> **1.** Switch to the **Journal**. The Journal opens.
> **2.** Change the view to **By Type**, and then review the Journal entries you created so far.

Outlook not only gives you various options for creating and sending new files from different Office programs, you can also work with existing files. In Session 5.2, you'll import and export files, and send and receive faxed documents.

Session 5.1 QUICK CHECK

1. What is the Journal?
2. Describe one benefit of using the Journal.
3. List the items you can record automatically in the Journal.
4. What are the two ways to send an Office document as an e-mail message?
5. When recipients receive an Office document as the message body, what access do they have to the data?
6. When you create an Office document from Outlook, what are your two options?
7. If you save an Office file you create in Outlook to your computer, where is it stored?
8. True or False: You must be in Outlook to open a posted file.

SESSION 5.2

In this session, you'll import data created in other Office programs and you'll export Outlook data into file formats that programs other than Outlook can use. Then you'll learn how to send and receive faxes right from Outlook.

Importing and Exporting Files

Importing and exporting are two sides of the same coin. Both copy data created in one program and transform it into another program's format. The difference is whether you're copying data into a program (**importing**) or moving data out of a program (**exporting**). For example, you might import e-mail messages from another program, such as Netscape Mail or Lotus Organizer, into your Outlook Inbox so that you can store all your messages in one location. Or, you might export your Outlook Contacts folder into an Access database of names and addresses so that someone else can work with the list.

You can import information into Outlook from a personal folder file (for example, to restore an archived folder), a Personal Address Book (such as to add names, addresses, and phone numbers from a contact list), or from a file (for example, to bring existing information from another program file, such as an Access database). When you import information, you copy the contents of the file into the Outlook folder that you specify.

You can export items from Outlook to a personal folder file or another file type. Personal folder files can be viewed only in Outlook. Other file types can be opened from or imported into other programs. If you plan to work with the exported data in Outlook, export to a personal folder file. If you plan to work with the data in another program, export to a file format that program can import. For example, if you wanted to work with your to-do list in Excel, you could export the Tasks folder into the Excel .xls file format.

You've already exported data into Outlook when you saved a contact as vCard. The Save As command is a simple way to change the format of Outlook items. However, the file format options available with the Save As command are limited and change, depending on the type of item.

The Import and Export Wizard provides a greater variety of file formats to choose from when exporting or importing. The wizard walks you through the steps for importing or exporting in Outlook. First you choose the action you want to perform (importing or exporting), then you select the file type you want to bring in or create, next you select the file you want to import or you select the folder items you want to export and the destination file, and finally you perform the import or export.

Importing from Other Mail Programs

When you've compiled an address book or messages in another program, such as Outlook Express, Eudora, Netscape, and so forth, you may want to import that information into Outlook. To import messages or addresses from another program, you must have that program installed on your computer.

One of the office assistants had been using Outlook Express to send and receive messages, and the address book contains a list of possible homebuyers that isn't stored elsewhere. Cassandra asks you to use the Import and Export Wizard to import this list from Outlook Express.

To import addresses from another mail program:

1. If you took a break after the previous session, make sure Outlook is running.

2. Click **File** on the menu bar, and then click **Import and Export**. The first Import and Export Wizard dialog box opens, so you can select what you want to do. See Figure 5-25.

Figure 5-25	IMPORT AND EXPORT WIZARD DIALOG BOX

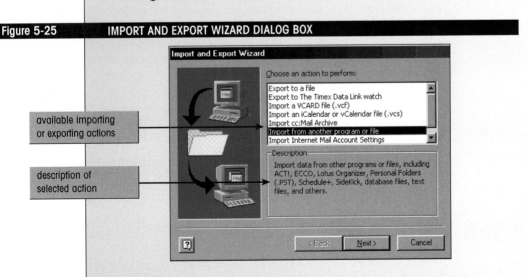

available importing or exporting actions

description of selected action

TROUBLE? If the Office Assistant appears, asking whether you want help, click the No, don't provide help now option.

3. Click **Import Internet Mail and Addresses** in the Choose an action to perform list box, and then click the **Next** button. You select which e-mail program you want to import from in the next wizard dialog box. See Figure 5-26.

Figure 5-26   **OUTLOOK IMPORT TOOL DIALOG BOX**

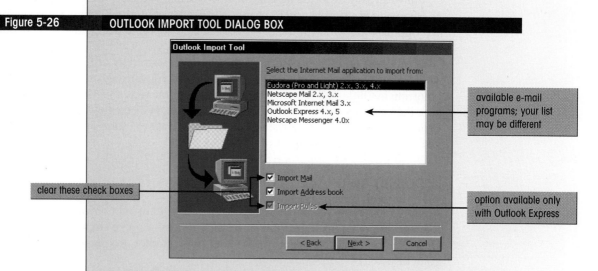

clear these check boxes

available e-mail programs; your list may be different

option available only with Outlook Express

TROUBLE? If your dialog box looks different, you might have selected the Import Internet Mail Account Settings action in the previous dialog box. Click the Back button, and then repeat Step 3, being careful to scroll down and click the correct option.

4. Click **Outlook Express** in the Select the Internet Mail application to import from list box. Because Outlook Express also uses rules, the selected Import Rules check box becomes active.

5. Click the **Import Mail** and **Import Rules** check boxes to remove the check marks, and then click the **Next** button.

In the third wizard dialog box, you specify where you want to place the imported addresses and how to handle addresses that duplicate those already in your folder. Whether you replace duplicates, create duplicates, or don't import duplicates depends on the list. If your list contains updated information, then you probably want to replace the duplicates with the items you are importing. If you know that you want to import all the items, regardless of duplicates, then you want to create duplicates. If duplicate items are older than the existing items, then you probably don't want to import duplicates.

6. Click the **Outlook Contacts Folder** option button if necessary, and then click the **Do not import duplicate items** option button. See Figure 5-27.

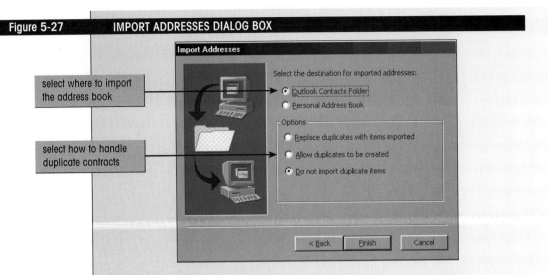

Figure 5-27   IMPORT ADDRESSES DIALOG BOX

select where to import the address book

select how to handle duplicate contracts

The wizard is all set up to import the addresses from Outlook Express into your Outlook Contacts folder. To copy the Outlook Express addresses into Outlook, you would click the Finish button. However, Cassandra realizes she has this data in another location, so you won't complete this action.

7. Click the **Cancel** button.

Instead, Cassandra asks you to import a contact list that is stored in an Office application.

Importing and Exporting with Office Applications

Cassandra has a list of current homebuyers that she created in an Access database. Rather than retyping the information into Outlook, risking typos and taking up time, you can import that list. The process for importing files is similar to importing from another mail program. The Import and Export Wizard walks you through the steps.

To import a contact list from Access:

1. Click **File** on the menu bar, and then click **Import and Export**.

   TROUBLE? If the Office Assistant appears, asking whether you want help, click the No, don't provide help now option.

2. Click **Import from another program or file** in the Choose an action to perform list box in the Import and Export Wizard dialog box, and then click the **Next** button. The second wizard dialog box shows a list of all the program files and formats you can import from. See Figure 5-28.

Figure 5-28   **IMPORT A FILE DIALOG BOX**

available file types
for importing

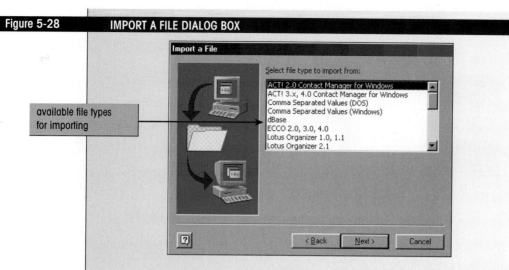

3. Click **Microsoft Access** in the Select file type to import from list box, and then click the **Next** button. The Import a File dialog box opens.

TROUBLE? If you get a message that Microsoft Outlook cannot start the Import/Export engine because the feature is not currently installed, click the Yes button to install it now and then follow the directions. You may need to insert the Office 2000 CD-ROM.

4. Click the **Browse** button, and then double-click **Homebuyers** in the **Tutorial** folder within the **Tutorial.05** folder on your Data Disk. The File to import text box shows the path, such as A:\Tutorial.05\Tutorial\Homebuyers.mdb.

5. Click the **Do not import duplicate items** option button. See Figure 5-29.

Figure 5-29   **SECOND IMPORT A FILE DIALOG BOX**

path of file being
imported

select how to treat
duplicates

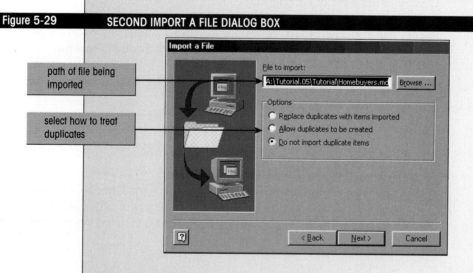

6. Click the **Next** button, and then click the **Contacts** folder in the Select destination folder list box. See Figure 5-30.

Figure 5-30	THIRD IMPORT A FILE DIALOG BOX

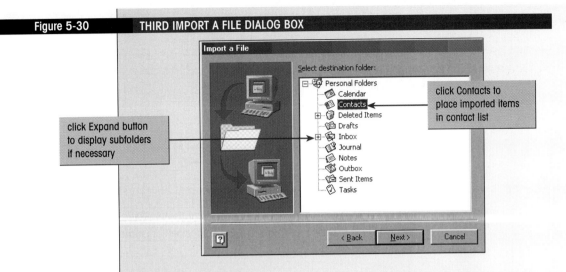

click Expand button to display subfolders if necessary

click Contacts to place imported items in contact list

7. Click the **Next** button. The dialog box shows what actions will be performed. See Figure 5-31. You are not quite done yet; you will complete the import process after you map fields.

Figure 5-31	FOURTH IMPORT A FILE DIALOG BOX

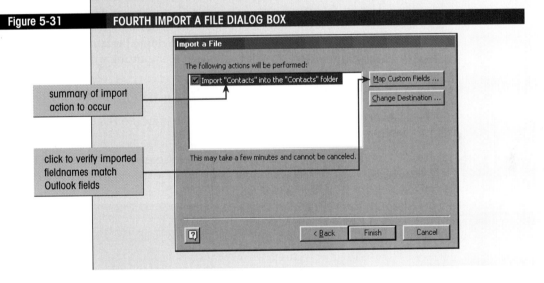

summary of import action to occur

click to verify imported fieldnames match Outlook fields

Information you are importing must fit the structure of the Outlook folder you select. For example, the field names used in a database or worksheet must match the ones used in the Outlook folder. Different programs distinguish between fields in different ways. For example, Excel stores each field in a different worksheet cell and Access stores each field in table cells. Another way to distinguish between fields is to separate them with a comma or tab character, called **comma-delimited** or **tab-delimited**, as shown in Figure 5-32. This way, Outlook knows to place the following data into a new field each time a comma or tab appears.

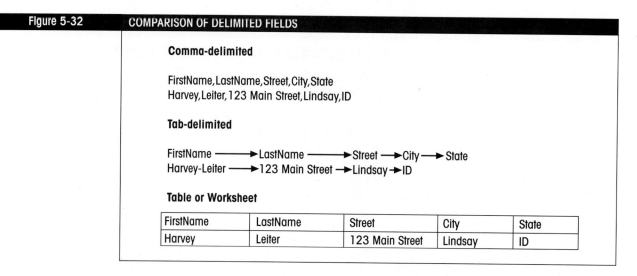

Figure 5-32   COMPARISON OF DELIMITED FIELDS

The first row in each example contains the field names, which label the columns. The data in each subsequent row is called a record and appears in the same order. The first field includes data until the comma or tab or cell border. Each column contains the data for the same field for all the records. For example, the first field is called FirstName, the first record in the second row begins with Harvey. If Outlook cannot determine how to insert information into the folder, an error message appears. If you know that field names in the imported file are different than what Outlook uses, you can map, or match, the imported fields to the appropriate Outlook fields.

You'll look at how the fields from the file you're importing will map into Outlook.

To map fields from an imported file to Outlook fields:

1. Click the **Map Custom Fields** button in the Import a File dialog box. The Map Custom Fields dialog box opens.

2. Click the **Expand** button next to Name to display the list of fields. As you can see, Outlook matches fields from the imported file to Outlook. See Figure 5-33.

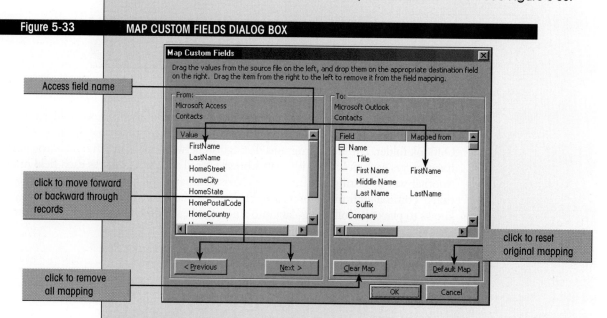

Figure 5-33   MAP CUSTOM FIELDS DIALOG BOX

3. Click the **Next** button to view how the first imported record will appear in Outlook. See Figure 5-34.

Figure 5-34	FIRST ACCESS RECORD MAPPED TO OUTLOOK

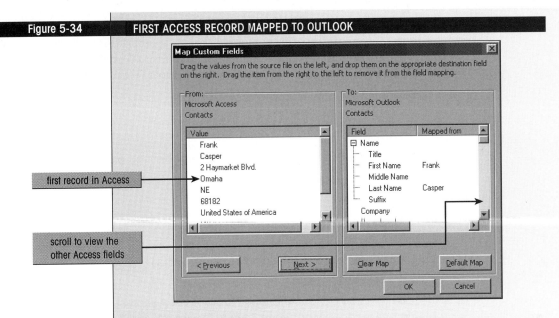

first record in Access

scroll to view the other Access fields

4. Scroll down and expand fields groups to view the remaining mapping, and then click the **Previous** button to return to the field names.

   If you needed to correct any field mapping, you would drag the field from the From box and drop it onto the appropriate Microsoft Outlook field in the To box. However, all the fields are mapping correctly.

5. Click the **Cancel** button to return to the Import a File dialog box. You are ready to complete the import process.

6. Click the **Finish** button. In a few moments, Outlook converts the information from the Access database into the Contacts folder.

7. Switch to the **Contacts** folder and view the imported entries. See Figure 5-35.

Figure 5-35	CONTACTS FOLDER WITH IMPORTED ACCESS RECORDS

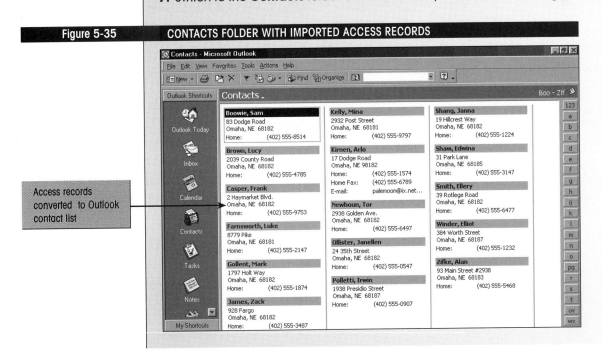

Access records converted to Outlook contact list

When you need to share some of your Outlook information with a person who uses another program, you can export the information into another format. Because you need to share this contact list with someone who uses only Excel, you'll export the Contacts folder to an Excel worksheet. You can also export the contact list to a Word, Access, comma-delimited, or tab-delimited file.

To export a contact list from Outlook:

1. Click **File** on the menu bar, and then click **Import and Export**.

2. Click **Export to a file** in the Choose an action to perform list box, and then click the **Next** button.

3. Click **Microsoft Excel** in the Create a file of type list box, and then click the **Next** button.

4. Click **Contacts** folder in the Select folder to export from list box, and then click the **Next** button.

5. Click the **Browse** button, and type **Homebuyer Addresses Worksheet** in the File name text box, change the Save in location to the **Tutorial** folder within the **Tutorial.05** folder on your Data Disk, and then click the **OK** button. The Save exported file as text box shows the path, such as A:\Tutorial.05\Tutorial\Homebuyer Addresses Worksheet.xls.

6. Click the **Next** button.

   In this final dialog box, you confirm the actions that will be performed and have the opportunity to map fields. You do not need to map the fields this time because you are creating a new workbook and there are no field names to match. If you were exporting data to an existing worksheet, you would verify that the Outlook fields mapped correctly to the Excel field names.

7. Click the **Finish** button. In a few moments, Outlook converts the information from the contact list into an Excel worksheet. The original information remains in the Contacts folder.

You want to check the Excel worksheet to see how the Contacts look in the worksheet file.

To verify the list in Excel:

1. Start Excel, and then open the **Homebuyer Addresses Worksheet** file that you just created in the **Tutorial** folder within the **Tutorial.05** folder on your Data Disk.

   The worksheet opens with the field names in the first row of the worksheet. Each column contains one field. Each row contains one record, starting in the second row.

2. Scroll down to view all the records.

3. Scroll to the right to see that fields extend all the way to columns CI.

4. Click **File** on the Excel menu bar, and then click **Exit** to close the worksheet and exit the program.

You can import or export to other applications using the same procedure.

Importing and Exporting Personal Folder Files

Recall that Outlook stores items in personal folder files (.pst), which you can import and export just like other files. You might import and export personal folder files so you can share your Outlook items with other users. Another reason might be to create a backup copy of all your data. Unlike archiving, exporting a personal folder file creates a copy of your data and leaves the items intact in Outlook so you can continue to work. If you experienced computer problems, you could import your personal folder file into Outlook on another computer and continue to work. Be aware that a personal folder file is often too large to fit on a standard floppy disk, so you'll need to copy it on a larger storage medium, such as a network server, Zip disk, or CD-ROM.

You want to back up the Contacts folder.

To back up your personal folder file:

1. Click **File** on the menu bar, and then click **Import and Export**.

2. Click **Export to a file** in the Choose an action to perform list box, and then click the **Next** button.

3. Click **Personal Folder File (.pst)** in the Create a file of type list box, and then click the **Next** button. You can choose to export any or all of the folders and subfolders in Outlook. See Figure 5-36.

| Figure 5-36 | EXPORT PERSONAL FOLDERS DIALOG BOX |

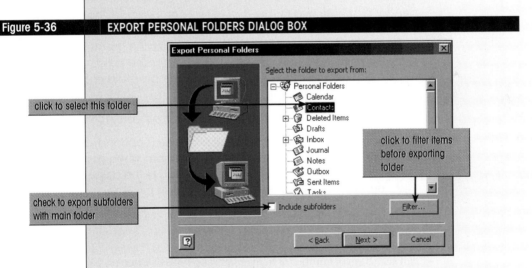

The Filter button enables you to specify a subset of items to export.

4. Click **Contacts** in the Select the folder to export from list box, and then click the **Next** button.

   You will create a .pst file and save it on your Data Disk.

5. Save the exported file as **Ace Contacts Backup** in the **Tutorial** folder within the **Tutorial.05** folder on your Data Disk.

   Because you're creating a new file, it doesn't matter which option you select for duplicated items.

6. Click the **Finish** button. The Create Microsoft Personal Folders dialog box opens. See Figure 5-37.

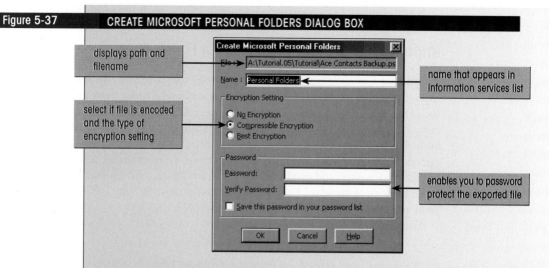

Figure 5-37 CREATE MICROSOFT PERSONAL FOLDERS DIALOG BOX

The Create Microsoft Personal Folders dialog box displays the path and file-name you specified when you named the exported file. You cannot change this setting from this dialog box. The Name text box displays the name that appears in the information services list. You'll leave the default, Personal Folders, which corresponds to the name of the personal folder in your information services. Encryption settings cannot be changed after you create the personal folder file. Encryption encodes the file to make it unreadable by other pro-grams. No encryption does not encode your file. Compressible encryption encodes the file in a format that allows compression; the file is compressed only if you have a compression program set up on your computer. Best encryption encodes file in a format that offers the greatest degree of protec-tion. If you have a disk-compression program, the file can be compressed but to a lesser degree than allowed by the Compressible encryption option.

7. Click the **No Encryption** option button. The other options allow the file to be compressed using a compression program on your computer.

Password-protecting your personal folder file is optional and provides added security. You will be prompted for the password when you start Outlook or con-nect to the personal folder file, unless you save the password in the password list. You will not set up password protection at this time.

8. Click the **OK** button. Outlook exports a copy of the folder as a personal folder file.

Even such a small number of items requires 64 KB of space on your disk. However, you could import this file into Outlook on your current computer or on another installation of Outlook.

Saving Items as Another File Format

As easy way to export Outlook items to another format is by using the Save As command. You've used the Save As command to save your calendar as a Web page in HTML format, which can be posted on intranets or the Internet. You can also use the Save As command to export other Outlook items, such as converting a posted item to an Office file to your com-puter (as you did earlier), an e-mail message into a Text Only (.txt) or a Rich Text Format (.rtf) file that most word processing programs can read, or a contact into a vCard File (.vcf) format that most mail programs can read.

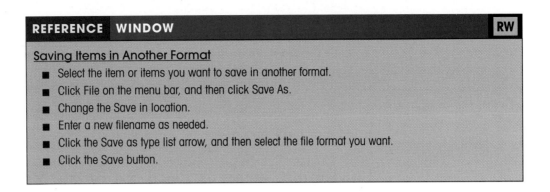

REFERENCE   WINDOW   **RW**

Saving Items in Another Format

- Select the item or items you want to save in another format.
- Click File on the menu bar, and then click Save As.
- Change the Save in location.
- Enter a new filename as needed.
- Click the Save as type list arrow, and then select the file format you want.
- Click the Save button.

You'll save one potential homebuyer entry from the Contacts folder as a Rich Text Format file.

To save a contact as a Rich Text Format file:

1. Click the **Luke Farnsworth** contact to select it.

2. Click **File** on the menu bar, and then click **Save As**. The Save As dialog box opens, with the contact name in the File Name text box.

3. Change the Save in location to the **Tutorial** folder within the **Tutorial.05** folder on your Data Disk.

4. Click the **Save as** type list arrow to display the file formats you can select from. See Figure 5-38.

Figure 5-38	SAVE AS DIALOG BOX

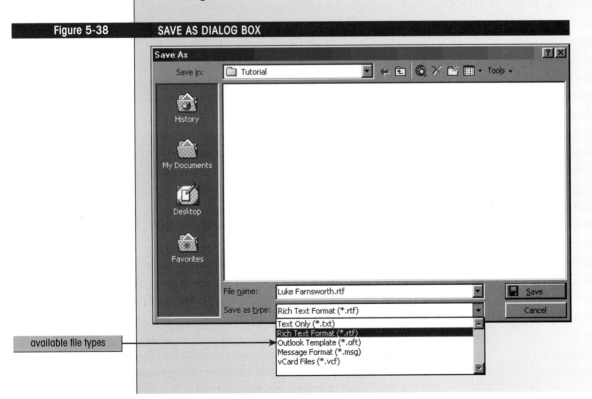

available file types

> **5.** Click **Rich Text Format (*.rtf)** to select that file format.
>
> **6.** Click the **Save** button. The Luke Farnsworth contact card is saved as a Rich Text Format file on your Data Disk.

You can share the exported file with others or open it in Word or any other program that can read Rich Text Format files.

> ### To view the Contact as a Rich Text Format file:
>
> **1.** Start Word, and then click the **Open** button 🗁 on the Standard toolbar. The Open dialog box opens.
>
> **2.** Change the Look in location to the **Tutorial** folder within the **Tutorial.05** folder on your Data Disk.
>
> **3.** Double-click **Luke Farnsworth**. The Convert File dialog box opens with Rich Text Format selected as the file type to convert from.
>
> **4.** Click the **Yes** button in the dialog box to open the Rich Text Format file in Word.
>
> **5.** Verify the information for Luke appears.
>
> **6.** Close the document and exit Word.

Faxing with Outlook

Sometimes, you'll want to share your document information, without distributing a file that others can use. Faxes are a popular way to send and receive information. Rather than printing a document and then sending it from a standalone fax machine, you can send and receive faxes right from Outlook. Faxing from Outlook saves you time and paper.

Before you can fax documents from Outlook, you must confirm that the fax service is part of your profile.

> ### To add fax service to your profile:
>
> **1.** Click **Tools** on the menu bar, and then click **Services**. The Services dialog box opens, with the Services tab selected.
>
> **2.** Verify that Microsoft Fax does *not* appear in list box, and then click the **Add** button. The Add Service to Profile dialog box opens.
>
> **TROUBLE?** If Microsoft Fax *does* appear in The following information services are set up in this profile list box, then you do not need to modify your profile. Click the Cancel button and continue with the Creating and Sending a Fax section.
>
> **TROUBLE?** If a dialog box opens saying, "A recently installed program may cause Microsoft Office or other email enabled programs to function improperly. Outlook can resolve this conflict without affecting the program that originally caused the problem. Do you want Outlook to resolve the problem?", click the Yes button. Then if a dialog box opens saying, "Outlook was unable to resolve the conflict between a recently installed program and Microsoft Office

or other e-mail enabled programs. Outlook needs to modify a system component that another program is currently using. To fix this problem, please restart Windows.", click the OK button.

3. Click **Microsoft Fax** in the Available information services list box, and then click the **OK** button.

TROUBLE? If Microsoft Fax does not appear in the list box, then the program is not installed on your system. Ask your instructor or technical support person for help.

4. Click the **Yes** button to set up the fax properties. You must enter a name and fax number, and select a modem. The User tab appears by default.

5. Enter your name and the fax number for your computer on the User tab of the Microsoft Fax Properties dialog box.

TROUBLE? If you don't know the fax number for your computer, ask your instructor or technical support person. If your computer is not connected to a phone line, you can read, but not complete, the remainder of the steps in this section; continue completing the steps in the Reviewing Journal Entries section.

6. Click the **Modem** tab, if necessary click your modem, and then click the **Properties** button. The Fax Modem Properties dialog box opens. See Figure 5-39.

Figure 5-39	FAX MODEM PROPERTIES DIALOG BOX

You select the Answer mode that best matches your setup. The Answer after option works well when the phone line is primarily dedicated to faxes; select 1 ring for a dedicated fax line, and select 3 or more rings if you want a chance to answer calls. The Manual option works well if the phone line is used for both voice and fax; click the Answer Now button in Microsoft Fax Status window when you answer the phone using the fax. The Don't answer option is used when you do not want to have Outlook receive faxes.

7. Click the **Manual** option button, and then click the **OK** button.

8. Click the **OK** button in the Microsoft Fax Properties dialog box.

9. If necessary, click the **OK** button in the dialog box to confirm that the changes won't take effect until you restart Outlook.

10. Click the **OK** button in the Services dialog box.

11. Exit and Log Off Outlook, and then restart Outlook.

Once your fax service is set up, you can send a fax.

Creating and Sending a Fax

The Compose New Fax Wizard walks you through the steps of creating a fax, complete with a cover page, and then sending it. You can send faxes to people and numbers you've already entered in your address book or contact list, or you can enter the name and number as you create the fax.

You'll send a fax with the Kirnens wish list for their dream house.

To create a fax with the Compose New Fax Wizard:

1. Click **Actions** on the menu bar, and then click **New Fax Message**. The Compose New Fax Wizard dialog box opens.

2. If necessary, select a new dialing location, and then click the **Next** button.

3. Type **Arlo Kirnen** in the To box, select United States from the list, type **555-555-5555** as the recipient's fax number, click the **Dial Area code** check box to select it, and then click the **Add to List** button. If you wanted to enter additional recipients, you would repeat this step for each recipient. See Figure 5-40.

Figure 5-40	COMPOSE NEW FAX DIALOG BOX

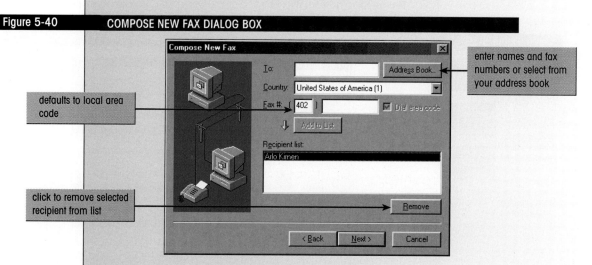

defaults to local area code

click to remove selected recipient from list

enter names and fax numbers or select from your address book

---

4. Click the **Next** button.

In the third Compose New Fax dialog box, you select the cover page you want. A **cover page** is a sheet that identifies the sender and receiver of the fax, lists how many pages the fax includes, and often contains a brief message.

5. Click the **Yes. Send this one** option button, and then click **Confidential!** in the list box. See Figure 5-41.

Figure 5-41 | SELECTING A COVER PAGE

available cover sheet styles

provides access to other settings

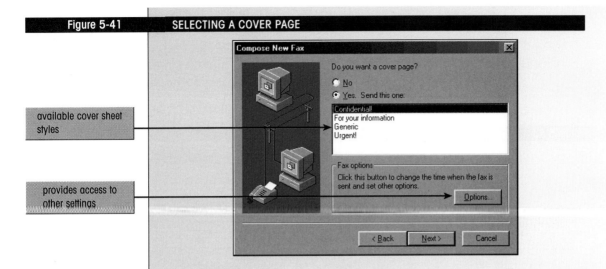

From this dialog box, you also have access to customizing fax options.

6. Click the **Options** button in the Compose New Fax dialog box. The Send Options for this Message dialog box opens. See Figure 5-42.

Figure 5-42 | SEND OPTIONS FOR THIS MESSAGE DIALOG BOX

select how recipient receives fax

select when to send fax

clear to send fax without cover page

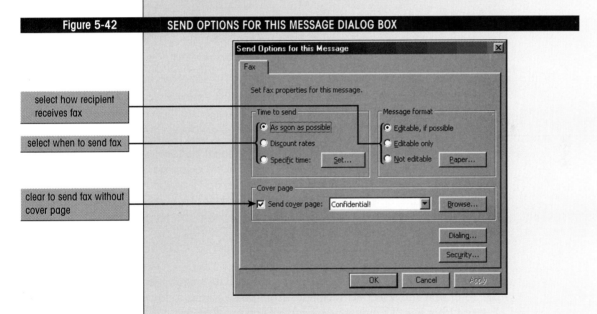

You can designate a time to send faxes, select whether recipients receive faxes in an editable form, and select a default cover page.

7. Click the **Cancel** button to close the Microsoft Fax Properties dialog box.

8. Click the **Next** button. In the fourth dialog box, you enter the fax message information.

Faxes are a quick way to send a copy of a document to someone. Their format is similar to e-mail messages, in that you need to enter a subject, a recipient name, and perhaps a short message. Instead of an e-mail address, however, you enter a fax number.

To finish and send a fax with the Compose New Fax Wizard:

1. Type **Your wish list** in the Subject text box, press the **Tab** key, and then type **Please review the following list to ensure that it includes the aspects of a home that are most important to you. Thank you**, double space and then type your name. See Figure 5-43.

Figure 5-43	COVER PAGE TEXT

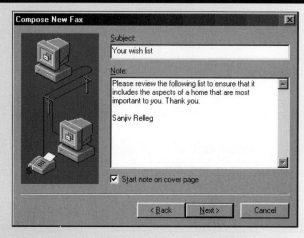

2. Click the **Next** button. The fifth dialog box enables you to attach document files that are sent along with your fax.

3. Click the **Add File** button, change the Look in location to the **Tutorial** folder within the **Tutorial.05** folder on your Data Disk, and then double-click **Wishlist**. The file and path appear in the Files to Send list box.

4. Click the **Next** button, and then click the **Finish** button. Microsoft Fax prepares the cover sheet, opens Word and prepares the document, and then dials the fax number you entered. If you are hooked up to a working fax modem, Outlook attempts to send the fax. However, because you entered a nonworking number, the fax cannot be sent. After a moment, the Microsoft Fax Status dialog box closes.

You can also send faxes just as you would e-mail messages. Just start a new message, click the To button and select fax recipients from those names followed by Business Fax, Home Fax, or Other Fax. Then you type a subject and message as usual, and attach any files. When you're done, click the Send button. The Microsoft Fax Status dialog box shows you the fax progress as Outlook sends the fax.

Receiving a Fax

Earlier, you set up Outlook to receive faxes. Incoming faxes appear in your Inbox just like e-mail messages. You can then open, read, and file faxes just as you would other messages.

To receive a fax from Outlook:

1. Open the document **Wishlist** in the **Tutorial** folder within the **Tutorial.05** folder on your Data Disk, print it, and then close the Word document and program.

2. If possible, fax the document to your computer. You can use a standalone fax machine or ask a classmate to fax the document from Outlook. When the phone line connected to your computer rings, the Microsoft Fax Status dialog box opens along with the Receive Fax Now? dialog box so you can answer the call. See Figure 5-44.

| Figure 5-44 | RECEIVE FAX NOW? DIALOG BOX |

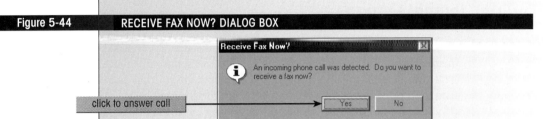

click to answer call

TROUBLE? If you don't see the Microsoft Fax Status window, double-click the Fax icon in the far right of the taskbar.

3. Click the **Yes** button in the Receive Fax Now? dialog box. Outlook recognizes the fax, and should hang up when the transmission is complete.

4. If necessary, click the **Hang Up** button in the Microsoft Fax Status dialog box when the fax is complete. The fax is posted in the Inbox.

5. Double-click the fax in the Inbox to open it. The Opening Mail Attachment dialog box opens.

6. Click the **Open it** option button, and then click the **OK** button. The fax opens in the Imaging window, which has features you can use to save, print, and modify the fax. See Figure 5-45.

| Figure 5-45 | FAX IN IMAGING WINDOW |

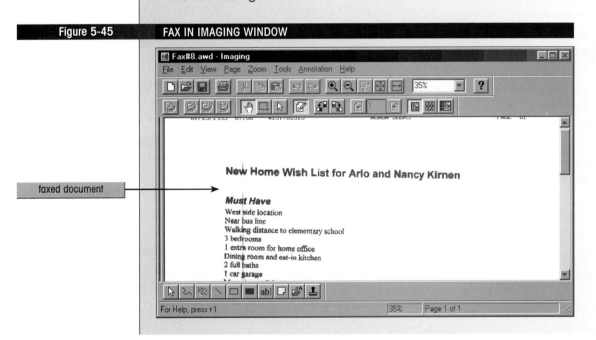

faxed document

7. Click the **Print** button 🖨 on the Standard toolbar, verify the settings in the Print dialog box, and then click the **OK** button. The fax document prints.

8. Click the **Close** button ☒ on the Imaging window title bar. The fax closes.

All the work you've done with importing and exporting files has been recorded in the Journal.

Reviewing **Journal Entries**

All the work you've done with Office files and e-mail is recorded in the Journal. This information is helpful if you want to see how you've spent your day, or locate the date and time you completed a specific activity. You'll review the Journal entries that were created today, and then print them. When you print from the Journal, only selected items or groups print. If you want to print for a selected timeframe, you must filter the Journal to display only items from that date.

To print journal entries:

1. Switch to the **Journal** folder, change the Journal view to **By Type**, and then click the **Day** button 📅Day on the Standard toolbar.

2. Click the **Go to Today** button Go to Today on the Standard toolbar to make sure the current day is visible.

3. Click the **Expand** button for each category in the Information viewer. See Figure 5-46.

| Figure 5-46 | JOURNAL WITH ENTRIES FOR TODAY |

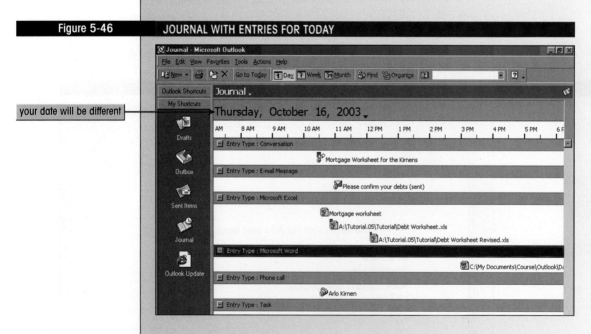

your date will be different

You'll filter the Journal to display only those items you created today.

4. Click **View** on the menu bar, point to **Current View**, and then click **Customize Current View**. The View Summary dialog box opens.

5. Click the **Filter** button in the View Summary dialog box. The Filter dialog box opens with options for selecting which Journal items you want to include in the view.

6. Click the **Time** list arrow, click **created**, click the right list arrow, and then click **today**. See Figure 5-47.

Figure 5-47	FILTER DIALOG BOX

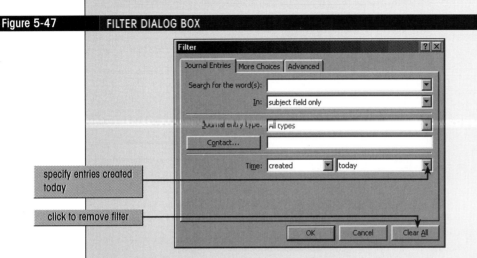

specify entries created today

click to remove filter

7. Click the **OK** button in the Filter dialog box, and then click the **OK** button in the View Summary dialog box. The Journal is filtered to show only those items you created today. The task still appears in the list because you filtered by the create date rather than the start date; the task's create date is today, and its start date is next Tuesday.

When you print the Journal, only the selected groups are included in the print-out. You want all the groups included.

8. Press and hold the **Shift** key, click each group heading to select all the entries, and then release the **Shift** key. The groups you want to include are selected.

9. Click the **Print** button 🖨 on the Standard toolbar. The Print dialog box opens.

10. If necessary, click the **Start each item on a new page** check box and the **Print attached file(s) with items** check box to remove the check marks. You will print only the Journal timeline on continuous pages.

TROUBLE? If the Start each item on a new page check box is unavailable, then the journal entries will print on one page; continue with Step 11.

11. Click the **Print** button in the Print dialog box. A dialog box opens, reminding you that the action will apply to all items in the selected groups.

12. Click the **OK** button. The entries you created today are printed. See Figure 5-48.

Figure 5-48   PRINTED JOURNAL ENTRIES

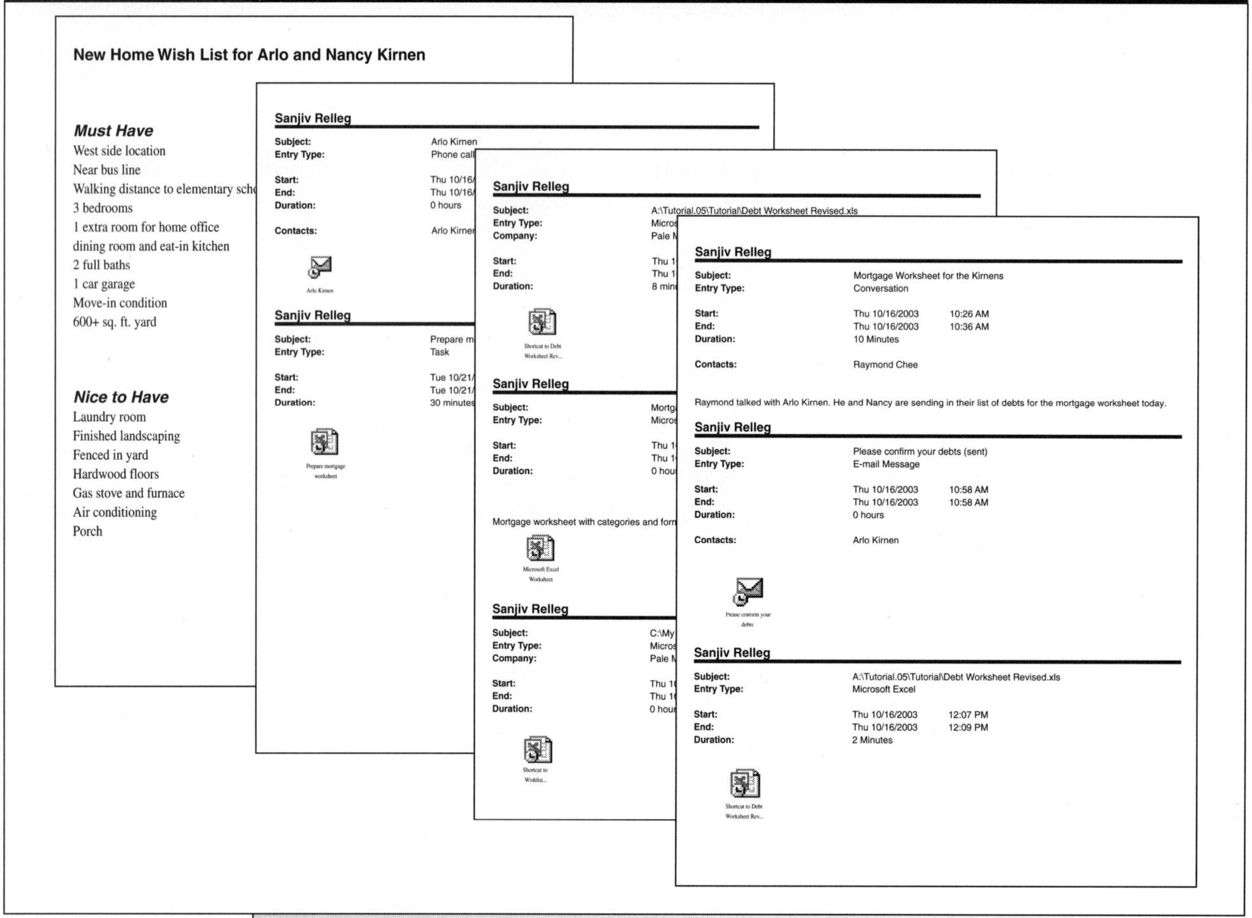

Now that you've finished, you can remove the filter and turn off the automatic Journal entries.

To remove the filter and turn off the Journal:

1. Click **View** on the menu bar, point to **Current View**, and then click **Customize Current View**. The View Summary dialog box opens.

2. Click the **Filter** button, click the **Clear All** button in the Filter dialog box, click the **OK** button in the Filter dialog box, and then click the **OK** button in the View Summary dialog box. All the items are again visible in the Journal By Type view.

   Next you'll turn off the automatic recording of Journal entries.

3. Click **Tools** on the menu bar, and then click **Options**. The Options dialog box opens.

4. Click the **Preferences** tab, and then click the **Journal Options** button. The Journal Options dialog box opens.

5. Click the **E-mail Message, Microsoft Access, Microsoft Excel, Microsoft PowerPoint**, and **Microsoft Word** check boxes to remove the check marks.

6. Click the **Arlo Kirnen** check box to remove the check mark.

7. Click the **OK** button in the Journal Options dialog box, and then click the **OK** button in the Options dialog box.

Next, you'll delete the existing Journal entries. Deleting Journal entries removes only the entry. Any associated Outlook items, files, or documents remain intact. You can remove individual entries, pressing the Shift or Ctrl key to select more than one item at a time. Or, you can remove an entire group of entries by selecting the group heading.

To delete journal entries:

1. Click the **Mortgage worksheet for the Kirnens** conversation entry in the Journal folder, and then press the **Delete** key. The selected entry is moved to the Deleted Items folder.

2. Click the **E-mail Message** group heading, press and hold the **Shift** key, click the **Microsoft Excel**, **Microsoft Word**, **Phone Call**, and **Task** group headings, and then release the **Shift** key. All the types of Journal entries you created in this tutorial are now selected.

3. Press the **Delete** key. A dialog box opens reminding you that this action will apply to all items in the selected groups.

4. Click the **OK** button. All the selected Journal entries are moved to the Deleted Items folder.

   Before you empty the Deleted Items folder, you will delete all the other Outlook items you created for this tutorial.

5. Delete the two messages and one post you created for this tutorial from the Inbox folder.

6. Delete the two messages you created in this tutorial from the Sent Items folder.

7. Delete the 16 contacts you created for this tutorial from the Contacts folder.

8. Delete the task you created for this tutorial in the Tasks folder.

9. Empty the Deleted Items folder.

As the Kirnens begin their search for a new home, you have sent and received e-mail messages with Office documents, created new Office documents from within Outlook, and faxed information. In addition, you have imported and exported contact information for potential clients. Cassandra will be busy for the foreseeable future working with these homebuyers.

Session 5.2 QUICK CHECK

1. Briefly explain importing as it relates to Outlook.

2. Briefly explain exporting as it relates to Outlook.

3. Why would you want to import files into Outlook?

4. List four formats to which you can export Outlook items.

5. What is a tab-delimited file?

6. Why would you need to map fields?

7. Why would you want to export a personal file folder?

8. True or False: You can send faxes from Outlook but you cannot receive faxes in Outlook.

REVIEW ASSIGNMENTS

Ty Mumford, the listing agent for Ace Realty, works exclusively with seller clients. He handles all aspects of listing properties, preparing properties for showings, and procuring purchase offers. His latest client is Margie Tackett, who is selling her home in Omaha and relocating to North Platte due to a promotion at work. You will help Ty work on the listing for Margie's house and enter contact lists of other potential seller clients.

1. Started Outlook and then create a task with the subject "Write listing for the Tackett house" and a due date of two days from now.

2. Create a contact for Margie Tackett, home phone number "402-555-7771", home fax "402-555-7782", address type Home, home mailing address "981 Lincoln Way, Omaha, NE 98182", and your e-mail address.

3. Turn on the Journal to automatically record e-mail messages for Margie Tackett and all Office files. (*Hint:* Use the Tools menu to get to the Journal Options dialog box.)

4. Create a new Journal entry to record a five-minute conversation with Margie Tackett about the "Listing for the Tackett home" with the note "Margie called to request that we add information about the new roof she installed on her home to the listing."

Explore   5. Right-drag the Write listing for the Tackett house task to the Journal folder, and then click Copy Here as Journal Entry with Attachment to create a Journal entry for the task. Change the duration to 30 minutes.

6. Create a Journal entry with the subject "Tackett house description" for the Microsoft Word document type. Insert the **Description** file in the **Review** folder within the **Tutorial.05** folder on your Data Disk displayed as an icon.

Explore   7. Create a new mail message using Microsoft PowerPoint Slide, addressed to Margie Tackett with the subject "Please review house highlights." Click the Click to add new slide box, which opens the New Slide dialog box. Click the Bulleted List button in the Choose an AutoLayout list box (the name of the AutoLayout will appear in the lower-right corner of the dialog box after you select a button), and then click the OK button. Click the Click to add title text box, type "Tackett Home Highlights", click the Click to add text box, type "2 bedroom home with 1260 sq. ft. living space", press the Enter key, type "Basement, large family room, 2 car detached garage", press the Enter key, type "Large fenced yard with pleasant landscaping", press the Enter key, type "Large redwood deck and enclosed porch with swing", press the Enter key, and type "Available for immediate occupancy". Send the slide.

8. Close PowerPoint without saving the slide you created.

9. Download the message, and then open and read it.

10. Right-click the message body, click Edit Message, and then save the PowerPoint slide as **Tackett Home Highlights** in the **Review** folder within the **Tutorial.05** folder on your Data Disk. Close the file and PowerPoint, and then close the message.

11. From the Outlook Inbox, create a new Office Document. Create a Word document that you post in the Inbox. Type the text "Please describe the unique features of your home to help Ace Realty find the best buyer.", press the Enter key twice, type "List all rooms, including bedrooms, baths, living/dining rooms, storage rooms, and so forth.", press the Enter key, type "Describe the kitchen, including size, cabinets, and appliances.", press the Enter key, type "Describe any attic, basement, and garage areas, including whether they are finished.", press the Enter key, and then type "Describe the yard, including size and landscaping". Press the Enter key twice and then type your name.

12. Format all paragraphs except the first one and your name as a bulleted list. (*Hint:* Select the lines and then click the Bullets button on the Word Formatting toolbar.)

13. Post the document in the Inbox folder. (*Hint:* If the Post button is not on the Standard toolbar, then use the File menu. If a discussion dialog box opens, enter "Home Description" as the subject.)

14. Open the posted document in the Inbox, save it as **Home Description** in the **Review** folder within the **Tutorial.05** folder on your Data Disk, and then close the document and exit Word.

15. Import the list of home sellers stored in the Contacts range in the Excel workbook **Homesellers** in the **Review** folder within the **Tutorial.05** folder on your Data Disk into the Contacts folder using the Import and Export Wizard. Do not import duplicates.

Explore 16. Map custom fields between the Excel worksheet and Outlook. Expand the Name field category. Drag the First value in the Excel worksheet to the First Name field in Outlook, and then drag the Last value to the Last Name field. Confirm the other fields map correctly, and then click the OK button.

17. Click the Finish button to import the Excel workbook data. Open the Contacts folder and review the new cards.

Explore 18. Export the contact list from the Outlook Contacts folder to an Access database. Save the database as **Home Seller Addresses Database** in the **Review** folder within the **Tutorial.05** folder on your Data Disk; you do not need to map any custom fields.

19. Back up the Outlook Contacts folder into a personal file folder saved as **Ty Contacts Backup** in the **Review** folder within the **Tutorial.05** folder on your Data Disk with no encryption.

Explore 20. Save the Joe Dundst contact as a vCard file; use the contact's name as the filename and save the file in the **Review** folder within the **Tutorial.05** folder on your Data Disk.

21. Review the Journal entries you created for these assignments in Entry List view.

22. Filter the list to display only those entries you created today.

23. Print all the Journal entries in all groups on one page; do not print any attached files.

24. Remove the filter, and then turn off the Journal.

25. Delete all the Journal entries, the e-mail message and the posting in the Inbox folder, the e-mail message in the Sent Items folder, the contacts, and the tasks you created in these Review Assignments, and then empty the Deleted Items folder.

26. Exit Outlook.

CASE PROBLEMS

Case 1. Space du Jour Space du Jour is a large open gallery that clients can rent for one- or multi-day events. The gallery has hosted all types of events, from art auctions to cooking demonstrations to small business workshops. Harriet Connors works with clients to arrange the open space as needed, whether split into partitioned rooms for seminars or divided by panels for hanging artwork. She uses Outlook to stay in touch with clients, record her daily activities, and organize her tasks.

1. Start Outlook, and then create a new contact for Mick Davis, using your telephone number, home address, and e-mail address.

2. Turn on the Journal to automatically record all Outlook items for Mick Davis and all Office files.

3. Create a new Journal entry to record a 45-minute phone call with Mick about arranging the space for a customer service training seminar for a local chain of clothing stores. Enter an appropriate subject and notes.

Explore ▶ 4. Switch to My Computer in the Other Shortcut group on the Outlook Bar, click the New Document button on the Standard toolbar, and then create a new Word document. The file will be saved as a Word file rather than posted to an Outlook folder.

5. Type "Mick Davis Seminar Setup" and format it as 14-point, bold, Arial; then press the Enter key twice, type your name, and then press the Enter key twice.

6. Insert the **Seminar** document located in the **Cases** folder within the **Tutorial.05** folder on your Data Disk. (*Hint:* Click Insert on the menu bar, click File, change the Look in location, select the file, and then click the Insert button.)

7. Save the Word document as **Mick Davis Seminar Setup** in the **Cases** folder within the **Tutorial.05** folder on your Data Disk, and then close the Word document and program.

Explore ▶ 8. Switch to the Tasks folder in Outlook, and then import the Tasks from the personal file folder **SeminarTasks** in the **Cases** folder within the **Tutorial.05** folder on your Data Disk into the Outlook Tasks folder using the Import and Export Wizard. Do not import duplicates. (*Hint:* Select Tasks as the folder to import from.)

Explore ▶ 9. Create a Journal entry for the two tasks that mention Mick's name. (*Hint:* Select the two tasks, drag them to the Journal folder on the Outlook Bar, type "Mick Davis" as the subject, change the Entry Type to Task, and then save and close the Journal entry.)

10. Switch to the Journal, and then change the view to Last Seven Days. Notice that Outlook applied a filter to display only the previous week's entries.

11. Sort the Journal in ascending order by Entry Type. (*Hint:* Click the Entry Type column heading.)

12. Print all rows of the Journal entries for the last seven days in Table Style.

13. Delete all the Journal entries you created in this Case.

14. Change the Journal view to By Type.

15. Turn off the Journal.

16. Delete the contact and all the tasks you created in this case, empty the Deleted Items folder, and then exit Outlook.

Case 2. Janise's Vegetarian Table   Janise Kellar runs a vegetarian gourmet catering business in Raleigh, North Carolina. She and her staff of four provide catering for business and personal events, ranging from hand-passed appetizers to sit-down multicourse meals. Janise uses Outlook to keep track of her clients and vendors, and to record her daily activities.

1. Start Outlook, and then turn on the Journal to automatically record all Outlook items and all Office files.

2. Create a contact for Janise Kellar, using your e-mail address, mailing address, and phone number.

Explore 3. Open the Journal Options dialog box, and set up the Journal to record entries for Janise.

Explore 4. Create a new Journal entry, and then click the Start Timer button to have Outlook determine the duration of the Journal entry. The hands on the stopwatch rotate to indicate the passage of time.

5. For the open Journal entry, enter "Fall mushroom supplies" as the subject, change the Entry type to conversation, and then type "Tanner expects a bountiful supply of wild mushrooms this autumn due to the unusual rainfall and temperature." in the notes box.

Explore 6. The timer has been running as you created the Journal entry. As each full minute passes, the time is recorded in the Duration text box. When the Duration text box reads at least 1 minute, click the Pause Timer button, and then save and close the entry.

7. Create a new mail message using Microsoft Excel Worksheet, addressed to Janise Kellar with the subject "Available mushroom types".

8. Type "Mushroom Type" in cell A1, type "Crimini" in cell A2, type "Oyster" in cell A3, type "Portobello" in cell A4, type "Shiitakes" in cell A5, type "Chanterelle" in cell A6, type "Hedgehog" in cell A7, and type "Morels" in cell A8.

Explore 9. Bold the text in cell A1, and then sort the column alphabetically by clicking the Sort Ascending button on the Excel Standard toolbar.

10. Send the message, and then close Excel without saving the worksheet.

11. Download the message, open it, and then save the message body as **Mushroom Availability** in the **Cases** folder within the **Tutorial.05** folder on your Data Disk. Leave the file and Excel open, but close the message window.

Explore 12. Create a new Office Document from the Inbox in Outlook. Create a Microsoft Excel Workbook that you send to someone else. Address the message to Janise Kellar on the Message tab, and then change the subject to "Mushroom order".

13. Switch to the Mushroom Availability worksheet that you left open, select cells A1 through A8, and then click the Copy button on the Excel Standard toolbar.

14. Switch to the Mushroom order document, click the Document tab, and then click the Paste button on the Excel Standard toolbar to duplicate the mushroom types in the message. Expand the width of column A to the longest cell entry.

15. Type "Pounds" in cell B1, type "20" in cell B2, type "10" in cell B4, type "10" in cell B5, and then type "2" in cell B8. Send the message, and then close Excel.

16. Download the message, and then save the attachment as **Mushrooms Order** in the **Cases** folder within the **Tutorial.05** folder on your Data Disk.

17. Back up the Inbox into a personal file folder saved as **Mushroom Messages Backup** in the **Cases** folder within the **Tutorial.05** folder on your Data Disk.

18. Review the Journal entries you created in this case in the By Type view, and then expand all the groups.

19. Change the view to show an entire Month, and then click the Go To Today button on the Standard toolbar.

Explore 20. Change the view to show a Day, click the date banner, and then change the date to next Friday.

21. Click the Go To Today button to display the entries you created in this case.

22. If necessary, filter the journal entries to display only those you created today.

23. Print all the Journal entries in all categories on one page; do not print any attached files.

24. Remove the filter, and then turn off the Journal.

25. Delete all the Journal entries, the e-mail messages in the Inbox and Sent Items folders, and the contacts you created in this case, empty the Deleted Items folder, and then exit Outlook.

Case 3. Pete's Frame Shop   Pete Lazaro opened a frame shop in 1992 to provide Cincinnati residents with access to quality framing at rock-bottom prices. Pete is able to keep his prices lower than his competitors by buying frames and other supplies in bulk, and cultivating artists and galleries with frequent framing needs as key customers—these savings are then also passed along to customers with occasional framing needs. Pete uses Outlook to track his work with suppliers and customers.

1. Start Outlook and then turn on the Journal to automatically record all Office files.

2. Create a new mail message from Microsoft Office using Microsoft Word Document. Click in the message body, and then type "Pete's Frame Shop provides the highest quality frames at the lowest cost. Whether you need to frame your college diploma, a special photograph, or your latest oil painting, Pete's Frame Shop has the frame to show it off. Our specially trained staff helps you select the frame, suggests complementary mats and borders, and then carefully frames your piece." Press the Enter key twice and then type your name.

3. Close the document and save the changes to the document as **Frame Shop Description** in the **Cases** folder within the **Tutorial.05** folder on your Data Disk.

4. Switch to the Contacts folder in Outlook, and then create a new Office Document. Post a Word document in the folder.

5. Insert the text from **Frame Shop Description** in the **Cases** folder in the **Tutorial.05** folder on your Data Disk. (*Hint:* Click Insert on the menubar, click File, change the Look in location, select the file, and then click the Insert button.)

6. In a new paragraph above your name, type "Mention this ad and receive an additional 20% off our already low prices." Post the file to the folder.

7. Open the posted document, save it as **Frame Shop Ad** in the **Cases** folder in the **Tutorial.05** folder on your Data Disk, and then close the Word document and program.

Explore 8. Import the list of customers and vendors stored in the tab-delimited text file **Frame** in the **Cases** folder in the **Tutorial.05** folder on your Data Disk into the Contacts folder using the Import and Export Wizard. (*Hint:* Use the Tab Separated Values (Windows) as the file type to import.)

Explore 9. Map custom fields to ensure all the fields import correctly. (*Hint:* Make sure Keywords maps to Categories in Outlook.)

10. Finish importing the text file to Outlook.

Explore 11. Create a mail merge Form letter to a New document, using all the imported contacts and the **Frame Shop Ad** in the **Cases** folder in the **Tutorial.05** folder on your Data Disk as the data file. Enter the appropriate fields to address the letter, and then type an appropriate salutation above your name at the bottom of the letter. Merge to a new document, and then save the merged document as **Frame Letter Merged** in the **Cases** folder in the **Tutorial.05** folder on your Data Disk. Close Word without saving the data file. (*Hint:* To start the mail merge, switch to the Contacts folder, click Tools on the menu bar, and then click Mail Merge.)

12. Export the contact list from the Outlook Contacts folder to an Excel workbook; save the file as **Frame Contact List** in the **Cases** folder in the **Tutorial.05** folder on your Data Disk.

13. Back up the Outlook Contacts folder into a personal file folder saved as **Frame Shop Contacts Backup** in the **Cases** folder in the **Tutorial.05** folder on your Data Disk.

14. Review the Journal entries in the By Category view.

15. Filter the list to display only those entries you created today.

16. Print all the Journal entries in the categories on one page; do not print any attached files.

17. Remove the filter, and then turn off the Journal.

18. Delete all the Journal entries and the contacts you created in this case, empty the Deleted Items folder, and then exit Outlook.

Case 4. Plan a Party   You're going to plan a party for the event of your choice—a favorite holiday, your birthday, or even TGIF. You'll create a contact list, write out an invitation, and then fax or e-mail the invitation to your guests.

1. Start Outlook, and then create new contact cards for yourself and at least five other people (real or fictional); include names, addresses, phone numbers, and your e-mail address.

2. Turn on the Journal to automatically record e-mail messages for yourself and the five contacts you created and for all Office files.

Explore ▷ 3. Create a new Journal entry with "Started party planning" as a subject by dragging your contact card to Journal on the Outlook Bar.

Explore ▷ 4. Create a new Journal entry to record a 10-minute conversation about your upcoming party. Enter one of the contacts you created in the Contacts text box at the bottom of the window.

5. Start a new Office Document from the Inbox. Post an Excel worksheet in the Inbox. Create the list of supplies that you'll need in column A and their estimated costs in column B. Use the AutoSum button on the Standard toolbar to total column B. Format the worksheet appropriately.

6. Open the posted document, save it as **Party Supplies** in the **Cases** folder in the **Tutorial.05** folder on your Data Disk, and then close the Excel workbook and program.

7. Create a new mail message using Microsoft Word Document. Address the message to the five contacts you entered earlier and enter the subject "Party Invitation."

8. In the message body, type the text for your party invitation, including your name as the party host, and then format the text appropriately. Send the message, and then close Word without saving changes.

9. Download the message, open it, edit the message, and then save the message in Word as **Party Invitation** in the **Cases** folder in the **Tutorial.05** folder on your Data Disk.

10. Close the document and Word, and then close the message.

11. Export the Contacts folder to a Microsoft Excel file; save the workbook as **Party Contacts Workbook** in the **Cases** folder in the **Tutorial.05** folder on your Data Disk.

Explore ▷ 12. Import the **Party Contacts Workbook** in the **Cases** folder in the **Tutorial.05** folder on your Data Disk, but do not allow duplicates.

13. Back up the Outlook Inbox folder into a personal file folder saved as **Party Messages Backup** in the **Cases** folder in the **Tutorial.05** folder on your Data Disk.

Explore   14. If you have the ability, fax the **Party Invitation** in the **Cases** folder in the **Tutorial.05** folder on your Data Disk to yourself or a classmate. Print the fax.

15. Review the Journal entries you created for this case in Entry List view.

16. Filter the list to display on the entries you created today.

17. Print all rows of the Journal entries in Table Style.

18. Remove the filter, and then turn off the Journal.

19. Delete all the Journal entries, the e-mail messages in the Inbox and Sent Items folders, and the contacts you created in this case, and then empty the Deleted Items folder.

20. Exit Outlook.

QUICK CHECK ANSWERS

Session 5.1

1. A diary that records the date, time, and duration of your actions with Outlook items, Office documents, and other activities.

2. The Journal enables you to look back at a timeline of your activities and locate a specific document or recall the events of a certain day.

3. E-mail messages; meeting requests, responses, and cancellations; task requests and responses; files you create, open, close, and save in Access, Excel, PowerPoint, and Word.

4. As an e-mail attachment or as the message body.

5. Recipients can save a message created from an Office file in its original program format, which they can then open and edit in that program, as long as they have the source program on their computer.

6. You can send the file as an e-mail attachment or you can save the file to your computer.

7. When you start an Office file from an Outlook folder, you post the file to that folder. When you start a new Office file from My Computer in the Other Shortcuts group on the Outlook Bar, you can save the file to any location on your computer or network.

8. True

Session 5.2

1. Copying data created in another program into Outlook.

2. Moving data out of Outlook into another program's format.

3. To bring into Outlook address books or messages you or someone else created in other programs.

4. Personal folder files, vCards, .rtf files, .txt files

5. A file of data in which fields for a record are separated by a tab character.

6. To let Outlook know where to store imported data that is set up with field names different from those used in Outlook.

7. To create a backup of an Outlook folder without removing the items from Outlook, as occurs when archiving.

8. False

CUSTOMIZING OUTLOOK

Creating Contributor Contact Forms for Luminescence

CASE

Luminescence

Luminescence is small nonprofit theater group that performs six original shows each year. The shows range from comedy to drama to experimental theater. Past shows have included singing jugglers, musical readings of poetry collections, dramatizations of children's tales, and environmental parables. The four founders—Fred O'Riordan, Ada Shubin, Bette Wattis, and Brian Cummings—write, direct, and act in all the shows. They hire a small staff to help with costumes, lights, and sound during productions. In addition, the staff manages the office and handles ticket sales, advertising, and promotion.

Although the shows are regularly sold out, ticket sales alone do not bring in enough money to support the group. This independent theater relies on outside funding to help pay its rent, utilities, and salaries, to purchase costumes and props, and hire visiting musicians and guest actors. To supplement its ticket sales, the group organizes an annual fundraiser. Brian wants to be able to collect the contributor information in Outlook. He needs to store each contributor's name, the contribution amount, and whether or not the contributor wants to be credited in the program that is handed out at each performance. You can customize Outlook to track this kind of information for Brian, as well to better match the specific needs and working style of the Luminescence team.

In this tutorial, you will create a new contact form based on the built-in contact form. You will use the form you created to enter contact information. Then you will create a mail form based on the built-in mail form and save it as a template. Next you will customize Outlook by adding fields to views, modifying Outlook Today, changing the Calendar options, adding groups and shortcuts to the Outlook Bar, and then creating a toolbar.

SESSION 6.1

In this session, you will learn how to customize forms and create fields. First you will modify the standard Contact form by displaying a hidden page and adding default and custom fields. Then you'll use the custom forms to record contacts and send messages. Finally you'll create a custom mail template.

Customizing Forms

Each time you write an e-mail message, record details about a contact, schedule an appointment, or create any other Outlook item, you type the appropriate data in a special window. The window in which you enter and view information about an item in Outlook is called a **form**. Outlook provides standard forms for each item, such as creating and viewing messages, appointments, and contact information. Forms are used to gather the required data in fields. For example, you have used the standard, built-in New Message form to compose e-mail messages and the New Contact form to enter information for a contact. Every Outlook item is based on a form. You can modify some of the built-in forms or create custom ones.

REFERENCE WINDOW	RW

Customizing a Form
- Open a blank item with the form you want to modify.
- Click Tools on the menu bar, point to Forms, and then click Design This Form.
- Customize the form by adding and deleting fields, options, tabs, and controls.
- Click Tools on the menu bar, point to Forms, and then click Publish Form.
  or
- Open the folder or item for which you want to create a new form.
- Click Tools on the menu bar, point to Forms, and then click Design A Form.
- Customize the form by adding and deleting fields, options, tabs, and controls.
- Click Tools on the menu bar, point to Forms, and then click Publish Form.

The four basic steps for customizing a form are:

1. Open an existing form in design mode.

2. Modify the form.

3. Test the form.

4. Publish the form.

Opening a Form in Design Mode

Custom forms are based on existing Outlook forms. When you want to modify a form, you need to switch the form to design mode. **Design mode** (also called the Outlook Form Designer) is the environment in Outlook where you create and customize forms. You know a form is in design mode because the word "(Design)" appears in the form's title bar, a dotted grid pattern appears in the background, and additional tabs appear in the window.

The form you choose to customize depends on what you want to accomplish. Select the existing form that best matches your goals for the custom form. For example, Brian wants you to create a custom form that collects information about people who make financial contributions to Luminescence. The existing form that has fields with information about individuals is the New Contact form. Therefore, you'll start by opening the New Contact form to which you can add fields to collect contributor information.

To open an Outlook form in design mode:

1. Start Outlook, and then open a new Contact window, as if you were creating a new contact. The Contact window is the form you want to modify.

2. Click **Tools** on the menu bar, point to **Forms**, and then click **Design This Form**. The form switches to design mode.

3. If necessary, maximize the form window. See Figure 6-1.

Figure 6-1	NEW CONTACT FORM IN DESIGN MODE

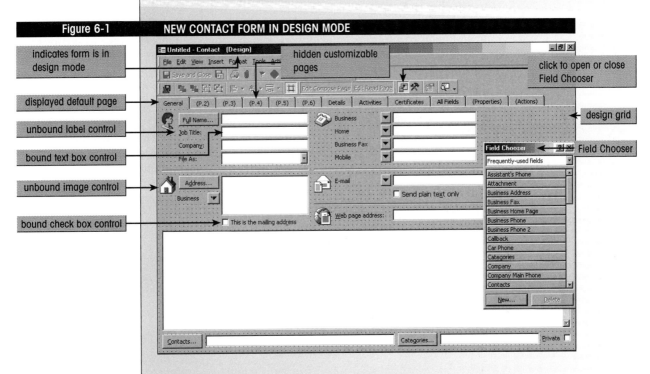

TROUBLE? If the Field Chooser doesn't appear, click the Field Chooser button on the Form Design toolbar.

TROUBLE? If the dotted grid background doesn't appear, click Layout on the menu bar, and then click Show Grid.

Each form is made up of pages, which appear on separate tabs in the item's window, as you can see in Figure 6-1. The first page contains the fields and organization you've seen before. On some forms, including the New Message and New Contact forms, you can modify this first page. For all forms, you can modify the next five pages, which are blank by default. These unused pages are hidden in the published form, but appear in design mode with parentheses around their names. When you modify a form, you can customize the existing fields, options, and layout on the default pages or you can display a blank page to create the layout you want.

Layout refers to the organization of the controls on the page. A **bound control** is an object on a form in which a user enters information that Outlook displays. Some common bound controls are check boxes, list boxes, and text boxes. An **unbound control** is an object that displays text, an image, or another design element for informational or decorative purposes that a user cannot edit (change). Some common unbound controls are text labels, lines, and pictures. Figure 6-1 identifies some of the controls on the General page of the New Contact form.

From design mode, you customize form pages by adding fields to collect and store information. Fields are made up of bound and unbound controls. The simplest way to add fields to a form is with the **Field Chooser**, a list of available fields that is available in design mode whenever a customizable page of a form is displayed. Not all the default fields in Outlook appear on a form; some default fields, such as the Customer ID and Referred By fields, are available in the Field Chooser but are not used. When you add a field to a form page with the Field Chooser, it appears as a bound control with a text label.

Modifying a Form

You add fields to a form page by dragging them from the Field Chooser to the location on the page where you want them to appear. The grid helps you to accurately position the fields on a form. The Field Chooser organizes all the available fields into field sets to make it easier for you to find the ones you want. Not all the built-in fields appear on the default forms. If you repeat a field from another page or on the same page, the same information appears in all locations when data is entered in one location.

Brian asks you to add fields to one of the blank form pages, rather than modify the standard General page of the form. You'll display a blank page for the contributor information, and then rename the page with a descriptive name: Contributions.

To display and rename a page:

1. Click the **(P.2)** tab on the form. This is the hidden page you want to display and customize. The grid fills the page.

2. Click **Form** on the menu bar, and then click **Display This Page**. The parentheses disappear from the tab name, indicating the page will appear in the finished form.

3. Click **Form** on the menu bar, and then click **Rename Page**. The Rename Page dialog box opens.

4. Type **Contributions** in the Page name text box, and then click the **OK** button. The tab is renamed on the form.

The next step for creating a form is to add fields to the layout. As you place fields on the grid, two features helps you align them neatly. Snap to Grid positions fields along the closest line of dots to where you drag them. AutoLayout aligns the fields in a column no matter where you drop the fields on the form.

To add fields to a form:

1. Click the list arrow in the Field Chooser, and then click **All Contact fields** to display the built-in Contact fields in the Field Chooser.

2. Scroll down the alphabetical list until you see Customer ID in the Field Chooser list.

3. Drag the **Customer ID** field from the Field Chooser to the page. No matter where you release the mouse button, Outlook places the field in the upper-left corner of the page and inserts the appropriate controls for the field—a label (Customer ID:) and a text box.

TROUBLE? If the field doesn't move to the upper-left corner of the form, AutoLayout is probably turned off. Click Layout on the menu bar, and then click AutoLayout. You'll reposition the Customer ID shortly.

4. Drag the **Referred By** field from the Field Chooser to below the Customer ID field, as shown in Figure 6-2.

Figure 6-2	CONTRIBUTIONS PAGE DISPLAYED WITH TWO FIELDS

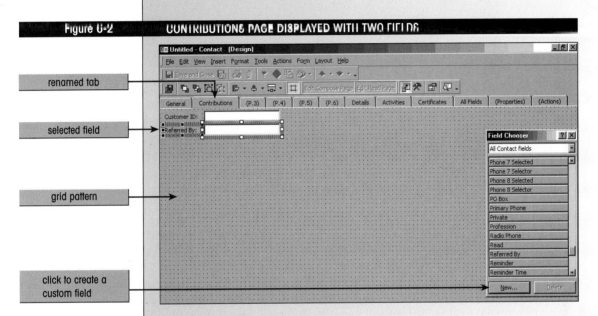

- renamed tab
- selected field
- grid pattern
- click to create a custom field

TROUBLE? If your fields don't align exactly as shown, don't worry. You'll fix the alignment later in this tutorial.

The other fields Brian wants on the form—Contributor, Donation, and Pledged—don't exist in any field set. You'll create these as custom fields in Outlook to meet your needs.

There are three types of fields—simple, combination, and formula. A **simple field** holds a basic piece of data, such as a name, amount, or date. A **combination field** combines existing fields into a single field, as you've seen with the Full Name field, which includes the Title, First Name, Middle Initial, Last Name, and Suffix fields. A **formula field** performs a calculation on data in other fields, such as the number of days until a specific date.

When you create a custom field, you'll need to supply three things: the custom field's name, type, and format. Each field is based on a specific data type, which is the kind of information you want to enter and display in that field. Figure 6-3 describes the field types available in Outlook. The format specifies how the data appears in that field; most data types have several format options. For example, a field with percentage data can be formatted to show all digits (32.8938%), two decimals (32.89%), one decimal (32.9%), or no decimals (33%). You enter the field's name, type, and format in the New Field dialog box.

Figure 6-3   **FIELD TYPES FOR CUSTOM FIELDS**

TYPE	DESCRIPTION	EXAMPLE
Combination	multiple fields and/or text	Harry and Sue Cozzel
Currency	numbers shown as money amounts	$123.45 ($123.45) £123.45
Date/Time	date and time	12/15/03 10 AM
Duration	numbers shown as minutes, hours, or days	10 hours 1.5 days
Formula	calculations based on fields	number of days until a contact's birthday
Integer	nondecimal (whole) numbers	123
Keywords	user-defined fields for grouping related items; similar to categories	Benefactor, Patron, Contributor
Number	nonfinancial numbers	323.313
Percent	numbers expressed as percentages	98%
Text	alphanumerical characters, up to 255 characters	987 Main Street (888) 555-1234
Yes/No	data that is restricted to one of two values; often shown as a check box	Yes or No, True or False, On or Off

You'll create three new fields for the custom form. The Contributor field has a text type and a text format; Brian will use it to list the name that contributors want to appear in the promotion, such as Anonymous, The Tiger Corporation, or The Worthnell Family. The second new field is named Donation and has a Currency field type without cents in the format; this field will be used to identify the amount of the financial contribution. The third new field is Pledged and has a Yes/No type with an Icon format; the pledged field will be checked when the contributor has not yet submitted the promised donation. A custom field is available only in the folder in which you create it. Therefore, the custom fields you'll create will be available only in the Contacts folder.

To create a new field:

1. Click the **New** button in the Field Chooser. The New Field dialog box opens. See Figure 6-4.

Figure 6-4   **NEW FIELD DIALOG BOX**

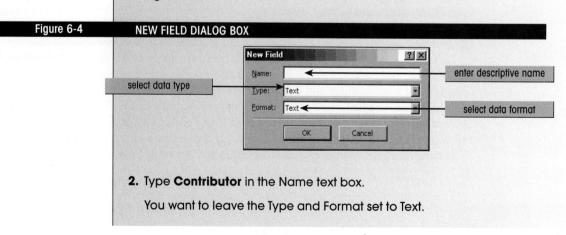

2. Type **Contributor** in the Name text box.

You want to leave the Type and Format set to Text.

3. Click the **OK** button. The Field Chooser switches to show the User-defined fields in folder and displays the custom field. See Figure 6-5.

Figure 6-5	FIELD CHOOSER WITH USER-DEFINED FIELD

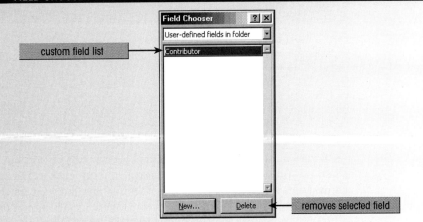

TROUBLE? If you see any other fields in the list, someone has defined Contact user fields previously on the Outlook installation you are working with.

4. Click the **New** button in the Field Chooser, and then type **Donation** in the Name text box.

5. Click the **Type** list arrow to display the available field types, and then click **Currency**.

6. Verify that the format is **$12,345.60 ($12,345.60)**.

7. Click the **OK** button. The Donation field appears as a user-defined field on the Field Chooser.

8. Create a new field named **Pledged** with the **Yes/No** type and **Icon** format. You should have three new fields in the User-defined fields in folder list.

The custom fields you created are placed on a page the same way as the default fields—by dragging them from the Field Chooser to the grid. You'll place the custom fields you created on the page. The fields are located in the User-defined fields in folder field set.

To place custom fields on a form page:

1. If necessary, click the list arrow in the Field Chooser, and then click **User-defined fields in folder**. The fields you created appear in the Field Chooser.

2. Drag the **Contributor** field from the Field Chooser to below the Referred By field. The field remains in the field list for you to use again on this form or another page.

3. Drag the **Donation** field from the Field Chooser below the Contributor field. The text box displays a default value of $0.00 because this has a currency format.

4. Drag the **Pledged** field from the Field Chooser to the right of the Donation field. The Pledged label and check box are grouped into one unit. See Figure 6-6.

Figure 6-6   CUSTOM FIELDS ON CONTRIBUTIONS PAGE

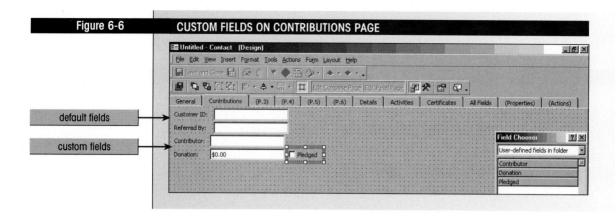

If you want to reposition any control for any reason, you can drag the selected control to a new position. To select a single control, you can click it. However, if you want to move an entire field, which includes the label and its text box, you need to select both controls. To select multiple controls, you can use the following selection methods:

- Press and hold the Ctrl key as you click controls to select nonadjacent ones.
- Select the first control, press and hold the Shift key, and then click the last control to select a group of adjacent ones.
- Drag a selection box around a group of controls, boxing in the ones you want to select.

You know a control is selected when sizing handles and a hatched border surround it. You'll use the sizing handles to reduce and expand fields later.

To reposition fields:

1. Click the **Referred By label** to select it.

2. Press and hold the **Ctrl** key, click the **Referred By text box** to select it, and then release the **Ctrl** key.

3. Drag the selected **Referred By** controls with the move pointer to below the **Donation** field, as shown in Figure 6-7.

Figure 6-7   REPOSITIONED FIELDS

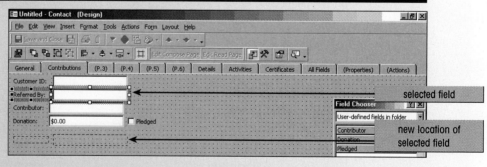

4. Select the **Contributor label** and **text box**, and then drag these selected controls to the right of the **Customer ID** field.

5. Select the **Pledged** field, and then drag it to below the **Customer ID** field.

6. Select the **Donation label** and **text box**, and then drag them to the right of the **Pledged** field.

7. Select the **Referred By label** and **text box**, and then drag them up to fill the empty space. See Figure 6-8.

| Figure 6-8 | FIELDS REORDERED ON CONTRIBUTIONS PAGE |

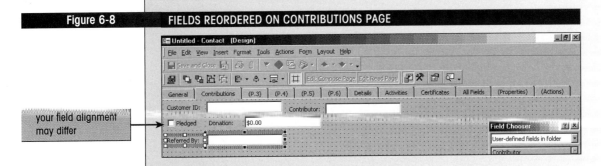

your field alignment may differ

TROUBLE? If your fields are not in the same basic position as shown in Figure 6-8, continue to select and reposition controls to approximate the placement in the figure.

This placement is a logical order for users to enter information in the fields. However, the order that fields are selected when users press the Tab key may not be logical. **Tab order** specifies the sequence that users move through fields on a form when they press the Tab key. Outlook matches the tab order to the sequence you selected fields from the Field Chooser. However, as you add, move, and replace fields, the tab order remains the same. As a result, pressing the Tab key may bounce users all over the page.

To test the tab order:

1. Click the **Customer ID label** to select it.

2. Press the **Tab** key. The Customer ID text box is selected, which makes sense, as it's the adjacent control.

3. Press the **Tab** key. The Referred By label is selected at the end of the page, which is not what users will expect.

4. Continue to press the **Tab** key, noticing the order controls are selected, until the Customer ID label is selected.

As you can see, the current tab order is not a logical sequence for the location of the controls. You can reset the tab order to better match the placement of the fields on the form page.

To set the tab order:

1. Click **Layout** on the menu bar, and then click **Tab Order**. The Tab Order dialog box opens. See Figure 6-9.

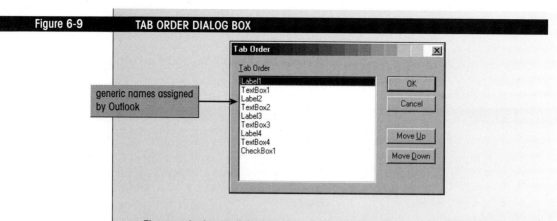

Figure 6-9   TAB ORDER DIALOG BOX

generic names assigned
by Outlook

The controls are listed by the default generic names given by Outlook—Label,
TextBox, and CheckBox—and are numbered in the order you placed them on
the form. Because you've repositioned the controls, it's difficult to know which
is which.

2. Click the **Cancel** button. The dialog box closes.

You can rename each control by changing its properties. A descriptive name enables you
to quickly identify each control. The simplest identification is to name the control using the
same text as the caption. For each control you can enter a descriptive name that Outlook
will use internally and modify the caption that users see. Avoid typing any spaces or punctuation in field names, which can cause problems if you later export the data in these fields
from Outlook to other Office applications. If your field name has two or more words, begin
the second word with a capital letter to make it easier to read. For example, use FirstName
rather than First Name or Firstname.

You also can determine how each control looks and functions by setting its properties.
The Display tab in the Properties dialog box shows how the selected control is referenced by
Outlook and how it looks on the form. The positions settings show the current size and location of the selected control; you can specify precise numbers here or modify the control on
the form with the mouse and let Outlook fill in these numbers. The font and color settings
let you modify the typeface and foreground and background colors of the control. For even
greater flexibility, you can modify the Settings options, which are described in Figure 6-10.

Figure 6-10   CONTROL PROPERTIES SETTING OPTIONS

SETTING	CHECKED	UNCHECKED
Visible	Displays the control on the finished form.	Hides the control on the finished form.
Enabled	Allows users to enter data in the control.	Prevents users from entering data in the control; control appears grayed out.
Read only	Allows users to only select or copy data in the control.	Allows users to edit the data in the control.
Resize with form	Enlarges or reduces the control proportionally with the form window.	Keeps the control the same size no matter how the form window is resized.
Sunken	Makes the control look three-dimensional.	Makes the control look two-dimensional.
Multi-line	Starts a new line within the control when users press the Enter key.	Selects next control when users press the Enter key.

You'll set the display properties for each of the fields you placed on the Contributor page.

To set a control's display properties:

1. Verify that the **Customer ID label** control is selected. Sizing handles and a hatch pattern appear around a selected control.

2. Click the **Properties** button 🖼 on the Form Design toolbar. The Properties dialog box opens. See Figure 6-11.

Figure 6-11   **CUSTOMER ID LABEL PROPERTIES DIALOG BOX**

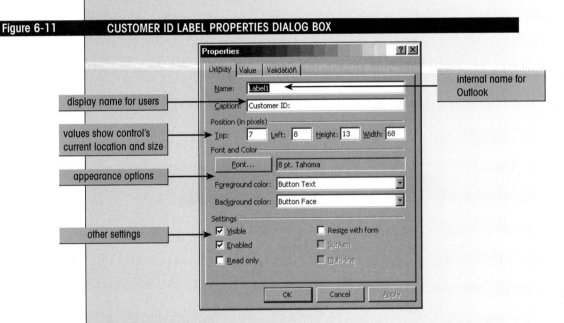

display name for users

internal name for Outlook

values show control's current location and size

appearance options

other settings

3. Type **CustomerIDLabel** in the Name text box; do not type any spaces between the words.

4. Verify that the **Visible** and **Enabled** check boxes contain check marks. The other check boxes should be unchecked.

5. Click the **OK** button.

The properties you set for this control did not change how it appears in the form, although they do affect how the control appears and works in the finished form. You need to set the properties for each of the other controls.

To set the display properties for the other controls:

1. Click the **Customer ID text box** to select it, and then click the **Properties** button 🖼 on the Form Design toolbar. The Properties dialog box opens for the text box.

2. Type **CustomerIDTextBox** in the Name text box. There is no caption for the text box because it will display the text you enter, not default text like a label.

3. Verify that the **Visible, Enabled,** and **Sunken** check boxes contain check marks and the others are unchecked.

4. Click the **OK** button.

5. Set the properties for each of the remaining controls: **Contributor label**, **Contributor text box**, **Pledged label and check box** (the Pledged label and check box are grouped so you can select them as one unit), **Donation label**, **Donation text box**, **Referred By label**, and **Referred By text box**. Use the caption name followed by the control type without spaces as the Name and verify that the Visible, Enabled, and, if necessary, Sunken check boxes are selected.

Now that the controls all have descriptive names, you can rearrange the tab order.

To set the tab order:

1. Click **Layout** on the menu bar, and then click **Tab Order**. The Tab Order dialog box opens. See Figure 6-12.

Figure 6-12	TAB ORDER DIALOG BOX WITH DESCRIPTIVE NAMES

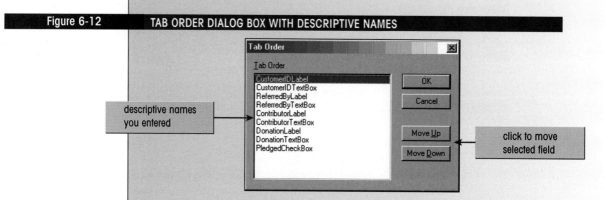

2. Click **ReferredByLabel** in the Tab Order list box.

3. Click the **Move Down** button until ReferredByLabel appears at the end of the list.

4. Click **ReferredByTextBox** in the Tab Order list box, and then click the **Move Down** button until it appears last in the list.

5. Click the **PledgedCheckBox**, and then click the **Move Up** button twice until it appears fifth in the list. See Figure 6-13.

Figure 6-13	COMPLETED TAB ORDER DIALOG BOX

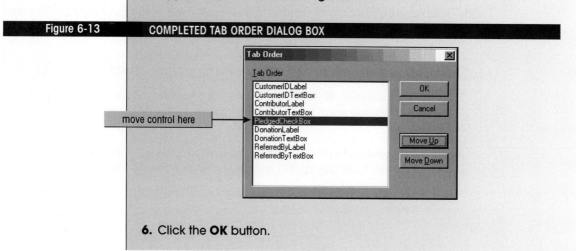

6. Click the **OK** button.

You'll check the tab order on the page to ensure the order is sequential and logical.

To test the revised tab order:

1. Click the **Customer ID label**, and then press the **Tab** key. The Customer ID text box is selected.

2. Press the **Tab** key to select Contributor label.

3. Press the **Tab** key to select the Contributor text box.

4. Press the **Tab** key five times to verify that the selection moves in the following order: Pledged check box, Donation label, Donation text box, Referred By label, and Referred By text box.

> TROUBLE? If your tab order differs, you need to reorder the controls in the Tab Order dialog box. Click Layout on the menu bar, and then click Tab Order to open the Tab Order dialog box. Move fields up and down as needed until the controls in the Tab Order list box match the order shown in Figure 6-13.

The Referred By field isn't really appropriate with the Contribution information. You'll delete it from the form.

To delete a field:

1. Select the **Referred By label** and the **Referred By text box**.

2. Press the **Delete** key. The two controls disappear from the form.

The form includes the appropriate fields in a logical arrangement with a tab order that will move users sequentially through the page. However, the fields may not be aligned precisely.

Professional forms carefully group related fields and align and size controls to make the form look neat and organized for users. For example, fields on the same row should be aligned horizontally. Fields in a column should be spaced equal distances apart. Figure 6-14 describes the layout tools available for forms.

Figure 6-14	LAYOUT TOOLS FOR FORMS

TOOL	DESCRIPTION
Alignment	Lines up selected controls along their left, right, center, middle, top, or bottom edges to the dominant control or to the grid.
Center in Form	Centers selected controls between the top and bottom or the left and right edges of the form.
Make Same Size	Resizes two or more controls to the same height, width, or height and width as the dominant control.
Spacing	Increases, decreases, removes, or makes even the horizontal or vertical spacing between selected controls.
Grouping	Combines two or more selected controls into one object so they can be moved or changed as one.

In many cases, the movement of selected controls depends on which control is dominant. The dominant control is determined by how you select controls. If you Shift+Click to select controls, the first selected control is dominant. If you Ctrl+Click to select controls, the last control selected is dominant. If you draw a rectangle around the controls you want to select, the control nearest the pointer when you started dragging the rectangle is dominant. No matter which selection method you used, you can Ctrl+Click twice the control you want to be dominant. You can always tell which control is dominant because it has the white selection handles; the other controls have black selection handles.

You'll use some of these tools to align the fields on your form. If any alignment changes have an unexpected result, you can press and hold the Ctrl key as you press the Z key to undo your previous action. *You can only undo one action*, so carefully look at your results before trying another option.

To align controls:

1. Click the **Customer ID label** to select it, press and hold the **Shift** key, click the **Contributor text box**, and then release the **Shift** key. The four controls on the first row are selected.

   The Customer ID label has the white selection handles and is the dominant control, so any alignment changes will reference that control's current placement.

2. Click **Layout** on the menu bar, and then point to **Align**.
   Left, Center, and Right provide vertical alignment options. Top, Middle, and Bottom provide horizontal alignment options.

3. Click **Middle**. The controls horizontally align at their center points to match the center point of the Customer ID label. See Figure 6-15.

Figure 6-15	HORIZONTALLY ALIGNED CONTROLS

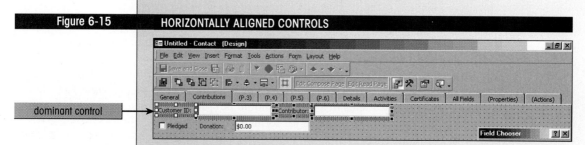

dominant control

   TROUBLE? If your controls do not align as shown in Figure 6-15, press Ctrl+Z to undo the action and carefully repeat Steps 1 through 3.

4. Click the **Pledged control** to select it, press and hold the **Shift** key, click the **Donation text box**, and then release the **Shift** key. The controls on the second row are selected.

5. Click **Layout** on the menu bar, point to **Align**, and then click **Middle**. Again, the controls align horizontally by their centers.

Next you'll resize some of the text boxes. The Customer ID text box has a lot of extra space as does the Donation text box.

To resize the text boxes:

1. Click the **Customer ID text box** to select it, and then point to the right-center sizing handle. The pointer changes to ↔.

2. Drag the right-center sizing handle to the left until the text box is about one-quarter its original size, and then release the mouse button.

3. Select the **Contributor label** and **text box**, point to the hatch pattern. The pointer changes to ✛.

4. Drag the controls left until they are close to the Customer ID text box (approximately four dots apart on the grid). See Figure 6-16.

Figure 6-16	EACH ROW OF CONTROLS ALIGNED HORIZONTALLY

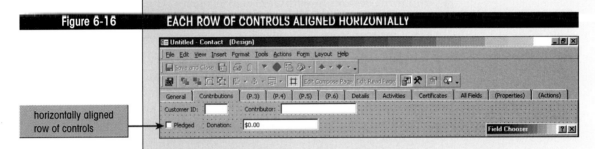

horizontally aligned row of controls

TROUBLE? If necessary, middle-align the controls in the first row again.

5. Click the **Donation text box**, press and hold the **Ctrl** key, click the **Contributor text box**, and then release the **Ctrl** key. The Contributor text box is the dominant selected control.

   TROUBLE? If a copy of the Donation text box appears, you dragged the control while holding the Ctrl key. Press Ctrl+Z to undo the copy action and then repeat Step 5.

6. Click **Layout** on the menu bar, point to **Align**, and then click **Right**. The Donation text box aligns vertically with the Contributor text box along its right edge.

7. Click the **Donation label**, hold the **Ctrl** key, click the **Contributor label**, and then release the **Ctrl** key. The Contributor label is the dominant selected control.

8. Click **Layout** on the menu bar, point to **Align**, and then click **Left**. The Donation label aligns vertically along the left edge of the Contributor label.

9. Align the **Pledged control** with the left edge of the Customer ID text box. See Figure 6-17.

Figure 6-17	COMPLETED REARRANGEMENT OF CONTROLS

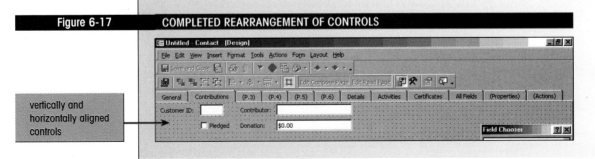

vertically and horizontally aligned controls

In addition to setting properties for individual controls, you can also set properties for the form itself. The form properties enable you to assign various elements to the form, including:

- **Category and Sub-category**—classifications to group forms; makes it easier to find and open a specific form.
- **Contact**—the name of the person whom users can contact for help or more information about the form.
- **Description**—comments about the form, its purpose, or how to use the form.
- **Version and Form Number**—an alphanumeric classification you create to track forms.
- **Send form definition with item**—saves the form's design information with the form so the layout is included when you share the form with others, such as by e-mail; uncheck if you plan to save the form in a forms library (see below for more details about forms libraries).

You can enter all this information on the hidden Properties page of the form. The information is displayed in the Choose Form dialog box, which is used to open a form, but is hidden in the opened form. Some of the information also appears in the form's Properties dialog box and in the About dialog box that opens from the Help menu.

To enter form properties:

1. Click the **(Properties)** tab in the form. The form properties page opens.

2. Right-click each item on the page to display its ScreenTip, read the information, and then click in the **Category** text box on the form.

3. Type **Contributions** in the Category text box.

4. Type **1** in the Version text box.

5. Type **Contributions** in the Form Number text box.

   TROUBLE? If you don't see the Form Number text box, the field may be called Form in your installation.

6. Type your name in the Contact text box.

7. Type **This form is used to collect information about contacts and their current contributions.** in the Description text box. See Figure 6-18.

Figure 6-18	PROPERTIES PAGE OF FORM

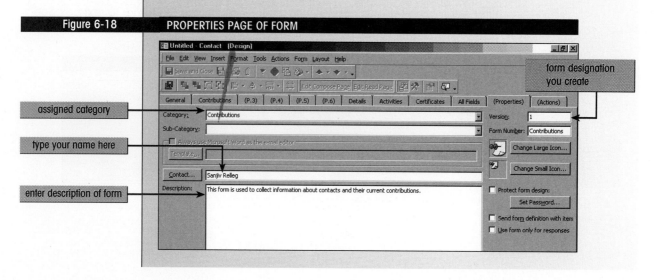

Once you are done modifying and documenting the form, you need to test it.

Testing a Custom Form

Before you finish creating a custom form you need to test it to ensure that the fields and controls you added work as expected. You test the form in **run mode**, which shows the form as it will appear when it's used. From run mode, you can enter information in the form, send or post it, and then open the form to make sure it appears correctly. If any aspect of the form is not correct, you can return to design mode and make changes to it.

To test the form:

1. Click **Form** on the menu bar, and then click **Run This Form**. The form switches from design mode to a new form in run mode. At first glance, the form looks like the same New Contact form you have been using; however, this version includes the new Contributions tab.

   You didn't modify the General page, so you'll switch to the Contributions tab and test that page.

2. Click the **Contributions** tab. The custom page of the form opens. See Figure 6-19.

Figure 6-19 **BLANK CONTRIBUTIONS PAGE**

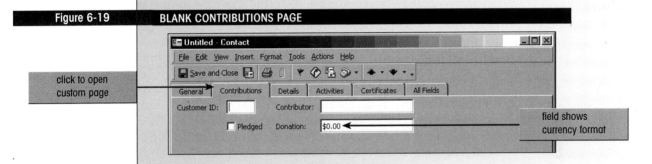

click to open custom page

field shows currency format

3. Type **D-12** in the Customer ID text box, and then press the **Tab** key. The insertion point appears in the Contributor text box.

4. Type **Bill Parker** in the Contributor text box, and then press the **Tab** key to move to the Pledged check box.

5. Press the **spacebar** to insert a check mark in the Pledged check box. When a check box is selected, pressing the spacebar inserts or removes a check mark from the box. The general rule for check boxes is that a check mark indicates yes, true, or on.

6. Press the **Tab** key, type **2500.9** in the Donation text box, and then press the **Tab** key. Outlook formats the amount as currency, inserting the necessary dollar sign, comma, and extra zero. See Figure 6-20.

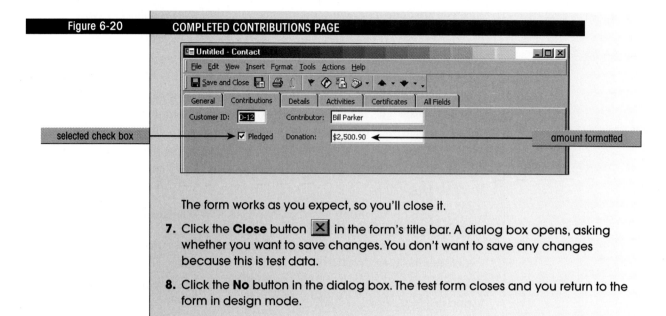

Figure 6-20   COMPLETED CONTRIBUTIONS PAGE

selected check box

amount formatted

The form works as you expect, so you'll close it.

7. Click the **Close** button [X] in the form's title bar. A dialog box opens, asking whether you want to save changes. You don't want to save any changes because this is test data.

8. Click the **No** button in the dialog box. The test form closes and you return to the form in design mode.

If you needed to make changes, you could revise the form as needed. After any revisions, you should retest the form to ensure you have achieved the results you intended.

Publishing a Form

After the form is complete, you can **publish** the form, which saves the form so it can be used in Outlook. If you make changes to a published form, you must republish the form to be able to use the updated form. There are three ways to publish a form. You can save the form in the Outlook folder where you want to use it, you can save the form in a forms library so that others can also use it, or you can save the form as a file so you or others can use it as a template or in other programs. These three options are detailed below:

■ **Outlook folder.** The form is saved in the open Outlook folder. Use this option when you don't want to share the form or when you want to send a form to someone by e-mail. The form is available from the Actions menu of that folder.

■ **Forms library.** The form is saved to the forms library you specify. A **forms library** is the location where Outlook stores published forms. Outlook has three forms libraries. The Personal forms library is stored on your computer and is accessible only to you. The Outlook Folders forms library saves the form to a public folder that is accessible to others or to a private folder that is accessible only to you. The Organizational forms library is stored on a corporate server and is accessible to everyone in an organization. The form is available from the Tools menu and Forms submenu.

■ **File.** The form is saved in another file type so you can work with it in another program or the form is saved as a template so you can create new items from it. Use this option when you don't want to share the form or when you want to send a form to someone by e-mail.

Once you select the location to save the form, you need to enter the display name and form name. The display name is the caption that appears at the top of the form as well as in the Forms menu and Choose Forms dialog box (from which you select a form to start a new item). The display name you enter also appears as the form name, unless you change the form name. The form name is the filename you assign to the form. You'll use Luminescence Contributors as the display name and Contributions as the form name.

The last item in the Publish Form As dialog box is the Message Class field. The **message class** is the internal identifier used by Outlook (and Microsoft Exchange) to locate and activate a form. Outlook generates the message class from the form name and assigns it to the form. The message class of all Outlook items begins with IPM, which is an acronym for Interpersonal Message. The second part of the message class specifies the type of form being used, such as Contact. The third part of the message class is the form name (or filename) you entered for the form. For example, the message class of the form you created will be IPM.Contact.Contributions.

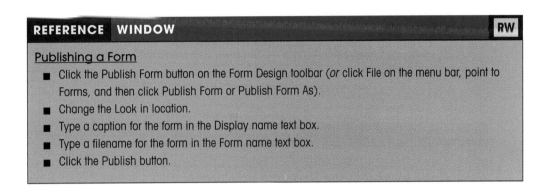

REFERENCE WINDOW   RW

Publishing a Form
- Click the Publish Form button on the Form Design toolbar (*or* click File on the menu bar, point to Forms, and then click Publish Form or Publish Form As).
- Change the Look in location.
- Type a caption for the form in the Display name text box.
- Type a filename for the form in the Form name text box.
- Click the Publish button.

You'll publish the form in the Contacts folder, the open Outlook folder. Then you'll assign the display name Luminescence Contributors and the form name Contributions.

To publish a form:

1. Click the **Publish Form** button 🖳 on the Form Design toolbar. The Publish Form As dialog box opens. You'll store the form in the open Outlook folder.

   TROUBLE? If you don't see the Publish Form button, click Tools on the menu bar, point to Forms, and then click Publish Forms.

2. Click the **Look In** list arrow, and then click **Contacts**. The Outlook folder in which you want to store the form is selected.

3. Type **Luminescence Contributors** in the Display name text box. The name is repeated in the Form name text box.

4. Press the **Tab** key, and then type **Contributions** in the Form name text box. Outlook generates the message class, IPM.Contact.Contributions, from the information you entered. Outlook uses the message class to locate and load the form. See Figure 6-21.

Figure 6-21   PUBLISH FORM AS DIALOG BOX

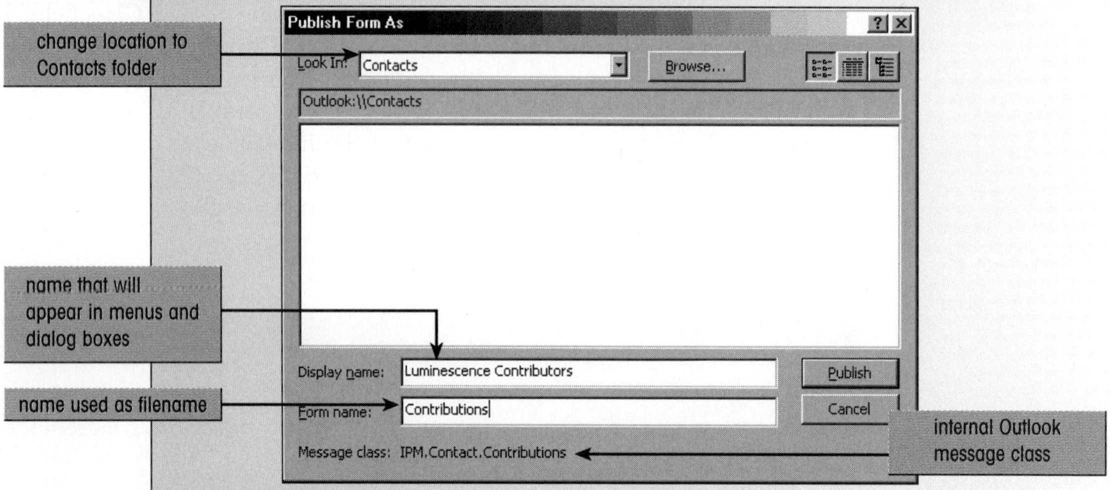

change location to
Contacts folder

Publish Form As

Look In: Contacts   Browse...

Outlook:\\Contacts

name that will
appear in menus and
dialog boxes

name used as filename

Display name: Luminescence Contributors   Publish

Form name: Contributions   Cancel

Message class: IPM.Contact.Contributions

internal Outlook
message class

5. Click the **Publish** button. The form is saved to the specified location.

   TROUBLE? If a dialog box opens asking if you want to clear the Form Definition while saving, click the No button.

You'll close the finished, published form. When you save a custom form based on a contact form without entering a name in the File As field (even if the field doesn't appear on the form), Outlook notifies you that the field is empty. You can then save the blank form or return to the form to enter information. If you enter data in the form, then that data will appear each time you create a new item based on that form. You'll want to save the form without any data.

To close the form:

1. Click the **Close** button ⊠ in the Contact window title bar. A dialog box opens, asking whether you want to save changes.

   If you save changes, then a blank contact card is saved in the Contacts folder.

2. Click the **No** button.

The process for creating custom mail forms is similar to the process you used to create a custom contact form. When you open a Message window and switch to design mode, you can customize all the pages of the mail form. The major difference is that each page of the mail form can have separate Compose and Read versions. The Compose page version shows what senders see when they create and send outgoing messages. The Read page version shows what recipients see when they open and read incoming messages. You switch between the Compose page version and the Read page version by clicking the appropriate button on the Form Design toolbar. Each version can be customized with different controls. If you want the Compose and Read versions of a page to be identical, you can disable the Separate Read Layout option.

You'll use the Contact form you created to enter new contacts for Brian.

Opening a Custom Form

You enter information in a custom form the same way as you do a standard form. The only difference between using a custom form and using a standard form is how you open the form. The process for opening a custom form varies, depending on where you saved the custom form, as described earlier.

REFERENCE WINDOW   **RW**

<u>Opening a Custom Form</u>
- Click Tools on the menu bar, point to Forms, and then click Choose Form (*or* click File on the menu bar, point to New, and then click Choose Form *or* click the New button list arrow, and then click Choose Form *or* switch to the Outlook folder in which you saved the form, click Actions on the menu bar, and then click the form name at the bottom of the menu).
- Click the Look In list arrow, and then click the location where you published the form you want to open.
- Click the form you want to open.
- Click the Details button to display or hide the description, contact, and message class of the selected form.
- Click the Open button.

You'll open the custom contact form and enter general contact information in the default page. Then you'll use the custom page you created to enter the contribution information for each contact.

To open the custom form:

1. Click **Tools** on the menu bar, point to **Forms**, and then click **Choose Form**. The Choose Form dialog box opens, showing the forms stored in the Standard Forms Library. You'll switch to the folder in which you stored the new form.

2. Click the **Look In** list arrow, and then click **Contacts**. Any forms available in that folder are listed in the dialog box. In this case, only the form you created is available.

3. Click the **Luminescence Contributors** form.

4. If necessary, click the **Details** button to display the description, contact, version, and message class of the selected form. See Figure 6-22.

Figure 6-22   **CHOOSE FORM DIALOG BOX**

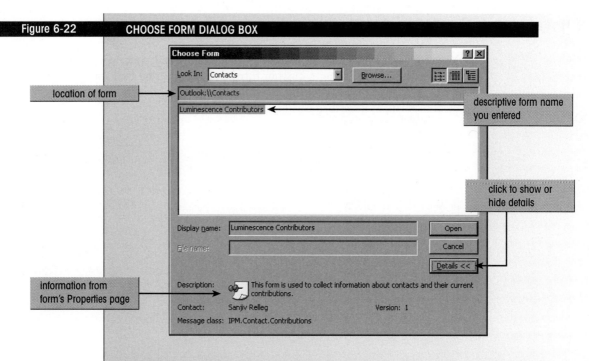

5. Click the **Open** button. A new Luminescence Contributors Contact window opens based on your custom form.

You enter information in the contact card as usual. The General page looks exactly as you would expect from your previous experience entering contact information. The Contributions page has the custom fields.

To enter information in the contact card:

1. Enter the following contact information on the General tab: full name **John Ravenfoot**, home phone **401-555-7526**, address type **Home**, home mailing address **12 Lake Shore, Kingston RI 02852**, and your e-mail address. See Figure 6-23.

Figure 6-23 GENERAL TAB COMPLETED FOR NEW CONTACT

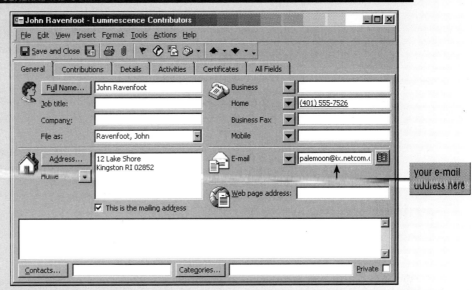

2. Click the **Contributions** tab to switch to the custom page you created.

3. Enter the following information: Customer ID **D-172**, Contributor **The Ravenfoot Family**, Pledged **unchecked**, Donation **2500**, and then press the **Enter** key. See Figure 6-24.

Figure 6-24 CONTRIBUTIONS TAB COMPLETED FOR NEW CONTACT

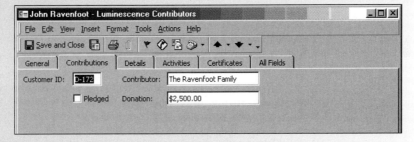

4. Save and close the form.

You'll enter a few more contacts for Brian. You can create a new contact card based on the form from the Actions menu, which is a bit faster than using the Choose Form dialog box.

To enter additional contacts:

1. Switch to the **Contacts Information viewer**, click **Actions** on the menu bar, and then click **New Luminescence Contributors**. A new Contact window based on the custom form opens.

2. Enter the following contact information: full name **Kara Martin**, home phone **401-555-1197**, address type **Home**, home mailing address **792 Oak Lane, Kingston RI 02852**, Customer ID **D-173**, Contributor **Anonymous**, Pledged **checked**, and Donation **1750**.

3. Click the **Save and New** button 📇 on the Standard toolbar to close the Kara Martin contact card and open a new contact card based on the custom form.

4. Enter the following contact information: full name **Mitch Elkin**, home phone **401-555-4967**, address type **Home**, home mailing address **11 Shady Brook Road, Kingston RI 02852**, Customer ID **D-174**, Contributor **In memory of Lillian Elkin**, Pledged **unchecked**, Donation **8575**.

5. Save and close the contact card.

The contacts you created appear in the Contacts Information viewer although you cannot see the information you entered on the Contributions page.

Creating Mail Templates

Rather than publish a custom form in Outlook, you might want to save the form as a template. A template is similar to a form in that both provide a blueprint of the fields and layout for an item. When you save a form as a template, Outlook creates a separate file with the .oft extension. In addition to customizing a form with fields, you can enter specific data in a field, and then publish or save the form. Any new items based on the form will include that data.

Brian wants to send an e-mail message to everyone who contributes to Luminescence, acknowledging the receipt of the contribution. Because Brian will use the same subject and message for each e-mail, you'll create a new e-mail, enter the standard subject and message body, and then save the e-mail as a template. You'll leave the To box blank, so that Brian can address the e-mail when he sends the message.

To create a mail template:

1. Create a new e-mail message in **Plain Text** format with the subject **Thank you for your support** and the message **The curtain will continue to rise on our stage thanks to your generous support. As a token of our appreciation, we are sending you a commemorative program with highlights from our past ten years. Thank you.** Press the **Enter** key twice, type your name, press the **Enter** key and then type **Luminescence**.

2. Click **File** on the menu bar of the Message window, and then click **Save As**. The Save As dialog box opens.

3. Type **Luminescence Mail Template** in the File name text box.

4. Click the **Save as type** list arrow, and then click **Outlook Template**.

5. Change the Save in location to the **Tutorial** folder within the **Tutorial.06** folder on your Data Disk.

6. Click the **Save** button. The mail form is saved as a template on your Data Disk.

7. Click the **Close** button ☒ on the Message window title bar to close it.

8. Click the **No** button to close the message without saving changes.

The template can be used several ways. You can create a new message from the template. You can e-mail the template to other users, who can then open the attachment from their computer. You can save the template to a disk, which is a convenient way to transfer the form to another computer or to create a backup of the form.

You'll use the mail template form to send a message to John Ravenfoot, one of the contacts who donated financial support to the theater group.

To send a message using the mail template:

1. Switch to the **Inbox**, click **Tools** on the Inbox menu bar, point to **Forms**, and then click **Choose Form**. The Choose Form dialog box opens.

   You need to change the Look In location to the folder on your Data Disk where you saved the template.

2. Click the **Look In** list arrow, click **User Templates in File System**, click the **Browse** button to open the Go to Folder dialog box, click the **Tutorial** folder within the **Tutorial.06** folder on your Data Disk in the folder list, and then click the **OK** button. The Luminescence Mail Template appears in the Choose Form dialog box.

3. Click **Luminescence Mail Template** in the list box in the Choose Form dialog box, and then click the **Open** button. A new Message window opens based on your mail template. See Figure 6-25.

| Figure 6-25 | MESSAGE BASED ON MAIL TEMPLATE |

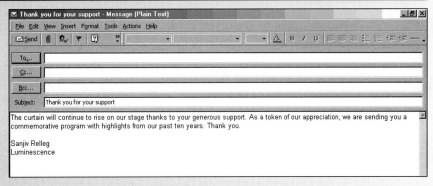

4. Address the message to **John Ravenfoot**, and then send the message.

5. If necessary, download the message, then read and print the message.

   TROUBLE? Depending on your Internet service and mail server, the message may not appear in the received e-mail.

So far, you have customized the contact form for Luminescence and used the custom form to create new contacts with specific data. You have also created a mail template with standard body text and then used the template to send an e-mail message. In Session 6.2, you'll learn other ways to view your items and customize Outlook.

Session 6.1 QUICK CHECK

1. What is a form?

2. List the four basic steps for customizing a form.

3. Explain the difference between a bound control and an unbound control.

4. Describe a simple field.

5. Define tab order.

6. What does it mean to publish a form?

7. Explain the difference between the Compose page and Read page in a mail form.

8. How does a form differ from a template?

SESSION 6.2

In this session, you will use fields to customize which data appears in the Information viewer. Then you'll review items in Outlook Today. Finally you'll customize Outlook by modifying the Calendar time zone, adding groups and shortcuts to the Outlook Bar, and creating a new toolbar.

Customizing Views with Fields

The default views that are available for each folder provide a good starting point for looking at items. But the ability to add or remove fields to any view as well as to select the order those fields appear is part of what makes Outlook so powerful. You can use the Show Fields dialog box or the Field Chooser to customize the views to show exactly the fields you want in the Outlook Information viewers.

REFERENCE WINDOW   **RW**

<u>Customizing Views with Fields</u>

- Switch to the view you want to customize.
- Click View on the menu bar, point to Current View, click Customize Current View, and then click the Field button in the View Summary dialog box (*or* right-click the column headings, click Customize Current View, and then click the Fields button in the View Summary dialog box *or* right-click the Information viewer background, and then click Show Fields).
- To display additional fields in the current view, select one or more fields in the Available fields list box, and then click the Add button.
- To remove displayed fields from the current view, select one or more fields in the Show these fields in this order list box, and then click the Remove button.
- To reorder fields displayed in the current view, select a field in the Show these fields in this order list box, and then click the Move Up or Move Down button as needed.
- When all fields you want to display in the current view are listed in the appropriate order, click the OK button.
- Click the OK button in the View Summary dialog box, if necessary.
  or
- Switch to the view you want to customize.
- To remove a field from the current view, drag the field from the column headings into the Information viewer.
- To add a field to the current view, right-click column headers, click Field Chooser, and then drag a field from the Field Chooser to the appropriate location within the column headings, using the red arrows to position the field.
- Click the Close button in the Field Chooser title bar to close the Field Chooser.
- To reorder column headings, drag a column heading to a new location within the column headings, using the red arrows to position the field.

The contacts you created include data for four fields that do not appear in any of the standard Contacts views. You'll customize the Address Cards view to display these fields.

To customize the Contacts folder view:

1. If you took a break after the last session, make sure Outlook is running.

2. Switch to the **Contacts** folder, and verify that the current view is **Address Cards**.

3. Right-click the background (not a contact card) of the Contacts Information viewer and then click **Show Fields** on the shortcut menu. The Show Fields dialog box opens. See Figure 6-26.

Figure 6-26   SHOW FIELDS DIALOG BOX

click to move selected
field into view

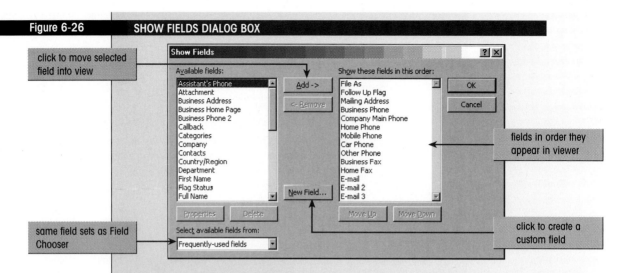

fields in order they
appear in viewer

same field sets as Field
Chooser

click to create a
custom field

4. Click the **Select available fields from** list arrow, and then click **User-defined fields in folder**. The three custom fields you created earlier appear.

   You'll add the Donation and Contributor fields below the File As name.

5. Click **Donation** in the Available fields list box to select it, and then click the **Add** button. The field moves to the end of the Show these fields in this order list box.

   You want to move up the fields to below the File As name.

6. Click the **Move Up** button until Donation appears as the second field in the list below File As.

7. Add the **Contributor** field to the Show these fields in this order list box. The field is added below the selected item, third in the list.

8. Click the **OK** button. The Donation and Contributor fields appear at the top of each contact card. See Figure 6-27.

Figure 6-27   CUSTOMIZED ADDRESS CARDS VIEW

data from custom fields

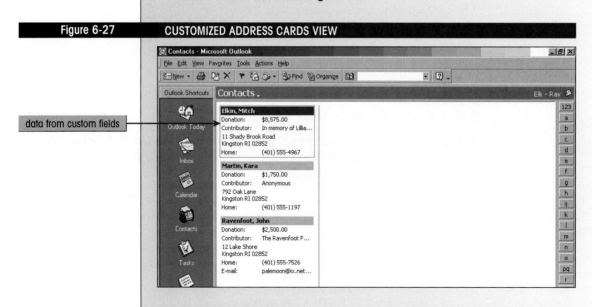

9. Print all the contacts you created in Card Style.

Next, you'll create an appointment with Mitch Elkin.

To create an appointment with a contact:

1. Click the **Mitch Elkin** contact card to select it.

2. Click **Actions** on the menu bar, and then click **New Appointment with Contact**. A new Appointment window opens with Mitch listed as the contact at the bottom of the window.

3. Set up an appointment with the subject **Funding a workshop for young actors** for **tomorrow** starting at **10 AM** and ending at **11 AM**.

4. Save and close the appointment.

With all your work on creating custom forms, you haven't updated your task list. You also want to create a folder in which to store the messages related to Luminescence contributions. You'll do both now.

To create tasks and a folder:

1. Create a new task with the subject **Confirm details of opening season gala**, a due date of **tomorrow**, a **High** priority, and no reminder.

2. Create a new task with the subject **Arrange audition with actor Aaron Geom**, a due date of **tomorrow**, a **Normal** priority, and no reminder.

3. Create a new task with the subject **Check on printing of program**, a due date of **yesterday**, a **Normal** priority, and no reminder.

4. Create a new folder named **Luminescence Mail** that contains **Mail Items** placed within the **Inbox**. If asked, do *not* create a shortcut to the folder on the Outlook Bar.

You could view all these items you created by opening the appropriate folders, but this doesn't give you the "big picture" that Outlook Today provides.

Navigating with Outlook Today

Each Outlook folder has a variety of views you can use to review the folder's active or overdue items. For example, you can view your incoming messages in Inbox, display your active appointments in Calendar, and show any in-progress or overdue to-do items in Tasks. Although the information in each folder is helpful, you need to do a lot of clicking around to attain a complete summary of the items. **Outlook Today** provides an overview of your current schedule, tasks list, and new e-mail messages. From there, you can quickly jump to any item or folder.

You'll use Outlook Today to view the calendar, task, and e-mail items in Outlook.

To view the Outlook Today page:

1. Click **Outlook Today** in the **Outlook Shortcuts** group on the Outlook Bar. The Outlook Today page appears in the Information viewer. Outlook Today displays Calendar, Tasks, and Messages. See Figure 6-28.

Figure 6-28   OUTLOOK TODAY

current task list and due dates

active appointments for the next several days

shows number of unread, unfinished, or unsent e-mails

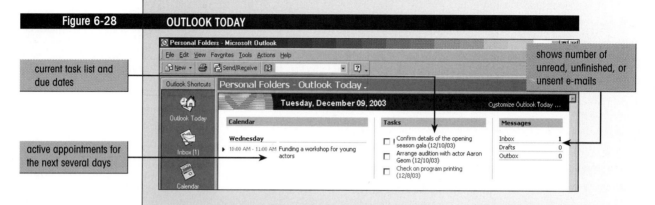

TROUBLE? If you don't see any information on the Outlook Today page, click View on the menu bar, and then click Show Folder Home Page.

TROUBLE? If the Outlook Today page appears to have a different style than the one in Figure 6-28, continue with the steps. You will learn about changing the Outlook Today style shortly.

Each task or appointment item or any listed folder in Outlook Today is a hyperlink that you can click to open the item's window or the folder's Information viewer.

2. Point to **Inbox** in the Messages area. The hand pointer indicates that the Inbox is a hyperlink you can click to jump to the folder.

3. Click **Inbox**. The Inbox Information viewer opens, so you can begin sending, replying to, and receiving e-mail messages.

4. Click **Outlook Today** in the **Outlook Shortcuts** group on the Outlook Bar to return to Outlook Today.

5. Click the **Check on printing of program** task (not the check box). The Task window opens, so you can review and modify the details as needed.

6. Change the task's due date to **tomorrow** and priority to **High**, and then save and close the task. The task information is updated in Outlook Today. See Figure 6-29.

Figure 6-29   UPDATED TASK LIST IN OUTLOOK TODAY

task with new due date

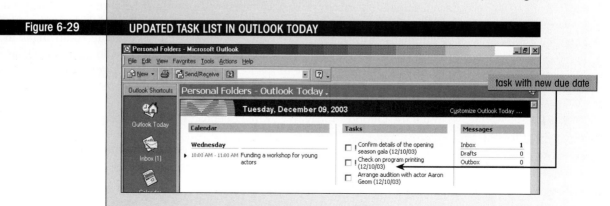

Many people start their day from Outlook Today. After reviewing this snapshot of their upcoming appointments and most pressing tasks, they begin working on their top priority item.

Customizing Outlook Today

Rather than manually opening Outlook Today when you begin working, you can set this page to open each time you start Outlook. This way, you can preview your activities before moving to a specific folder. You also can change how much information appears on the page and what the page looks like. For example, you can view appointments for the next 1 to 7 days, see a count of unread messages for the e-mail folders you select, choose which tasks to view and in what order, and even decide on the layout you prefer.

You'll customize Outlook Today to better meet your needs.

To customize Outlook Today:

1. Click the **Customize Outlook Today** button in the upper-right corner of the Information viewer.

   TROUBLE? If the Outlook Today page has a different style, the Customize Outlook Today button may be located elsewhere in the Information viewer.

   The Outlook Today Options page opens in the Information viewer. See Figure 6-30.

Figure 6-30	OUTLOOK TODAY OPTIONS FOR CUSTOMIZATION

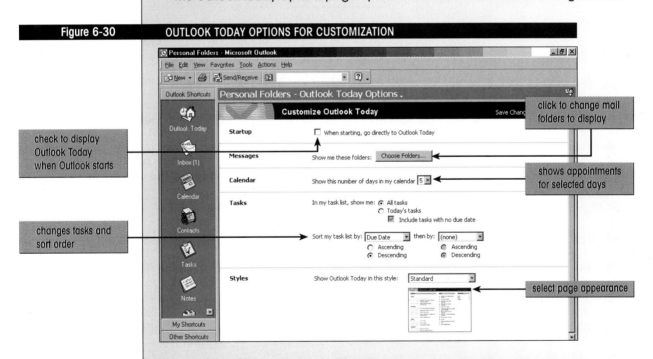

2. Click the **When starting, go directly to Outlook Today** check box to insert a check mark. Each time you start Outlook, Outlook Today will open in the Information viewer.

   You can select which mail folders appear in the Messages area. If you display a folder that does not store mail items, then the messages count on the Outlook Today page will always be 0.

3. Click the **Choose Folders** button. The Select Folder dialog box opens; checked message folders appear on the Outlook Today page.

4. Expand the **Inbox** folder, if necessary, and then click the **Luminescence Mail** folder check box to insert a check mark. See Figure 6-31.

Figure 6-31   SELECT FOLDER DIALOG BOX

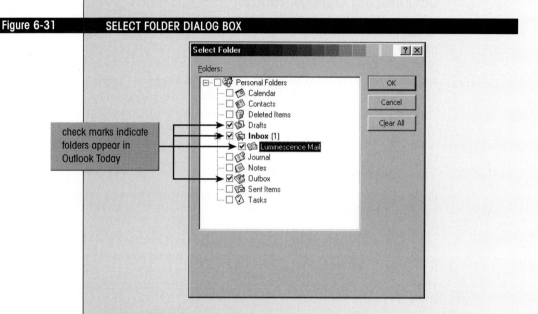

check marks indicate
folders appear in
Outlook Today

5. Click the **OK** button. The folder will appear on the Outlook Today page when you save the options.

   You can organize your task list to better reflect the way you work by setting the two sort criteria.

6. Click the **Sort my task list by** list arrow, and then click **Due Date**. You can select a second criterion by which to sort the task on the Outlook Today page.

7. Click the **then by** list arrow, and then click **Importance**. Tasks will be sorted in descending order by their priority level within due dates groups.

   The default three-column layout is functional, but you may prefer another style.

8. Click the **Show Outlook Today in this style** list arrow, and then click **Summer**. The graphic shows how the Outlook Today page will appear.

9. Change the Outlook Today style to **Standard (two column)**.

   When you finish customizing Outlook Today Options, you must save your selections to have them take effect.

10. Click the **Save Changes** button near the top of the window. The customized Outlook Today page appears with the changes you specified. See Figure 6-32.

Figure 6-32   **CUSTOMIZED OUTLOOK TODAY**

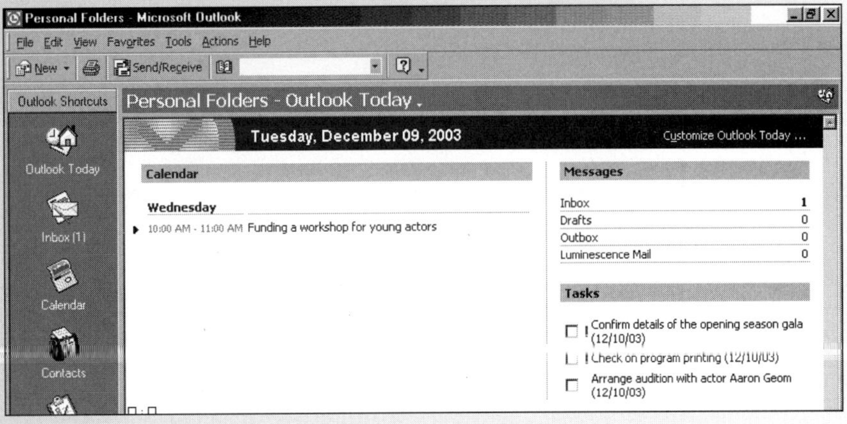

You'll switch to the Calendar, and then customize the TaskPad to show the Priority field. This time you'll use the Field Chooser to customize the view.

To customize the Calendar TaskPad:

1. Click the **Calendar** link in Outlook Today to open that folder, and then if necessary change the current view to **Day** within the **Day/Week/Month** view.

2. Display tomorrow in the planner to review the appointment with Mitch.

   The TaskPad shows the Icon, Complete, and Subject fields. You want to display the Priority field.

3. Right-click the **TaskPad** column heading, and then click **Field Chooser** from the shortcut menu. The Field Chooser opens, displaying the Frequently-used fields list.

4. Drag the **Priority** field from the Field Chooser to the right of the TaskPad field, using the red placement arrows to position the field. The field is inserted at the right side of the TaskPad.

   The field would be better if it were to the left of the TaskPad field.

5. Drag the **Priority** field using ⬚ between the Complete and TaskPad fields, as shown in Figure 6-33, and then release the mouse button.

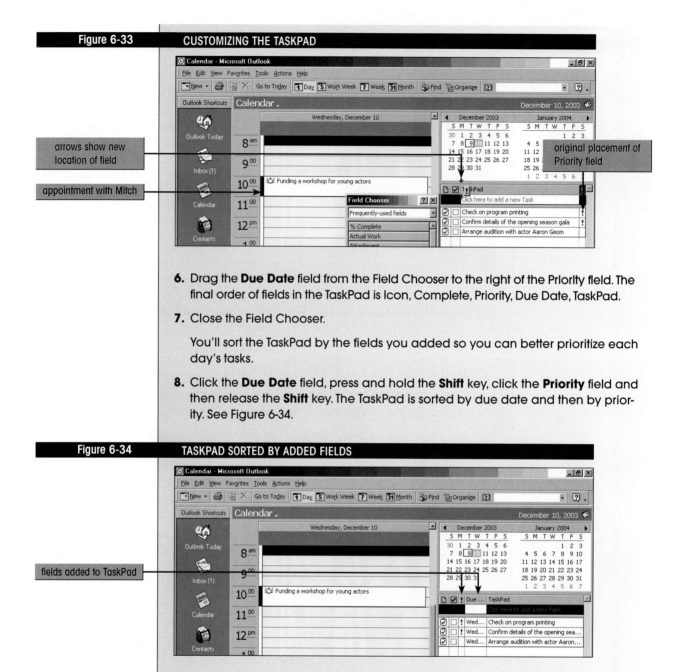

Figure 6-33 CUSTOMIZING THE TASKPAD

arrows show new location of field

appointment with Mitch

original placement of Priority field

6. Drag the **Due Date** field from the Field Chooser to the right of the Priority field. The final order of fields in the TaskPad is Icon, Complete, Priority, Due Date, TaskPad.

7. Close the Field Chooser.

You'll sort the TaskPad by the fields you added so you can better prioritize each day's tasks.

8. Click the **Due Date** field, press and hold the **Shift** key, click the **Priority** field and then release the **Shift** key. The TaskPad is sorted by due date and then by priority. See Figure 6-34.

Figure 6-34 TASKPAD SORTED BY ADDED FIELDS

fields added to TaskPad

You'll find that this flexibility for adding and removing fields makes Outlook a useful place to review files anywhere on your computer. In addition to Outlook Today, you can configure other Outlook options.

Configuring Outlook Options

Outlook is quite functional with its default settings. However, it also has many optional settings. After a time, you may want to fine-tune some of these settings to better fit the way you work. There are options available for each Outlook folder and function. The complete list of options available depends on whether you have Outlook installed for Corporate and Workgroup, Internet Only, or No E-mail as well as which Add-Ins are installed.

Configuring Calendar Options

The Options dialog box provides access to most of the customization options for Outlook. They are organized by categories and subcategories within the tabs. You'll open the Options dialog box and change some of the Calendar options.

You'll start by modifying the times Outlook displays as the workday, or usual business hours. Because of its evening shows, the theater group starts its day at 10 AM and closes its office at 6 PM—an hour later than usual business hours. You can change the Calendar options to reflect this shifted workday.

To configure Calendar options:

1. Click **Tools** on the menu bar, click **Options**, and then if necessary click the **Preferences** tab. The Preferences tab in the Options dialog box opens.

2. Click the **Calendar Options** button. The Calendar Options dialog box opens. See Figure 6-35.

Figure 6-35	CALENDAR OPTIONS DIALOG BOX

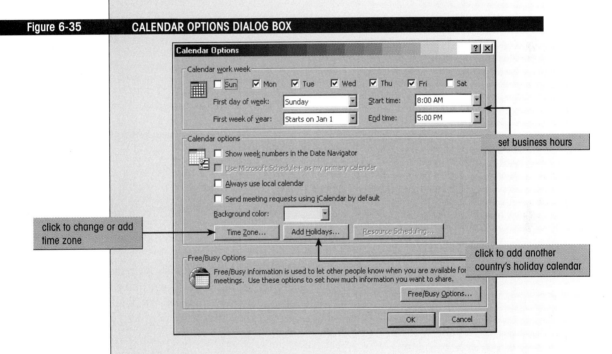

You can change the days considered part of the workweek, specify the standard hours counted as the workday, and set which days at the start of the year are counted as workdays. You also can add another country's holidays to the Calendar.

3. Click the **Start time** list arrow, and then click **10:00 AM**.

4. Click the **End time** list arrow, and then click **6:00 PM**.

5. Click the **OK** button in the Calendar Options dialog box, and then click the **OK** button in the Options dialog box. The light and dark yellows, indicating the workday, are shifted to reflect your changes. See Figure 6-36.

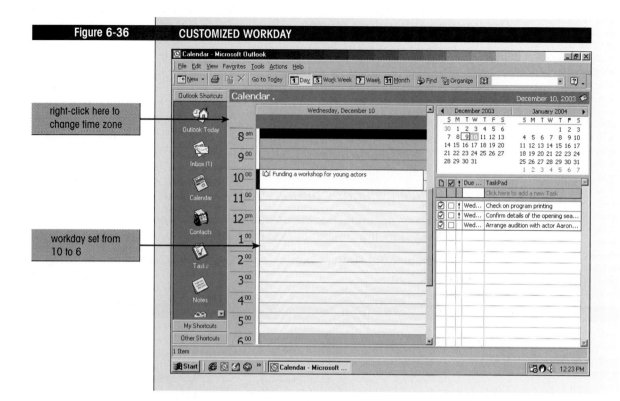

Figure 6-36   CUSTOMIZED WORKDAY

right-click here to change time zone

workday set from 10 to 6

In addition to these daily settings, there are some settings you can change based on your location.

Changing Time Zones

If you regularly work with others in another time zone, you can set up Outlook to display both zones. In addition, if you travel, you can then swap the time zones so your calendar and messages are converted to the time zone you're currently visiting.

Ada will be teaching a theater class in Athens for the next six months. Because she will remain active in the theater's planning and activities, the group will need to pay attention to time zone differences when setting up conference calls. You'll add the Athens time zone to the Calendar. Rather than reopening the Options dialog box, you can go directly to the Time Zone dialog box using a shortcut menu.

To change the time zone settings:

1. Right-click the space above the times in the daily planner, and then click **Change Time Zone** on the shortcut menu. The Time Zone dialog box opens. See Figure 6-37.

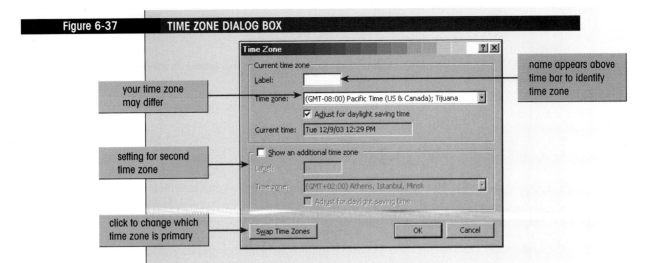

Figure 6-37   TIME ZONE DIALOG BOX

your time zone may differ

setting for second time zone

click to change which time zone is primary

name appears above time bar to identify time zone

2. Type **Here** in the Label text box. This identifies your current time zone. Your time zone, daylight savings time, and current time are set for your location.

3. Click the **Show an additional time zone** check box to insert a check mark.

4. Type **Athens** in the Label text box. This identifies Ada's time zone.

5. Click the **Time zone** list arrow, and then click **(GMT+02:00) Athens, Istanbul, Minsk**.

6. Click the **OK** button in the Time Zone dialog box. The two time zones appear in the daily planner. See Figure 6-38.

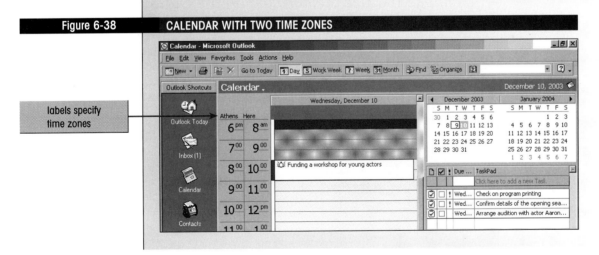

Figure 6-38   CALENDAR WITH TWO TIME ZONES

labels specify time zones

There are many other options you can use to customize Outlook to match your personal work style and preferences.

Customizing the Outlook Bar

Earlier you created a mail folder within the Inbox and added the folder to Outlook Today. You want to move the mail messages related to Luminescence from the Inbox into that folder. The folder you created doesn't appear on the Outlook Bar, so you'll use the Folder List.

> *To move e-mail messages from the Inbox to the Luminescence Mail folder:*
>
> **1.** Display the Folder List, and then expand the **Inbox** to display the Luminescence Mail folder.
>
> **2.** Drag the **Thank you for your support** message from the Inbox to the **Luminescence Mail** folder.

Some people prefer to use the Folder List to navigate around Outlook because all the folders automatically appear on it. However, you can customize the Outlook Bar to show other folders as well.

As you've seen, the Outlook Bar is one of the main navigation tools in Outlook. The default shortcuts give you basic access to the Outlook folders as well as the My Computer, My Documents, and Favorites folders on your computer. You can add more icons to any group and create additional groups on the Outlook Bar to more quickly access Outlook folders and items you create and any files and folders on your computer.

Resizing the Outlook Bar Icons

Even with only the default icons displayed on the Outlook Bar, some of the icons move out of view. Although you can scroll to see these out-of-view icons, you also can reduce their size so you see more icons at once on the Outlook Bar. Then you can access any shortcut icon without scrolling through a long list of icons.

> *To change the size of shortcuts on the Outlook Bar:*
>
> **1.** If necessary, display the **Outlook Shortcuts** group on the Outlook Bar.
>
> **2.** Right-click the background of the Outlook Bar, and then click **Small Icons** on the shortcut menu. The icons are resized. See Figure 6-39.

| Figure 6-39 | RESIZED ICONS ON OUTLOOK BAR |

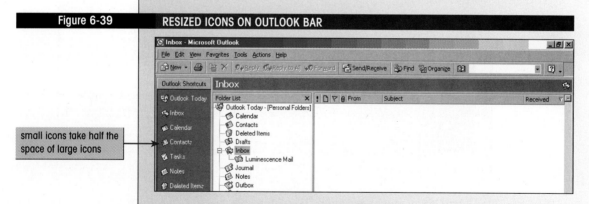

small icons take half the space of large icons

> TROUBLE? If you don't see Small Icons on the shortcut menu, you probably right-clicked a shortcut on the Outlook Bar. Click in the Information viewer to close the shortcut menu, and then repeat Step 1 being sure to right-click the gray background of the Outlook Bar.
>
> **3.** Right-click the background of the Outlook Bar, and then click **Large Icons** on the shortcut menu. The icons return to their original size.

Each shortcut group on the Outlook Bar is resized separately, so you can resize the icons for the My Shortcuts group differently than the Outlook Shortcuts. Use the large and small icons in whichever way works best for you.

Adding and Renaming a Group

As you add shortcuts to a group, the icon list may become very long, even when you're using small icons. One way to manage the list is to create additional groups on the Outlook Bar to organize shortcut icons into related categories. For example, the Outlook Shortcuts group includes icons for the most commonly used folders in Outlook—Outlook Today, Inbox, Calendar, Contacts, Tasks, Notes, and Deleted Items. You might create another group on the Outlook Bar to store shortcut icons related to a particular project, company, or person. The Outlook Bar can support a maximum of 12 groups.

You'll create a new group for Luminescence.

To add a group to the Outlook Bar:

1. Right-click the Outlook Bar background, and then click **Add New Group** on the shortcut menu. The new group appears at the bottom of the Outlook Bar. See Figure 6-40.

Figure 6-40	ADDING A NEW GROUP

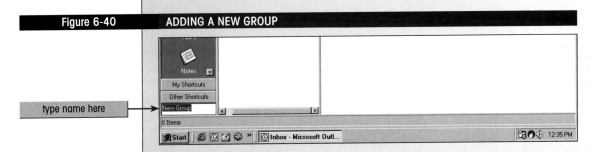

type name here

2. Type **Contributors** as the name for the group, and then press the **Enter** key. The new group is added to the Outlook Bar, ready for you to add shortcuts.

You can change the name of a group on the Outlook Bar at any time to better describe the shortcut items it contains. You'll change the Contributors group to Luminescence because you'll be adding shortcuts related to the company in the group.

To rename a group on the Outlook Bar:

1. Right-click the **Contributors** group, and then click **Rename Group** on the shortcut menu. The group button becomes a text box with the text selected, so you can type a new name.

2. Type **Luminescence** as the new name for the group, and then press the **Enter** key. The group is renamed.

You can add shortcuts to any group on the Outlook Bar.

Adding Shortcuts to the Outlook Bar

When you create a new folder in Outlook, unless this option is turned off in your Outlook installation, you will be given the option to create a shortcut to that folder on the Outlook Bar. If you choose not to create a shortcut icon for the Outlook Bar at that time, you can always add one later. In addition to creating Outlook Shortcut icons to existing folders, you also can create Outlook Bar shortcuts to Outlook items, folders or files on your computer, Web pages, and items on the Windows desktop.

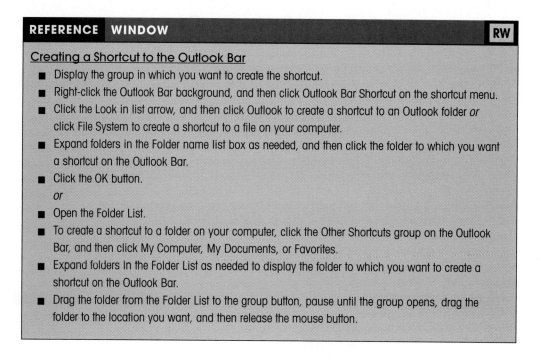

REFERENCE WINDOW   RW

Creating a Shortcut to the Outlook Bar

- Display the group in which you want to create the shortcut.
- Right-click the Outlook Bar background, and then click Outlook Bar Shortcut on the shortcut menu.
- Click the Look in list arrow, and then click Outlook to create a shortcut to an Outlook folder *or* click File System to create a shortcut to a file on your computer.
- Expand folders in the Folder name list box as needed, and then click the folder to which you want a shortcut on the Outlook Bar.
- Click the OK button.
  or
- Open the Folder List.
- To create a shortcut to a folder on your computer, click the Other Shortcuts group on the Outlook Bar, and then click My Computer, My Documents, or Favorites.
- Expand folders in the Folder List as needed to display the folder to which you want to create a shortcut on the Outlook Bar.
- Drag the folder from the Folder List to the group button, pause until the group opens, drag the folder to the location you want, and then release the mouse button.

You'll create a shortcut on the Outlook Bar to the Luminescence Mail folder to provide easy access to that folder.

To create an Outlook Bar shortcut to an existing Outlook folder:

1. Click the **Luminescence** group button to display the group. This is the group to which you want to add the shortcut.

2. Right-click the Outlook Bar background, and then click **Outlook Bar Shortcut** on the shortcut menu. The Add to Outlook Bar dialog box opens. See Figure 6-41.

Figure 6-41   ADD TO OUTLOOK BAR DIALOG BOX

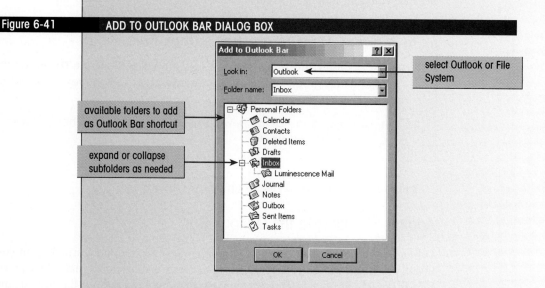

3. Click the **Luminescence Mail** folder within the Inbox. You want to add a shortcut to this folder to the Outlook Bar.

4. Click the **OK** button. A shortcut icon to the Luminescence Mail folder is added to the Luminescence group on the Outlook Bar. The shortcut icon reflects the type of item that the folder stores, in this case, messages.

In addition to Outlook folder shortcuts, you can create shortcuts for folders and files on your computer and to Web sites.

Managing Files from Outlook

With the Outlook Bar and Folders List both displayed, Outlook looks similar to Windows Explorer. In fact, Outlook is even more functional than Windows Explorer because you can customize the Information viewer to add or remove displayed fields, using the Field Chooser, as well as filter, group, and sort the items listed. With Windows Explorer, you can only reorder and sort items using the provided fields. Similar to the Folders and file panes in Windows Explorer, you single-click an item in Folder List to display its content in the Information viewer; you double-click an item in the Information viewer to open it.

You'll use the Outlook Bar, Folder List, and Information viewer to display files on your Data Disk.

To view files on your computer:

1. Make sure your Data Disk is in the proper drive.

2. Click the **My Computer** icon in the **Other Shortcuts** group on the Outlook Bar. The items on your desktop appear in the Folder List.

3. Expand the **My Computer** group, expand **3½ Floppy (A:)** or the drive that contains your Data Disk, and then click the **Tutorial.06** folder. A list of subfolders and files appears in the Information viewer. See Figure 6-42.

| Figure 6-42 | VIEWING MY COMPUTER FROM OUTLOOK |

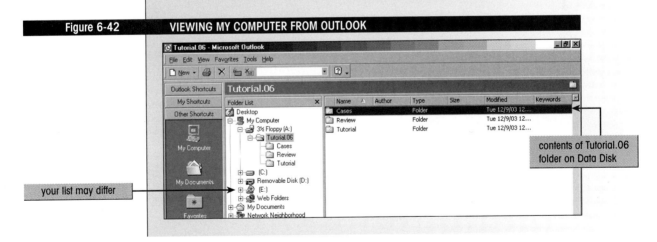

When My Computer is displayed in the Information viewer, you can create folders anywhere on your system using the same procedure as you did to create a new folder in Outlook. You can move files from one folder to another by opening the folder with the file you want to move, and then dragging the file from the Information viewer to another folder in the Folder List.

Creating Shortcuts to Files and Folders on Your Computer

You also can create shortcuts on the Outlook Bar to any files or folders on your computer. You want to add a shortcut to the mail template you saved. Earlier you used the Add to Outlook Bar dialog box to create an Outlook folder shortcut to the Outlook Bar. You can use this same method to create a shortcut to any folder on your computer. However, a simpler method is to simply drag the folder from the Folder List to the location where you want the shortcut on the Outlook Bar. You can also drag a particular item or file from the Information viewer to the Outlook Bar to create a shortcut to that item or file. You'll use this drag method to create an Outlook Bar shortcut to the mail template file you saved in the Tutorial folder within the Tutorial.06 folder on your Data Disk.

To create a shortcut to a file:

1. In the Information viewer, double-click the **Tutorial** folder within the **Tutorial.06** folder on your Data Disk. The folder is selected in the Folder List and the folder's items appear in the Information viewer.

2. Click the **Luminescence Mail Template** in the Information viewer. The file is selected.

   You could double-click the template file to open a new Message window based on the template. Instead, you'll create a shortcut to the file.

3. Drag **Luminescence Mail Template** to the **Luminescence** group Bar on the Outlook Bar, pause until the group opens, and then continue to drag the file to below the Luminescence Mail folder icon. When you release the mouse button, the shortcut appears. See Figure 6-43.

Figure 6-43	CREATING A SHORTCUT TO A FILE

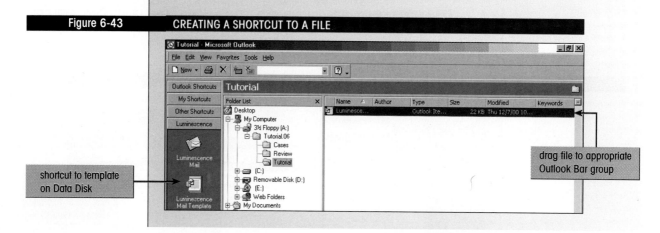

shortcut to template on Data Disk

drag file to appropriate Outlook Bar group

When you click the mail template shortcut on the Outlook Bar, a new Message window based on the template opens. Because the shortcut appears on the Outlook Bar, you can open a new message based on the template with any Outlook folder displayed.

To use the mail template shortcut:

1. Click the **Luminescence Mail Template** shortcut in the **Luminescence** group on the Outlook Bar. A new Message window opens based on the template you created.

   You don't need to create a message at the moment, so you'll close the window without saving it.

2. Click the **Close** button ☒ on the title bar to close the window.

Anytime you create a shortcut to a file, clicking the shortcut opens the application associated with that file and displays the file. If you had dragged a Windows folder to the Outlook Bar, clicking the shortcut would display the contents of that folder in the Information viewer. If you had dragged an executable file, clicking the shortcut would run the program.

Moving Shortcuts on the Outlook Bar

As you add shortcuts to the Outlook Bar, you might want to reorder them to better reflect the frequency or order that you access them. You can move a shortcut to a different location in the same group or to a new group by dragging it. As you drag the shortcut, a positioning line appears to indicate where the shortcut will be dropped when you release the mouse button.

To move a shortcut on the Outlook Bar:

1. Drag the **Luminescence Mail** folder shortcut below the Mail Template shortcut, but do not release the mouse button. The placement marker indicates where the shortcut will be moved. See Figure 6-44.

Figure 6-44	REPOSITIONING A SHORTCUT

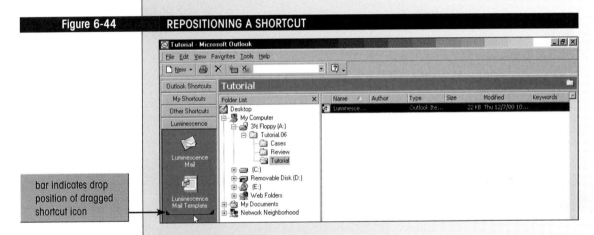

bar indicates drop position of dragged shortcut icon

2. Release the mouse button to reposition the shortcut. The shortcut positions are reversed.

   TROUBLE? If a dialog box opens, indicating that you cannot move the icon, then you probably released the mouse button while pointing to a group name. Click the OK button, and then repeat Steps 1 and 2.

Shortcuts can be moved between groups as well. To move a shortcut to a new group, drag the shortcut to the group button, pause for a few seconds until the group opens, and then continue to drag the shortcut to the location you want. You can scroll to a position out of view by pointing to the top or bottom of the group.

Sometimes the shortcut names are not descriptive enough or are so long that only part of the name is visible. In either case, just as you renamed the group, you can rename the shortcut. Right-click the shortcut you want to rename, click Rename Shortcut on the shortcut menu, type a new name in the text box that opens, and then press the Enter key. Only the shortcut is renamed, the file or folder to which the shortcut points retains the original name.

Customizing Menus and Toolbars

As you work with Outlook, you'll find that some menus and buttons you use frequently; others you'll use rarely, if at all. In addition, sometimes, you'll wish that certain commands would appear on a specific menu or toolbar. In these cases, you can customize the menus and toolbars.

Most menus are located on the menu bar, which is considered a toolbar. Toolbars can contain buttons, menus, or both. You can add and remove buttons and menus on the built-in toolbars or custom toolbars you create. You can customize the menu bar the same way you customize toolbars, adding or removing commands and menus, however, unlike toolbars you cannot hide the menu bar nor can you add a second menu bar.

Creating a Custom Menu or Toolbar

You can create additional menus and toolbars for Outlook. You might create a custom menu or toolbar to keep the list of commands and buttons on a built-in menu or toolbar a manageable length. Or, you might want to group commands or buttons related to a specific task in one location.

You'll create a new toolbar, called Navigate, that contains buttons for moving around in Outlook.

To create a toolbar:

1. Right-click any toolbar, and then click **Customize** on the shortcut menu. The Customize dialog box opens.

2. If necessary, click the **Toolbars** tab. Check marks next to the toolbar names indicate that the toolbar is visible. See Figure 6-45.

Figure 6-45   CUSTOMIZE DIALOG BOX

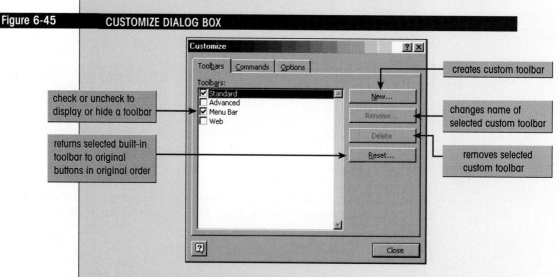

3. Click the **New** button. The New Toolbar dialog box opens so you can enter a descriptive name for the toolbar.

4. Type **Navigate** in the Toolbar name text box, and then click the **OK** button. The new, descriptive toolbar name appears in the Toolbars list box with a check mark, and the empty toolbar appears in the Outlook window.

Once you create a toolbar, you can add buttons to it.

Adding Commands to a Toolbar or Menu

Opening the Customize dialog box enables you to edit the toolbars. You can add or remove a command from any toolbar or menu that is visible in the Information viewer. The process for adding commands is the same whether you're adding them to a built-in menu or toolbar, menu bar, or a custom menu or toolbar.

You'll add two buttons to the Navigate toolbar. One button will open or close the Folder List so you can quickly make more room on the screen. The second button will open the Go to Folder dialog box so you can easily switch to a folder when the Folder List is closed.

To add commands to a toolbar:

1. Click the **Commands** tab in the Customize dialog box. Commands are organized by logical categories so you can quickly find the ones you need. See Figure 6-46.

Figure 6-46	COMMANDS TAB OF CUSTOMIZE DIALOG BOX

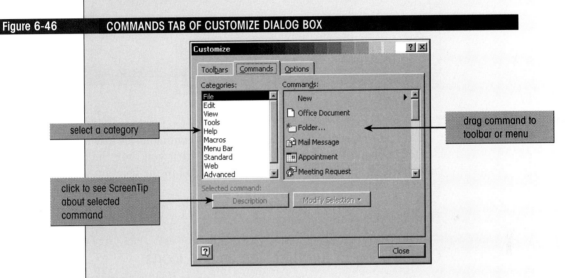

2. Click **View** in the Categories list box. The various tools available in that category appear in the Commands list box.

3. Scroll down, and then drag **Folder List** from the Commands list box to the Navigate toolbar. The command appears on the toolbar as a button with an icon.

   If you closed the dialog box, you could click the command on the toolbar. As long as the Customize dialog box is open, you can drag the command to a new location or continue to add other commands.

4. Scroll up, click **Folder**, press and hold the mouse button, drag **Folder** from the Commands list box to the right of the Folder List button on the Navigate toolbar, but do not release the mouse button. A placement bar appears, indicating the drop location. See Figure 6-47.

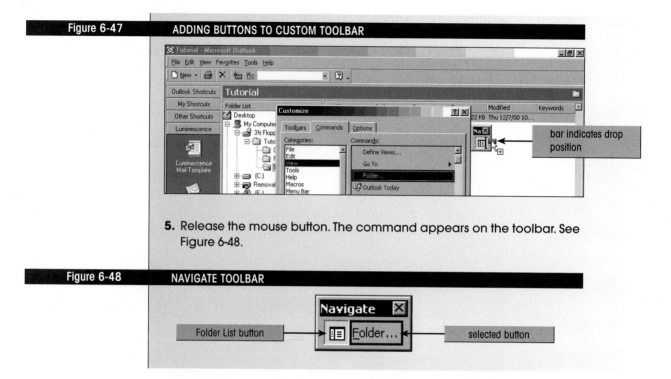

Figure 6-47   ADDING BUTTONS TO CUSTOM TOOLBAR

bar indicates drop position

5. Release the mouse button. The command appears on the toolbar. See Figure 6-48.

Figure 6-48   NAVIGATE TOOLBAR

Folder List button → ← selected button

You could repeat this process to add other commands to the toolbar. The process is similar for adding commands to a menu, except that you drag the command onto the menu, pause until the menu opens, drag the command to the location you want, and then release the mouse button.

If you closed the Customize dialog box, you could use the new toolbar and its buttons. However, you want to make one more change.

Customizing Command Names and Icons

Right now the Folder button on the Navigate toolbar shows text rather than an icon on the button. You can modify the icon for any button or the text for any menu.

To customize a toolbar button icon:

1. Verify that the Customize dialog box is open and that the **Folder** button on the Navigate toolbar is selected.

2. Click the **Modify Selection** button in the Customize dialog box. The shortcut menu provides information about the command's name, image, and style, and provides a variety of ways to modify the selected command.

3. Point to **Change Button Image** on the shortcut menu. A palette of pictures opens from which you can select an image for the button. See Figure 6-49.

Figure 6-49	CHANGING A BUTTON ICON

specifies when text and icon display

click to customize selected button

click this icon

You can use the eye image to remind you that this button will enable you to see another folder.

4. Click the **Eye** button from the image palette. The image appears next to the text. To make the toolbar button more consistent with other buttons, you'll set the button text to appear only in menus.

5. Click the **Modify Selection** button in the Customize toolbar, and then click **Text Only (in Menus)**. The icon shows only the eye image because the button is located on a toolbar rather than in a menu.

6. Click the **Close** button in the Customize dialog box.

Once the Customize dialog box is closed, you can no longer add commands to the toolbars and menus. You hide and display and move the custom toolbar the same way as you would any other toolbar.

To use the custom toolbar:

1. Drag the Navigate toolbar up and to the right of the Standard toolbar. The toolbar docks next to the existing toolbars and behaves just like the other toolbars.

2. Right-click the toolbar area. The Navigate toolbar is listed with the other available toolbars.

3. Press the **Esc** key, and then point to each button on the Navigate toolbar. ScreenTips appear just like on the other toolbars.

4. Click the **Folder List** button on the Navigate toolbar. The Folder List closes. The button works as a toggle to open and close the Folder List.

5. Click the **Folder** button on the Navigate toolbar. The Go to Folder dialog box opens.

6. Look in **Outlook**, select **Contacts** as the folder name, and then click the **OK** button. The Contacts Information viewer appears.

You can customize any toolbar or menu to match the way you work or the tasks you perform regularly.

Adding/Removing a Menu or Toolbar Button

If you want to delete a toolbar button you must display the toolbar from which you want to delete the button. You can then press and hold the Alt key as you drag the button off the toolbar. Once the button is off the toolbar, you can release the Alt key and the button is removed from the toolbar. To delete a menu and all the items it contains from the menu bar you would use the same procedure. *You cannot undo this procedure nor will a dialog box confirm your action.*

Removing Customizations from Outlook

Before you finish, you'll remove all the customizations you made to Outlook. This includes removing the contact and mail forms you created and deleting the custom fields. You'll also return Address Cards view, Outlook Today, Calendar, and the TaskPad to their default settings, and delete any messages, contacts, and toolbars you created in this tutorial.

To remove a form from a forms library:

1. Click **Tools** on the menu bar, and then click **Options**. The Options dialog box opens.

2. Click the **Other** tab, and then click the **Advanced Options** button. The Advanced Options dialog box opens.

3. Click the **Custom Forms** button, and then click the **Manage Forms** button. The Forms Manager dialog box opens. The form has two identical list boxes so you can manage forms in two locations and copy or move forms between locations.

4. Click the **Set** button above the left list box in the dialog box. The Set Library To dialog box opens.

5. Expand the folders as needed, select **Contacts** in the Folder Forms Library list box, and then click the **OK** button. The Luminescence Contributors form appears in the left list box.

6. Click **Luminescence Contributors**, click the **Copy** button, click **Luminescence Contributors** in the right list box, click the **Save As** button, switch the Save in location to the **Tutorial** folder within the **Tutorial.06** folder on your Data Disk, type **Luminescence Contributors** as the filename, select **Form Message** as the file type, and then click the **Save** button.

   Now that the form is saved on your Data Disk, you can delete it.

7. Click the **Delete** button, click **Luminescence Contributors** in the left list box, and then click the **Delete** button.

8. Click the **Yes** button to confirm that you want to delete the form.

9. Click the **Close** button in the Forms Manager, and then click the **OK** button in each of the remaining dialog boxes to close them.

Next you'll remove the fields from the Address Cards view, and then delete the custom fields you created. When you return to the Address Cards view, you'll delete the contact cards you created in this tutorial.

To remove fields from a view, delete custom fields, and delete contact cards:

1. Right-click the Contacts Information viewer background, and then click **Show Fields**. The Show Fields dialog box opens.

   You can remove the fields you added to the Address Cards view and delete the custom fields.

2. Click the **Donation** field in the Show these fields in this order list box, press and hold the **Shift** key, click the **Contributor** field, and then release the **Shift** key. Both custom fields are selected.

3. Click the **Remove** button to place the fields back into the Available fields for User-defined fields in folder.

4. Click the **Contributor** field in the Available fields list, press and hold the **Shift** key, click the **Pledged** field, and then release the **Shift** key. All three custom fields are selected.

5. Click the **Delete** button, and then click the **OK** button in the dialog box to confirm the deletion.

6. Click the **OK** button to close the Show Fields dialog box.

7. Delete the contact cards for **Mitch Elkin**, **Kara Martin**, and **John Ravenfoot** from the Contacts Information viewer.

Next you'll return the Calendar and TaskPad to their default views. You can quickly remove unwanted fields from a table view, like the TaskPad, by dragging the fields off the table by their column headings.

To remove customizations from the TaskPad:

1. Switch to the **Calendar** Information viewer.

2. Drag the **Priority** field by its column heading out of the TaskPad until a big X appears over the field, and then release the mouse button. The field is removed from the TaskPad.

3. Drag the **Due Date** field off the TaskPad.

4. Delete the tasks you created.

Next, you'll remove the extra time zone and labels from the planner, and return the workday to its default setting of 8 AM to 5 PM.

To remove the Calendar customizations:

1. Click **Tools** on the menu bar, click **Options**, and then if necessary click the **Preferences** tab. The Preferences tab in the Options dialog box opens.

2. Click the **Calendar Options** button. The Calendar Options dialog box opens.

3. Click the **Start time** list arrow, and then click **8:00 AM**.

4. Click the **End time** list arrow, and then click **5:00 PM**.

5. Click the **Time Zone** button. The Time Zone dialog box opens.

6. Delete **Here** from the top Label text box, and then delete **Athens** from the additional time zone Label text box.

7. Click the **Show an additional time zone** check box to remove the check mark.

8. Click the **OK** button in the Time Zone dialog box, click the **OK** button in the Calendar Options dialog box, and then click the **OK** button in the Options dialog box.
9. Delete the appointment you created.

The Calendar is returned to its default settings. Next you'll reset the default Outlook Today options.

To reset the Outlook Today defaults:

1. Switch to **Outlook Today**, and then click the **Customize Outlook Today** button.
2. Click the **When starting, go directly to Outlook Today** check box to remove the check mark.
3. Click the **Choose Folders** button, click the **Luminescence Mail** check box to remove the check mark, and then click the **OK** button.
4. Sort the task list by **Due Date** in **Descending** order and then by **(none)**.
5. Click the **Show Outlook Today in this style** list arrow, and then click **Standard**.
6. Click the **Save Changes** button. Outlook Today returns to its default settings.

You'll remove the shortcuts and group you added to the Outlook Bar. When you remove a shortcut icon on the Outlook Bar, only the shortcut is removed, not the file or folder to which it pointed. The process is the same to remove a group or shortcut. If you remove a group, all the shortcuts it contains are also deleted.

To remove a shortcut and group from the Outlook Bar:

1. Right-click the **Luminescence Mail** shortcut icon in the **Luminescence** group on the Outlook Bar, and then click **Remove from Outlook Bar** on the shortcut menu. A dialog box opens, confirming the deletion.
2. Click the **Yes** button to confirm that you want to remove the shortcut.
3. Right-click the **Luminescence** group button, and then click **Remove Group** on the shortcut menu.
4. Click the **Yes** button to confirm that you want to remove the group from the Outlook Bar. The group and the remaining shortcut are deleted.

You can delete a toolbar button or menu command without opening the Customize dialog box. However, when you want to delete a custom toolbar, you must do so from the dialog box. You'll delete the custom Navigate toolbar. When you delete the toolbar, you delete all its buttons as well, although the commands are still available from their original categories in the Customize dialog box.

To delete a custom toolbar:

1. Right-click any toolbar, click **Customize** to open the Customize dialog box, and then click the **Toolbars** tab.
2. Click the **Navigate** toolbar in the Toolbars list box, and then click the **Delete** button.

3. Click the **OK** button in the dialog box to confirm that you want to delete the Navigate toolbar.

4. Click the **Close** button. The Customize dialog box closes and the toolbar no longer exists.

Your final task is to delete the Luminescence Mail folder you created along with any copies of the message in the Sent Items folder. Then, you'll empty the Deleted Items folder.

To remove the mail folder and e-mail items:

1. Display the Folder List.

2. Right-click the **Luminescence Mail** folder, and then click **Delete "Luminescence Mail"** on the shortcut menu.

3. Click the **Yes** button to confirm the deletion and move all of its contents to the Deleted Items folder.

4. Delete any messages you sent from the **Sent Items** folder.

5. Empty the **Deleted Items** folder.

6. Hide the Folder List.

The custom forms and fields you created will make it easier for Brian to keep track of current contributors and their donations and to respond with an appropriate message. In addition, the customization options ensure that Brian is working most efficiently in Outlook.

Session 6.2 QUICK CHECK

1. Why would you add a field to a view?

2. Describe the two ways you can add fields to a view.

3. What is Outlook Today?

4. Give two reasons why you might display two time zones in the Calendar planner.

5. What are three ways you can customize the Outlook Bar?

6. In what ways is Outlook a more functional Windows Explorer?

7. Why would you create a custom toolbar or menu?

8. True or False: Toolbars can only contain buttons with images and menus must always have only text.

REVIEW ASSIGNMENTS

Luminescence records information about its series subscribers in the Outlook Contacts folder. The group has been running an early-bird promotion that gives series subscribers an additional 25% off the regular prices. Many people have responded, and Fred wants you to create a form to record the data. The information collected includes whether the subscription is new or a renewal, which series package the subscriber wants (categorized as

Series A through Series G), and the number of tickets the subscriber is purchasing.

1. Start Outlook, open a new Contact window, click Tools on the menu bar, point to Forms, and then click Design this Form to create a new form based on a blank Contact window.

2. Display page 2 and use the Form menu to rename the tab "Subscription".

3. Switch the Field Chooser to display All Contact fields, and then add the Customer ID field and the Account field to the form.

4. Create three new fields: "Series" with a Text data type and a Text format; "Renewal" with a Yes/No data type and an Icon format; and "Tickets" with an Integer data type and a 1,234 format.

5. Drag the custom fields to the form.

6. Arrange the fields on the form so that Customer ID and Renewal appear on the first row, Tickets and Series appear on the second row, and Account appears on the third row.

7. For each control, open the Properties dialog box and rename the control, entering its caption name plus control type without any spaces as the Name and verifying that the Visible, Enabled, and, if appropriate, Sunken check boxes are selected.

8. Rearrange the tab order so the controls appear in the following sequence: CustomerIDLabel, CustomerIDTextBox, RenewalCheckBox, TicketsLabel, TicketsTextBox, SeriesLabel, SeriesTextBox, AccountLabel, and AccountTextBox.

9. Reduce the Customer ID text box to ¼ its size, reduce the Tickets text box to ¼ its size, and then align the fields using an organized, attractive, and logical layout.

10. Delete the Account field from the form.

11. Switch to the form's Properties page, and then enter "Subscriptions" as the Category, "1.0" as the Version, "Series" as the Form Number, your name as the Contact, and the description "This form is used to collect information about series subscribers."

12. Test the form, and then close the test form without saving it. Make any changes needed.

13. Publish the form in the Outlook Contacts folder with the display name "Luminescence Subscribers" and the Form name "Subscribers".

Explore ▷ 14. Save the form as a template with the name **Luminescence Subscribers Contact Template** in the **Review** folder within the **Tutorial.06** folder on your Data Disk, and then close the form without saving changes.

15. Create a new contact based on the custom form for the following information: full name "Pam Shephard"; home phone "401-555-3457"; address type "Home"; home mailing address "41 Larkin Street, Kingston RI 02852"; Customer ID "S-544"; Renewal checked; Tickets "4"; and Series "A".

16. Create a new contact based on the custom form for the following information: full name "Ralph Salvas"; home phone "401-555-3778"; address type "Home"; home mailing address "112 Quenton Street, Kingston RI 02852"; Customer ID "S-545"; Renewal unchecked; Tickets "1"; and Series "C".

17. Create a new contact based on the custom form for the following information: full name "Garret Bruneau"; home phone "401-555-7431"; address type "Home"; home mailing address "981 Center Road, Kingston RI 02852"; Customer ID "S-546"; Renewal checked; Tickets "2"; and Series "A".

18. Display the contacts you created in Address Card view in the Contacts Information viewer.

19. Customize the Address Card view to display the Customer ID, Renewal, Tickets, and Series fields below the File As name.

Explore ▷ 20. Sort the cards in ascending order by Customer ID, and then print the view in Card Style.

Explore ▷ 21. Filter the cards to display only those that have a check mark in the Renewal check box. (*Hint:* In the Advanced tab of the Filter dialog box, create a criterion for the Renewal field equals yes.)

22. Print the cards in Card Style and then remove the filter, sort, and custom fields you added to the view.

23. Use the Actions menu to create a half-hour appointment with Pam Shephard for tomorrow at 10 AM with a Normal importance to confirm the number of tickets she requested.

24. Create an appointment with Garret Bruneau for tomorrow at 11 AM with a High importance to confirm that he wants Series A.

Explore ▷ 25. Create a new mail message with the subject "Series rates increase on Monday" and the message text "Friday is the last day to receive the 25% early-bird discount for the series subscription for the new season. Subscribe today to lock in the best rates. Thank you." Press the Enter key twice and then type your name. Save the message as a Draft by clicking the Save button, and then close the message.

26. Switch to Outlook Today, and then print the view.

Explore 27. Customize Outlook Today to use the Winter style and show 3 days in the calendar.

Explore 28. Click the link for the appointment with Pam tomorrow at 10 AM, and then click the Delete button on the Standard toolbar in the Appointment window. The window closes, and in a moment the appointment is removed from Outlook Today and your calendar. (If this were a recurring appointment, the entire series would be deleted.)

29. Click the Drafts link to open the Drafts folder, and then open the saved message.

Explore 30. Save the message as an Outlook Template with the filename **Early Bird Discount** in the **Review** folder within the **Tutorial.06** folder on your Data Disk, and then close it.

31. Open the Folder List, and then use the Outlook Bar and Folder List to display the files in the Review folder in the Information viewer.

Explore 32. Drag the Early Bird Discount template to the end of the Other Shortcuts group on the Outlook Bar to create a shortcut.

33. Click the shortcut you created to open a new message based on the template to verify the shortcut works, and then close the window.

Explore 34. Create a new group on the Outlook Bar called "Luminescence", and then drag the Early Bird Discount shortcut from the Other Shortcuts group to the Luminescence group.

35. Click the Early Bird Discount shortcut in the Luminescence group on the Outlook Shortcut Bar, address the message to yourself, send the message, and then print the received message.

36. Save the Luminescence Subscribers form from the forms library in the Outlook Contacts folder as **Luminescence Subscribers** in the **Review** folder within the **Tutorial.06** folder on your Data Disk, remove the form from the forms library, and then delete the custom fields you created for the form.

37. Delete any items or customizations you created in these assignments, including the contacts, the appointments, the e-mail messages from the Inbox, Drafts, and Sent Items folders, the Luminescence group and the shortcut from the Outlook Bar, and then empty the Deleted Items folder.

38. Return Outlook Today to Standard style and show 5 days in the calendar.

39. Exit Outlook.

CASE PROBLEMS

Case 1. Sexton Jewels   Beverly Sexton makes and sells custom jewelry, from high-quality costume jewelry to high-end gemstone and precious metals jewelry. Her clients include individuals as well as boutiques and independent shops. Beverly contacts her regular clients once each month to solicit new orders. She asks you to create a custom Outlook form she can use to track her last conversation with contacts.

1. Start Outlook, and then create a new form based on a blank Contact window.

2. Delete the Business phone label, button, and text box controls from the second column in the General tab of the Contact form.

Explore 3. Create a new field named "Last Talked To" with a Date/Time data type in the Tues 12/12/03 4:30 PM format.

4. Drag the Last Talked To custom field to the space you created above the phone fields on the General tab.

5. Change the field's properties so that each control's name reflects the field caption and control type.

6. Adjust the tab order so that the Last Talked To field is selected after the File As field. (*Hint:*

Hold the Shift key as you click each control to select and move both controls at one time.)

7. Adjust the size and alignment of the field you added to the form as needed.

8. Switch to the form's Properties page, and then enter "Follow up" as the Category, your name as the Contact, and the description "This form is used to record the date and time of the last conversation with the contact."

9. Test the form by entering "yesterday 10 AM" in the Last Talked To text box, and then close the test form without saving it. Make any changes needed.

10. Publish the form in the Outlook Contacts folder with the display name "Contact Follow Up" and the Form name "Follow Up". Close the form without saving changes.

11. Create a new contact based on the custom form with the following information: full name "Claire Wagstaffe"; last talked to "yesterday 7 AM"; home phone "407-555-2117".

12. Create a new contact based on the custom form for the following information: full name "Wesley Rider"; last talked to "one month ago 3 PM"; home phone "407-555-8718".

13. Create a new contact based on the custom form with the following information: full name "Florence Peterson"; last talked to "four Wed ago noon"; home phone "407-555-5534".

14. Create a new contact based on the custom form with the following information: full name "Margaret Wong"; last talked to "yesterday noon"; home phone "407-555-4719".

15. Create a new folder named "Follow Up" that contains Contact items placed within the Contacts folder. Create a shortcut to the new folder below the Contacts shortcut on the Outlook Bar.

16. Move the four contacts you created to the Follow Up folder.

17. Use the Outlook Bar shortcut you created to open the Follow Up folder.

 Explore   18. Click View on the menu bar, point to Current View, and then click Define Views. The Define Views for "Follow Up" dialog box opens. You'll use this dialog box to create a new custom view.

Explore   19. Click "Phone List" in the Views for folder list box, click the Copy button to open the Copy View dialog box, type "Last Called" in the Name of new view text box, click the All Contact folders option button if necessary, and then click the OK button.

Explore   20. Click the Fields button in the View Summary dialog box, and then use the Show Fields dialog box to display only the following fields in this order: Icon, Attachment, Flag Status, Full Name, Home Phone, and Last Talked To. (*Hint:* You'll need to recreate the Last Talked To Date/Time field in this folder.)

21. Click the OK button in the Show Fields dialog box, click the OK button in the View Summary dialog box, review the new view in the Define Views for Follow Up dialog box, and then click the Apply View button.

22. Sort the fields in descending order by the Last Talked To field.

23. Print the view in Table Style.

Explore   24. Delete the Last Called view. Open the Define Views for Follow Up dialog box, select the Last Called view, click the Delete button, click the OK button to confirm the deletion, and then click the Close button.

25. Save the Contact Follow Up form from the forms library in the Outlook Contacts folder as **Contact Followup** in the **Cases** folder within the **Tutorial.06** folder on your Data Disk, remove the form from the forms library, and then delete the custom fields you created for the form.

26. Delete any items or customizations you created in this case, including the contacts, the Follow Up folder, and the Outlook Bar shortcut.

27. Empty the Deleted Items folder, and then exit Outlook.

Case 2. Zafforini Bed & Breakfast Zafforini Bed & Breakfast organizes its staff into three teams—Red, Yellow, Blue—to foster a sense of commitment and community among employees. Each team is responsible for a variety of jobs, and selects a different team leader (or contact) for each task. In addition, Vicki Zafforini, owner of the B&B, rotates the tasks among the three teams. She asks you to create a custom Task form to help organize the team's responsibilities.

Explore   1. Start Outlook, and then create a new form based on a blank Task window.

2. Display page 2 and rename the tab "Teamwork".
3. Display All Task fields in the Field Chooser, and then add the Contact field (be sure you don't use the Contacts field), the Role field, the Sensitivity field, and the Team Task field to the form.
4. Rearrange the fields so that they appear in one column in the following order: Team Task, Role, Contact, Sensitivity.
5. Change the field's properties so that each control's name reflects the field caption and control type.
6. Adjust the tab order so that pressing the Tab key moves users consecutively through the controls.
7. Center align the text boxes and Left align the labels on the form. You can center the check box.
8. Switch to the form's Properties page, and then enter your name as the Contact, and the description "This form is used to record information about the tasks being completed by the team."
9. Test the form, and then close the test form without saving it. Make any changes needed.
10. Delete the Sensitivity field.

Explore ▷ 11. Publish the form in the Outlook Tasks folder with the Display name "Team Tasks" and the Form name "Team Tasks". Close the form without saving changes.
12. Create a new folder named "Red Team" that contains Task Items placed within the Tasks folder; create a shortcut to the Outlook Bar.
13. Create a new group on the Outlook Bar called "Red", and then move the Red Team folder shortcut to the new group.
14. Use the shortcut to open the Red Team folder, and then switch to the Simple List view.

Explore ▷ 15. Use the Field Chooser to add the Contact, Role, and Team Task fields to the Simple List view.

Explore ▷ 16. Create a new task from the custom Simple List view with the following information: subject "Housecleaning"; Due Date "next Monday"; Team Task checked; Role "Primary"; and Contact "Simone Turner".

Explore ▷ 17. Create a new task from the custom Simple List view with the following information: subject "Dining Room Setup"; Due Date "next Monday"; Team Task checked; Role "Secondary"; and Contact "Irving Shearn".

Explore ▷ 18. Create a new task from the custom Simple List view with the following information: subject "Guest Check-in"; Due Date "next Monday"; Team Task unchecked; Role "Primary"; and Contact "Gayle Sufy".

Explore ▷ 19. Create a new task from the custom Simple List view with the following information: subject "Guest Check-out"; Due Date "next Monday"; Team Task unchecked; Role "Primary"; and Contact "Gayle Sufy".

Explore ▷ 20. Create a new task from the custom Simple List view with the following information: subject "Room Service Delivery"; Due Date "next Monday"; Team Task checked; Role "Primary"; and Contact "Irving Shearn".
21. Sort the tasks in ascending order by Team Task, and then Role. (*Hint:* Click the Team Task column heading, press and hold the Shift key, click the Role column heading, and then release the Shift key.)
22. Print all rows of the task list in Table Style.
23. Save the Team Tasks form from the forms library in the Outlook Tasks folder as **Team Tasks** in the **Cases** folder within the **Tutorial.06** folder on your Data Disk, and then remove the form from the forms library.
24. Delete any items or customizations you created in this case, including the tasks, the Red Team folder, and the Outlook Bar shortcut and group.
25. Empty the Deleted Items folder, and then exit Outlook.

Case 3. Steindler Travel Newsletter Steindler Travel Newsletter provides travel and destination information to budget vacationers. The weekly newsletter includes information about little-known sales from airlines, hotels, and tour packagers. New subscribers are given a choice of promotional welcome gifts—a tote bag, a travel alarm clock, or a sleep mask. Barry Steindler, the founder of the newsletter, uses Outlook to store contact information about subscribers. He asks you to create a custom combination field that displays both partners names and to create a list box (called combo box) from which he can select the promotional gift the new subscribers requested.

1. Start Outlook, open a new Message window, right-click the menu bar, and then click Customize. Switch to the Commands tab in the Customize dialog box.

Explore   2. Click Tools in the Categories list box, and then drag the Design This Form command to the leftmost position on the Standard toolbar.

3. Close the Customize dialog box, and then close the Message window.

Explore   4. Open a new Contact window, and click the Design This Form button on the Standard toolbar to switch to design mode. (*Hint:* The button may not be in the leftmost position.)

5. On the General tab, delete the Job Title and Company fields.

6. Insert the Spouse field from the Personal fields list below the Full Name field, and then left-align each control with the appropriate control above it, and then horizontally align the Spouse controls with the Home controls in the next column.

Explore   7. Expand the Spouse text box so that it is the same width as the Full Name text box. (*Hint:* Make the Full Name text box the dominant control, click Layout on the menu bar, point to Make Same Size, and then click Width.)

Explore   8. Click the Control Toolbox button on the Form Design toolbar to open the Toolbox, click the TextBox button, and then click below the Spouse text box to add a text box to the form.

9. Resize and align the text box to match the dimensions and left-alignment of the Spouse text box. Middle align the textbox with the Business Fax field.

Explore   10. Open the text box control's Properties dialog box, and then click the New button on the Value tab.

Explore   11. Create a new field with the name "Household" and the type Combination, and then click the Edit button to open the Combination Formula Field dialog box.

Explore   12. Click the Field button, point to Name fields, click Spouse, type "and" (without the quotation marks), press the spacebar, click the Field button, point to Name fields, and click Full Name. The text "[Spouse] and [Full Name]" appears in the Formula text box.

13. Click the OK button in the Combination Formula Field dialog box, click the OK button in the New Field dialog box, click the Display tab, change the name to "HouseholdTextBox", and then click the OK button to close the Properties dialog box. The value will appear by default in the blank form.

Explore   14. Click the Label button in the Toolbox, click below the Spouse label to add a label to the left of the Household text box; open the label's Properties dialog box, and then change the name to "HouseholdLabel" and the caption to "Household:".

15. Resize and align the label to match the dimensions and left-alignment of the Spouse label box. Middle align the label with the Household text box.

16. Test the form in run mode; type "Lisa Taylor" in the Full Name text box, type "Mark Quince" in the Spouse text box, verify that "Mark Quince and Lisa Taylor" appear in the Household text box, and then close the form without saving changes.

17. Delete the Business Fax and Mobile fields from the right side of the form page.

Explore   18. Click the ComboBox button in the toolbox, click the form below the Home field, and then open the combo box control's Properties dialog box.

Explore   19. Click the New button on the Value tab, create a custom field called "Promo" with Text as its type and format, and then click the OK button.

Explore   20. Click in the Possible values text box, and then type "Tote bag;Travel clock;Sleep mask" to enter the list box options. A semicolon separates each selection in a list.

21. On the Display tab, type "PromoComboBox" as the name, and then click the OK button.

22. Add a label to the left of the Promo combo box with the caption "Promo Gift:" and the name "PromoLabel".

23. Align the Promo controls appropriately on the form.

24. Change the tab order as needed.

25. Test the form in run mode using fictitious data to verify the three selections in the list box, and then close the form without saving changes.

Explore   26. Hide the Details tab in the form. (*Hint:* Click the Details tab, click Form on the menu bar, and then click Display This Page to remove the check mark.)

27. Save the form as a template with the name **Promotions Contact Template** in the **Cases** folder within the **Tutorial.06** folder on your Data Disk, and then close the form without saving changes.

28. Display the Promotions Contact Template file in the Information viewer, and then double-click the file to open a new window using the form.

29. Enter the following contact: full name "Lisa Taylor"; spouse "Mark Quince"; address type "Home"; home mailing address as your address; and Promo list "Travel clock".

30. Print the contact, and then close the contact card without saving it.

Explore 31. Open a new Task window, remove the Design This Form button from the Standard toolbar, and then close the form without saving. (*Hint:* Press and hold the Alt key, drag the Design This Form button off the Standard toolbar, and then release the mouse button and Alt key.)

32. Delete the custom Promo and Household fields you created in the Contacts folder and then exit Outlook.

Case 4. Urban Camp Services Urban Camp Services (UCS) is a volunteer organization in Vancouver, Washington, that provides camp activities to children ages 5 through 18. UCS matches children with adult volunteers who have similar interests. In many cases, the children's parents or guardians request an adult counselor of a specific gender. UCS wants to track all this information in Outlook, and asks you to create a custom form.

1. Start Outlook, and then create a new form based on a blank Contact window.

2. Drag the Gender field and the Hobbies field from the Personal fields in the Field Chooser to page 2 of the form.

3. Rename the page 2 tab "Counselors".

Explore 4. Press Ctrl+A to select all the fields on the form.

Explore 5. Press the Group button on the Design Form toolbar to combine the controls into one group. Now you can move the two fields as one group.

Explore 6. Drag down the grouped fields to make room for two fields above them.

Explore 7. Click the Ungroup button on the Design Form toolbar to separate the fields.

8. Show the Name fields in the Field Chooser, drag the Full Name field to the empty space you created at the top of the page, and then drag the Nickname field to the space below the Full Name field.

9. Change the fields' properties so that each control's name reflects the field caption and control type.

10. Adjust the tab order so that the user moves sequentially through the fields you added to the form.

11. Fix the alignment of the fields you added to the form as needed.

12. Switch to the form's Properties page, and then enter "Volunteers" as the Category, your name as the Contact, and the description "This form is used to record the gender and interests of volunteer counselors."

13. Test the form, and then close the test form without saving it. Make any changes needed.

14. Publish the form in the Outlook Contacts folder with the display name "UCS Volunteer Counselors" and the Form name "Counselors". Close the form without saving changes.

15. Create a new contact based on the custom form, and then enter the following information in the Counselors tab: full name "Matthew Riker"; nickname "Matt"; gender "Male"; Hobbies "football".

Explore 16. Switch to the General tab, and verify that Matt's full name appears on the page.

17. Create a new contact based on the custom form, and then enter the following information in the Counselors tab: full name "Marilyn Rosow"; nickname "Rosie"; gender "Female"; Hobbies "softball and archery".

18. Create a new contact based on the custom form, and then enter the following information in the Counselors tab: full name "Susan Parvin"; nickname none; gender "Female"; Hobbies "soccer".

19. Create a new contact based on the custom form, and then enter the following information in the Counselors tab: full name "Jesse Haskins"; nickname "Jess"; gender "Male"; Hobbies "computer games and chess".

20. Customize the Address Cards view to show the following fields below the File As field: Full Name, Nickname, Gender, and Hobbies. (You can leave the other fields in the view.)

21. Filter the contact list to show only the Male counselors in the custom Address Cards view, and then print all items in the filtered contact list in Card Style.

22. Remove the filter, and then print all the contacts in the custom Address Cards view in Card Style.

23. Remove the fields you added to the Address Cards view, and then delete the contacts you created.

24. Save the UCS Volunteer Counselors form from the forms library in the Outlook Contacts folder as **UCS Volunteer Counselors** in the **Cases** folder within the **Tutorial.06** folder on your Data Disk, and then remove the form from the forms library.

25. Empty the Deleted Items folder and then exit Outlook.

QUICK CHECK ANSWERS

Session 6.1

1. **A form is a window in which you enter and view information about an item electronically.**

2. (1) open an existing form in design mode; (2) modify the form; (3) test the form; (4) publish the form.

3. A bound control is an object on a form in which a user enters information that Outlook displays (check boxes, list boxes, and text boxes); an unbound control is an object that displays text or images that users cannot edit (change) for informational or decorative purposes (text labels, lines, and images).

4. A simple field holds basic pieces of data, such as a name, amount, or date.

5. Tab order is the sequence that users move through fields on a form when they press the Tab key.

6. Publishing a form saves the form so you or others can use it in Outlook.

7. The Compose page shows what senders see when they create and send outgoing messages; the Read page shows what recipients see when they open and read incoming messages.

8. A template and a form both provide a blueprint of the fields and layout for an item, but a template is a separate file with the .oft extension.

Session 6.2

1. Adding a field to a view enables you to see the exact data you want in an Information viewer.

2. (1) Drag fields from the Field Chooser in any table view; (2) Open the Show Fields dialog box, and select and order the fields that will be displayed in any view.

3. Outlook Today provides an overview of your current schedule, task list, and unread e-mail messages.

4. (1) If you regularly work with others in another time zone, displaying both time zones enables you to see the time differences without mental calculations. (2) If you regularly travel between time zones, you can swap time zones so your calendar and messages are converted to the time zone you're in.

5. Any three of the following: (1) add shortcuts to Outlook items or folders, folders and files on your computer, or Web pages; (2) add and/or rename groups; (3) reorder shortcut icons; (4) switch from Large Icons to Small Icons, or vice versa.

6. Outlook enables you to add or remove fields as well as filter, group, and sort the listed items. In Windows Explorer, you can only reorder and sort items using the provided fields.

7. To group commands or buttons related to a specific task in one location.

8. False

OBJECTIVES

In this tutorial you will:

- View Web pages from Outlook

- Save a Web page as a favorite

- Create a folder home page

- Participate in a newsgroup

- Create a Net Folder to share items

- Schedule online meetings and presentations

USING OUTLOOK WITH THE INTERNET

Collaborating on a Computer Workstation for ErgoDesign

ErgoDesign

Six years ago, Eric Latmer, Chelsie Gradle, and Ian Zelinsky were commiserating on a newsgroup about the lack of functional and comfortable computer workspaces for their home offices. When they couldn't find the inexpensive quality furniture they wanted, they decided to join forces to create workspaces that match their financial means, physical needs, and aesthetic senses. The three founded ErgoDesign, which designs, manufactures, and sells attractive, affordable, ergonomic computer furniture that fits the needs of home office workers. They currently have 15 workspace designs constructed from quality woods that can be customized to an individual's requirements.

Because the three partners live hundreds of miles apart in different states, they rely on the Internet to collaborate and run their business. Eric, Chelsie, and Ian are working on adding a new workspace design to their company's catalog. Before they finalize the design, though, they want to check the latest ergonomic guidelines put out by the Occupational Safety and Health Administration (OSHA), which is part of the U.S. Department of Labor, and get feedback from some of their potential customers. Then they want to set up a project folder that distributes all items and files related to the project within the group and to select others. Once they have gathered and distributed all this information, the entire group will participate in an online meeting to discuss their next steps. Outlook enables them to complete all these tasks.

In this tutorial, you'll view Web pages from within Outlook. Then you'll learn how to participate in newsgroups. Next you'll create a Net Folder and set it up to distribute information to a select group of people. With all that information in place, you'll learn how to schedule an online meeting with NetMeeting so attendees can collaborate actively.

SESSION 7.1

In this session, you will learn how to view Web pages from Outlook. Then you'll set up a folder home page for an Outlook folder. Finally you'll learn how to participate in online newsgroups.

Viewing Web Pages

There are many ways to find information and collaborate with people on the Internet or an intranet. The **Internet** is a worldwide collection of computer networks where users at one computer can access information on other computers. The most popular part of the Internet is the **World Wide Web (WWW** or **Web),** an Internet service that stores and provides information. An **intranet** is a private internal corporate network that uses Internet and Web technology to enable employees in an organization to share computing resources and information. An intranet might be used to make a company policy manual available internally within the company but not to the general public. When access to the intranet is provided to people outside the organization, it is called an **extranet.**

People frequently rely on the Web to locate specific data. A **Web page** is an HTML document with text, graphics, sound, and links that is accessible on the Web or an intranet. **HTML (Hypertext Markup Language)** is a standard coding system that specifies how to display the text, graphics, and links on a Web page for a viewer. Web pages provide a great way for individuals, organizations, and businesses to share information with people around the world or within the same organization. Web pages are used to dispense such information as the price of a product, the latest news, or a description of a company's services. They can also provide a host of information—from family photo albums and happenings to the goals and memberships of associations, from businesses' catalogs of products or services to schools' programs, faculty, and syllabi. A collection of related Web pages is called a **Web site.**

Anyone who knows how to post pages on the Web, can do so. The content of the pages is neither regulated nor verified. Whenever you research information on the Web, you should assess data you find for:

- ■ **Authorship.** Determine who wrote the information and assess whether the author has the credentials or expertise to write on the topic.

- ■ **Currency.** Try to find out when the information was last updated; most Web pages include a last revision date at the bottom of the page. Consider whether timeliness affects the reliability of the information.

- ■ **Validity.** Look at the source of the site to determine whether this is a trustworthy resource of information.

- ■ **Accuracy.** Evaluate the content for validity, relevance, and correctness. Confirm the information with a second source, like you would other research materials.

Web pages are viewed with a **Web browser,** a program such as Internet Explorer or Netscape Navigator that enables you to access, display, and interact with the Web. You can open your Web browser directly from Outlook or you can use Outlook as a Web browser. The former launches a separate program each time you want to review information on the Web; the latter opens a Web page right from Outlook.

Using Outlook as a Web Browser

You can view Web pages in any Outlook Information viewer. In this way, Outlook acts like a Web browser, similar to Internet Explorer. You move among Web pages in Outlook just as you do in a Web browser—by clicking links, clicking navigation buttons, or typing a URL. The Web toolbar provides all the features you need to navigate Web pages from Outlook. You'll use the Web toolbar to open and view a Web page from the Outlook Inbox.

To open the Web toolbar:

1. Start Outlook, and then switch to the **Inbox**.

2. Right-click the **Standard** toolbar, and then click **Web** on the shortcut menu. The Web toolbar opens. See Figure 7-1.

Figure 7-1 ◂	OUTLOOK WINDOW WITH WEB TOOLBAR

Web toolbar; yours might be in a different location

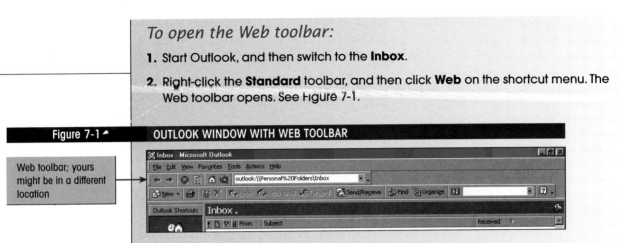

You can use the buttons on the Web toolbar to navigate through the Web. Many of the buttons are the same as the ones you use with Internet Explorer. Figure 7-2 lists and describes these buttons.

Figure 7-2	WEB TOOLBAR BUTTONS

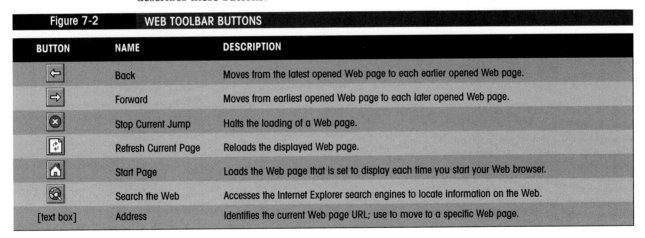

BUTTON	NAME	DESCRIPTION
⬅	Back	Moves from the latest opened Web page to each earlier opened Web page.
➡	Forward	Moves from earliest opened Web page to each later opened Web page.
⊗	Stop Current Jump	Halts the loading of a Web page.
↻	Refresh Current Page	Reloads the displayed Web page.
⌂	Start Page	Loads the Web page that is set to display each time you start your Web browser.
🔍	Search the Web	Accesses the Internet Explorer search engines to locate information on the Web.
[text box]	Address	Identifies the current Web page URL; use to move to a specific Web page.

You'll use the Web toolbar to open Web pages in Outlook. When you know what Web page you want to view, you can enter its **URL (Uniform Resource Locator)**, the address or location of a Web page. A URL is split into several parts separated by slashes (/): the Web protocol, the Web server name, and possibly the path to a specific page. The **Web protocol** is HTTP (Hypertext Transfer Protocol), the communications system that enables Web browsers to access Web pages. Outlook assumes that all URLs begin with "http://" so you don't have to type these characters. A **Web server** is the name of the computer that stores the Web page. The Web server is also the home page for most Web sites. A **home page** is the main page of a Web site, and usually provides general introductory information with links to more specific content within the site. Home page can also refer to the Web page that opens when you start a browser. The Web server can be followed by one or more folder names and a filename and extension that access a particular page. For example, look how each part makes up the OSHA Web site URL shown in Figure 7-3.

Figure 7-3	PARTS OF A URL

You'll start by viewing the OSHA home page. Web pages change frequently, so the headlines and content and even design of the OSHA home page you see may be different from that shown in the figures in the steps.

To view the OSHA Web site in Outlook:

1. If necessary, connect to the Internet.

2. Type **www.osha.gov** in the Address text box on the Web toolbar, and then press the **Enter** key. The progress of the Web page loading appears in the status bar. After a moment, the OSHA home page finishes loading in the Inbox Information viewer. See Figure 7-4.

Figure 7-4	OSHA HOME PAGE

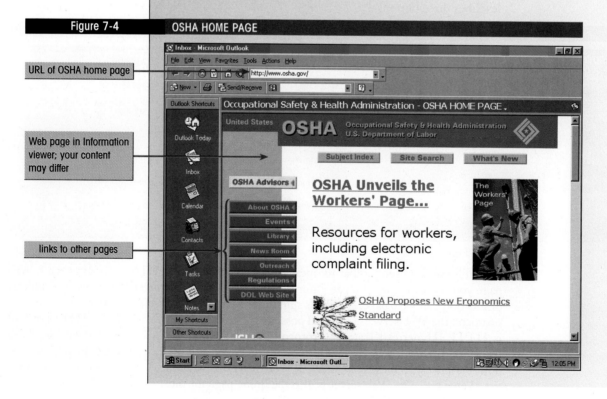

URL of OSHA home page

Web page in Information viewer; your content may differ

links to other pages

TROUBLE? If the Web page you see looks different from the one shown in Figure 7-4, the content or layout of the page may have changed since this book was printed. Web pages are constantly changing and being updated. However the major links should still be available.

The home page contains some basic information along with many links to other pages on the site.

3. Click the **About OSHA** link on the Web page. A second page opens in the Information viewer. This page contains links to specific topics about OSHA.

4. Click **OSHA Facts** link near the bottom of the page. This page contains a document of text that you can read, scrolling as necessary to bring more text into view. Also, the URL shows the address of the current page you are viewing. See Figure 7-5.

| Figure 7-5 | WEB PAGE WITH TEXT |

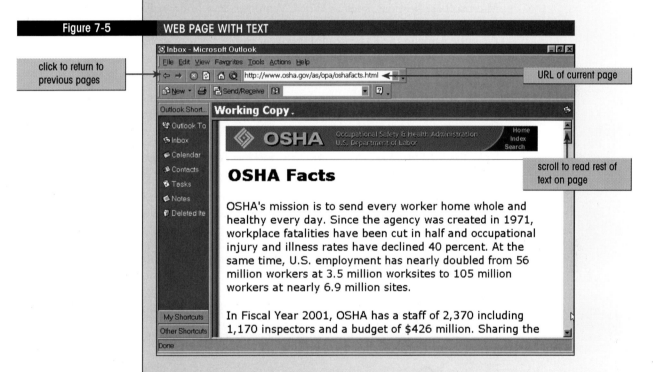

click to return to previous pages

URL of current page

scroll to read rest of text on page

TROUBLE? If you don't see The New OSHA-Reinventing Worker Safety and Health link, the link may no longer be available. Click another link to view a third page on the OSHA site.

Once you read this document, you might want to return to the previous page to select a different link. You can use the Web toolbar to navigate between the pages you have already viewed. Because you have opened several pages, the Back button is active; the Forward button remains inactive until you back up one or more pages.

5. Click the **Back** button ⇐ on the Web toolbar. The previous page you loaded— the About OSHA page—reappears in the Information viewer.

Now that you have gone back one page, the Forward button is available. You can use it to return to the OSHA facts page or you could continue back to the OSHA home page.

> **6.** Click the **Forward** button ➡ on the Web toolbar. The New OSHA-Reinventing Worker Safety and Health page you loaded reappears.
>
> **7.** Click ⬅ twice to return to the OSHA home page.

Ian has requested that you regularly look up information on the OSHA Web site. Rather than retype the URL each time, you can save the URL.

Saving Your Favorite Web Addresses

When you come across Web pages that you think you'll return to frequently, you can save their URLs as favorites. **Favorites** is a list of shortcuts that you set up to commonly used items, files, folders, or URLs. It also shows items you added to the Favorites folder in other Microsoft applications, such as Word, Windows, and Internet Explorer. You can open any favorite Web page from within Outlook by selecting it from the Favorites menu. (Clicking the same name in the Favorites Information viewer opens the page in Internet Explorer.)

You can add Web pages that you want to visit again to the Favorites folder as you locate them. In this case, you'll create a new folder within the Favorites folder to store the shortcuts.

To add a new folder and Web page shortcut to the Favorites folder:

1. Click **Favorites** on the menu bar, and then click **Add to Favorites**. The Add To Favorites dialog box opens with the Favorites folder displayed.

2. Click the **Create New Folder** button 📁 in the dialog box. The New Folder dialog box opens, displaying the path to the current folder where the new folder will be created—C:\Windows\Favorites.

TROUBLE? If you cannot create a new folder on the computer system you're using, create the folder on your Data Disk. Click the Cancel button in the New Folder dialog box, if necessary. Change the Save in location to the Tutorial folder within the Tutorial.07 folder on your Data Disk, and then repeat Step 2.

3. Type **ErgoDesign** in the Name text box, and then click the **OK** button. The new folder is added and opens within the Favorites folder.

Outlook inserts the name of the Web page as a suggested filename in the File name text box. You can change this to be more succinct or descriptive, as needed.

4. Type **OSHA Home Page** in the File name text box.

5. Verify **Internet Shortcuts** appears in the Save as type text box. See Figure 7-6.

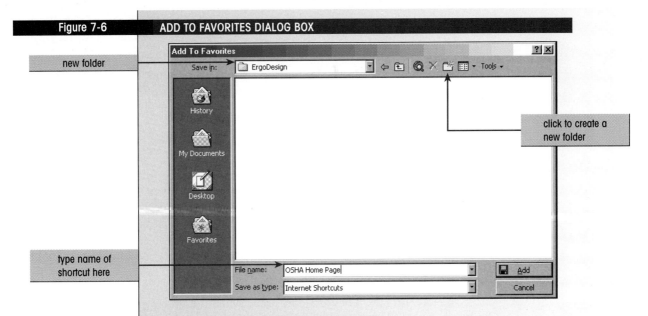

Figure 7-6   ADD TO FAVORITES DIALOG BOX

new folder

click to create a
new folder

type name of
shortcut here

TROUBLE? If you see Internet Shortcuts (*.url), then your computer system is set
up to show file extensions. Click Internet Shortcuts (*.url), and then continue
with Step 6.

6. Click the **Add** button. The dialog box closes, and the shortcut is added to the
Favorites list within the folder you created.

Favorites provide an easy way to return to Web pages. They are easier to manage if you
group related shortcuts in folders by topic. You can use the shortcut to return to the OSHA
Web page.

To display a favorite Web page in Outlook:

1. Click the **Forward** button ⇨ on the Web toolbar. You want to display a different page so you can see how the Favorites shortcut works.

2. Click **Favorites** on the menu bar, point to the **ErgoDesign** folder, and then click
OSHA Home Page. The Web page associated with the favorites shortcut opens
in the Information viewer.

TROUBLE? If you don't see the ErgoDesign folder on the Favorites menu, then
you saved the ErgoDesign folder on your Data Disk. Click Open Favorites, and
then change the Look in location for the Favorites dialog box to the
ErgoDesign folder within the Tutorial folder within the Tutorial.07 folder on your
Data Disk. Double-click OSHA Home Page.

The Favorites menu is available from any Information viewer. The folder and Web page
shortcut you added to Favorites are also accessible in any Office application with a Favorites
menu or from the Open, Save As, and Insert File dialog boxes.

When you're done viewing Web pages, you can return to the Inbox folder content.

> ### To return to the Inbox folder:
>
> 1. Click the **Back** button ⇐ on the Web toolbar.
>
> 2. Click **Inbox** in the **Outlook Shortcuts** group on the Outlook Bar. The Inbox folder content reappears; in this case, there are no items to view.

Creating a Home Page for an Outlook Folder

In Outlook, you can assign one Web page to each Outlook folder, called a **folder home page**. When you open the folder, you switch between displaying the assigned Web page and the folder contents. You can assign a Web page to a default Outlook folder or create your own. Eric frequently asks you to visit the Center for Office Technology Web site, which is devoted to health and safety issues related to technology. If you assign the Center for Office Technology Web page to the Inbox as its folder home page, you can view that Web page whenever you click the folder.

Folder home pages can be located anywhere—on the Internet, on your local hard disk, or on a corporate intranet. They are most useful when the Web page is updated frequently to display the most current information, reminders, or messages. For example, an Internet Web page that lists the current membership of an association might be associated with the Contacts folder so you can see the latest list of members each time you open the folder. Or, you might associate an intranet Web page with the company's calendar to the Calendar folder so you can switch between your personal calendar and the corporate schedule.

The folder home page can be set as the default view when you first select the folder or as an optional view. If you choose to set it as the default view, then each time you open the folder the Web page appears. To display the folder's content, you click the folder icon a second time. If you want to return to the Web page or set the folder home page as an optional view, then you can switch manually to the Web page at any time.

If you use Microsoft Exchange Server and work remotely, you can store folder home pages for viewing offline.

You'll create a new folder, and then assign the Center for Office Technology Web page as the folder home page.

> ### To assign a Web page to a folder:
>
> 1. Click the **New Mail Message** button list arrow [📄 New ▾] on the Standard toolbar, and then click **Folder**. The Create New Folder dialog box opens.
>
> 2. Create a new folder named **Ergonomics** that contains **Note Items** placed in **Personal Folders**. Do *not* add a shortcut to the folder to the Outlook Bar. The Folder List opens so you can access the folder.
>
>   TROUBLE? If the Folder List doesn't open, click View on the menu bar, and then click Folder List.
>
> 3. Click the **Ergonomics** folder in the Folder List. The new folder opens in the Information viewer.
>
> 4. Create a new yellow note with the text **Should we search for other Web sites with current ergonomic information?**, and then close the note.
>
> 5. Right-click the **Ergonomics** folder, and then click **Properties** on the shortcut menu. The Ergonomics Properties dialog box opens.

6. Click the **Home Page** tab. This tab contains information related to the selected folder's home page.

7. Type **www.cot.org** in the Address text box. This is the URL for the Web page you want to associate with the Ergonomics folder. See Figure 7-7.

Figure 7-7	HOME PAGE TAB IN THE ERGONOMICS PROPERTIES DIALOG BOX

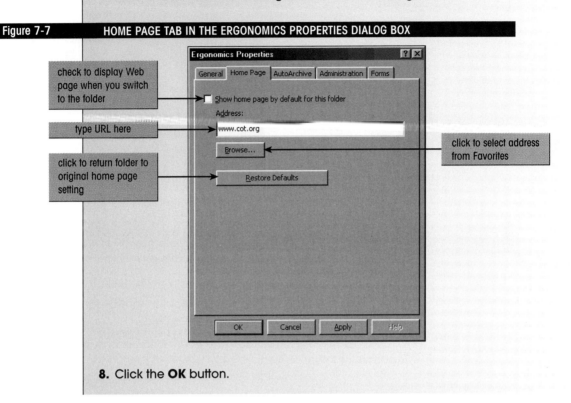

check to display Web page when you switch to the folder

type URL here

click to return folder to original home page setting

click to select address from Favorites

8. Click the **OK** button.

When you want to view the Web page, you need only to open the associated folder. After you associate a Web page with a folder, a new command, Show Folder Home Page, appears on the View menu. You can use this command to switch between viewing the folder's contents and the Web page. If Show Folder Home Page is selected, the Web page appears in the Information viewer whenever you select the folder.

To view a folder home page:

1. Click **Inbox** in the Folder List.

2. Click **Ergonomics** in the Folder List. A dialog box opens, indicating that the folder has a Web page associated with it and to use the Show Folder Home Page command to view the page.

   TROUBLE? If you don't see the dialog box, then the reminder was turned off for your installation of Outlook. Continue with Step 4.

3. Click the **OK** button. The Information viewer contains a list of the Outlook items in the folder—in this case, there is one note.

4. Click **View** on the menu bar, and then click **Show Folder Home Page**. This command is available only when a Web page is assigned to the selected folder. The Web page associated with the folder appears in the Information viewer. See Figure 7-8.

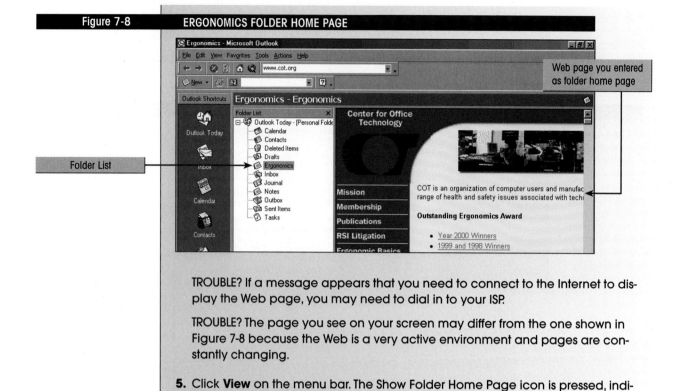

Figure 7-8   ERGONOMICS FOLDER HOME PAGE

TROUBLE? If a message appears that you need to connect to the Internet to display the Web page, you may need to dial in to your ISP.

TROUBLE? The page you see on your screen may differ from the one shown in Figure 7-8 because the Web is a very active environment and pages are constantly changing.

5. Click **View** on the menu bar. The Show Folder Home Page icon is pressed, indicating that the command is selected.

6. Click **Show Folder Home Page**. The Information viewer redisplays the Ergonomics folder contents.

You can switch between the folder contents and the folder home page at any point. To remove the folder home page from a folder, you delete the URL from the Home Page tab in the folder's Properties dialog box.

Participating in Newsgroups

Web pages enable you to research and gather information about a particular topic right from your computer. However, if you want to participate in a discussion about a topic, then you can turn to a newsgroup. A **newsgroup** is a collection of messages related to a specific subject written by individuals, and then posted to a news server. A **news server** is a computer that hosts newsgroups. Many ISPs, online services, universities, and other organizations have news servers, with a variety of newsgroups.

You can find newsgroups on practically any subject, from antique collecting to electronic music to politics to Xtreme skateboarding to Zen Buddhism. There is no membership or joining fee to participate in an Internet newsgroup. The entire collection of newsgroups on the Internet is called **Usenet**.

Newsgroups are organized into forums, discussion groups that focus on a particular topic. Forum names are hierarchical: The first few letters of the form indicate the main subject category. The main category is followed by a subtopic that further clarifies the newsgroup's focus. Newsgroups can have multiple levels of subtopics. Each level of the forum name is separated by a period. Figure 7-9 lists some examples of newsgroup hierarchies and forum names.

Figure 7-9	NEWSGROUP FORUM HIERARCHIES	
CATEGORY	**DESCRIPTION**	**SAMPLE FORUM**
biz	business	biz.entrepreneurs
comp	computer	comp.graphics.animation
misc	miscellaneous	misc.jobs.resume
rec	recreation	rec.collecting.books
sci	science	sci.anthropology.paleo
soc	society	soc.politics.marxism

These are just a few examples of the categories and forums. There are dozens of categories and countless forums with thousands of participants. To access a newsgroup, you need to open a newsreader and set up an account with a news server.

Setting Up the Outlook Express Newsreader and a News Account

Before you can access a newsgroup, you must set up a newsreader. A **newsreader** is a program that enables you to access newsgroups, download and read messages, and post replies to newsgroups. In that way, a newsreader is similar to an e-mail program. Outlook uses the Outlook Express newsreader to access newsgroups. **Outlook Express** is a component of Internet Explorer, which is a component of Windows, that provides access to e-mail and newsgroups. Outlook Express is automatically installed with Outlook and uses the Internet account that you set up in Outlook. Depending on the option selected in Internet Explorer, the newsreader opens in either the Outlook Express window or in the Outlook newsreader window. If you prefer a different newsreader, you also can start that newsreader from Outlook.

Once the newsreader is ready to go, you need to set up an account for each news server you want to access. The Internet Connection Wizard takes you through the process of setting up a news account. You'll need to supply your name, your e-mail address, and the server you want to access.

Once you set up a news account you can read and post messages in any of the newsgroups stored on that news server. News servers can be private or public (or open). Private news services may require participants to enter a user name and password to join the discussion, which limits access to their newsgroups to authorized members. Public news services do not require a name or password. For example, a newsgroup could be an Internet Usenet group or an internal company newsgroup. You can find newsgroups and news servers by referrals, through your ISP, through portals such as Yahoo, or through your school or company.

Setting Up a News Server Account

- Click View on the menu bar, point to Go To, and then click News (*or* start Outlook Express).
- If the Internet Connection Wizard does not open, click the Set up a Newsgroups account link (*or* click Tools on the menu bar, click Accounts, click the Add button in the Internet Accounts dialog box, and then click News).
- Type your name in the Display Name text box, and then click the Next button.
- Type your e-mail address in the E-mail address text box, and then click the Next button.
- Type the news server you want to use in the News (NNTP) server text box.
- If necessary, click the My news server requires me to log on check box, and enter a name and password when requested.
- Click the Next button, and then click the Finish button.
- If necessary, click the Close button in the Internet Accounts dialog box.

You'll start the newsreader and set up an account with Microsoft's public news server.

To start the newsreader and set up a news account:

1. Click **View** on the menu bar, point to **Go To**, and then click **News**. The Outlook Express window or the Outlook newsreader window opens.

   TROUBLE? If a dialog box opens, asking whether you want to set Outlook Express as your default newsreader, click the No button.

2. If necessary, click **Set up a Newsgroups account** to open the Internet Connection Wizard, type your name in the Display name text box, and then click the **Next** button. The name you enter will appear in the From box on any e-mail or newsgroup messages you send.

3. Type your e-mail address in the E-mail address text box, and then click the **Next** button. People in the newsgroup will be able to send you private messages at this address.

4. Type **msnews.microsoft.com** in the News (NNTP) server text box to specify the news server you want to use.

5. Make sure the **My news server requires me to log on** check box does *not* contain a check mark. When you select the My news server requires me to log on check box, the wizard will ask you to provide a name and password. However, the Microsoft news server does not require a password.

6. Click the **Next** button, and then click the **Finish** button. A dialog box opens. If you have not subscribed to newsgroups before, the message will tell you that you are not subscribed to any newsgroups in this account, and ask whether you want to view a list of available newsgroups now. If you had subscribed before, the message will ask if you want to download newsgroups from the news account you just added.

7. Click the **Yes** button. The list of newsgroups available on the server from the account you just added downloads and appears in the Newsgroups Subscriptions dialog box. This may take a few moments. See Figure 7-10.

Figure 7-10	NEWSGROUP SUBSCRIPTIONS DIALOG BOX

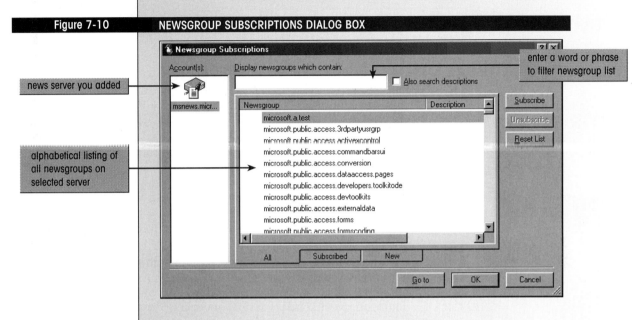

TROUBLE? If a dialog box opens, saying that Outlook Express was unable to retrieve a list of newsgroups available on the server, you may have clicked the password required check box. Right-click the Newsgroups from the list, click Properties, click the Server tab, click the Password required check box to remove the check mark, and then click the OK button.

You can review the list of newsgroups available on that server by scrolling or searching for a keyword, and then select one that interests you. Eric wants to find out whether there are any modifications they should make to their latest computer workspace design to accommodate people with special physical needs. You'll look for a newsgroup that focuses on disability issues; these newsgroups include the word "enable" in their name.

Although newsgroups are intended to focus on a specific issue or topic, adult content finds its way into most newsgroups. If you are offended by adult content, skip the rest of the steps in this section.

To go to a newsgroup:

1. Type **enable** in the Display newsgroups which contain text box. As you type, the list is filtered to display only those newsgroups that include the text you enter. See Figure 7-11.

Figure 7-11 FILTERED NEWSGROUPS LIST

newsgroups related to disability issues; your list may differ

click to view messages for selected newsgroup

drag column heading right to expand Newsgroup column width

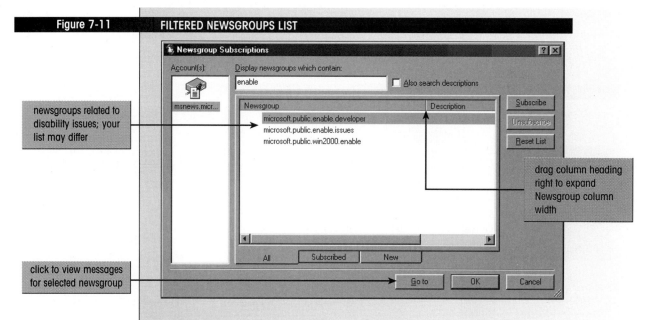

TROUBLE? If you can't see the entire name of the newsgroups, you can widen the Newsgroup column by dragging the border of its column heading to the right.

2. Click the **microsoft.public.enable.issues** newsgroup to select it.

   TROUBLE? If you don't see the microsoft.public.enable.issues newsgroup, then select another newsgroup of your choice.

3. Click the **Go to** button. All the message headers related to the topic appear in the newsreader. See Figure 7-12.

Figure 7-12 DOWNLOADED NEWSGROUP MESSAGES

news server and newsgroup listed in Folders pane

preview pane

downloaded message headers

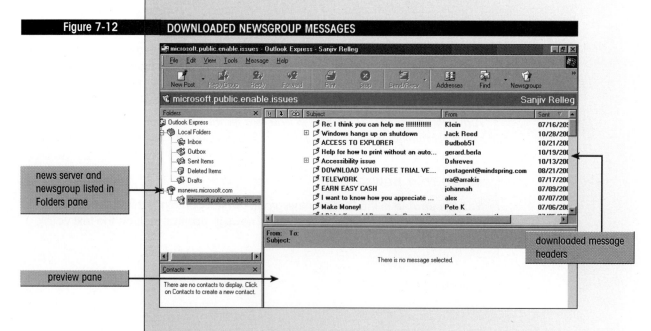

TROUBLE? If a dialog box opens, asking whether you'd like to make Outlook Express your current default news client, click the No button.

Outlook Express downloads the message headers rather than the complete message to save downloading time. You then review the headers and decide which messages you want to read. You'll review the message headers for the microsoft.public.enable.issues newsgroup.

Reading Newsgroup Messages

Newsgroups can contain thousands of messages, also called **articles** or **postings**, which can be time-consuming to sift through. Outlook Express has a variety of features that make it easier to find the information you want. Posted messages are sorted first by subject and then by their sent date (although you can change the sort order by clicking the column headers). Replies to a particular message are grouped with the original message, creating a **thread** or threaded discussion. Participants who are interested in a thread can expand the message group and read all the postings. Anyone uninterested in that thread then can scroll past that collapsed message thread to other postings. You read and reply to messages in the newsreader in much the same way as you do e-mail messages—select a message header to read the message in the preview pane. Unread messages appear in boldface.

To read newsgroup postings:

1. Click any message header. The message appears in the preview pane. If you prefer to read the message in its own window, you would double-click the message header.

2. Click the **Expand** button ⊞ next to a message. The threaded discussion expands to display all the replies. See Figure 7-13.

Figure 7-13	EXPANDED MESSAGE THREAD

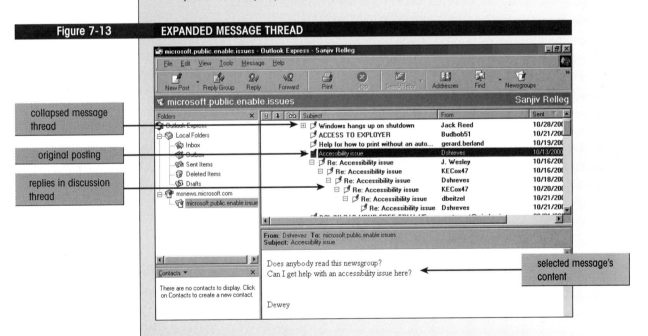

3. Click each message in the thread to display it in the preview pane, and then read it.

Some threads you'll find interesting and want to continue to review; others you'll want to ignore. You can choose to watch or ignore any message thread by clicking in the Watch/Ignore column next to that header. The first click inserts the watch icon 👓; the second click changes the icon to ignore 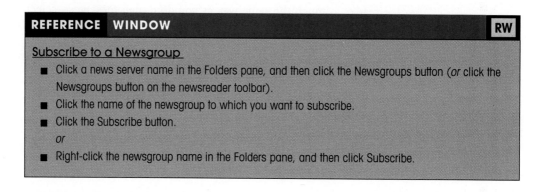; a third click removes any icon from the column. Then you can change the current view to control whether you see previously read or ignored messages. You also can set the Watch/Ignore status for any selected messages by clicking Message on the menu bar, and then clicking Watch Conversation or Ignore Conversation.

Subscribing to a Newsgroup

Some news servers contain thousands of newsgroups. Once you find a newsgroup you like and plan to access frequently, you can subscribe to it. Subscribing adds the newsgroup to the Folders pane, which makes it easier for you to return to that newsgroup. Although you can visit a newsgroup without subscribing to it, you would have to open the news server, scroll through a long list of newsgroups, and then select the newsgroup each time. A subscription is basically a shortcut to the specific newsgroup you want.

REFERENCE WINDOW   **RW**

<u>Subscribe to a Newsgroup</u>

- Click a news server name in the Folders pane, and then click the Newsgroups button (*or* click the Newsgroups button on the newsreader toolbar).
- Click the name of the newsgroup to which you want to subscribe.
- Click the Subscribe button.

   or
- Right-click the newsgroup name in the Folders pane, and then click Subscribe.

You'll subscribe to this newsgroup.

To subscribe to a newsgroup:

1. Click the **Newsgroups** button [Newsgroups] on the Outlook Express or Outlook news-reader toolbar. The Newsgroups Subscription dialog box opens.

   You'll again filter the list of available newsgroups so you can quickly find the one to which you want to subscribe.

2. Type **enable** in the Display newsgroups which contain text box.

3. Click the **microsoft.public.enable.issues** newsgroup to select it.

   TROUBLE? If you don't see the microsoft.public.enable.issues newsgroup, then select another newsgroup of your choice.

4. Click the **Subscribe** button. A subscription icon appears next to the newsgroup. See Figure 7-14.

Figure 7-14 | FILTERED NEWSGROUPS WITH SUBSCRIPTION

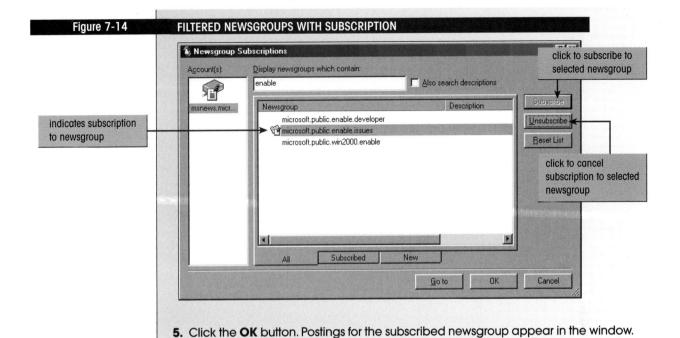

indicates subscription to newsgroup

click to subscribe to selected newsgroup

click to cancel subscription to selected newsgroup

5. Click the **OK** button. Postings for the subscribed newsgroup appear in the window.

You can subscribe to as many newsgroups as you like. You also can create accounts to other news servers and subscribe to newsgroups on them.

If you find messages that are particularly useful or relevant, you may want to print those postings for later reference. You can print newsgroups postings in the newsreader just like you would e-mail messages in Outlook. You can select multiple postings by pressing the Ctrl or Shift keys as you click postings.

To print newsgroup postings:

1. Click a posting to select it.

2. Click the **Print** button on the newsreader toolbar. The Print dialog box opens.

3. Verify your printer, and then click the **OK** button.

After subscribing to a newsgroup, you can select how you want to **synchronize** or update the newsgroup postings. Right now, the newsreader downloads the message headers, and you review the headers and read postings much as you would e-mail messages. If you prefer, you can choose to download the complete messages or only the new messages so you can disconnect from the Internet and work offline. You also can check for new postings at any time by clicking the Synchronize button. You'll review the settings.

To review newsgroups settings:

1. Click **msnews.microsoft.com** in the Folders pane.

TROUBLE? If a dialog box opens asking whether you want to subscribe to the newsgroup, click the No button.

The Information viewer shows any newsgroups to which you've subscribed, and provides options for changing the newsgroup settings. See Figure 7-15.

Figure 7-15   NEWS SERVER INFORMATION VIEWER

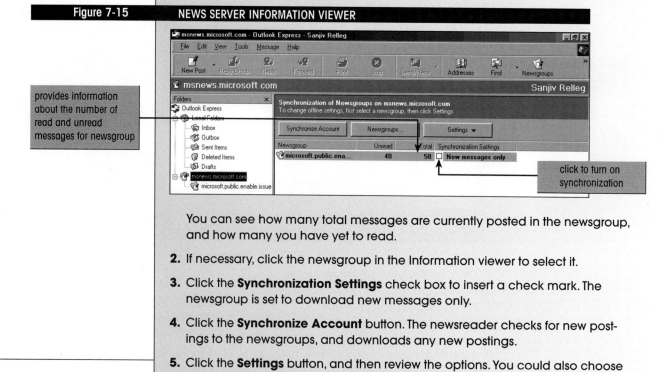

provides information about the number of read and unread messages for newsgroup

click to turn on synchronization

You can see how many total messages are currently posted in the newsgroup, and how many you have yet to read.

2. If necessary, click the newsgroup in the Information viewer to select it.

3. Click the **Synchronization Settings** check box to insert a check mark. The newsgroup is set to download new messages only.

4. Click the **Synchronize Account** button. The newsreader checks for new postings to the newsgroups, and downloads any new postings.

5. Click the **Settings** button, and then review the options. You could also choose to download all messages or only the headers.

6. Click **Don't Synchronize**, and then click the **Settings** button to verify that you selected the Don't Synchronize option.

You can return to the newsgroup you subscribed to by double-clicking its name in the Information viewer or clicking its name in the Folders pane.

7. Click the newsgroup name in the Folders pane to return to the postings.

After reading messages, you may want to post your own message. There doesn't seem to be a thread about Eric's issue—special desk design considerations for people with physical disabilities. You can post the questions on the newsgroup.

Posting Messages to a Newsgroup

Anyone who has access to a newsgroup can post and read messages as well as reply to previous postings. Some newsgroups are **moderated**, or monitored by a designated person who reviews all the postings and removes any that are inappropriate. However, most newsgroups are not moderated. This means that all messages, whether relevant or inappropriate, are posted to the newsgroup.

The Outlook Express newsreader toolbar provides access to working with messages in a newsgroup. Figure 7-16 describes the toolbar buttons.

Figure 7-16	OUTLOOK EXPRESS NEWSREADER TOOLBAR BUTTONS

BUTTON	ACTION
New Post	Creates a new message to post on the newsgroup.
Reply Group	Posts your reply to the selected message to the newsgroup.
Reply	Sends your reply as an e-mail message to only the person who posted the original message.
Forward	Sends the selected message to someone else as an e-mail message.
Print	Prints a copy of the selected message.
Stop	Terminates the sending and receiving of messages.
Send/Receive	Sends outgoing messages and downloads new messages.
Find	Opens the Find Message dialog box so you can locate a specific person or message.
Newsgroups	Opens the Newsgroup Subscriptions dialog box.

When you create a new posting or reply to posting, the Message window that opens looks similar to the e-mail Message window you worked with in Outlook. You have many of the same options as well. You can format your messages, and add your signature, business card, or links to files. Some of these options require that recipients use a newsreader that can read HTML—be aware that many newsreaders cannot.

Like e-mail, newsgroups follow some basic netiquette for sending out messages. Keep in mind the following guidelines as you participate in newsgroups:

- **Familiarize yourself with the newsgroup.** Read past messages *before you start posting* to find out what has already been discussed. Don't repeat what has already been said.
- **Use descriptive subject headers for your postings.** You want others to be able to determine the topic of your posting from the header.
- **Summarize what you are following up.** When posting a reply, include enough of the original message so others can tell what thought or comment you're responding to.
- **Follow the guidelines for sending e-mail messages.** Reread your messages; be concise; use standard capitalization; check spelling and grammar; avoid sarcasm; and don't send confidential information.

Remember that this is a public form of communication, and people around the globe can read your postings. You are not anonymous: your name and e-mail address are connected to your postings. Moreover, use common sense: only reveal ideas and thoughts you want the world to know, and don't give out your address or phone number.

For more information about newsgroups, you can search the Web using the keyword newsgroups or visit Web sites such as: **http://groups.google.com**; **http://www.liszt.com/select/news**, or **dir.yahoo.com/Computers_and_Internet/Internet/Chats_and_Forums/Usenet**.

Eric decides that he'll post his question later. For now, you'll cancel your subscription to the newsgroup.

To cancel a subscription and remove a newsgroup account:

1. Right-click **microsoft.public.enable.issues** in the Folders pane, and then click **Unsubscribe**. A dialog box opens, asking you to confirm that you want to unsubscribe from the newsgroup.

2. Click the **OK** button. The newsgroup is removed from the Folders pane.

    If you are not subscribed to any other newsgroups on the server, a dialog box opens, asking whether you want to view a list of available newsgroups.

3. Click the **No** button.

4. Right-click **msnews.microsoft.com** in the Folders pane, and then click **Remove Account**. A dialog box opens, asking you to confirm that you want to delete the newsgroup account.

5. Click the **Yes** button. The news server account is removed.

    You're done with the newsreader so you can close the newsreader.

6. Click the **Close** button ☒ on the title bar to close the newsreader program.

You now know how to view Web pages from Outlook to research information for ErgoDesign, and set up a folder home page and favorites shortcuts to return to certain pages quickly. You learned how to find and subscribe to newsgroups so you can participate in discussions with others interested in the same topic.

There may be times, however, when you want to share specific information that you gather or develop with people that you designate. In Session 7.2, you'll share the project folder you created with others by designating it as a Net Folder. Then you'll learn how to schedule an online meeting for NetMeeting and a presentation for NetShow.

Session 7.1 QUICK CHECK

1. List two ways you can open a Web page in Outlook.

2. What is a folder home page? Why would you use one?

3. What is a newsgroup?

4. How do you access newsgroups, download and read messages, and post replies to a newsgroup from Outlook?

5. Explain the difference between a private newsgroup and a public newsgroup.

6. List two other ways to refer to newsgroup messages.

7. What is a threaded discussion?

8. List three guidelines for posting messages to a newsgroup.

SESSION 7.2

In this session, you'll set up a Net Folder to share items with selected people. You'll set up the Net Folder, assign permission, and share items. Finally you'll schedule an online meeting with NetMeeting and NetShow.

Sharing Information over the Internet

A **Net Folder** is an Outlook folder that you share over the Internet or an intranet with anyone to whom you can send e-mail. You can use Net Folders to share messages, calendars, tasks, contacts, journals, or notes, as long as the other people are using Outlook. For example, you might create a Net Folder to send messages to a selected group of people. Be aware that anything you share in a Net Folder is not secure; the information is not encrypted in any way.

If someone is not using Outlook, you can still share e-mail messages, which that person receives in the Inbox or equivalent folder in their e-mail system. However, the remaining Outlook items are not shared because other e-mail programs cannot decipher them.

Creating Net Folders

The basic process for using Net Folders is to select or create the folder you want to share, make the folder sharable, and then permit specific people access to the folder. You can share any folder in Outlook as a Net Folder except the Inbox, the Outbox, Exchange folders, or Exchange Offline Folders.

Eric wants the Ergonomics folder you created earlier to be a Net Folder so the entire workstation design team for ErgoDesign can share notes as well as any documents that are posted in the folder.

To create a Net Folder:

1. If you took a break after the last session, make sure Outlook is running and the Ergonomics folder is displayed in the Information viewer.

2. Click **File** on the menu bar, and then point to **Share**. The menu shows the default Outlook folders you can share: Calendar, Tasks, and Contacts. The This Folder option enables you to share the displayed folder, as long as it is not the Inbox, the Outbox, or an Exchange folder.

   TROUBLE? If you don't see Share on the File menu, then the Net Folders add-in is not installed. Click Tools on the menu bar, click Options, and then click the Other tab in the Options dialog box. Click the Advanced Options button, and then click the Add-In Manager button. If Net Folders does not appear in the Add-In Manager dialog box, click the Install button, and then double-click the fldpub.ecf file. Click the Net Folders check box to insert a check mark, and then click the OK button in each dialog box.

3. Click **This Folder**. The first Net Folder Wizard dialog box opens, displaying information about sharing a folder.

OUT 7.22 TUTORIAL 7 USING OUTLOOK WITH THE INTERNET

> TROUBLE? If a dialog box opens, indicating that you need to install the feature and asking whether you want to install this feature now, click the Yes button. You may need the Office 2000 CD-ROM. Once the feature is installed, continue with Step 4.
>
> TROUBLE? If the Office Assistant opens, click the No, don't provide help now option.

4. Click the **Next** button. The second Net Folder Wizard dialog box opens, listing the people with whom you will share the folder. See Figure 7-17.

Figure 7-17   NET FOLDER WIZARD DIALOG BOX

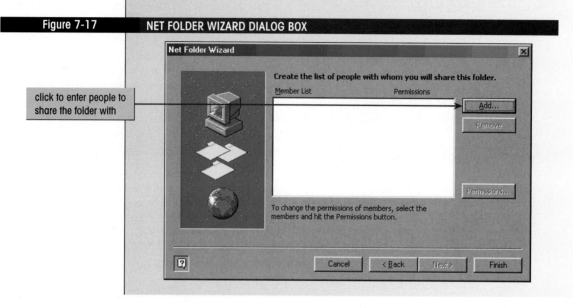

click to enter people to share the folder with

You can share a folder with one or more people.

Adding Subscribers

A person with whom you share a folder is called a **subscriber**. All subscribers duplicate the Net Folder in their Folder List just like they see their own folders. For example, after Eric sets up the Ergonomics folder to share with Chelsie, Ian, and the rest of the project team, they receive a copy of the Ergonomics folder in their Folder Lists. When Eric adds an item to his Ergonomics folder, the subscribers automatically receive that item in their folders; when Eric modifies an item in the shared folder, everyone else receives the update.

You can enter or select contacts for the Net Folder just like you select recipients for an e-mail message. You can add new subscribers at this time or select from people already entered in your contacts list, Address Book, or Global Address Book.

To add a subscriber to a Net Folder:

1. Click the **Add** button in the Net Folder Wizard dialog box. The Add Entries to Subscriber Database dialog box opens.

2. Click the **New** button to open the New Entry dialog box.

3. Verify that **New Contact** is selected in the Select the Entry type list box and that **Contacts** is selected in the Put this entry in the list box, and then click the **OK** button. A new Contact window opens.

TROUBLE? If you are using Lotus Notes or cc:Mail, you must add the contact to the Personal Address Book, rather than the Contacts folder. Click the Personal Address Book (your name) in the Put this entry in the list box, select Internet Mail Address in the Select the Entry type list box, and then click the OK button. In Step 5, you'll need to Show Names from the Personal Address Book.

4. Type **Chelsie Gradle** in the Full Name dialog box, and then type your e-mail address in the E-mail text box.

5. Right-click the e-mail address, click **Properties** on the shortcut menu, click the **Always send to this recipient in Microsoft Outlook rich-text format** check box to insert a check mark, and then click the **OK** button.

6. Click the **Save and Close** button ⊞ Save and Close on the Standard toolbar

7. Click **Contacts** in the Show Names from the list box, and then double-click **Chelsie Gradle (E-mail)** to move her name to the Entries to Add to Subscriber Database list. See Figure 7-18.

| Figure 7-18 | ADD ENTRIES TO SUBSCRIBER DATABASE DIALOG BOX |

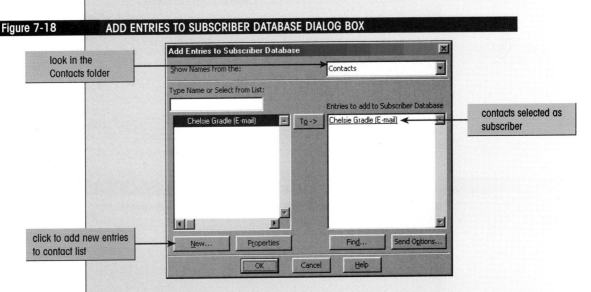

look in the Contacts folder

contacts selected as subscriber

click to add new entries to contact list

8. Click the **OK** button. Chelsie's name is added to the Member List in the Net Folder Wizard. See Figure 7-19.

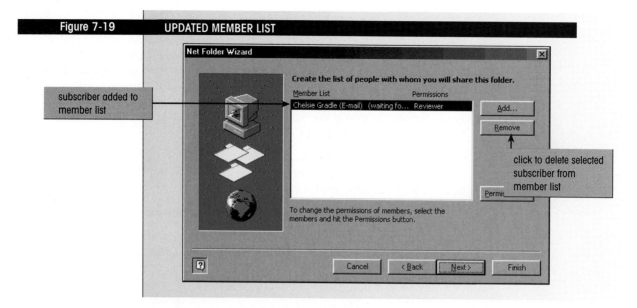

Figure 7-19   UPDATED MEMBER LIST

subscriber added to member list

click to delete selected subscriber from member list

The next step is to set the permissions level for each subscriber.

Setting Permissions

The level of permission assigned to a subscriber determines how that subscriber can work with items in the Net Folder. Permissions access ranges from read-only access to full editing access. Figure 7-20 lists and describes the subscriber access for each permission level.

Figure 7-20   PERMISSION LEVELS FOR NET FOLDERS

PERMISSION LEVEL	SUBSCRIBER ACCESS
Reviewer	Read any items and files but cannot create, modify, or delete items or files.
Contributor	Read and create items and files but cannot edit or delete any items or files, even the ones he or she created.
Author	Read and create items and files, and modify and delete only the items he or she created.
Editor	Read, create, modify, and delete all items and files.
Minimum (for subscribers who do not use Outlook)	Receive all items as attachments to e-mail messages. Any changes he or she makes to items are not updated to other members' folders.

When you add a subscriber to the Member List, Outlook assigns that person Reviewer permission, the lowest level of access. Reviewers can only read items in the shared folder, which provides the most security to the creator of the folder. Editors have the most access, which means they can alter the folder and its contents just like the creator. As the folder owner, Eric can change the access for any subscriber. For example, Eric might decide to give Editor permission to Chelsie so that she can add new items or change existing items in the Net Folder. Be aware that any items modified by qualified subscribers are updated in the original folder as well as in all subscriber folders.

To set permissions level:

1. If necessary, click **Chelsie Gradle** in the Member List to select the name.

You could use the Shift and Ctrl keys as needed to select multiple names if you wanted to give more than one person the same level of permission.

2. Click the **Permissions** button. The Net Folder Sharing Permissions dialog box opens.

3. Click the **Editor** option button to assign that permission level to Chelsie. See Figure 7-21.

Figure 7-21	NET FOLDER SHARING PERMISSIONS DIALOG BOX

permission level options

available when selected subscriber does not use Outlook

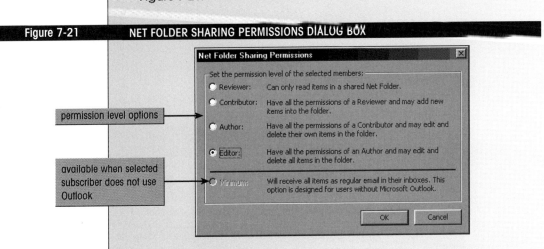

4. Click the **OK** button. The Permissions is updated for the member. See Figure 7-22.

Figure 7-22	MEMBER LIST WITH UPDATED PERMISSIONS

summary of subscriber status

click to set permissions for selected subscriber

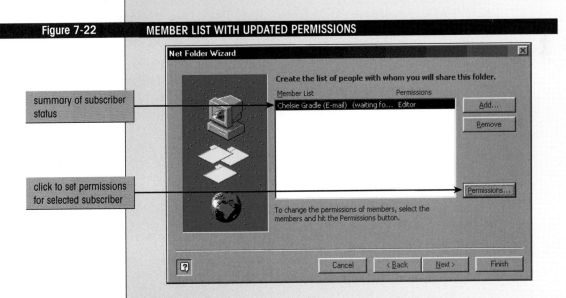

5. Click the **Next** button. The next Net Folders Wizard dialog box enables you to enter a fairly detailed description of the Net Folder. You should be concise and accurate. This description will appear in two places: (1) the e-mail message that subscribers receive notifying them about the Net Folder, and (2) the Description text box in the Properties dialog box for the folder.

6. Type **ErgoDesign's new workstation design** to describe the folder for the subscribers. See Figure 7-23.

Figure 7-23   **NET FOLDER DESCRIPTION**

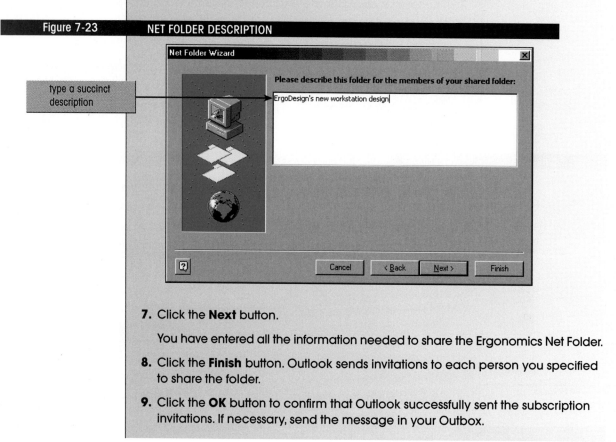

type a succinct
description

7. Click the **Next** button.

You have entered all the information needed to share the Ergonomics Net Folder.

8. Click the **Finish** button. Outlook sends invitations to each person you specified to share the folder.

9. Click the **OK** button to confirm that Outlook successfully sent the subscription invitations. If necessary, send the message in your Outbox.

At this point, each person you specified receives an invitation to subscribe to the folder. The invitation that subscribers receive describes how Net Folders work. They must accept the invitation to be subscribed to the folder. People who are not using Outlook will receive a notification message. You cannot subscribe yourself to someone else's Net Folder; the Net Folder owner must add you to the shared folder.

To accept a subscription to Net Folder:

1. If necessary, download your message. You must open the subscription message to read the invitation and accept the invitation to subscribe to a Net Folder.

2. Open the **New subscription to Ergonomics** message and read it. See Figure 7-24.

Figure 7-24	NEW SUBSCRIPTION TO ERGONOMICS MESSAGE

information about Net Folders and your permission level

specifies the Net Folder name on your computer

edit name to Ergonomics Copy

click to reject invitation to subscribe to folder

3. Type **Copy** after Ergonomics in the Local Folder Name text box. Usually, you would keep the name the same, but you want to be able to distinguish between the original folder and the Net Folder copy on your computer.

4. Click the **Accept** button. A dialog box opens, confirming that you have accepted the Net Folder and notifying you that the folder contents will be available shortly.

5. Click the **OK** button.

6. If necessary, send the message.

Now you're subscribed and have access to the Net Folder according to the permission level set by the Net Folder owner. If you need a higher level of permission access, you must ask the Net Folder owner to change your permission level.

The process for adding additional subscribers or removing current subscribers and changing subscriber permission levels is the same as the process for adding the original subscribers. You open the wizard dialog box with the members list, and then add or remove subscribers or modify permission levels as needed.

Updating a Net Folder

The benefit of using a Net Folder to share information becomes apparent once you send a note. You'll create a note in the Ergonomics folder and then see it appear in the Ergonomics Copy folder.

To create a note to share in the Net Folder:

1. Open the **Ergonomics** folder using the Folder List.

2. Create a new yellow note with the text **I'll plan a meeting for all of us to discuss the design features for the new workstation.**, and then close the note.

By default, updates are sent out from the Net Folder every ten minutes. You can change this frequency by selecting from a list of interval options that spans from five minutes to one day to better suit your needs. Because Outlook sends updates in the background during your computer's idle time, the frequency interval you select is approximate. If the computer is processing other tasks, the update may be delayed until the computer is free. You also can choose to send out the Net Folder update immediately, which you'll do for the note you created.

To send out an immediate update of a Net Folder:

1. Right-click the shared **Ergonomics** folder, and then click **Properties** on the shortcut menu. The Ergonomics Properties dialog box opens.

2. Click the **Sharing** tab. You can review all the default update settings. See Figure 7-25.

Figure 7-25 | **SHARING TAB IN THE ERGONOMICS PROPERTIES DIALOG BOX**

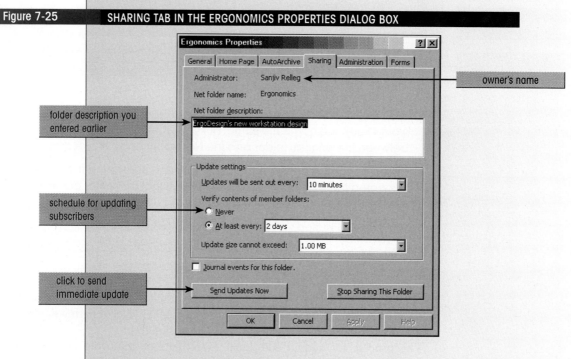

owner's name

folder description you entered earlier

schedule for updating subscribers

click to send immediate update

3. Click the **Send Updates Now** button.

4. Click the **OK** button to close the Ergonomics Properties dialog box.

The Sharing tab enables owners to verify that subscribers have received all the items in the Net Folder, set by default to two days. Outlook sends hidden messages between the owner and all subscribers to check the contents of the shared folder. This process adds extra traffic to the mail system, slowing down the delivery of all messages, so you should use the longest verification interval you can.

Stop Sharing a Net Folder

At a certain point either a subscriber or owner may decide not to share a folder, such as when a subscriber is reassigned to a different department or when a project is completed. The way you stop sharing a Net Folder depends on whether you're the subscriber or the owner. If you're the subscriber, you can cancel your subscription and stop receiving updates to the folder. The folder remains in your Folder List and any items previously received are still stored there until the subscriber deletes them. When you cancel your subscription, the original Net Folder and other subscribers remain unaffected. If you're the Net Folder owner, you can choose to stop sharing the folder. This procedure affects all subscribers to the folders.

First, cancel your subscription to the Ergonomics Copy folder.

To cancel your subscription to a Net Folder:

1. Right-click the shared **Ergonomics Copy** folder, and then click **Properties** on the shortcut menu. The Ergonomics Copy Properties dialog box opens.

2. Click the **Sharing** tab. See Figure 7-26.

Figure 7-26	SHARING TAB IN THE ERGONOMICS COPY DIALOG BOX

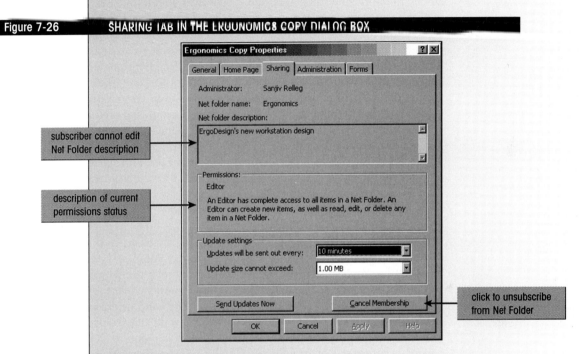

subscriber cannot edit Net Folder description

description of current permissions status

click to unsubscribe from Net Folder

3. Click the **Cancel Membership** button. A dialog box opens, asking you to confirm that you want to cancel your membership to the Net Folder, and reminding you that the Net Folder on your computer will remain intact although you will not receive any updates.

4. Click the **Yes** button. A message to the Net Folder owner is sent with notification that you have cancelled your membership.

Next, you'll stop sharing the Ergonomics folder, which you own.

To stop sharing a Net Folder you own:

1. Right-click the shared **Ergonomics** folder, and then click **Properties** on the shortcut menu.

2. Click the **Sharing** tab.

3. Click the **Stop Sharing This Folder** button. A dialog box opens, informing you that all subscribers will be removed and the folder will not longer be a Net Folder.

4. Click the **Yes** button. A notification of the change in the Net Folder status is sent by e-mail to all subscribers.

5. If necessary, send and receive your messages.

The folder is no longer shared and all subscriptions are cancelled. Former subscribers will no longer receive any updates. The folder, with the last updates they received, remains on subscribers' computers until they delete it.

Scheduling Online Meetings and Presentations

Business trips are becoming an expense of the past. It is no longer necessary to gather colleagues from around the country or world in one room to discuss an ongoing project, project financial status for the upcoming quarter, or plan a presentation. Nowadays, people can be scattered around the world and still collaborate effectively. For example, Eric, Chelsie, and Ian no longer have to meet in the same room to discuss their latest workstation design as long as they have access to the Internet and a program like NetMeeting. **NetMeeting**, a program that comes with Internet Explorer, enables two or more participants to communicate over the Internet or an intranet. In addition to the speech interaction of a telephone conference call, NetMeeting participants can also communicate by typing messages to each other, and even sharing files and applications. With the proper equipment they can even use real-time video. This is useful for providing technical support, conducting training sessions, and offering distance learning classes.

The amount of extra equipment you need depends on how you plan to use NetMeeting. You can use NetMeeting without video or audio. If you want to use the sound capabilities of NetMeeting, you will need a microphone, sound card, and speakers, which are fairly common today. You don't need any extra equipment to view another participant's video; if you want to send video you will need a camera and video card. Such collaboration allows two or more people to work on one document at the same time, or see each other and converse even if the people are in different locations.

All attendees must be running NetMeeting to participate in the online meeting. One way to ensure that the participants are available and running NetMeeting is to schedule a NetMeeting. You can schedule a NetMeeting in much the same way as you schedule a regular meeting. After opening a Meeting window, you schedule the meeting as usual, and then specify that the meeting is an online meeting. The window expands so that you can specify the directory service, select whether you want to send all participants a reminder notice and start the meeting automatically, and select a document to collaborate on. A **directory server** or **Internet Locator Server (ILS)** is a server that lists individuals who are available for a NetMeeting. If you don't have access to a private ILS, you can find a listing of public ILSs at **www.netmeet.net**, **www.visitalk.com**, **www.netmeetinghq.com**, and other Web sites. NetMeeting has a Directories Information viewer, which displays a list of people who are connected to the selected directory server.

You must be using NetMeeting 2.1 or later to schedule a NetMeeting.

Another online meeting option is NetShow. A **NetShow** is an audiovisual presentation that people you specify can view online from the Internet or an intranet. NetShow broadcasts the presentation as **streaming** content, sound or video that is played as it is downloaded. For example, Eric can set up a presentation about the latest ErgoDesign desk for potential customers to view with NetShow.

REFERENCE WINDOW   RW

Scheduling a NetMeeting or NetShow

- Create a meeting request, fill out the meeting information.
- Click the This is an online meeting using check box to insert a check mark.
- Click Microsoft NetMeeting, verify the directory server, and then select a document if necessary (or click Microsoft NetShow and enter the address of the broadcast).
- Send the meeting request.
- Click Start Meeting on the reminder message.

You'll schedule a meeting with Chelsie for tomorrow to discuss the workstation design.

To schedule a NetMeeting:

1. If necessary click the **Outlook** button on the taskbar, click the **New** button list arrow 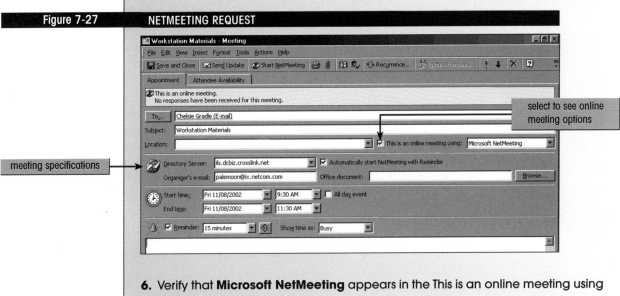 on the Standard toolbar, and then click **Meeting Request**. A new Meeting window opens.

2. Click the **To** button to open the Select Attendees and Resources dialog box.

3. Verify that Show names from the **Contacts** is selected, double-click **Chelsie Cradle** to add her to the list of required attendees, and then click the **OK** button.

4. Type **Workstation Materials** in the Subject text box. This meeting description will appear as the NetMeeting conference name.

5. Click the **This is an online meeting using** check box to insert a check mark. The window expands to show additional options, as shown in Figure 7-27.

Figure 7-27	NETMEETING REQUEST

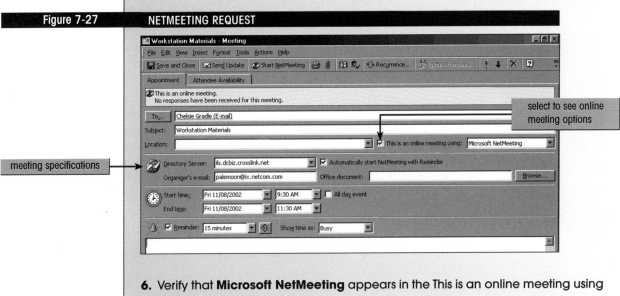

6. Verify that **Microsoft NetMeeting** appears in the This is an online meeting using list box.

7. Type **ils.dcbiz.crosslink.net** in the Directory Server list box, and then verify your e-mail address.

   If you had selected NetShow Services, you would enter the address of the broadcast rather than the directory server.

8. Click the **Automatically start NetMeeting with Reminder** check box to insert a check mark.

   Participants will receive a reminder notice before the meeting by the amount of time specified in the Reminder text box, and NetMeeting will start automatically.

9. Enter a Start time of **tomorrow** at **9:30 AM** and then enter an End time of **tomorrow** at **11:30 AM**.

10. Send the meeting invitation, and then verify the NetMeeting appears on your calendar for tomorrow.

Recipients must reply to the NetMeeting invitation just as they would a regular meeting invitation. Before the meeting, scheduled attendees will receive a message with a reminder that the meeting will begin shortly.

When you want to join a NetMeeting as a participant, you can click the Join Meeting button on the meeting request or the Reminder message. You also can right-click the meeting item on your calendar, and then click the Join Meeting option. The meeting organizer will see Start Meeting rather than Join Meeting.

All participants in the current call are listed in the NetMeeting Current Call Information viewer along with information about their audio, video, and file and application sharing capabilities.

Depending on their capabilities, participants can collaborate in a variety of ways. NetMeeting participants can see what other meeting participants are doing, exchange text messages with Chat, draw with others on an electronic Whiteboard, share applications and documents, or transfer files.

Cleaning Up

As you work in Outlook, you should continually remove outdated items. For example, you no longer need the shortcut you added to the Favorites folder. You'll delete it to keep the list streamlined and current.

To delete a shortcut from Favorites:

1. Click **Favorites** on the menu bar and then click **Open** Favorites. The Favorites dialog box opens, showing the folders and shortcuts saved in Favorites.

   TROUBLE? If you created the ErgoDesign folder and favorites shortcut on your Data Disk, click the Cancel button in the Favorites dialog box and then skip this set of steps.

2. Click the **ErgoDesign** folder, and then press the **Delete** key. A dialog box opens, asking you to confirm the deletion.

3. Click the **Yes** button. The folder and shortcut are moved to the Deleted Items folder.

4. Click the **Cancel** button to close the Favorites dialog box.

You also want to delete other Outlook items you created in this tutorial.

To delete the other Outlook items:

1. Delete the **Ergonomics** folder and the **Ergonomics Copy** folder from the Folder List.

2. Delete any e-mail messages you created in this tutorial from the Inbox, Outbox, and Sent Items folders.

3. Delete **Chelsie Gradle** from the Contacts folder.

4. Delete the notes in the Notes folder.

5. Delete the meeting scheduled for tomorrow from the Calendar folder.

6. Empty the **Deleted Items** folder.

> **7.** Close the Folder List.
>
> **8.** Right-click the **Web** toolbar, and then click **Web** to close the toolbar.

The design for the latest addition to the ErgoDesign catalog is coming along nicely. The team appreciates all the information you collected on the Web. The online meeting and collaboration tools are speeding up the planning and production phases.

Session 7.2 QUICK CHECK

1. What is a Net Folder?

2. If you want a subscriber to be able to read items and files in a Net Folder but not create, modify, or delete them, what level of permissions would you assign that person?

3. True or False: Once you are subscribed to a Net Folder, you can change your permission level at any time without asking the Net Folder owner.

4. Outlook sends updates at intervals set on the Sharing tab in the Net Folder's Properties dialog box. Why is the interval approximate?

5. What is a drawback of verifying every five minutes that subscribers have received items during Net Folder updates?

6. What happens when a subscriber cancels a subscription to a Net Folder?

7. Explain the purpose of NetMeeting.

8. What is a NetShow?

REVIEW ASSIGNMENTS

Ian Zelinsky is working on the marketing plan for the upcoming workstation from ErgoDesign. Ian wants you to look for similar products available from ErgoDesign's competitors. Then you'll look for a newsgroup that discusses information technology issues, and watch for relevant messages. Finally you'll create a Net Folder to share information related to marketing ErgoDesign's products.

1. Start Outlook, switch to the Contacts folder, create a contact card for Ian Zelinsky with your e-mail address, and then display the Web toolbar.

2. Open the Computer Furniture Direct Web page at **www.cf-direct.com** using the Web toolbar.

3. Click the link to the online catalog, and then click the link to the Power Works series. (If these links are not available, then choose two links of your choice.)

Explore ▷ 4. E-mail the Web page you are viewing to Ian. Click Actions on the menu bar, and then click Send Web Page by E-mail. A Message window opens with the subject completed and the Web page included as an attachment. Click the To button, select Ian from your contact list, then type the message "This is our biggest competitor. Let's review the catalog carefully.", press the Enter key twice, and then type your name. Send the message.

5. Go back to the previous page, and then click the link to the Enthusiasts series (or another link).

6. Return to the company's home page, and then add it to your Favorites list in a new folder named "Competitors"; use the company name as the shortcut name. (If you can't

modify the Favorites list, create the new folder in the Review folder within the Tutorial.07 folder on your Data Disk.)

7. Click the FAQs link (or another link if this is not available), and then use the shortcut you added to Favorites to return to the company's home page.

8. Create a new folder named "Marketing" that contains Mail Items placed in Personal Folders; do not add a shortcut to the Outlook Bar.

9. Download the Computer Furniture Direct message, and then move the message from the Inbox to the new Marketing folder.

 10. Create a folder home page for the Marketing folder with the URL **www.office-ergo.com**; show the home page by default. The folder home page appears in the Information viewer. If you don't see the folder home page, click the Marketing folder in the Folder List.

 11. Click the Marketing folder again. The folder content appears in the Information viewer.

12. Open the newsreader, set up a new account to the **msnews.microsoft.com** news server, and then download the newsgroups.

 13. Filter the newsgroups to display those related to "tool," subscribe to the **microsoft.public.it.tool** newsgroup, filter the list using the keyword "news," and then subscribe to the **microsoft.public.news.server** newsgroup. Click the OK button in the Newsgroup Subscriptions dialog box.

14. Click the **microsoft.public.news.server** newsgroup in the Folders pane to download the message headers.

15. Read some of the latest messages, expanding and collapsing message threads as necessary. Watch one that interests you and ignore one that doesn't.

 16. Return to the message thread you watched, and print one of the messages. (*Hint:* Select the message header of the article you want to print, click File on the menu bar, click Print, verify the settings in the Print dialog box, and then click the OK button.)

17. Cancel your subscription to the **microsoft.public.it.tool newsgroup**.

18. Remove the news account from the Folders pane using the shortcut menu. Any newsgroup subscriptions are deleted with the account.

19. Close the newsreader.

20. Create a Net Folder from the Marketing folder with Ian as a subscriber with Contributor permission and the description "Use the Marketing folder for any material related to competitive information or our selling points, such as ergonomics."

21. Accept the subscription, but change the Net Folder name to "Marketing Copy".

 22. Change Ian's permission level to Editor. (*Hint:* Open the Net Folder Wizard, select Ian in the Members List, and then click the Permissions button to change the level.)

23. Move the Net Folder Notification message from the Inbox to the Marketing folder, and then Send Updates Now.

24. Print the messages in the Marketing Copy folder in Memo Style. The Marketing Copy has the same folder home page as the Marketing folder.

25. Cancel your subscription to the Marketing Copy folder, stop sharing the Marketing folder, and then remove the folder home page from the Marketing folder.

26. Verify that the folder home page still exists for the Marketing Copy folder.

27. Schedule an hour NetMeeting with Ian on the subject "Competitive Analysis" for next Tuesday starting at 2 PM using **ils.dcbiz.crosslink.net** as the directory server. Do not start the meeting with a reminder. Send the request.

28. Verify the appointment in your calendar. Open and print the appointment, and then delete it from the calendar.

29. Delete the Competitors folder and shortcut you added to Favorites, delete the Marketing and Marketing Copy folders, delete Ian's contact card, and then delete any messages in the Inbox, Outbox, and Sent Items folders.

30. Empty the Deleted Items folder, close the Folder List, and then hide the Web toolbar.

31. Exit Outlook.

CASE PROBLEMS

Case 1. Plan for Visitors Friends will be visiting you in several weeks. In preparation, you want to plan events and activities for their stay. You'll search the Web for information about your state or province.

1. Start Outlook, and then display the Web toolbar.

2. Enter **www.towd.com** in the Address text box of the Web toolbar in Outlook. The Web site for the Tourism Offices Worldwide Directory opens.

3. Save the Web page as a Favorite in a new folder called "Tourism" with its default name.

Explore ▶ 4. Open the Internet Explorer Web browser from Outlook. Click View on the menu bar, point to Go To, and then click Web Browser. Internet Explorer displays the default start page.

> TROUBLE? If you see the message This page cannot be displayed, Internet Explorer isn't set up to connect automatically to the Internet. Click the OK button in the dialog box, click File on the menu bar, and then click Work Offline. Click Tools on the Internet Explorer menu bar, click Internet Options, click the Connections tab, select a dial-up setting, click the Set Default button, click the Always dial my default connection option button, click the OK button, and then close Internet Explorer.

Explore ▶ 5. Using the Favorites menu in Internet Explorer, click add the shortcut to the URL you just created.

6. Select your state or province, click the Search button, and then click the link to open the Web page of the tourism office for your state or province. (*Hint:* You may need to click several links to get to the tourism office's Web page.)

7. Save the URL for the tourism office's home page in the Tourism folder, and then close Internet Explorer.

8. Use the Favorites list in Outlook to open the tourism office page.

Explore ▶ 9. E-mail the Web page you're viewing to yourself. Click Actions on the menu bar, and then click Send Web Page by E-mail. Complete the Message window as usual, and then send the message.

10. Create a folder named "Tourism" that contains Mail Items in the Inbox; do not add a shortcut to the Outlook Bar.

11. Download your messages, and then move the message to the Tourism folder.

Explore ▶ 12. Set up a folder home page for the Tourism folder using the URL listed in the message you just received; show the home page by default.

13. Switch to the Inbox, and then return to the Tourism folder. The folder home page appears in the Information viewer.

14. Click a link on that page, and then click the Back button to return to the previous page.

15. Click the Tourism folder again to display the folder content.

Explore ▶ 16. Search for other Web pages about tourism for your state or province. Click the Search button on the Web toolbar, enter appropriate search text (such as your state name) and start the search.

17. Click a link in the search results to view a Web page, and then click the Back button to return to the search results. After viewing at least three sites, display a Web page that includes interesting information about your state or province. Print the Web page.

18. Save the e-mail message and the attachment in the Tourism folder as a Text Only file with the name **My State** followed by the default name assigned by Outlook in the **Cases** folder within the **Tutorial.07** folder on your Data Disk.

19. Remove the folder home page from the Tourism folder.

20. Delete any Outlook items you created in this case, including the Favorites shortcut and folder and e-mail messages, empty the Deleted Items folder, and then exit Outlook.

Case 2. Participate in a Newsgroup   Newsgroups are a fun way to carry on discussions with like-minded people about a certain topic. Even if your family and friends don't share your interest, there is sure to be a newsgroup of others who are just as intrigued by that topic, hobby, or activity, whether an unusual music type, a favorite food, an obscure sport, or rare collection.

1. Start Outlook, and then open the newsreader from Outlook.
2. Set up a new account to a news server of your choice. One option is: **msnews.microsoft.com**.
3. Download the newsgroups on the server, and then search for a newsgroup that interests you.
4. Go to the newsgroup to ensure that it is one you like. If not, continue to look for and go to newsgroups until you find one you like.
5. Subscribe to the newsgroup.
6. Download the message headers for the newsgroup.

Explore   7. Click the Subject column heading to sort list by topic.

Explore   8. Click the Sent column heading to sort list by date.

9. Read the past message to get a sense of what the newsgroup is currently discussing as well as past topics. You may want to do this over the course of a few days.

Explore   10. If the newsgroup has more than 300 messages, only the first 300 headers are downloaded. Click Tools on the menu bar, and then click Get Next 300 headers to review more messages.

11. Watch any messages or threads you find interesting; ignore those you don't.

Explore   12. Post a message or respond to a current message thread.

13. Continue responding to the discussion thread as needed.
14. Print all the messages related to the thread you initiated or participated in.
15. Unsubscribe to the newsgroup.
16. Delete the news account from the Folders pane using the shortcut menu.
17. Close the newsreader and then exit Outlook.

Case 3. Insight Productions   Insight Productions produces independent films and documentaries that explore events, people, and issues that are rarely profiled. The company is ready to begin a new project about the electoral process in the United States. You will use Net Folders to make sure the entire project team is kept up to date. If possible, complete this case with a classmate.

1. Start Outlook, create a new contact card using a classmate's name and e-mail address (or a fictional name and your e-mail address).
2. Create a new folder named "Insight" that contains Mail Items placed in the Personal Folders; do not add a shortcut to the Outlook Bar.
3. Create a Net Folder from the Insight folder.
4. Add the contact you created as a subscriber with Editor permission.
5. Enter an appropriate description about the project for the Net Folder.
6. Accept the subscription, but change the Net Folder name to "Project Info".

Explore   7. Change the subscriber's permission level to Contributor.

Explore   8. Add a subscriber to the Insight folder by creating a new contact (use a fictional name and your e-mail address); give the new subscriber Reviewer permission. (*Hint:* Select the folder, click File on the menu bar, point to Share, and then click This Folder.)

Explore   9. Decline the subscription for the new contact. (If you are working alone, click the OK button in the dialog box, and then delete the message as recommended.)

10. Switch to the Insight folder, create a new Office document, create a new Word document to post in the folder. Type "Before we begin, we'll need to decide whether to focus on presidential elections, local elections, or both." Post the document.
11. Send updates now for the Insight Net Folder.
12. Switch to the Project Info folder, create a new Office document, and create a new Excel worksheet to post in the folder. Enter possible titles for the new film in cells A1, A2, and A3, and then post the worksheet.

Explore   13. Send updates now for the Project Info Net Folder.

14. Cancel your subscription to the Project Info Net folder.

Explore   15. Stop sharing the Insight folder from the Net Folder Wizard. (*Hint:* Select the folder, click File on the menu bar, point to Share, and then click This Folder. Click the Stop Sharing This Folder button.)

16. Delete the Insight and Project Info folders, delete the contact cards you created, and delete any messages from the Inbox, Outbox, and Sent Items folders.

17. Empty the Deleted Items folder, close the Folder List, and then exit Outlook.

Case 4. My Landscaping   When a group of people need to collaborate actively, a NetMeeting enables everyone to gather together without having to be in the same physical location. Attendees can then have voice discussions, exchange written messages, share files and documents, and even draw on a community whiteboard. To ensure participants are available and running the program, you can schedule a NetMeeting in Outlook.

As owner of a landscaping company, you often meet with potential clients to discuss how they would like to landscape their yards. If possible, conduct a NetMeeting with a classmate to discuss the possible landscaping for a home. You will need to have NetMeeting set up and access to a directory server.

1. Start Outlook, create a new contact card using a fictional name and your e-mail address (or use a classmate's name and address, if you will be working with a partner).

2. Schedule a NetMeeting for a convenient time with the contact you created. Print the meeting invitation, and then send it.

3. Accept the invitation to the NetMeeting.

4. Start NetMeeting, if necessary. Click View on the menu bar, point to Go To, point to Internet Call, and then click Internet Call.

Explore   5. If you are working with a classmate, host a meeting and have your classmate join you. Communicate by speaking or video if you both have those capabilities. (*Hint:* Log onto the directory server, click Call on the menu bar, and then click Host Meeting. Your classmate then double-clicks your name in the directory.)

6. Click Tools on the NetMeeting menu bar, and then click Chat to open Chat.

Explore   7. Exchange at least three messages about landscaping for a home. You can discuss such things as types of trees, grass, and flowers, the necessary amount of upkeep, and a possible budget. (*Hint:* Type a message in the Chat Message text box, and then press the Enter key.)

8. Save your Chat session as **My Meeting Chat** in the **Cases** folder within the **Tutorial.07** folder on your Data Disk. (*Hint:* Click File on the menu bar, and then click Save.)

9. Click the Close button in the Chat title bar to close Chat.

10. Click Tools on the menu bar, and then click Whiteboard to open the Whiteboard.

11. Start Word, and open the file called **House** in the **Cases** folder within the **Tutorial.07** folder on your Data Disk.

Explore   12. Copy the image from the document you opened onto the page. Return to the Whiteboard. Click the Select Area button on the toolbar, and then click the OK button in the dialog box if necessary. The Word document reappears. Drag the pointer from the upper-left corner of the image to the lower-right corner of the image in the document window to select the area you want to copy. When you release the mouse button, the image is pasted into the Whiteboard. (*Hint:* If you run into problems, clear the partial image from the Whiteboard by clicking the Eraser button and clicking the image. Then, try again.)

Explore   13. You (and your classmate) draw on the image to indicate where you would plant flowers, grass, and trees. Experiment with the drawing tools, line widths, and colors. (*Hint:* Click a drawing tool and then drag the pointer on the Whiteboard page.)

Explore   14. Magnify the image by clicking the Zoom button, and then reduce the image by clicking the button again. (*Hint:* There are only two zoom levels.)

15. Save the Whiteboard as **My Meeting Whiteboard** in the **Cases** folder within the **Tutorial.07** folder on your Data Disk.

Explore 16. If you are working with a classmate, share your Word program which already is open. Click Tools on the menu bar, point to Share Applications, and then click Word. Your classmate sees the program and your name appears in the upper-right corner of the window.

Explore 17. In the Word document, type "My Landscaping Company" and then press the Enter key. Click the Collaborate button on the toolbar. Your classmate can now use the program. Together, write a paragraph that accurately describes your views about landscaping as a business. (*Hint:* The person who wants to take control of the program, double-clicks the shared program.) When you're done, press the Esc key.

18. Save the Word document as **My Landscaping Business** in the **Cases** folder within the **Tutorial.07** folder on your Data Disk. Exit Word.

19. Click the Hang Up button to end the call, if necessary, and then close NetMeeting.

20. Delete any items you created in this case, including the contact card, e-mail messages, and calendar appointments.

21. Empty the Deleted Items folder, and then exit Outlook.

QUICK | CHECK ANSWERS

Session 7.1

1. Type its URL in the Address list box of the Web toolbar; select the shortcut from the Favorites menu.

2. A Web page you assign to an Outlook folder; you switch between displaying the folder contents and the assigned Web page. Useful when you frequently visit a Web page or the Web page contains updated information such as a roster of employees.

3. A collection of messages related to a specific subject written by individuals and then posted to a news server.

4. By using the Outlook Express newsreader.

5. A private newsgroup requires participants to enter a user name and password to join the discussion, limiting access to authorized members. A public newsgroup is open to everyone.

6. Articles or postings

7. Replies to a particular message in a newsgroup that is grouped with the original message.

8. Any three of the following: familiarize yourself with the newsgroup; use descriptive subject headings for your postings; summarize what you are following up; reread your messages; be concise; use standard capitalization; check spelling and grammar; avoid sarcasm; don't send confidential information.

Session 7.2

1. An Outlook folder that you share over the Internet or an intranet with anyone to whom you can send e-mail.

2. Reviewer

3. False; only the Net Folder owner can change permission levels for subscribers.

4. Outlook sends updates in the background during the computer's idle time. If the computer is processing other tasks, the update may be delayed until the computer is free.

5. Outlook sends hidden messages to verify the contents of shared folders between the owner and subscribers, which adds extra traffic to the mail system, slowing down the delivery of all messages.

6. The subscriber stops receiving updates to the folder, but the folder and any items previously received remain there until deleted.

7. NetMeeting is a program that enables two or more participants to communicate over the Internet or an intranet.

8. A NetShow is an audiovisual presentation that people you specify can view online from the Internet or an intranet.

OBJECTIVES

In this appendix you will:

- Grant delegate access

- Generate an out-of-office message

- Create Exchange offline folders

- Synchronize offline folders

USING OUTLOOK WITH MICROSOFT EXCHANGE

CASE

Microsoft Exchange Server (or just **Exchange**) is a mail server used for corporate messaging and collaboration systems that runs under Windows 2000 and Windows NT Server. To use Outlook with Exchange, you must add the Exchange Server information service to your profile. Then you have access to all of the capabilities in Outlook, including such features as:

- Message recall to retrieve or replace messages that recipients have not yet opened (see Tutorial 4)
- Voting buttons to gather and track responses about topics by polling recipients through e-mail (see Tutorial 4)
- Group scheduling to plan a meeting, using the free/busy times of attendees, locations, and equipment (see Tutorial 3)
- Public folders to share files and Outlook items among a group
- Delegate access permission to allow another person to work in your folders
- Out of Office Assistant to send an automatic response to incoming messages
- Offline folders to work remotely and synchronize folder contents with those on the Exchange Server computer

Exchange saves information on the server in **stores**. The Public store is used for shared information. Any user can create a public folder within the store, and then allow a specific group of people to access it, such as a workgroup, department, or entire organization. For example, Human Resources might post the company's calendar of upcoming events and holiday schedule for the year in a public folder so all employees can read it, rather than creating and distributing paper copies each time the calendar is updated. The Private store is used for your e-mail messages and other personal information. If you'd like, you can grant specific people access to folders in your Private store. You also can choose to save your e-mail messages and other information in a Personal Folder file on your computer's hard drive.

Grant **Delegate Access**

If you have a secretary, an assistant, or others whom you have send e-mail messages or schedule your appointments and meetings for you, then you can make those people delegates so they can perform these actions on your behalf right from Outlook. A **delegate** is a person who has permission to access someone else's folders. Depending on the assigned permission level, a delegate may read, create, modify, and delete items from those folders. The folder owner determines which folders delegates can access and what permission levels the delegates have. You can grant others delegate access to your Calendar, Tasks, Inbox, Contacts, Notes, and Journal folders, choosing one of the following permission levels for each folder:

- **None**—no permission; delegates cannot open a folder and cannot read, create, or modify items.
- **Reviewer**—delegates can only read items.
- **Author**—delegates can read and create items, and can modify and delete items they created.
- **Editor**—delegates can read, create, modify, and delete any items.

You might give an administrative assistant Editor delegate access to your Inbox, Calendar, Tasks, and Contacts folders, which enables that person to manage your messages, your schedule, send and reply to meeting and task requests, and update your contact list. Or, you might allow a colleague Reviewer access to your Inbox so that person can read your messages while you're out of the office but cannot create or modify or delete any items. You decide how much you want a delegate to be able to do for you and from which folders. If you assign more than one delegate to the same folder, all delegates receive the same permission level.

The Delegate Access feature is available only in Exchange Server. You must be connected to the server and the Delegate Access add-in must be installed.

To set sharing permissions for a delegate:

1. Click **Tools** on the menu bar, click **Options** to open the Options dialog box, and then click the **Delegates** tab. See Figure A-1.

Figure A-1	DELEGATES TAB OF OPTIONS DIALOG BOX

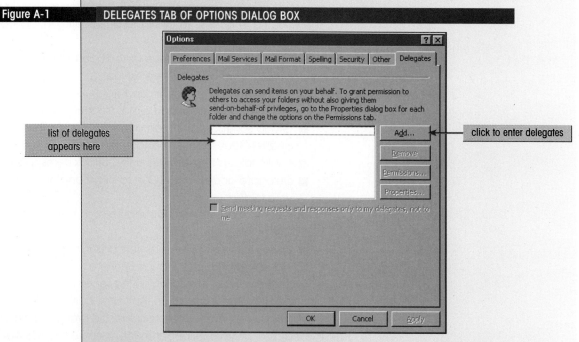

list of delegates appears here

click to enter delegates

TROUBLE? If the Delegates tab is not available, then you may need to install the Delegate Access add-in. Click the Other tab in the Options dialog box, click the Advanced Options button, and then click the Add-in Manager button in the Advanced Options dialog box. Click the Delegate Access check box to insert a check mark, and then click the OK button. If the Delegate Access check box is not available, click the Install button, and then set up the add-in. Click the OK button in the Add-in Manager dialog box, and then click the OK button in the Advanced Options dialog box. If you still have trouble, ask your instructor or technical support person for help.

2. Click the **Add** button. The Add Users dialog box opens. See Figure A-2.

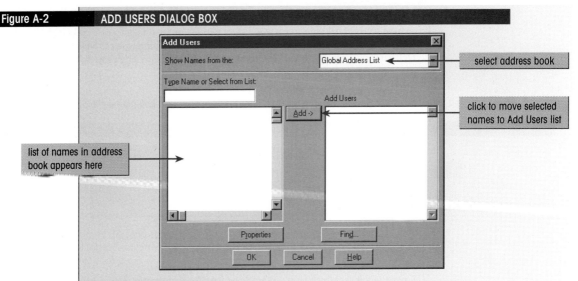

Figure A-2 ADD USERS DIALOG BOX

- select address book
- click to move selected names to Add Users list
- list of names in address book appears here

The Add Users dialog box shows the contacts in the selected address book; you can change this to another address book if needed.

3. Click the **Show Names from the** list arrow, and then click the address book you want.
4. Click the name of each person for whom you want to set delegate permission in the list box, and then click the **Add** button.
5. Click the **OK** button in the Add Users dialog box. A dialog box opens, prompting you to set permission levels for the delegates.
6. Click the **OK** button. The Delegate Permissions dialog box opens, enabling you to assign a permission level for the users you selected. See Figure A-3.

Figure A-3 DELEGATE PERMISSIONS DIALOG BOX

- delegate's name or Multiple Delegates appears here
- click to select permission level for each folder
- check to send e-mail notification to delegate

7. For each Outlook item, click the list arrow and then select the appropriate permissions level.
8. Click the **Automatically send a message to delegate summarizing these permissions** check box to insert a check mark. Outlook will send an e-mail message to the delegates notifying them of their delegate status and permissions.
9. Click the **Delegate can see my private items** check box to insert a check mark. The delegates will be able to view your private items.
10. Click the **OK** button in the Delegate Permissions dialog box, and then click the **OK** button in the Options dialog box.

The delegates you specified now have **send-on-behalf-of permission**, which means that they can send messages for you. Messages sent this way contain both your name and the delegate's name. Message recipients see your name in the Sent On Behalf Of box and the delegate's name in the From box in the Message window.

A delegate must have Editor permission for your Calendar or Tasks folder and Reviewer permission in your Inbox to accept meeting or task requests for you. If you check the Send meeting requests and responses only to my delegates, not to me check box on the Delegates tab in the Options dialog box, then the delegate does not need Reviewer permission for the Inbox. The delegate receives any meeting requests and responses directly in his or her Inbox.

Set Delegate Access to Share Tasks

If you have received delegate access with Editor permission to someone else's Tasks folder, you have a shared task list and can read, create, and modify that person's tasks. In addition, you can send and respond to task requests.

Delegates then can open the folders you specified. Any items a delegate with Author or Editor permission creates while the shared folder is active are stored in your folder.

To open another person's folder:
1. Click **File** on the menu bar, point to **Open**, and then click **Other User's Folder**. See Figure A-4.

| Figure A-4 | OPEN OTHER USER'S FOLDER DIALOG BOX |

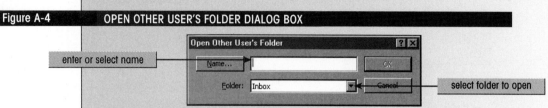

enter or select name

select folder to open

2. Click the Name button and then double-click the name of the folder owner in the text box.
3. Click the **Tasks** folder (or the folder you want to open) in the Folder list box.
4. Click the **OK** button.

Once the folder is open, you can create an item for that person. The item's window, such as a Task window or Contact window, has the same options as when you create that item in your own folder. The task would appear on the task list in the owner's Tasks folder; a contact would appear in the owner's Contacts folder.

To create a task in another person's Tasks folder:
1. Click the **New Task** button ☑ New on the Standard toolbar. A new Task window opens.
2. Type a task name in the Subject box and set a due date.
3. Set any other task options, just like a task you would create from your own Tasks folder.
4. Close the task. The task appears on the task list in the owner's Tasks folder.

If you don't have an assistant or someone else who can review your messages as a delegate when you're out of the office, then you might want to create an out-of-office message.

Setting an Out-of-Office Message

When you are on vacation or away from e-mail access for a time, anyone who sends a message and doesn't receive a timely response will think that you are ignoring the message or never received it—either is a bad business practice. Rather than leave senders wondering, you can set up the Out of Office Assistant to respond to messages that arrive during your absence. The activated **Out of Office Assistant** sends an automated reply that you create to all the senders of incoming messages. Before you leave, turn on the Out of Office Assistant, type the message you want sent, and then set up rules for any exceptions. While you're enjoying time away, Outlook automatically replies to every message with your preset response.

To use the Out of Office Assistant, you must be using Outlook with Microsoft Exchange Server and have the Exchange Extensions add-in installed.

To set up the Out of Office Assistant:
1. Click **Tools** on the menu bar, and then click **Out of Office Assistant**. The Out of Office Assistant dialog box opens. See Figure A-5.

| Figure A-5 | OUT OF OFFICE ASSISTANT DIALOG BOX |

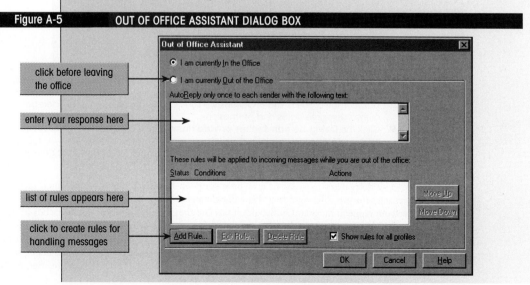

click before leaving the office

enter your response here

list of rules appears here

click to create rules for handling messages

> **TROUBLE?** If you don't see Out of Office Assistant on the Tools menu, the feature may not be available. Make sure you are using Outlook with Exchange Server and have the Exchange Extensions add-in installed. If you need further assistance, ask your instructor or technical support person for help.
>
> 2. Click the **I am currently Out of the Office** option button to turn on the Out of Office Assistant.
> 3. Click in the **AutoReply only once to each sender with the following** text box, and then type your message.
>   You could set up rules to have some messages handled differently, such as deleted or forwarded to another person. Each rule you add slows down the processing of your mail so you might consider responding to all messages with the same generic reply without exception.
> 4. Click the **OK** button.

When you return to the office and start Outlook and connect to your e-mail server, a dialog box will remind you that the Out of Office Assistant is turned on. You then can choose to leave it on or turn it off. If you turn off the AutoReply, any rules you created remain intact (but inactive) so you can reuse them next time. All the mail that arrived while the Out of Office Assistant was turned on appears in the Inbox or in folders according to the rules you set up.

> ### To turn off the Out of Office Assistant:
> 1. Click **Tools** on the menu bar, and then click **Out of Office Assistant**. The Out of Office Assistant dialog box opens.
> 2. Click the **I am currently In the Office** option button to turn off the Assistant.
> 3. Delete any rules and the text you typed in the AutoReply text box, as needed. Any text or rules that you leave in the dialog box will be available next time you use the Out of Office Assistant.
> 4. Click the **OK** button.

If you are enrolled in any listservs, be aware that the Out of Office Assistant will respond to every posting you receive, which in turn will be distributed to the group. Instead, don't use the AutoReply, add the listservs to your exception list, or unsubscribe from the listservs.

Working **Remotely with Exchange**

If you often spend time at various locations, you might find it convenient to be able to use a laptop computer to send and receive messages and schedule upcoming events on the calendar. By setting up Outlook to **work offline** (disconnected from a server), you can manage e-mail messages and other items when you are away from your office.

Working with Offline Folders

The simplest way to work offline with Exchange is with offline folders, which enable you to keep identical information on the server and your remote computer. **Offline folders** are folders on your remote computer's hard drive that duplicate the contents of Outlook folders stored on the server, including the Inbox, Outbox, Deleted Items, Sent Items, Calendar, Contacts, Tasks, Journal, Notes, and Drafts folders. You work with the contents of these offline folders just as you do with folders on Exchange Server. For example, you can edit and move items in your offline Inbox and send messages that are placed in your offline Outbox. Offline folders are stored in the **offline folder file** on your computer's hard disk that is available even when the network is down.

The basic process for setting up offline folders for a remote computer to work with Exchange Server is:

1. Install Outlook on the remote computer. When creating your profile, click the Yes button in response to the question "Do you travel with this computer?"
2. Create an offline folder file.
3. Specify the dial-up connection you want to use.
4. Download the Global Address List.
5. Add shortcuts to the public folders you want available.
6. Specify folders you created that you want available.
7. Synchronize the offline folders.
8. Set Outlook to start offline.
9. Exit Outlook, and then start Outlook from a remote location.

After you have Outlook set up on your remote computer, you create the offline folder file. An offline folder file can be created automatically when you set up Outlook, or you can create one when you first make a folder available offline.

> ### To create an offline folder file:
> 1. Click **Tools** on the Inbox menu bar, and then click **Services**. The Services dialog box opens.
> 2. Click **Microsoft Exchange Server** in The following information services are set up in this profile list box.
> 3. Click the **Properties** button, and then click the **Advanced** tab in the Microsoft Exchange Server dialog box. See Figure A-6.

Figure A-6   ADVANCED TAB OF MICROSOFT EXCHANGE SERVER DIALOG BOX

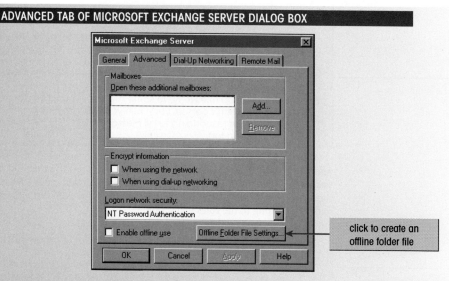

click to create an
offline folder file

4. Click the **Offline Folder File Settings** button. The Offline Folder File Settings dialog box opens.
   See Figure A-7.

Figure A-7   OFFICE FOLDER FILE SETTINGS DIALOG BOX

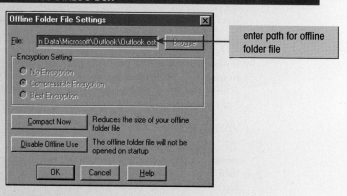

enter path for offline
folder file

5. Type the path for your offline folder file in the File text box.
6. Click the **OK** button in each dialog box.

To work offline, you'll need to set up a dial-up connection on the Dial-Up Networking tab in the
Microsoft Exchange Server Properties dialog box. Your computer must have a modem and Dial-up
Networking software, and be connected to a telephone line. This way you can connect to the server and
send your messages and other items.

You'll also need to download the Global Address List to your remote computer. Recall that the Global
Address List is an address book created and maintained by a network administrator that contains all user, group,
and distribution list e-mail addresses in your organization.

To copy the Global Address List to a remote computer:
1. Click **Tools** on the menu bar, point to **Synchronize**, and then click **Download Address Book**. Your
   computer connects to the server, downloads the offline address book, and then disconnects.

If you are working with Outlook on Exchange Server, you have the added advantage of working with public
folders. A **public folder** (also called an Exchange folder) is a folder stored on an Exchange Server computer
that holds any type of file or Outlook item and that you and others can access to share information. For
example, an employer can include a Word file with employer guidelines or Outlook items with upcoming work
schedules and tasks lists in a public folder that all current staff members can read. To set up a public folder or
access and read items in a public folder, you must have the appropriate permission, assigned by the server
administrator. You can add shortcuts to the public folders you want to be able to access when working remotely
in the Public Folders Favorites folder.

To add a public folder shortcut:
1. Click **Public Folders** in the Folder List, and then click the public folder you want to add to the
   Favorites folder.
2. Click **File** on the menu bar, point to **Folder**, and then click **Add to Public Folder Favorites**.
3. If necessary, type a name in the Favorite folder name text box.

4. Click the **Add** button.
5. Repeat Steps 1 through 4 for each public folder to which you want a shortcut.

The Inbox, Outbox, Deleted Items, Sent Items, Calendar, Contacts, Tasks, Journal, Notes, and Drafts folders are automatically available offline when you set up offline folders. If you want to use any other folders offline, you must set them up for offline use.

To make a folder available offline:
1. Switch to the **Inbox**.
2. Click **Tools** on the menu bar, click **Options** to open the Options dialog box, and then click the **Mail Services** tab.
3. Click the **Enable offline access** check box to insert a check mark, and then click the appropriate options.
4. Click the **Offline Folder Settings** button.
5. Select the folders you want to use offline in addition to your default folders.
6. Click the **OK** button in each dialog box.

The next step is to synchronize the folders on your remote computer with those on your desktop computer.

Synchronizing Folders

Once you have determined which folders will be available offline, you synchronize the offline folders with the Exchange folders. **Synchronizing** is the process of updating the folders on your remote computer and the corresponding folders on the server so their contents are identical. You can choose to manually synchronize a selected offline folder, a group of offline folders, or all of your offline folders. From the Mail Services tab in the Options dialog box, you can set up Outlook to synchronize your offline folders when you disconnect your connection or during specified time intervals while you are working. You need to synchronize your folders when you set up your offline folders, and then periodically as you work offline to ensure that the folders on both your remote computer and the server folders contain the same files and information.

To manually synchronize offline folders:
1. If necessary, select the offline folder you want to synchronize.
2. Click **Tools** on the menu bar, point to **Synchronize**, and then click **This Folder** to synchronize the selected folder or click **All Folders** to synchronize all offline folders.

Outlook copies the changes made in each folder to the other folder, and then disconnects. Any item that is deleted from either the offline folder or the corresponding Exchange folder is deleted from both.

The last step before working from a remote location is to set Outlook to start offline.

To set Outlook to start offline:
1. Click **Tools** on the menu bar, and then click **Services**. The Services dialog box opens
2. Click **Microsoft Exchange Server** in The following information services are set up in this profile list box.
3. Click the **Properties** button, and then click the **General** tab in the Microsoft Exchange Server dialog box.
4. Click the **Manually control connection state** option button. See Figure A-8.

| Figure A-8 | GENERAL TAB OF MICROSOFT EXCHANGE SERVER DIALOG BOX |

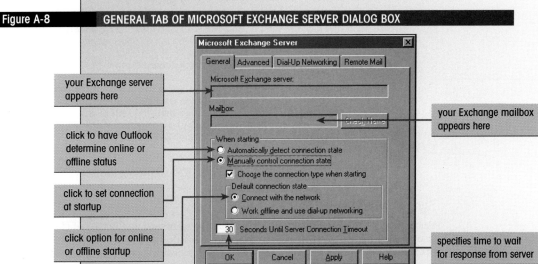

your Exchange server appears here

click to have Outlook determine online or offline status

click to set connection at startup

click option for online or offline startup

your Exchange mailbox appears here

specifies time to wait for response from server

5. Click the **Work offline and use dial-up networking** option button. This sets Outlook to always start offline.
6. Click the **Advanced** tab.
7. Click the **Enable offline use** check box to insert a check mark, if necessary.
8. Click the **OK** button in each dialog box.

When you exit Outlook, you can start Outlook from an offline location. As you work offline, you'll need to periodically synchronize your folders. As you did above, you can manually synchronize an individual folder or all your offline folders at one time. Or to save space and downloading time, you can create a subset of your offline folders and synchronize them as a **quick synchronization group**.

To create a quick synchronization group:
1. Click **Tools** on the menu bar, point to **Synchronize**, and then click **Offline Folder Settings**.
2. Click the **Quick Synchronization** tab.
3. Click the **New** button, type a name for the group, and then click the **OK** button.
4. Select the name of the new group, and then click the **Choose Folders** button.
5. Click the check box for each folder you want to include in the group.
6. Click the **OK** button.

You can prevent large messages from downloading when you synchronize by setting a message size limit. If you use a dial-up connection with your remote computer, large messages can take a long time to download, tying up your computer and phone line. Instead, you can create a Large Messages folder on your server and create a rule that moves large messages to this folder. The Large Messages folder is not included when you synchronize your Inbox, but its contents are still available on the mail server the next time you work online. You can add exceptions to the Large Message rule; for example, you might specify that messages from current clients be delivered regardless of their size.

To synchronize by message size:
1. Click **Tools** on the menu bar, point to **Synchronize**, and then click **Offline Folder Settings**.
2. Click the **Download Options** button.
3. Click the **Don't download messages larger than** check box to insert a check mark.
4. Type the maximum number of kilobytes per message that you want to download. Messages larger than this size will be moved to the Large Messages folder on the Exchange server.

When you are done working remotely, you can reset Outlook to work online and then either disable or delete the offline folders file you created.

To set Outlook to start online:
1. Click **Tools** on the menu bar, and then click **Services**. The Services dialog box opens.
2. Click **Microsoft Exchange Server** in The following information services are set up in this profile list box.
3. Click the **Properties** button, and then click the **General** tab in the Microsoft Exchange Server Properties dialog box.
4. Click the **Automatically detect connection state** option button.
5. Click the **Advanced** tab.
6. Click the **Enable offline use** check box to remove the check mark.
7. Click the **OK** button in each dialog box.

At some point, you many no longer have the ability or need to work remotely. If you are passing the laptop to someone else in your organization, you may want to remove your personal files and folders from the computer. You can delete the offline folder file you created.

To delete an offline folder file:
1. Click **Tools** on the Inbox menu bar, and then click **Services**. The Services dialog box opens.
2. Click **Microsoft Exchange Server** in The following information services are set up in this profile list box.
3. Click the **Properties** button, and then click the **Advanced** tab in the Microsoft Exchange Server Properties dialog box.
4. Click the **Offline Folder File Settings** button. The Offline Folder File Settings dialog box opens.
5. Click the **Browse** button to open the New Offline File Folder dialog box.
6. Click the offline folder file you created, and then press the **Delete** key.
7. Click the **Yes** button to confirm the deletion.
8. Click the **Cancel** button to close the New Offline File Folder dialog box.
9. Click the **OK** button in each dialog box.

In addition to synchronizing your Outlook folders with a remote computer, you may want to synchronize them with a portable device.

Synchronizing Outlook with a PIM

Personal Information Managers (PIMs), Personal Digital Assistants (PDAs), and Handheld or Pocket PCs are so convenient that many people carry these portable devices everywhere. Some devices include a pocket version of Outlook, which means that users can enter contacts, schedule appointments, create a task, and jot down notes at any time. When they return to the office, they can synchronize Outlook folders on the portable device with the Outlook folders on their desktop computer. Any new items in either location are duplicated in the other location, ensuring that the portable device and the desktop contain identical information. When you connect the portable device with your desktop, they automatically synchronize.

merge field, OUT 3.40
repositioning, OUT 6.08–6.09
simple field, OUT 6.05
sorting contacts by, OUT 3.38–3.40
tab-delimited field, OUT 5.27
file. *See also* **importing/exporting**
creating shortcuts to, OUT 6.42–6.43
document file, OUT 3.40
folder file, OUT 5.31–5.32
form publishing, OUT 6.18–6.20
managing from Outlook, OUT 6.41
filter, OUT 3.36
filtering
e-mail message, OUT 4.32
junk mail, OUT 4.37
turning on filter, OUT 4.38–4.39
removing, OUT 5.42–5.43
view, OUT 3.36–3.38
folder, OUT 1.04. *See also* **Net Folder; Outlook folder**
adding to Favorites, OUT 7.06–7.08
creating, OUT 4.13–4.14, OUT 6.29
deleting, OUT 4.41
grouping items, OUT 4.29–4.32
navigating between, OUT 1.11–1.13
offline, APP 5–7
public folder shortcut, APP 6
retrieving archived items, OUT 4.36
subfolder creation, OUT 4.14
synchronizing, APP 7–8
folder banner, OUT 1.10
folder file. *See also* **file**
importing/exporting, OUT 5.31–5.32
folder home page. *See also* **Web page**
creating, OUT 7.08–7.10
viewing, OUT 7.09–7.10
folder list, OUT 1.09
navigating with, OUT 1.11–1.13
form
adding fields to, OUT 6.04–6.05
bound control, OUT 6.03
closing, OUT 6.20

custom
opening, OUT 6.21–6.24
testing, OUT 6.17–6.18
entering information in contact card, OUT 6.22–6.23
entering properties, OUT 6.16–6.17
in general, OUT 6.02
layout, OUT 6.03
Mail templates, OUT 6.24–6.26
message class, OUT 6.19
modifying, OUT 6.04–6.17
opening
custom, OUT 6.21–6.24
in design mode, OUT 6.02–6.04
placing custom fields on, OUT 6.07–6.08
publishing, OUT 6.18–6.20
Tab order, OUT 6.09
setting, OUT 6.09–6.10, OUT 6.12–6.13
testing, OUT 6.09, OUT 6.13
testing, OUT 6.17–6.18
text box resizing, OUT 6.15
unbound control, OUT 6.03
form library
form publishing, OUT 6.18–6.20
removing form from, OUT 6.48–6.51
formatting, e-mail message, OUT 1.38–1.39

G

group, OUT 1.09
adding and renaming, OUT 6.39
grouping. *See also* **e-mail message**
folder items, OUT 4.29–4.32

H

Help
in general, OUT 1.43–1.44
Office Assistant, OUT 1.43
ScreenTip, OUT 1.43
What's This?, OUT 1.43

TASK REFERENCE

TASK	PAGE #	RECOMMENDED METHOD
Address Book, create new entry	OUT 1.22	Click 📖, click ▭, select your address book from the In the list, select an entry type, click OK, enter contact information, click OK
Appointment, schedule one-time	OUT 2.24	See Reference Window: Scheduling an Appointment
Appointment, schedule recurring	OUT 2.25	Create appointment, click 🔄 Recurrence..., select recurrence pattern and range, click OK
Archive, create automatically	OUT 4.33	See Reference Window: Setting Up AutoArchive
Archive, create manually	OUT 4.36	Click File, click Archive, select folders, enter date, select save in location, click OK, click Yes
Attachment, add to e-mail	OUT 1.40	From Message window, click 📎, select file location, double-click file to insert
Attachment, open	OUT 1.42	Double-click attachment icon in Message window, read, edit, format, and save as usual
Attachment, save	OUT 1.42	Right-click attachment icon in Message window, click Save As, change select save location, enter filename, click Save button
AutoArchive, turn off	OUT 4.41	Click Tools, click Options, click Other tab, click AutoArchive button, remove check mark, click OK, click OK, click OK
Calendar, configure options	OUT 6.35	Click Tools, click Options, click Preferences tab, click Calendar Options button, make changes as needed, click OK, click OK
Calendar, printing	OUT 2.32	Switch to Calendar, display view and dates, click 🖨, select print style and range, click Preview button, click Print
Calendar, save as Web page	OUT 2.43	See Reference Window: Saving a Calendar as a Web Page
Categories, adding to master list	OUT 2.14	Click Categories button in item's window, click Master Category List button, type category name, click Add button, click OK
Categories, assign to item	OUT 2.13	See Reference Window: Assigning a Category
Categories, remove from item	OUT 2.15	Select category including the comma, press Delete
Clipboard toolbar, clear	OUT 2.40	Click 📋
Clipboard toolbar, open	OUT 2.39	Right-click toolbar, click Clipboard
Commands, add to or remove from toolbars or menus	OUT 6.53	Display toolbar, right-click toolbar, click Customize, click Commands tab, click category, drag command to or from toolbar or menu
Contact list, print	OUT 3.18	Select contact or contacts, click 🖨, select print style and range, click Print
Contact, create	OUT 3.04	See Reference Window: Creating a Contact
Contact, edit from Information viewer	OUT 3.17	Switch to Address Cards or Detailed Address Cards view, click in contact card, edit text as usual, click outside contact card
Contact, flag for follow up	OUT 3.33	See Reference Window: Flagging a Contact for Follow Up
Contact, link activity to	OUT 3.32	See Reference Window: Linking an Activity to a Contact

TASK	PAGE #	RECOMMENDED METHOD
Contact, view activities	OUT 3.12	Open contact card, click Activities tab
Contact, write a letter to	OUT 3.29	See Reference Window: Writing a Letter to a Contact
Contacts, accept duplicate names	OUT 3.14	Click Add this as a new contact anyway option button in Duplicate Contact Detected dialog box, click OK, click File as list arrow to save with different file as name
Contacts, change views	OUT 3.15	Click View, point to Current View, click a view, if necessary expand and collapse groups as necessary to view contacts
Contacts, merge with a Word document	OUT 3.41	See Reference Window: Merging Outlook Contacts and a Word Document
Contacts, organize by category	OUT 3.36	Switch to Contacts Information viewer, click [Organize], click Using Views, click a view
Contacts, send by e-mail	OUT 3.21	See Reference Window: Sending Contact Information by E-mail
Contacts, sort by field	OUT 3.39	See Reference Window: Sorting by Fields
Contacts, view by flag	OUT 3.34	Switch to Contacts Information viewer, click View, point to Current View, click By Follow-up Flag, expand and collapse each flag as needed
Control properties, set	OUT 6.11	Select control, click [icon], set properties, click OK
Control, resize	OUT 6.15	Select controls, drag sizing handles using ↔ or ↕
Controls, align on form	OUT 6.14	Select controls, click Layout, point to Align, select option
Controls, delete from form	OUT 6.13	Select control, press Delete key
Deleted Items folder, empty	OUT 1.45	Right-click Deleted Items folder, click Empty "Deleted Items" Folder, click Yes
Distribution list, create from Contacts	OUT 3.19	See Reference Window: Creating a Distribution List
e-mail message, check spelling	OUT 1.18	Click Tools, click Spelling, click Change or Ignore to correct spelling, click OK to confirm spell check is complete
e-mail message, create and send	OUT 1.16	See Reference Window: Sending an E-mail Message
e-mail message, create with stationery	OUT 1.36	See Reference Window: Creating an E-mail with Stationery
e-mail message, format	OUT 1.38	Select text, click appropriate buttons on Formatting toolbar
e-mail message, send to contact distribution list	OUT 3.27	Select contact or distribution list, click [icon], create or and send message as usual
e-mail messages, forward	OUT 1.33	Select message, click [Forward], enter e-mail address, type message, click [Send]
e-mail messages, reply	OUT 1.32	Select message, click [Reply], type reply message, click [Send]
e-mail messages, send or receive from mail server	OUT 1.30	Switch to Inbox or Outbox, click [Send/Receive]

TASK REFERENCE

TASK	PAGE #	RECOMMENDED METHOD
Event, scheduling	OUT 2.31	See Reference Window: Scheduling an Event
Favorites shortcut, delete	OUT 7.32	Click Favorites, click Open Favorites, select shortcut, press Delete key, click Yes, click Cancel
Fax, send from Outlook	OUT 5.36	Click Actions, click New Fax Message, supply information requested by wizard
Field, create new	OUT 6.06	Click New button in Field Chooser, type name, select type, select format, click OK
Field, reposition	OUT 6.08	Select fields, use ✛ to drag to new location on form
Fields, map imported fields to Outlook fields	OUT 5.29	Click Map Custom Fields button in Import a File dialog box, drag fields as needed between From box and To box, click OK
Fields, delete	OUT 6.49	Right-click Information viewer background, click Show Fields, click field in left list box, click Delete button, click OK, click OK
Fields, remove from view	OUT 6.49	Right-click Information viewer background, click Show Fields, click field in right list box, click Remove button, click OK
Files, import or export	OUT 5.24	Click File, click Import and Export, select action and other options as needed in wizard
Files, view from Outlook	OUT 6.41	Click Other Shortcuts group button, click My Computer, expand a drive and folder as needed in Folder List, click folder to view files in Information viewer
Filter, remove	OUT 3.47	Click View, point to Current View, click Customize Current View, click Filter button, click Clear All button, click OK, click OK
Folder home page, create	OUT 7.08	Right-click folder, click Properties, click Home Page tab, type URL for Web page, click OK
Folder home page, view or hide	OUT 7.09	Switch to folder, click OK if needed, click View, click Show Folder Home Page
Folder List, display or hide	OUT 4.13	Click View, click Folder List
Form page, display or hide	OUT 6.04	Click tab, click Form, click Display This Page
Form page, rename	OUT 6.04	Click tab, click Form, click Rename Page, type name, click OK
Form properties, enter	OUT 6.16	Click (Properties) tab, enter form properties as needed
Form, add fields	OUT 6.06	Drag field from Field Chooser to form
Form, open	OUT 6.21	See Reference Window: Opening a Custom Form
Form, publish	OUT 6.19	See Reference Window: Publishing a Form
Form, remove from forms library	OUT 6.48	Click Tools, click Options, click Other tab, click Advanced Options button, click Custom Forms button, click Manage Forms button, click Set button in left list box, select library location, click form, click Delete button, click Yes, click Close, click OK in each dialog box

TASK	PAGE #	RECOMMENDED METHOD
Form, save to a new location	OUT 6.48	Click Tools, click Options, click Other tab, click Advanced Options button, click Custom Forms button, click Manage Forms button, click Set button in right list box, select library location, click form, click Save As button, select save location and name and type, click Save button, click Close, click OK in each dialog box
Form, test	OUT 6.17	Click Form, click Run This Form, enter data and select options as usual, click ☒, click No
Forms, customize	OUT 6.02	See Reference Window: Customizing a Form
Help, get from Office Assistant	OUT 1.43	Click ②, type question, click Search, click topic, click ☒
Item, save and close	OUT 2.15	Click 🖫 Save and Close
Items, delete	OUT 1.45	Select item or items, click ☒
Items, move between folders	OUT 4.15	See Reference Window: Moving Outlook Items Between Folders
Items, save in another format	OUT 5.33	See Reference Window: Saving Items in Another Format
Journal entries, filter	OUT 5.41	Right-click Journal folder background, click Customize Current View, click Filter button, specify filter as needed, click OK
Journal entries, print	OUT 5.40	Select entry or entries, click 🖨, select print style and range, click Print
Journal entries, record automatically	OUT 5.03	See Reference Window: Recording Journal Entries Automatically
Journal entry, record manually for existing items	OUT 5.06	Right-drag item from Information viewer to Journal folder, click option, complete Journal window, click 🖫 Save and Close
Journal entry, record manually for new items	OUT 5.05	Click 🖫 New, type subject, select entry type, set duration, enter notes, click 🖫 Save and Close
Journal entry, view	OUT 5.11	Switch to Journal, folder, select view, expand or collapse groups
Junk mail, setting up filter	OUT 4.38	See Reference Window: Filtering Junk Mail
Mail template, create	OUT 6.24	Click 🖹 New, enter text, click File, click Save As, enter filename, select Outlook Template as Save as type, change save in location, click Save button, close Message window without saving changes
Mail template, open	OUT 6.25	Switch to Inbox, click Tools, point to Forms, click Choose Form, change look in location, select template, click Open button
Meeting attendees, review or add	OUT 2.36	Double-click meeting in Calendar, click Attendee Availability tab, click Invite Others button
Meeting, scheduling	OUT 2.35	See Reference Window: Planning a Meeting
Message flag, change to complete or clear	OUT 4.05	Right-click flag icon, click Flag Complete or Flag Clear
Message flag, create	OUT 4.02	In Message window, click ⚑, select preset text or type custom text in Flag to box, set due date, click OK

TASK	PAGE #	RECOMMENDED METHOD
Message format, select default	OUT 1.14	Click Tools, click Options, click Mail Format tab, click Send in this message format list arrow, click format, click OK
Message options, set	OUT 4.06	See Reference Window: Setting Message Options
Message, print	OUT 1.34	Select message or messages, click File, click Print, select print style, click OK
Messages, find	OUT 4.25	See Reference Window: Finding Messages
Messages, group	OUT 4.30	See Reference Window: Grouping Messages
Messages, sort	OUT 4.28	Click column heading
Messages, sort by two or more columns	OUT 4.29	Click column heading, hold down Shift, click additional column headings, release Shift
Net Folder, cancel your subscription	OUT 7.29	Right-click shared folder, click Properties, click Sharing tab, click Cancel Membership button, click Yes
Net Folder, create	OUT 7.21	Click File, point to Share, click This Folder, follow wizard instructions to add subscriber, set permissions, and sent notification
Net Folder, stop sharing	OUT 7.28	Right-click shared folder, click Properties, click Sharing tab, click Stop Sharing This Folder button, click Yes
Net Folder, update	OUT 7.28	Right-click shared folder, click Properties, click Sharing tab, click Send Updates Now button, click OK
NetMeeting, scheduling	OUT 7.31	See Reference Window: Scheduling a NetMeeting or NetShow
NetShow, scheduling	OUT 7.31	See Reference Window: Scheduling a NetMeeting or NetShow
Newsgroup account, delete	OUT 7.20	Right-click newsgroup in Folders pane, click Remove Account, click Yes
Newsgroup message, print	OUT 7.17	Click a posting, click the Print button on newsreader toolbar, verify settings, click OK
Newsgroup message, read	OUT 7.15	Click a message header
Newsgroup subscription, cancel	OUT 7.20	Right-click newsgroup in Folders pane, click Unsubscribe, click OK, click No
Newsgroup, setting up	OUT 7.12	See Reference Window: Setting Up a News Server Account
Newsgroup, subscribe	OUT 7.16	See Reference Window: Subscribing to a Newsgroup
Note, create	OUT 2.02	Click New, type text, click X
Note, customize look	OUT 2.04	See Reference Window: Customizing Notes
Note, open and edit	OUT 2.04	Double-click note, edit as usual
Notes, copy to Clipboard	OUT 2.39	Select text and click for each phrase
Notes, insert into meeting request	OUT 2.38	In meeting request window, click Insert, click Item, click Notes in Look in list, select notes, click Text only option button, click OK
Notes, organize	OUT 2.06	Click Organize, click Using Views, click desired view in Change your view list

TASK	PAGE #	RECOMMENDED METHOD
Notes, paste from Clipboard	OUT 2.39	Move insertion point to paste location, click icon on Clipboard toolbar for item to paste
Notes, print	OUT 2.07	Select note or notes, click 🖨, select print style and other options, click OK
Office document, create new from Outlook	OUT 5.19	See Reference Window: Starting New Office Documents from Outlook
Office document, send as e-mail	OUT 5.14	See Reference Window: Mailing Office Documents
Outlook Bar, add new group	OUT 6.39	Right-click Outlook Bar background, click Add New Group, type name, press Enter
Outlook Bar, add shortcuts	OUT 6.40	See Reference Window: Creating a Shortcut to the Outlook Bar
Outlook Bar, shortcuts	OUT 6.43	Drag shortcut to new location
Outlook Bar, remove group	OUT 6.50	Right-click group button, click Remove Group, click Yes
Outlook Bar, remove shortcut	OUT 6.50	Right-click shortcut, click Remove from Outlook Bar, click Yes
Outlook Bar, rename group	OUT 6.39	Right-click group button, click Rename Group, type name, press Enter
Outlook Bar, resize icons	OUT 6.38	Switch to group, right-click Outlook Bar background, click Small Icons
Outlook Today, customize	OUT 6.31	Click Customize Outlook Today in Outlook Today window, select options, click Save Changes button
Personal distribution list, create	OUT 1.24	See Reference Window: Creating a Distribution List
Personal distribution list, delete	OUT 1.28	Click 📖, select your Address Book, select distribution list, click ✕, click Yes
Profile, add an information service	OUT 1.06	Click Tools, click Services, click Add button, click service, click OK, select options for service as needed, click OK in each dialog box, exit Outlook, and then restart Outlook
Remote Mail, check messages	OUT 4.43	Switch to Inbox, click Tools, click Remote Mail, click Connect, specify connections in wizard, click Mark to Retrieve on Remote toolbar, retrieve messages, click Finish, disconnect
Remote mail, set up	OUT 4.42	Add Personal Folders Information service to profile, specify mail delivery service and dial-up connections, click Tools, click Services, click Delivery tab, specify location, click OK
Rule, run	OUT 4.21	Click Tools, click Rules Wizard, click Run Now button, check rule(s) to run, select folder(s) to apply rule to, and what to apply rules to, click Run Now button, click Close button, click OK
Rules, create	OUT 4.17	See Reference Window: Creating a Rule with the Rules Wizard
Rules, export	OUT 4.23	Click Tools, click Rules Wizard, click Options button, click Export Rules button, enter filename and save location, click Save button, click OK, click OK

TASK	PAGE #	RECOMMENDED METHOD
Signature picker, delete	OUT 1.45	Click Tools, click Options, click Mail Format tab, click Signature Picker button, click name of signature to delete, click Remove button, click Yes or No to confirm deletion
Signature, create	OUT 1.35	Click Tools, click Options, click Mail Format tab, click Signature Picker button, click New button, type signature, format as needed, click Finish, click OK, select when to include, click OK
Sort, remove	OUT 3.47	Click View, point to Current View, click Customize Current View, click Sort button, click Clear All button, click OK, click OK
Subfolders, create	OUT 4.14	Click [New], click Folder, type folder name, select item you want folder to contain, select new folder location, click OK
Subfolders, delete	OUT 6.51	Right-click subfolder in Folder List, click Delete folder, click Yes
Tab order, set	OUT 6.12	Click Layout, click Tab Order, click control, click Move Up or Move Down button to reposition, click OK
Task request, accept	OUT 2.19	Open task request message, click [Accept], click option for sending response with or without adding message, send message
Task, create a one-time	OUT 2.10	See Reference Window: Creating a Task
Task, create recurring	OUT 2.11	See Reference Window: Creating a Recurring Task
TaskPad, customize	OUT 6.33	Right-click TaskPad column, click Field Chooser, drag fields from Field Chooser to TaskPad, drag fields to new positions as needed, click column headings to sort as needed
Tasks, assigning	OUT 2.17	See Reference Window: Assigning a Task
Tasks, check off completed	OUT 2.42	Click task's completed check box
Tasks, view by category	OUT 2.16	Click View, point to Current View, click By Category
Time zone, show additional	OUT 6.37	Right-click gray space above times in daily planner, click Change Time Zone, enter current time zone label, click Show an additional time zone check box, type a label, select time zone, click OK
Toolbar, create custom	OUT 6.44	Right-click a toolbar, click Customize, click Toolbars tab, click New button, type name, click OK
Toolbar, delete	OUT 6.50	Right-click a toolbar, click Customize, click Toolbars tab, click toolbar, click Delete, click OK, click Close
Vcard, forward contact information by e-mail	OUT 3.23	Select contact, click Actions, click Forward as vCard, create and send message as usual
View, filter	OUT 3.37	See Reference Window: Filtering a View
Views, customize with fields	OUT 6.27	See Reference Window: Customizing Views with Fields
Vote, respond to	OUT 4.10	Open message, click voting button, edit response if necessary, send message
Votes, track	OUT 4.12	Open original message in Sent Items folder, click Tracking tab, close message

TASK	PAGE #	RECOMMENDED METHOD
Voting buttons, create	OUT 4.07	Click **Options...** in Message window, click Use voting buttons list arrow, make selection or create new buttons, set options as needed, click Close
Web page, browse	OUT 7.04	Click links in page, click ⇨ and ⇦ on Web toolbar as needed
Web page, open Favorite	OUT 7.07	Click Favorites, click favorite filename
Web page, save as Favorite	OUT 7.06	Display Web page, click Favorites, click Add to Favorites, select location, type filename, click Add
Web page, view in Outlook Information viewer	OUT 7.05	Type URL in Address text box of Web toolbar, press Enter
Web toolbar, display	OUT 7.03	Right-click a toolbar, click Web

Standardized Coding Number	Certification Skill Activity — Activity	Tutorial Pages	End-of-Tutorial Practice — End-of-Tutorial Pages	Exercise	Step Number
OL2000.1	Use Outlook 2000 Mail to communicate with others inside and outside your company				
OL2000.1.1	Read mail	1.30–1.31	1.51	Case Problem 4	13
OL2000.1.2	Send mail	1.19–1.21	1.46–1.47	Review Assignment	3, 5, 7, 14, 16
			1.47–1.48	Case Problem 1	5, 6, 8
			1.48–1.49	Case Problem 2	3, 9, 12
			1.50	Case Problem 3	17, 18
			1.51	Case Problem 4	2, 11, 13
OL2000.1.3	Compose mail by entering text	1.15–1.19	1.46	Review Assignment	2, 5, 7
			1.47–1.48	Case Problem 1	2, 6, 7, 10
			1.48–1.49	Case Problem 2	3, 8, 10
			1.49–1.50	Case Problem 3	3, 12, 18
			1.51	Case Problem 4	2, 9, 13
OL2000.1.4	Print mail	1.33–1.34	1.47	Review Assignment	20, 21
			1.48	Case Problem 1	11
			1.49	Case Problem 2	16
			1.51	Case Problem 4	15
OL2000.1.5	Address mail by entering text	1.15–1.17	1.46	Review Assignment	2
			1.47	Case Problem 1	2
			1.48	Case Problem 2	3
			1.49	Case Problem 3	3
			1.51	Case Problem 4	2
OL2000.1.6	Use mail features (forward, reply, recall)	1.31–1.33	1.46, 1.47	Review Assignment	10, 15
			1.47, 1.48	Case Problem 1	6, 7, 10
		4.8–4.9	1.48, 1.49	Case Problem 2	8, 10
			1.50	Case Problem 3	18
			1.51	Case Problem 4	13
OL2000.1.7	Use address book to address mail	1.21–1.24	1.46, 1.47	Review Assignment	5, 15
		1.27–1.28	1.48	Case Problem 2	6
		1.33	1.50	Case Problem 3	8, 11, 15
			1.51	Case Problem 4	3–5, 8
OL2000.1.8	Flag mail messages	4.2–4.5	4.45	Review Assignment	2, 5
			4.47	Case Problem 1	2
			4.48, 4.49	Case Problem 2	3, 16
			4.50	Case Problem 3	12
			4.51	Case Problem 4	5
OL2000.1.9	Navigate within mail	1.11–1.13	1.46, 1.47	Review Assignment	1, 22
			1.47	Case Problem 1	1
			1.48	Case Problem 2	1
			1.49, 1.50	Case Problem 3	1, 14, 18
			1.51	Case Problem 4	1

CORE SKILLS GRID

Standardized Coding Number	**Certification Skill Activity** Activity	Tutorial Pages	**End-of-Tutorial Practice** End-of-Tutorial Pages	Exercise	Step Number
OL2000.1.10	Find messages	4.24–4.28	4.46 4.50	Review Assignment Case Problem 3	19, 22, 23 18–21
OL2000.1.11	Configure basic mail print options	1.33–1.34	1.47 1.48 1.49 1.51	Review Assignment Case Problem 1 Case Problem 2 Case Problem 4	20, 21 11 16 15
OL2000.1.12	Work with attachments	1.40	1.47 1.49	Review Assignment Case Problem 2	13, 19, 20 9, 16
OL2000.1.13	Add a signature to mail	1.35–1.36	1.46 1.50	Review Assignment Case Problem 3	8 6, 7, 16
OL2000.1.14	Customize the look of mail	1.34–1.39	1.46 1.47 1.48, 1.49 1.49, 1.50 1.51	Review Assignment Case Problem 1 Case Problem 2 Case Problem 3 Case Problem 4	11, 12 3, 4 2, 4, 8, 11 2, 7, 17 10
OL2000.1.15	Use mail templates to compose mail	1.36–1.38	1.51	Case Problem 4	7
OL2000.1.16	Integrate and use mail with other Outlook components	2.59 2.69–2.73 2.85–2.90	2.47, 2.48 2.48, 2.49 2.51	Review Assignment Case Problem 1 Case Problem 4	21, 22 2, 3, 4, 5, 11 13, 16
OL2000.1.17	Customize menu and task bar	1.10	6.56, 6.57	Case Problem 3	1–4, 31
OL2000.2	**Use Outlook 2000 to manage messages**	6.44–6.48			
OL2000.2.1	Create folders	4.13–4.14	4.46 4.47 4.48, 4.49 4.50 4.51	Review Assignment Case Problem 1 Case Problem 2 Case Problem 3 Case Problem 4	13, 14 12–14 6, 7, 18 8 1
OL2000.2.2	Sort mail	4.28–4.29	4.46 4.51	Review Assignment Case Problem 4	20 6
OL2000.2.3	Set viewing options	4.29–4.32	4.46 4.49 4.50 4.51	Review Assignment Case Problem 2 Case Problem 3 Case Problem 4	24, 25 19–21 16 11, 13, 15, 16
OL2000.2.4	Archive mail message	4.32–4.36	4.46 4.48 4.49 4.51 4.51–4.52	Review Assignment Case Problem 1 Case Problem 2 Case Problem 3 Case Problem 4	26, 27 20 24 22 19–23

Standardized Coding Number	Certification Skill Activity		Tutorial Pages	End-of-Tutorial Practice		
	Activity			End-of-Tutorial Pages	Exercise	Step Number
OL2000.2.5	Filter a view		3.36–3.38 4.32	3.49	Review Assignment	19
				3.51	Case Problem 1	11
				3.52	Case Problem 2	19
				3.54	Case Problem 3	13, 16, 17
				3.55	Case Problem 4	8
				4.49	Case Problem 2	22
OL2000.3	**Use the Outlook 2000 calendar**					
OL2000.3.1	Navigate within the calendar		2.22–2.24	2.47	Review Assignment	13, 16
				2.48	Case Problem 1	7
				2.49	Case Problem 2	13
				2.50	Case Problem 3	6
OL2000.3.2	Schedule appointments and events		2.22–2.29 2.30–2.32	2.47	Review Assignment	15, 16
				2.48	Case Problem 1	8, 10
				2.49–2.50	Case Problem 2	14–18
				2.50–2.51	Case Problem 3	6–10
				2.51	Case Problem 4	8
OL2000.3.3	Set reminders		2.26	2.47	Review Assignment	12
				2.48	Case Problem 1	10
				2.50	Case Problem 2	16–18
				2.50–2.51	Case Problem 3	6-8, 10
OL2000.3.4	Print in calendar		2.32–2.33	2.47	Review Assignment	17
				2.49	Case Problem 1	12
				2.50	Case Problem 2	20
				2.51	Case Problem 3	11
				2.51	Case Problem 4	17
OL2000.3.5	Schedule multi-day events		2.30–2.32	2.47	Review Assignment	14
				2.51	Case Problem 3	10
OL2000.3.6	Configure calendar print options		2.32–2.33	2.47	Review Assignment	17
				2.49	Case Problem 1	12
				2.50	Case Problem 2	20
				2.51	Case Problem 3	11
				2.51	Case Problem 4	17
OL2000.3.7	Customize the calendar view		2.22–2.23	2.48	Case Problem 1	7
				2.49	Case Problem 2	13
			6.26–6.29	6.52	Review Assignment	19, 22
				6.54	Case Problem 1	18–24
				6.55	Case Problem 2	15
OL2000.3.8	Schedule recurring appointments		2.29–2.30	2.47	Review Assignment	15
				2.48	Case Problem 1	8
				2.51	Case Problem 3	9

CORE SKILLS GRID

Standardized Coding Number	Certification Skill Activity — Activity	Tutorial Pages	End-of-Tutorial Practice — End-of-Tutorial Pages	Exercise	Step Number
OL2000.3.9	Customize menu and task bars	1.10 6.44–6.48	6.56, 6.57	Case Problem 3	1–4, 31
OL2000.3.10	Add and remove meeting attendees	2.33–2.36 2.40–2.41	2.47, 2.48 2.49 2.51	Review Assignment Case Problem 1 Case Problem 4	19, 22 11 12
OL2000.3.11	Plan meetings involving others	2.33–2.41	2.47, 2.48 2.49 2.51	Review Assignment Case Problem 1 Case Problem 4	19, 22 11 12
OL2000.3.12	Save a personal or team calendar as a Web page	2.42–2.44	2.48 2.49 2.52	Review Assignment Case Problem 1 Case Problem 4	24 13 18
OL2000.3.13	Book office resources directly (e.g., conference rooms)	2.33–2.34	2.47 2.49	Review Assignment Case Problem 1	19 11
OL2000.3.14	Integrate calendar with other Outlook components	2.25–2.27 2.34–2.89	2.47, 2.48 2.48 2.50 2.50	Review Assignment Case Problem 1 Case Problem 2 Case Problem 3	13, 23 9 19 6, 7
OL2000.4	**Navigate and use Outlook 2000 effectively**				
OL2000.4.1	Use Outlook Help and Office Assistant	1.43–1.44	1.49 1.50	Case Problem 2 Case Problem 3	14 4
OL2000.4.2	Move items between folders	2.8–2.9 2.25 4.15–4.16	2.47, 2.48 2.48 2.49, 2.50 2.50 2.51 4.46 4.47, 4.48 4.48, 4.49 4.50 4.51	Review Assignment Case Problem 1 Case Problem 2 Case Problem 3 Case Problem 4 Review Assignment Case Problem 1 Case Problem 2 Case Problem 3 Case Problem 4	5, 12, 13,20 2, 4 8, 19 4, 6, 7 8, 14 15 15, 19 7, 18 9–10, 17 2
OL2000.4.3	Navigate between Outlook components	1.11–1.13	1.46 1.47 1.48 1.49, 1.50 1.51	Review Assignment Case Problem 1 Case Problem 2 Case Problem 3 Case Problem 4	1 1 1 1, 14, 21 1
OL2000.4.4	Modify the Outlook Master Categories List	2.14–2.15	2.47, 2.48 2.48, 2.49 2.49, 2.50 2.51,2.52	Review Assignment Case Problem 1 Case Problem 2 Case Problem 4	4, 26 6,14 8,21 3,22

Standardized Coding Number	Certification Skill Activity Activity	Tutorial Pages	End-of-Tutorial Practice End-of-Tutorial Pages	Exercise	Step Number
OL2000.4.5	Assign items to a category	2.13–2.16	2.47	Review Assignment	4, 7, 8, 10
			2.48	Case Problem 1	6
			2.49	Case Problem 2	2, 8, 14
			2.51	Case Problem 4	4, 7, 9, 12
OL2000.4.6	Sort information using categories	2.16–2.17	2.47	Review Assignment	11
			2.49	Case Problem 2	10
			2.52	Case Problem 4	19
OL2000.4.7	Use the Office Clipboard	2.38–.39	2.49	Case Problem 2	3
OL2000.5	**Use Contacts**				
OL2000.5.1	Create, edit, and delete contacts	3.4–3.15 3.17-3.18 3.47	3.48–3.49	Review Assignment	1–7, 9, 14
			3.50	Case Problem 1	2–6
			3.51–3.52	Case Problem 2	2–7, 9-11
			3.53	Case Problem 3	2–7
			3.54	Case Problem 4	1, 3
OL2000.5.2	Send contact information via e-mail	3.21–3.25	3.49	Review Assignment	12
			3.53	Case Problem 3	9, 10
OL2000.5.3	Organize contacts by category	3.35–3.38	3.49	Review Assignment	19
			3.51	Case Problem 1	11
			3.53, 3.54	Case Problem 3	8, 9, 10, 17
			3.54, 3.55	Case Problem 4	4, 6, 8
OL2000.5.4	Manually record an activity in a journal	5.2–5.11	5.44–5.45	Review Assignment	4–7
			5.46	Case Problem 1	3, 9
			5.47	Case Problem 2	4–6
			5.49	Case Problem 4	3, 4
OL2000.5.5	Link activities to a Contacts	3.32–3.33	3.51	Case Problem 1	9
			3.52	Case Problem 2	7, 8
OL2000.5.6	Sort contacts using fields	3.38–3.40	3.49, 3.50	Review Assignment	20, 28
			3.51	Case Problem 1	20
			3.55	Case Problem 4	8
OL2000.6	**Use Tasks**				
OL2000.6.1	Create and update one-time tasks	2.8–2.10	2.47	Review Assignment	5, 10
			2.48	Case Problem 1	4, 6
			2.49, 2.50	Case Problem 2	8, 11, 19
			2.50	Case Problem 3	4, 5
			2.51	Case Problem 4	6
OL2000.6.2	Accept and decline tasks	2.19–2.20	2.48	Case Problem 1	5
			2.51	Case Problem 4	10

Standardized Coding Number	Certification Skill Activity — Activity	Tutorial Pages	End-of-Tutorial Practice — End-of-Tutorial Pages	Exercise	Step Number
OL2000.6.3	Organize tasks using categories	2.13–2.17	2.47	Review Assignment	10, 11
			2.48	Case Problem 1	6
			2.49	Case Problem 2	8
			2.51	Case Problem 4	7
OL2000.6.4	Assign tasks to others	2.17–2.21	2.48	Case Problem 1	5
			2.51	Case Problem 4	9
OL2000.6.5	Create tasks from other Outlook components	2.8–2.9	2.47	Review Assignment	5
			2.48	Case Problem 1	4
			2.49, 2.50	Case Problem 2	8, 19
			2.50	Case Problem 3	4
OL2000.6.6	Change the view for tasks	2.16	2.47	Review Assignment	11
			2.49	Case Problem 2	10
OL2000.7	**Integrate Office applications and other applications with Outlook 2000 components**				
OL2000.7.1	Create and use Office documents inside Outlook 2000	3.28–3.31	3.49–3.50	Review Assignment	16–18, 22–27
		3.40–3.46	3.51	Case Problem 1	7–8, 12–18
			3.52–3.53	Case Problem 2	15–19
			3.55	Case Problem 4	9–13
		5.19–5.22	5.45	Review Assignment	11–14
			5.46	Case Problem 1	4–7
			5.47	Case Problem 2	7–16
			5.48-5.49	Case Problem 3	2-8, 11, 12
			5.49-5.50	Case Problem 4	5–12
OL2000.8	**Use Notes**				
OL2000.8.1	Create and edit notes	2.2–2.4	2.47	Review Assignment	2–4, 6, 8
			2.48	Case Problem 1	1
			2.49	Case Problem 2	1–3
			2.50	Case Problem 3	1–3
			2.51	Case Problem 4	1
OL2000.8.2	Organize and view notes	2.6	2.47	Review Assignment	4, 7, 8, 9
			2.49	Case Problem 2	7
			2.51	Case Problem 4	14
OL2000.8.3	Customize notes	2.4–2.6	2.47	Review Assignment	2–4, 6, 8
			2.48	Case Problem 1	1
			2.49	Case Problem 2	1, 2
			2.50	Case Problem 3	1, 2
			2.51	Case Problem 4	2

Standardized Coding Number	Certification Skill Activity Activity	Tutorial Pages	End-of-Tutorial Practice		
			End-of-Tutorial Pages	Exercise	Step Number
OL2000E.1	**Use Outlook 2000 Mail to communicate with others inside and outside your company**				
OL2000E.1.1	Work off-line or use remote mail	4.42–4.44 APP 5–APP 6			
OL2000E.1.2	Add a vcard to a message	3.23	3.49 3.52 3.53	Review Assignment Case Problem 2 Case Problem 3	12 13 10
OL2000E.1.3	Create re-usable mail templates	6.24–6.25	6.52, 6.53 6-57–6.58	Review Assignment Case Problem 3	1–14, 30 1–27
OL2000E.1.4	Use mail with Office applications	5.14–5.22	5.44–5.45 5.47 5.48 5.50	Review Assignment Case Problem 2 Case Problem 3 Case Problem 4	7–14 7–16 2, 3 7–10
OL2000E.2	**Use Outlook 2000 to manage messages**				
OL2000E.2.1	Customize the look of mail	1.34–1.39	1.46 1.47 1.48 1.49, 1.50 1.51	Review Assignment Case Problem 1 Case Problem 2 Case Problem 3 Case Problem 4	11, 12 3, 4 2, 4, 8 2, 17 10
OL2000E.2.2	Create a personal address book	1.21–1.26 1.28	1.46 1.48 1.50 1.51	Review Assignment Case Problem 2 Case Problem 3 Case Problem 4	4 6 8 3
OL2000E.2.3	Customize menu and task bars	1.10 6.44–6.48	6.56–6.57	Case Problem 3	1–4, 31
OL2000E.2.4	Track when mail messages are delivered or read	4.5–4.8 4.11–4.12	4.47	Case Problem 1	8, 11
OL2000E.2.5	Create a personal distribution list	1.24–1.26 1.28	1.46 1.48 1.50 1.51	Review Assignment Case Problem 2 Case Problem 3 Case Problem 4	6 7 9, 10 4, 5
OL2000E.2.6	Create a Quick Synchronization group	APP 7–APP 8			
OL2000E.2.7	Synchronize by message size	APP 8			
OL2000E.2.8	Organize mail using the Rules Wizard	4.16–4.23 4.36–4.40	4.46 4.48 4.48 4.51	Review Assignment Case Problem 1 Case Problem 2 Case Problem 4	16–18, 28 16–18 2-5, 8–10 2-4

CORE SKILLS GRID

Standardized Coding Number	Certification Skill Activity / Activity	Tutorial Pages	End-of-Tutorial Practice		
			End-of-Tutorial Pages	Exercise	Step Number
OL2000E.3	**Use the Outlook 2000 calendar**				
OL2000E.3.1	Configure calendar options	6.35–6.37			
OL2000E.3.2	Share calendar information with other applications over the Internet	2.42–2.44	2.48 2.49 2.52	Review Assignment Case Problem 1 Case Problem 4	24 13 18
OL2000E.3.3	Schedule real-time meetings (NetMeeting)	7.30–7.32	7.34 7.38	Review Assignment Case Problem 4	27 2, 3
OL2000E.3.4	Schedule times to watch broadcasts using NetShow	7.31–7.32			
OL2000E.4	**Share folders and files with other Outlook users and with users inside and outside of the company**				
OL2000E.4.1	Use Net folders and public folders	7.24–7.30	7.35 7.37–7.38	Review Assignment Case Problem 3	20–26 2–15
OL2000E.4.2	Grant delegate access	APP 2–APP 4			
OL2000E.4.3	Grant permissions to folders	7.24–7.26	7.35 7.37–7.38	Review Assignment Case Problem 3	20–22 4, 6–9, 14–15
OL2000E.5	**Navigate and use Outlook 2000 effectively**				
OL2000E.5.1	Customize and use Outlook Today	6.29–6.33	6.52–6.53	Review Assignment	26–29, 38
OL2000E.5.2	Configure time zone information	6.36–6.37			
OL2000E.5.3	Manage favorite Web site addresses	7.6–7.10	7.34 7.35–7.36	Review Assignment Case Problem 1	2–7, 10–11 2–8, 12–18
OL2000E.5.4	Import and export data between Outlook and other mail applications	5.23–5.26			
OL2000E.5.5	Create Outlook forms	6.2–6.21	6.52 6.53–6.54 6.55 6.56–6.57 6.58	Review Assignment Case Problem 1 Case Problem 2 Case Problem 3 Case Problem 4	1–13 1–10 1–11 1–27 1–14
OL2000E.5.6	Create a shortcut to a file on your Outlook Bar	6.40–6.41	6.53 6.54 6.55	Review Assignment Case Problem 1 Case Problem 2	32–35 15 12–13

Standardized Coding Number	Certification Skill Activity		Tutorial Pages	End-of-Tutorial Practice		
	Activity			End-of-Tutorial Pages	Exercise	Step Number
OL2000E.6	**Use Contacts**					
OL2000E.6.1	Flag contacts for follow-up (reminder)		3.33–3.35	3.51 3.54	Case Problem 1 Case Problem 3	10 12, 14, 15
OL2000E.6.2	Customize Contacts menu and task bars		1.10 6.44–6.48	6.56, 6.57	Case Problem 3	1–4, 31
OL2000E.6.3	Integrate Contacts with other Outlook components		3.21–3.25 3.26–3.28 3.329	3.49 3.51 3.53, 3.54	Review Assignment Case Problem 1 Case Problem 3	12–14 9 9, 10, 11
OL2000E.6.4	Use Contacts with Office applications		3.28–3.31 3.40–3.46	3.49–3.50 3.51 3.52–3.53 3.55	Review Assignment Case Problem 1 Case Problem 2 Case Problem 4	16–18, 22–27 7–8, 12–18 15–19 9–13
OL2000E.7	**Use Tasks**					
OL2000E.7.1	Create and update recurring tasks		2.10–2.13	2.49	Case Problem 2	9, 11
OL2000E.7.2	Customize menu and task bars		1.10 6.44–6.48	6.56, 6.57	Case Problem 3	1–4, 31
OL2000E.7.3	Record tasks for any Office file with the journal		5.02–5.04 5.09–5.11	5.44–5.45 5.46 5.47 5.48, 5.49 5.49	Review Assignment Case Problem 1 Case Problem 2 Case Problem 3 Case Problem 4	3–6 2, 3, 9 1, 3, 4–6 1 2–4
OL2000E.7.4	Set delegate access to share tasks with two or more people.		APP 4			
OL2000E.8	**Integrate Office applications and other applications with Outlook 2000 components**					
OL2000E.8.1	Import and export data between Outlook and other Office applications		5.26–5.32 5.34–5.35	5.46–5.47 5.47–5.48 5.49 5.49, 5.50 5.51	Review Assignment Case Problem 1 Case Problem 2 Case Problem 3 Case Problem 4	6, 10, 15–20 4–8 11, 16, 17 3, 5, 7–10, 12–13 6, 9, 11–13
OL2000E.8.2	Use Mail Merge with Word		3.40–3.46	3.49–3.50 3.51 3.52–3.53 3.55	Review Assignment Case Problem 1 Case Problem 2 Case Problem 4	22–27 12–18 15–19 9–13

CORE SKILLS GRID

CORE SKILLS GRID

Standardized Coding Number	Certification Skill Activity / Activity	Tutorial Pages	End-of-Tutorial Practice		
			End-of-Tutorial Pages	Exercise	Step Number
OL2000E.9	**Use the fax service from within Outlook 2000**				
OL2000E.9.1	Receive a fax	5.40–5.41	5.50	Case Problem 4	14
OL2000E.9.2	Create and send a fax from within Outlook 2000	5.36–5.40	5.50	Case Problem 4	14
OL2000E.9.3	Customize a fax	5.37–5.40	5.50	Case Problem 4	14
OL2000E.10	**Use Newsreader**				
OL2000E.10.1	Send and receive information through Newsreader	7.13–7.20	7.34–7.35 7.37	Review Assignment Case Problem 2	12–18 3–14
OL2000E.10.2	Set up Newsreader	7.10–7.13	7.34 7.37	Review Assignment Case Problem 2	12–13 1–2

Outlook File Finder

Location in Tutorial	Name and Location of Data File	Student Saves File As...	Student Creates New File
TUTORIAL 1			
Session 1.1			
Session 1.2	Tutorial.01\Tutorial\Sales.xls	Tutorial.01\Tutorial\Second Quarter Sales.xls	
Review Assignment	Tutorial.01\Review\Tea.doc	Tutorial.01\Review\Tea Health Benefits.doc	
Case Problem 1			Tutorial.01\Cases\Free Trees.htm Tutorial.01\Cases\RE Free Trees.htm Tutorial.01\Cases\FW Free Trees.htm
Case Problem 2	Tutorial.01\Cases\Amendments.doc		Tutorial.01\Cases\History Questions.htm or .txt Tutorial.01\Cases\RE History Questions.htm or .txt Tutorial.01\Cases\FW History Questions.htm or .txt
Case Problem 3			Tutorial.01\Cases\RE Referral.txt
Case Problem 4			Tutorial.01\Cases\Graduation Party.htm or .txt Tutorial.01\Cases\Celebrate.htm or .txt Tutorial.01\Cases\RE Graduation Party.htm or .txt
TUTORIAL 2			
Session 2.1			
Session 2.2			Tutorial.02\Tutorial\Calendar.htm
Review Assignment			Tutorial.02\Review\Schedule.htm
Case Problem 1			Tutorial.02\Cases\Movie Schedule.htm
Case Problem 2			
Case Problem 3			
Case Problem 4			Tutorial.02\Cases\Fundraiser Calendar.htm
TUTORIAL 3			
Session 3.1			
Session 3.2	Tutorial.03\Tutorial\LinkUp Letter.doc	Tutorial.03\Tutorial\New Cars Document File.doc	Tutorial.03\Tutorial\Jill White Letter.doc Tutorial.03\Tutorial\New Cars Letters.doc
Review Assignment	Tutorial.03\Review\Frieda Cohn.vcf (vCard file) Tutorial.03\Review\Supplier Letter.doc	Tutorial.03\Review\Supplier Referral Document File.doc	Tutorial.03\Review\Felicia Rogers Letter.doc Tutorial.03\Review\Supplier Referral Letters.doc
Case Problem 1			Tutorial.03\Cases\Ross Letter.doc Tutorial.03\Cases\Ulvang Mailing Labels.doc Tutorial.03\Cases\Ulvang Document File.doc
Case Problem 2	Tutorial.03\Cases\Natalie.doc	Tutorial.03\Cases\Natalie Data File.doc	Tutorial.03\Cases\Natalie Thiboau.vcf Tutorial.03\Cases\Pierre Thiboau.vcf Tutorial.03\Cases\Channing Thiboau.vcf Tutorial.03\Cases\Ari Finley.vcf Tutorial.03\Cases\Orlando Parkes.vcf Tutorial.03\Cases\Natalie Contacts Merged.doc
Case Problem 3			
Case Problem 4			Tutorial.03\Cases\Student Name vCard.vcf Tutorial.03\Cases\Fan Club Document File.doc Tutorial.03\Cases\Fan Club Letters.doc

Outlook File Finder

Location in Tutorial	Name and Location of Data File	Student Saves File As...	Student Creates New File
TUTORIAL 4			
Session 4.1			Tutorial.04\Tutorial\Gormann Party Rules.rwz
Session 4.2			Tutorial.04\Tutorial\Gormann Archive.pst
Review Assignment			Tutorial.04\Review\Conference Rule.rwz Tutorial.04\Review\Conference Archive.pst Tutorial.04\Review\Nadya Archive.pst
Case Problem 1			Tutorial.04\Cases\Carroll Rule.rwz Tutorial.04\Cases\Customer Archive.pst
Case Problem 2			Tutorial.04\Cases\Getaway Rules.rwz Tutorial.04\Cases\Important Messages Modified.rwz Tutorial.04\Cases\Getaway Archive.pst
Case Problem 3			Tutorial.04\Cases\Viewpoint Search Tutorial.04\Cases\Viewpoint Archive.pst
Case Problem 4			Tutorial.04\Cases\Actor Rule.rwz Tutorial.04\Cases\Actors Archive.pst
TUTORIAL 5			
Session 5.1	Tutorial.05\Tutorial\Mortgage.xls	Tutorial.05\Tutorial\Debt Worksheet.xls Tutorial.05\Tutorial\Debt Worksheet Revised.xls	Tutorial.05\Tutorial\Dream Home.doc
Session 5.2	Tutorial.05\Tutorial\Homebuyers.mdb Tutorial.05\Tutorial\Wishlist.doc		Tutorial.05\Tutorial\Homebuyer Addresses Worksheet.xls Tutorial.05\Tutorial\Ace Contacts Backup.pst Tutorial.05\Tutorial\Luke Farnsworth.rtf
Review Assignment	Tutorial.05\Review\Description.doc Tutorial.05\Review\Homeseller.xls	Tutorial.05\Review\Home Description.doc	Tutorial.05\Review\Tackett Home Highlights.ppt Tutorial.05\Review\Home Seller Addresses Database.mdb Tutorial.05\Review\Ty Contacts Backup.pst Tutorial.05\Review\Joe Dundst.vcf
Case Problem 1	Tutorial.05\Cases\Seminar.doc Tutorial.05\Cases\SeminarTasks.pst	Tutorial.05\Cases\Mick Davis Seminar Setup.doc	
Case Problem 2			Tutorial.05\Cases\Mushroom Availability.htm Tutorial.05\Cases\Mushrooms Order.xls Tutorial.05\Cases\Mushrooms Messages Backup.pst
Case Problem 3	Tutorial.05\Cases\Frame.txt		Tutorial.05\Cases\Frame Shop Description.doc Tutorial.05\Cases\Frame Shop Ad.doc Tutorial.05\Cases\Frame Letter Merged.doc Tutorial.05\Cases\Frame Contact List.xls Tutorial.05\Cases\Frame Shop Backup.pst
Case Problem 4	Tutorial.05\Cases\		Tutorial.05\Cases\Party Supplies.xls Tutorial.05\Cases\Party Invitation.doc Tutorial.05\Cases\Party Contacts Workbook.xls Tutorial.05\Cases\Party Messages Backup.pst